JOURNAL FOR THE STUDY OF THE NEW TESTAMENT
SUPPLEMENT SERIES

251

The Unity of the Corinthian Correspondence

David R. Hall

T & T CLARK INTERNATIONAL
A Continuum imprint
LONDON • NEW YORK

Copyright © 2003 T&T Clark International
A Continuum imprint

Published by T&T Clark International
The Tower Building, 11 York Road, London SE1 7NX
15 East 26th Street, Suite 1703, New York, NY 10010

www.tandtclark.com

British Library Cataloguing-in-Publication Data
A catalogue record for this book is available from the British Library

Library of Congress Cataloging-in-Publication Data
A catalogue record for this book is available from the Library of Congress

Typeset by TMW Typesetting, Sheffield
Printed on acid-free paper in Great Britain by Cromwell Press, Trowbridge, Wiltshire

ISBN 0-8264-6987-6 (hb)
      0-5670-8422-1 (pb)

CONTENTS

Preface   vii
Abbreviations   viii
Introduction   1

Chapter 1
PAUL'S OPPONENTS IN 1 CORINTHIANS   3
    Excursus A: The Meaning of μετασχηματίζειν
      in 1 Corinthians 4.6   19
    Excursus B: The Translation of 1 Corinthians 4.15   25

Chapter 2
THE UNITY OF 1 CORINTHIANS   30

Chapter 3
THE SOCIAL BACKGROUND TO 1 CORINTHIANS   51
    Excursus C: The Meaning of ἤδη in 1 Corinthians 4.8   79

Chapter 4
THE UNITY OF 2 CORINTHIANS   86
    Excursus D: The Meaning of
    αὐτὸς ἐγὼ Παῦλος in 2 Corinthians 10.1   106

Chapter 5
THE INTERNAL UNITY OF 2 CORINTHIANS 1–9   113
    Excursus E: The Connection between
    2 Corinthians 1.11 and 1.12   124

Chapter 6
THE BACKGROUND OF PAUL'S OPPONENTS   129

Chapter 7
THE TEACHING OF PAUL'S OPPONENTS   149
    Excursus F: The Interpretation of 1 Corinthians 11.10   170

Chapter 8
THE QUESTION OF SELF-SUPPORT   174
    Excursus G: The Interpretation of 1 Corinthians 9.17   190

Chapter 9
THE VOCABULARY OF PAUL'S OPPONENTS   199

Chapter 10
THE TEARFUL LETTER   223

Chapter 11
PAUL'S TRAVELS AND TRAVEL PLANS   236
    Excursus H: The Journeys of Titus   248

Chapter 12
PAUL'S PASTORAL STRATEGY   254

Bibliography   258
Index of References   266
Index of Authors   278

This book has been a long time in the making. My love affair with the Corinthian letters began with the study of 1 Corinthians in college study groups, and has extended through the teaching of 1 Corinthians to students in India to the long days of leisure afforded by retirement. I have learned much from the critical comments of various scholars on earlier drafts—especially from Andrew Clarke, Paul Ellingworth, Michael Goulder and Howard Marshall. But as I have frequently failed to take their advice, they should not be held responsible for the deficiencies in the finished product. In preparing the text for the press, Simon Duckett has been more than generous with his time and his computer skills. Above all, it is my wife Janet's unfailing love and support that has kept me going over many years.

One of the most valuable second-hand books I acquired in my student days was Frederick Field's *Notes on the Translation of the New Testament*. Field's comment on 1 Cor. 4.6 introduced me to John Chrysostom's interpretation of that verse—an interpretation that I have increasingly come to view as the key to understanding the Corinthian correspondence. It is one of those 'old treasures' which, as described in Mt. 13.52, scholars apprenticed to the kingdom of heaven keep on discovering in the storehouse of knowledge. It is therefore to the memory of 'John of the golden mouth' that this book is dedicated.

ABBREVIATIONS

AB	Anchor Bible
AGJU	Arbeiten zur Geschichte des antiken Judentums und des Urchristentums
AusBR	*Australian Biblical Review*
BA	*Biblical Archaeologist*
BAGD	Walter Bauer, William F. Arndt, F. William Gingrich and Frederick W. Danker, *A Greek–English Lexicon of the New Testament and Other Early Christian Literature* (Chicago: University of Chicago Press, 2nd edn, 1958; 3rd edn, 2000)
BDF	Friedrich Blass, A. Debrunner and Robert W. Funk, *A Greek Grammar of the New Testament and Other Early Christian Literature* (Cambridge: Cambridge University Press, 1961)
BJRL	*Bulletin of the John Rylands University Library of Manchester*
BT	*The Bible Translator*
CBQ	*Catholic Biblical Quarterly*
EBib	Etudes bibliques
EKKNT	Evangelisch-Katholischer Kommentar zum Neuen Testament
EvT	*Evangelische Theologie*
ExpTim	*Expository Times*
HTR	*Harvard Theological Review*
HUT	Hermeneutische Untersuchungen zur Theologie
ICC	International Critical Commentary
Int	*Interpretation*
JBL	*Journal of Biblical Literature*
JRH	*Journal of Religious History*
JSNT	*Journal for the Study of the New Testament*
JSNTSup	*Journal for the Study of the New Testament*, Supplement Series
JTS	*Journal of Theological Studies*
LCL	Loeb Classical Library
LSJ	H.G. Liddell, Robert Scott and H. Stuart Jones, *Greek–English Lexicon* (Oxford: Clarendon Press, 9th edn, 1968)
MeyerK	Meyer Kommentar
MM	J.H. Moulton and G. Milligan, *The Vocabulary of the Greek Testament Illustrated from the Papri and Other Non-literary Sources* (London: Hodder & Stoughton, 1914–29)
MPG	Migne's *Patrologia Graeca*

NEB	*New English Bible*
NICNT	New International Commentary on the New Testament
NIGTC	The New International Greek Testament Commentary
NIV	New International Version
NovT	*Novum Testamentum*
NTS	*New Testament Studies*
NTTS	New Testament Tools and Studies
OGIS	W. Dittenberger (ed.), *Orientis Graeci Inscriptiones Selectae* (Leipzig: Hirzel, 1903–1905)
RB	*Revue biblique*
RV	Revised Version
SBLDS	Society of Biblical Literature Dissertation Series
SJT	*Scottish Journal of Theology*
SNTSMS	Society for New Testament Studies Monograph Series
SNTU	*Studien zum Neuen Testament und seiner Umwelt*
TDNT	Gerhard Kittel and Gerhard Friedrich (eds.), *Theological Dictionary of the New Testament* (trans. Geoffrey W. Bromiley; 10 vols.; Grand Rapids: Eerdmans, 1964–76)
TynBul	*Tyndale Bulletin*
TJ	*Trinity Journal*
TU	Texte und Untersuchungen
WBC	Word Biblical Commentary
WC	Westminster Commentary
WUNT	Wissenschaftliche Untersuchungen zum Neuen Testament
ZNW	*Zeitschrift für die neutestamentliche Wissenschaft*

INTRODUCTION

The thesis of this book is that 1 and 2 Corinthians, in the form in which we now have them, represent two stages in a single conflict; that in both letters Paul faces the same opponents; and that the references in 2 Corinthians to a tearful letter and to the punishment of an offender are references to 1 Corinthians.

A close connection between the two letters was generally assumed until well into the nineteenth century. In H.A.W. Meyer's commentary on 1 and 2 Corinthians this view was stoutly upheld. In reply to G.H.A. Ewald's theory of a visit and (lost) letter between the two canonical epistles, he replied that this proposal 'finds...no sufficient confirmation in the passages concerned'.[1] In the fifth edition of the commentary on 2 Corinthians, published in 1870, he noted that the theory of an intermediate letter was by then widely adopted. But after careful investigation he found himself compelled to reject it.[2]

Since that time, however, Ewald's theory has become generally accepted, though with variations. Some have argued that the supposed intermediate letter is wholly lost; others believe that part of it has been preserved in 2 Cor. 10–13. In my opinion Meyer's judgment still stands: the modern theory is not confirmed by the passages concerned. 2 Corinthians is a follow-up to 1 Corinthians, in which Paul brings to a conclusion the plan of campaign he began to implement in the earlier letter. My main contentions are as follows:

1. 1 Corinthians reveals the presence at Corinth of preachers from elsewhere, who gathered groups of disciples in the manner of the sophists, and taught their disciples an ethical theory and lifestyle that were contrary to those of Paul.
2. Paul's references to his opponents in 2 Corinthians reflect the same background situation as 1 Corinthians.

1.   H.A.W. Meyer, *Critical and Exegetical Handbook to the Epistles to the Corinthians* (2 vols.; Edinburgh: T. & T. Clark, 1877 and 1879), II, p. 131.
2.   Meyer, *Corinthians*, II, p. vii.

3. Paul's opponents (in both letters) came probably from a Hellenistic–Jewish background, and combined a sophistic lifestyle with the teaching of a form of 'wisdom' based on allegorical interpretation of Scripture.
4. Most of the problems dealt with in 1 Corinthians were offshoots of the wisdom teaching of Paul's opponents.
5. The references in 2 Corinthians to a previous letter are references to 1 Corinthians.
6. The references in 2 Corinthians to Paul's travel plans are a follow-up to the travel plans announced in 1 Corinthians.
7. Throughout the Corinthian correspondence Paul implements a consistent pastoral strategy.
8. Attempts to divide 1 and 2 Corinthians into a number of separate letters fail to appreciate Paul's pastoral strategy, and employ arguments that are logically flawed.
9. Leadership in the church at Corinth was related primarily to charismatic endowment, not to social class.

Chapter 1

PAUL'S OPPONENTS IN 1 CORINTHIANS

In this chapter I shall examine the opposition that Paul faced in 1 Corinthians. I shall seek to show that this opposition was inspired by teachers who had come to Corinth from elsewhere. In subsequent chapters I shall argue that these teachers were the same as those attacked in 2 Cor. 10–13.

This view runs contrary to the generally accepted opinion today. It is commonly assumed that the 'false apostles' whom Paul confronts in 2 Cor. 10–13 had arrived in Corinth after 1 Corinthians was written, and that there is no trace of their activity in the earlier letter. Typical of this consensus is the comment of Carson, Moo and Morris:

> One must not read the situation of 2 Corinthians back into 1 Corinthians—at least, not without observing several distinctions. In particular, there is no evidence whatsoever that at the time of writing 1 Corinthians the apostle Paul was facing a church that had been taken over by leaders *from the outside*. By the time of 2 Corinthians 10–13, that has certainly happened.[1]

This opinion, though widespread, is not universal. C.K. Barrett is one of the few modern commentators to admit the possibility that the opponents of 2 Corinthians may have been already present at Corinth at the time 1 Corinthians was written. Commenting on 1 Cor. 4.6, he writes: 'He [Paul] has deliberately omitted other names (notably Peter's; but it may be that "false apostles" were already at work in Corinth)'.[2] Again, in his introduction to 2 Corinthians, he states that 'very soon after 1 Corinthians had been written—possibly indeed before—Corinth was entered by a group of persons who gave themselves out to be, and were accepted as, Christian

---

1. D.A. Carson, D.J. Moo and L. Morris, *An Introduction to the New Testament* (Grand Rapids: Zondervan, 1992), p. 279 (original italics).
2. C.K. Barrett, *A Commentary on the First Epistle to the Corinthians* (London: A. & C. Black, 2nd edn, 1971), p. 106.

apostles'.[3] Similarly Colin Kruse, when discussing the offender referred to in 2 Corinthians (2.5-11; 7.12), states that 'the "false apostles" may have been in Corinth during the first phase of opposition, and an undercurrent of criticism emanating from them may have strengthened the attacks of the offending individual'.[4] However, although Barrett and Kruse admit the possibility that the rival apostles of 2 Corinthians were present in Corinth at the time of 1 Corinthians, they do not believe their presence at that time was a major factor in the situation. The thesis of the present chapter, by contrast, is that incoming teachers were not only present in Corinth at the time of writing of 1 Corinthians, but were the major influence behind the problems discussed in that letter.

1. *The Divisions at Corinth*

In 1 Cor. 1.11-12 Paul writes as follows:

> Chloe's people have told me, my brothers, that there are divisions among you. What I mean is, each of you is saying, 'I belong to Paul', 'I belong to Apollos', 'I belong to Cephas', 'I belong to Christ'.

There are passages later in the letter that can help us to understand this statement. In ch. 3 Paul repeats the slogans 'I belong to Paul' and 'I belong to Apollos' as evidence that the Corinthians were living at a merely human (or 'fleshly') level (vv. 3-4). He insists that he and Apollos are colleagues, not rivals, employed by God and rewarded by God (vv. 5-9). He then goes on to compare the church at Corinth to a building of which he laid the foundation but others are building the superstructure (vv. 10-17). Some of these other teachers are building with gold, silver and precious stones; some are building with wood, hay and stubble. The course of Paul's argument in ch. 3 raises the question: who are these teachers who are building the church at Corinth with wood, hay and stubble, and what is the connection between their activity and that of Paul and Apollos?

The key verse for answering this question is 4.6.[5] The verse reads:

---

3.   C.K. Barrett, *A Commentary on the Second Epistle to the Corinthians* (London: A. & C. Black, 2nd edn, 1990), p. 6.

4.   C.G. Kruse, *The Second Epistle of Paul to the Corinthians* (Leicester: Inter-Varsity Press, 1987), pp. 40-41.

5.   For a more detailed discussion of this verse see D.R. Hall, 'A Disguise for the Wise: μετασχηματισμός in 1 Corinthians 4.6', *NTS* 40 (1994), pp. 143-49. My interpretation has been challenged by J.S. Vos, 'Der Μετασχηματισμός in 1 Kor.

ταῦτα δέ, ἀδελφοί, μετεσχημάτισα εἰς ἐμαυτὸν καὶ Ἀπολλῶν δι᾽
ὑμᾶς, ἵνα ἐν ἡμῖν μάθητε τὸ Μὴ ὑπὲρ ἃ γέγραπται, ἵνα μὴ εἷς ὑπὲρ
τοῦ ἑνὸς φυσιοῦσθε κατὰ τοῦ ἑτέρου

I have altered the form of what I have been saying into myself and Apollos
for your sake, my brothers, so that you may learn from our example the
principle 'not beyond what is written', so that you may not be puffed up,
each of you supporting one person in opposition to another.

The verb μετασχηματίζω has a clear and consistent meaning in ancient
Greek literature—to alter the form or appearance of something into something else. In some contexts it can be translated 'disguise' (e.g. 2 Cor.
11.13-15). In other contexts it can be translated 'transform' (e.g. Phil.
3.21). Where the verb is followed by the preposition εἰς (into), the noun or
pronoun governed by εἰς denotes the end product of the transformation.
For example, in 2 Cor. 11.14 Satan transforms himself into (εἰς) an angel
of light. In 1 Cor. 4.6 the words governed by εἰς are ἐμαυτὸν καὶ
Ἀπολλῶν. The meaning is that Paul has disguised his argument, so that
what really applies to other people has been applied to himself and
Apollos.[6]

Paul is here referring particularly to 3.5-9—to his portrayal of Apollos
and himself as colleagues rather than rivals. In the light of what Paul says
about disguise in 4.6 it is clear that his main concern was not with the
relationship between himself and Apollos.[7] His concern was with other
people whom he does not name, who had set themselves up as rivals
competing for the allegiance of the Corinthian church. That is why the
comparison between the ministries of Apollos and himself in 3.4-9 is
immediately followed by the allusion to a variety of teachers in 3.10-17.

The 'disguise' mentioned in 4.6 was not limited to the comparison
between Paul and Apollos twenty verses earlier in 3.4-9. The passage 3.4-
9 is itself a commentary on 1.12, and its opening reference to people saying 'I support Paul' and 'I support Apollos' echoes the words of 1.12. If
the mention of Paul and Apollos in 3.4-9 is a disguised reference to other

---

4.6', *ZNW* 86 (1995), pp. 154-72. For a critique of Vos's article see Excursus A at the
end of this chapter.

6.   Meyer (*Corinthians*, I, p. 116) paraphrases 4.6: 'I have changed the form of it
into myself and Apollos, i.e. I have, instead of directing my discourse to others, upon
whom it might properly have been moulded, written in such fashion in an altered form,
that what has been said now applies to myself and Apollos'.

7.   The fact that Paul had no quarrel with Apollos is also clear from 1 Cor. 16.12,
unless the first half of that verse is regarded as a deliberate falsehood.

teachers, the same will be true of the mention of Paul, Apollos, Cephas and Christ in 1.12.

There are three possible interpretations of 1.12—the literal, the semi-literal and the cryptic. Representative of the literal interpretation is H.A.W. Meyer:

> There can be no reduction of the number of the parties below four. Paul, in fact, sets forth quite uniformly four definite diversities of confession standing in contrast, and then shows in ver. 13 how sad and how preposterous this state of division was.[8]

This is a logical position: 1.12 is a literal description of the state of affairs at Corinth, and there were therefore precisely four parties, claiming allegiance to the four names given. However, most scholars are justifiably unwilling to regard this verse as a literal statement, because the rest of the letter does not seem to reflect such a fourfold division.

The semi-literal interpretation regards some of the four names mentioned in 1.12 as more significant than others. The main conflict is seen to be between followers of Peter and followers of Paul, or between followers of Apollos and followers of Paul, or the fourth slogan (ἐγὼ δὲ Χριστοῦ) is thought to be of a different order to the other three.[9] But, once it is conceded that 1.12 as a whole is not a literal statement, there is no logical reason for assuming the literal truth of any one part of it.

The cryptic interpretation understands 1.12 in the light of 4.6. The preceding verse (1.11) reporting the information from Chloe's people is literally true—the church was divided. But the association of the groups with the names of Paul, Apollos, Cephas and Christ in v. 12 is part of the disguise. The real group leaders are not named—let us call them A, B, C and D. Paul does not name them partly, perhaps, for reasons of tact; partly, perhaps, because he had only heard about them at second hand and it is dangerous to name names on hearsay evidence; partly, perhaps, 'following the ancient rhetorical convention of denying one's enemies even such status as the use of their names could accord them'.[10] The Corinthians

---

8.   Meyer, *Corinthians*, I, p. 26.

9.   For a survey of various interpretations see A.C. Thiselton, *The First Epistle to the Corinthians: A Commentary on the Greek Text* (NIGTC; Grand Rapids: Eerdmans; Carlisle: Paternoster, 2000), pp. 123-33.

10.   V.P. Furnish, *II Corinthians: A New Translation with Introduction and Commentary* (AB, 32A; Garden City, NY: Doubleday, 1984), p. 49, following P. Marshall, *Enmity in Corinth: Social Conventions in Paul's Relations with the Corinthians* (WUNT [2nd Series] 23; Tübingen: J.C.B. Mohr, 1987), pp. 528-38. Furnish is commenting on

would immediately realize what Paul meant, and would also read between the lines of 3.1-9 and understand what Paul was saying: if I Paul who first brought you the gospel and Apollos who confirmed it are not rivals but colleagues, how much more should this be true of your new teachers A, B, C and D!

This interpretation is not new, but goes back to Chrysostom. Its advantage is not only that it gives a proper sense to the verb μετασχηματίζω but also that it fits in with 1 Corinthians as a whole. Those who take 1.12 literally (or semi-literally) run into great difficulties, because it is not possible to find the parties named in 1.12 reflected in the rest of the letter.

The aim of Paul's 'disguise' in 4.6 is to teach the Corinthians a lesson, 'so that you may not be puffed up, each supporting one person in opposition to another'.[11] The word φυσιοῦσθαι (be puffed up) describes the pride of the Corinthians in their own particular leader and their feeling of superiority to those who follow other leaders.[12] Paul has disguised his argument under the names of himself and Apollos so that the Corinthians

---

Paul's use of terms such as τις and τινες in 2 Corinthians. Despite the fact that Paul does refer openly to his opponents in 2 Cor. 11 and 12, for most of the letter, as Furnish says, he refers to them only obliquely. This is one of the many points of similarity between the two letters.

11. There are three referents in 4.6—εἷς ὑπὲρ τοῦ ἑνὸς κατὰ τοῦ ἑτέρου. The terms 'one' and 'another' are generic, and do not refer to a specific individual. This is a different construction from Mt. 6.24, where a reference to two masters is followed by two pronouns, which can therefore be translated 'the one' and 'the other'. The closest NT parallel to the construction of 4.6 is 1 Thess. 5.11, where οἰκοδομεῖτε εἷς τὸν ἕνα means 'build up one another'. M.D. Goulder ('Σοφία in 1 Corinthians', *NTS* 37 [1991], pp. 516-34 [519]) argues that τοῦ ἑνός refers to Cephas. But if the second εἷς refers to an individual, so must the first, and we must translate: 'so that you may not be puffed up, one specific individual (unnamed) in support of another specific individual (Cephas) in opposition to a third specific individual (unnamed)'. This would mean that only three individuals were involved in the Corinthian divisions.

12. L.L. Welborn, 'On the Discord in Corinth: 1 Corinthians 1–4 and Ancient Politics', *JBL* 106 (1987), pp. 85-111 (88), followed by D. Litfin, *St. Paul's Theology of Proclamation: 1 Corinthians 1–4 and Greco-Roman Rhetoric* (SNTSMS, 79; Cambridge: Cambridge University Press, 1994), p. 168, sees in the word φυσιοῦσθαι a reflection of the widespread ancient caricature of 'the political windbag, the orator inflated at his success..., the young aristocrat, the aspiring tyrant, filled with a sense of his own power..., the supercilious office-holder'. But had Paul meant the word in this way he would have written ἵνα μὴ φυσιοῦσθε εἷς κατὰ τοῦ ἑτέρου. By adding the words ὑπὲρ τοῦ ἑνός he makes it clear that the pride of the Corinthians was not in their own ability but in the particular party leader they were supporting.

could learn 'through us' (ἐν ἡμῖν)—that is, through our example[13]—not to be puffed up in this way. The whole argument presupposes that the party leaders were teachers and preachers on a par with Apollos, so that a comparison could appropriately be drawn between the co-operative attitude of Paul and Apollos on the one hand and the competitive attitude of the new arrivals on the other.

2. *The Builders at Corinth*

In 3.10-17 Paul refers to people who are building the superstructure of the Corinthian church upon the foundation he laid. The passage begins: 'By virtue of the grace of God that was given me I laid a foundation like a skilful master-builder, and someone else builds on it. But each one should take care how he builds on it' (3.10). The clause ἕκαστος δὲ βλεπέτω πῶς ἐποικοδομεῖ ('but each one should take care how he builds on it') is a commentary on the immediately preceding clause ἄλλος δὲ ἐποικοδομεῖ ('someone else builds on it'). The fact that ἄλλος and ἕκαστος are parallel words indicates that ἄλλος is used in a generic sense.[14] It does not refer to one particular other person but to other people in general. 'Each one' (ἕκαστος) means 'each of the builders who are included within the collective term ἄλλος'.

Who, then, are these builders? The idea that Paul is referring to Apollos or Peter is ruled out by the present tense employed throughout the passage.[15] Fee comments that Paul 'is concerned to warn...those who are

---

13. On the meaning of ἐν ἡμῖν see J.T. Fitzgerald, *Cracks in an Earthen Vessel: An Examination of the Catalogues of Hardships in the Corinthian Correspondence* (SBLDS, 99; Atlanta, GA: Scholars Press, 1988), p. 122 n. 18.

14. Cf. G.D. Fee, *The First Epistle to the Corinthians* (NICNT; Grand Rapids: Eerdmans, 1987), p. 136: 'The paragraph [3.10-15] is dominated by the indefinite pronouns "someone else", "no one", "each one", and "anyone". Since Apollos is not mentioned, and since the urgency both here and in the further application of the metaphor that follows (vv. 16-17) is specifically with what was happening in the church at the time of Paul's writing, the particulars therefore shift from Paul and Apollos to Paul and those responsible for the current "wood, hay and straw" of σοφία (wisdom)'. For the generic use of ἄλλος cf. 1 Cor. 12.8-10.

15. Failure to realize this is a weakness in Gerd Theissen's analysis. He writes (with regard to both 1 and 2 Corinthians): 'The origin of the conflict lies in the fact that various missionaries have achieved influence within the community, giving rise to group divisions and arguments. The missionaries themselves have moved on. Apollos is no longer in Corinth when 1 Corinthians is written (1 Cor. 16.12), and the mission-

currently "building the church" '.[16] 'Each one should take care how he builds' is not a natural expression to use of people whose building work lay in the past.[17] As Ben Witherington says, 'clearly this whole passage cannot be directed just against Apollos or Peter, neither of whom is in Corinth *when Paul writes*'.[18]

One commonly held opinion today is that Paul is referring to 'the Corinthians themselves, and in particular those who are leading the way in their strife and divisions'.[19] But there are several difficulties with this opinion. The builders are continuing the work Paul began and erecting a superstructure on his foundation. The metaphor suggests that they are people whose teaching is treated as authoritative by their disciples. It is

aries of 2 Corinthians have been given letters of recommendation to help them on their further travels (2 Cor. 3.1). In their wake they leave problems which also must have had causes within the Corinthian community itself' (G. Theissen, *The Social Setting of Pauline Christianity* [Edinburgh: T. & T. Clark, 1982], p. 54). In two respects Theissen has correctly analysed the situation at Corinth. The conflict was indeed caused by the influence of incoming missionaries; and this is indeed a problem common to both letters. Where Theissen is mistaken is in thinking that the missionaries have moved on. In the case of 1 Corinthians this view rests on an over-literal understanding of 1.12, whereby Peter and/or Apollos are the missionaries concerned. In the case of 2 Corinthians the reference to letters of recommendation written by the Corinthians does not mean that *all* visiting missionaries had left Corinth. Verses such as 11.22 imply their continuing presence.

16. Fee, *First Epistle*, p. 136.

17. According to Litfin (*Proclamation*, p. 225), 'Paul's warning, unlike the material surrounding it, is directed to ministers who *had* worked within the congregation' (my italics). It is his treatment of Paul's present tenses as though they were past tenses that forces Litfin to believe that this section is 'unlike the material surrounding it' and alien to its context.

18. B. Witherington, *Conflict and Community in Corinth: A Socio-Rhetorical Commentary on 1 and 2 Corinthians* (Grand Rapids: Eerdmans; Carlisle: Paternoster, 1995), p. 133 (his italics). The political overtones of Paul's language also suggest its current relevance. M.M. Mitchell (*Paul and the Rhetoric of Reconciliation: An Exegetical Investigation of the Language and Composition of 1 Corinthians* [HUT, 28; Tübingen: J.C.B. Mohr, 1991], pp. 82-83), following Welborn, 'Discord', pp. 90-92, correctly emphasizes the 'common and recognizable aspect of ancient party politics, the dependence of factions upon a leader'. But she fails to see the logic of this parallel when she argues that the Corinthian factions claimed allegiance to Paul, Apollos and Cephas. A leader is not the same as a figurehead. The leaders of the Corinthian parties, like the political leaders of ancient Greece, were people actively influencing their followers, not absentee figureheads.

19. Fee, *First Epistle*, p. 138.

hard to imagine members of the Corinthian church, all fairly recent converts, exercising this kind of teaching authority over their fellow-members.[20]

Corinth was an international city with a constant influx of new people.[21] For a young church of relatively immature Christians the attraction of teachers from older, more established churches would be more potent than the pretensions of their own members. The principle enunciated by Jesus applies here: 'A prophet is not without honour except in his own country' (Mk 6.4).

Moreover, v. 17 refers to builders who cause damage to God's holy temple, the church.[22] The temple is identified as 'you' in the second person. The causers of damage are distinguished from this temple and are referred to in the third person. This would be a strange way of speaking if the builders were church members and were thus causing damage to themselves. It is much more likely that they were Apollos-type figures who had come from Alexandria or elsewhere with all the glamour and authority their provenance gave them.

3. *The Pedagogues at Corinth*

In 4.15 Paul declares: ἐὰν γὰρ μυρίους παιδαγωγοὺς ἔχητε ἐν Χριστῷ, ἀλλ᾿ οὐ πολλοὺς πατέρας. The present tense of the verb ἔχητε refers, as I seek to demonstrate in Excursus B,[23] to the present situation at Corinth, and to specific individuals who are described metaphorically as pedagogues: 'for even if you have ten thousand pedagogues, you do not have many fathers'. This raises two questions: who are the people referred to as pedagogues, and what is the force of the metaphor?

---

20. Vos, 'Μετασχηματισμός', p. 168, comments on the function of the builders as follows: 'Es gibt im Bezug auf diese Funktion kein einziges Textsignal, das den Leser veranlassen könnte, an eine andere Person als einen Mitarbeiter vom Schlage des Apollos, also an einen von aussen kommenden Missionar zu denken'.

21. Cf. Litfin, *Proclamation*, p. 165: 'Paul was in many superficial ways similar to other travelling speakers. The Corinthians were used to a more or less steady stream of such speakers and typically registered in some way their own judgments about these speakers' eloquence or the lack of it'.

22. J. Shanor ('Paul as Master Builder: Construction Terms in First Corinthians', *NTS* 34 [1988], pp. 461-71 [470]) illustrates the meaning 'damage' for φθείρειν from a building inscription of Arcadian Tegea, and argues that 'destroy' is an inappropriate translation.

23. Excursus B, 'The Translation of 1 Corinthians 4.15'.

The pedagogue (παιδαγωγός) has been defined by David Lull as 'a household slave responsible for accompanying children from six to sixteen on their journeys away from home'.[24] Tales were told of pedagogues who were loyal to the point of death, defending their charges from attacks in the street. Because their role included the protection of minors from moral as well as physical dangers they were often strict disciplinarians (though Philo defends their hard discipline as that of a friend). Plutarch tells a story about Diogenes, who saw a child eating delicacies and struck the child's pedagogue, 'showing that the fault belonged not to the one who had not learned but to the one who had not taught'. Plutarch also quotes the remark of a Spartan pedagogue that his task was to cause his ward to take pleasure in the noble and to be offended by the shameful.[25]

It is clear from this that pedagogues, though slaves, were regarded by children as people with authority. Their task was to teach the child how to behave. Good pedagogues, according to Plutarch, 'by their habits shape the child's character and start the child on the path of virtue'.[26] A bad pedagogue could, in Philo's words, be a 'teacher of sin'.[27]

It is significant that Paul's reference to pedagogues comes in a section dealing with the moral behaviour of the Corinthians. In the following verse (v. 16) he urges the Corinthians to imitate him, and he goes on to say that he has sent Timothy to Corinth to remind them of his Christian life-style—his 'ways in Christ' (v. 17). This suggests that the pedagogues were claiming the right to be moral guides of the Corinthian Christians and were teaching them an alternative lifestyle.

According to Fee, the reference to pedagogues has been interpreted in two main ways. The standard view sees an allusion to Apollos and Peter; an alternative view sees an allusion to 'those within the community who are presently leading them astray'.[28] What Fee calls the standard view is untenable, for three reasons. (i) Whenever Paul refers to Apollos and Peter in 1 Corinthians, he treats them as fellow apostles of equal status to his own (1.12; 3.4-6; 3.22; 4.6; 9.5; 15.5; 16.12). It is difficult to believe that

---

24. D.J. Lull, ' "The Law was our Pedagogue": A Study in Galatians 3.19-25', *JBL* 105/3 (1986), pp. 481-98 (489). All the references in this and the next paragraph are taken from Lull's article.

25. Philo, *Migr. Abr.* 116; Appian, *B.C.* 4.30; Plutarch, *Mor.* 452D, 439E.

26. Plutarch, *Mor.* 439F.

27. Philo, *Rer. Div. Her.* 295.

28. Fee, *First Epistle*, p. 185 n. 20.

he could have attributed to them in 4.15 the status of a slave.[29] (ii) The contrast between 'ten thousand pedagogues' and one single father would lose its point if only Peter or Apollos were in view. (iii) The pedagogue was in daily attendance on his charges and the metaphor would be inappropriate for someone not currently resident in Corinth. Apollos had visited Corinth in the past (Acts 18.24-28) but had since moved away (1 Cor. 16.12). Peter may well have visited Corinth (the four references to Cephas in 1 Corinthians suggest someone known to the congregation) but there is no indication that he was resident there at the time 1 Corinthians was written.[30]

We should therefore accept the view that the pedagogues were people currently living in Corinth. But they are unlikely to have been members of the local church. In the metaphor the church members are compared to children, and are distinguished from the pedagogues who are their guardians. These pedagogues should be identified, along with the builders of 3.10-17, as the visiting teachers to whom Paul has been alluding in a disguised fashion throughout chs. 1–4.

4. *The Examiners at Corinth*

The main theme of ch. 9 is Paul's refusal to accept the material support to which, as an apostle, he was entitled.[31] It is remarkable, however, that Paul only begins to expound this theme in v. 15. The earlier half of the chapter (vv. 1-14) consists of a series of arguments to prove that he has the right to support in the first place. The reason for this procedure is revealed in v. 3—Paul is on the defensive. 'This is my defence against those who are examining me' (ἡ ἐμὴ ἀπολογία τοῖς ἐμὲ ἀνακρίνουσίν ἐστιν αὕτη).

The word ἀνακρίνω was often used of the judicial examination (ἀνάκρισις) that preceded a Roman trial (cf. Acts 25.26). Paul talks of being 'examined' not only here but also in 4.1-5 where, as L.L. Welborn says, 'we must think of a kind of ecclesiastical court, where the legitimacy of Paul's apostleship is to be tested'.[32] The 'examiners' were apparently

---

29. A good illustration of the social status of the pedagogue is Plato, *Lys.* 208C. Plato comments on the fact that, when a child is under the control of a pedagogue, a free person is being ruled by a slave.

30. According to Thiselton (*First Epistle*, p. 128), 'we cannot be certain whether Peter actually visited Corinth'.

31. See the discussion of 1 Cor. 9 in Chapter 8.

32. Welborn, 'Discord', p. 108. Barrett (*First Epistle*, pp. 201-202) argues that ἀνακρίνουσιν is conative and translates 'those who would like to examine me'. But

calling into question Paul's right to receive support on the grounds that he was not a proper apostle. This is implied by the fact that he begins the chapter with the rhetorical question, 'Am I not an apostle?' and goes on to refer to 'others' (ἄλλοι) who do not accept his apostleship.[33] Presumably the 'others' of v. 2 are closely related to the 'examiners' of v. 3, since vv. 1-2 have no obvious purpose if they are divorced from v. 3 and left hanging in the air.

Fee suggests two possible understandings of the 'others'. Either Paul is 'allowing the hypothetical possibility that others outside their immediate circle may have some reason for not thinking of him as an apostle'; or the reference is to 'some outsiders, such as those taken on in vigorous confrontation in 2 Cor. 10–12, who have already entered the community and begun to sow seeds of discord'.[34] The latter view is far more probable. The vehemence of Paul's language, and the space he devotes to his ἀπολογία, are inexplicable if this is only a theoretical issue. The 'others' (who are expressly distinguished from the church members in v. 2) were probably the wisdom teachers pictured as builders and pedagogues in chs. 3 and 4, to whom Paul has already applied the generic term ἄλλος in 3.10. The 'examiners' (at least some of whom seem, in the light of 4.3, to have been members of the church) may have comprised both the wisdom teachers and some of their Corinthian disciples.

5. *Wisdom at Corinth*

Throughout chs. 1–4 of 1 Corinthians the themes of party spirit and of wisdom are intertwined. This is true of chs. 1 and 2, where Paul's initial

the term 'conative' is only applicable to verbs that indicate a process leading to a conclusion. For example, πείθειν in the present and imperfect means 'to urge' or 'to try to persuade', but in the aorist means 'to succeed in persuading'. In the case of a verb such as ἀνακρίνειν, the only way to 'try to examine' people is actually to examine them. The present tense indicates a present activity.

W. Willis ('An Apostolic Apologia? The Form and Function of 1 Corinthians 9', *JSNT* 24 [1985], pp. 33-48 [34]) regards ἀνακρινοῦσιν as a future participle and alleges that Paul is 'giving a "reasoned response" (ἀπολογία) to anyone who might contest his exhortation in 8.9-12'. But if this were a future participle, it would indicate not what these people *might* do but what they definitely *would* do. Paul could not give a 'reasoned response' to an examination that was still in the future.

33. For a detailed discussion of 9.1, and the meaning of the word ἐλεύθερος in that verse, see Chapter 9.

34. Fee, *First Epistle*, p. 396.

condemnation of divisions in the church (1.10-16) is followed by a lengthy discussion of false and true wisdom (1.17–2.16). It is also true of ch. 3, where his scornful reference to divisions as a sign of childishness (3.1-4) and his warning to the 'builders' who are fomenting them (3.10-17) are followed by a condemnation of the wisdom of this world (3.18-20). The clearest indication of the close connection between divisions and wisdom is 3.20-21. Paul there quotes the words of scripture: 'The Lord knows that the reasonings of the wise are foolish', and comments: 'therefore no one should make human beings the object of their boasting'. The word 'therefore' (ὥστε) only makes sense if the Corinthian pride in their party leaders was also a pride in the wisdom of those leaders.[35] If the reasonings of the wise are useless, Paul is saying, then it is also useless to boast about people who claim to be wise and engage in reasonings.

There has been much discussion about the nature of the wisdom that the party leaders were claiming. Duane Litfin lists three main interpretations— rhetorical wisdom, gnostic wisdom and Hellenistic–Jewish wisdom.[36] The view that there was a kind of 'gnostic' wisdom at Corinth is nowadays discredited, since there is no evidence for Gnosticism as an identifiable movement at the time 1 Corinthians was written.[37] The two main possibilities are that 'wisdom' refers mainly to style and presentation—to the kind of oratory practised by the sophists; and that 'wisdom' refers mainly to the content of what was taught—for example, to the kind of wisdom taught in Hellenistic Judaism and exemplified in Philo and Sirach. But these interpretations are not mutually exclusive. In the words of Edwin Judge:

35. W. Schrage, *Der erste Brief an die Korinther* (3 vols.; EKKNT, 7/1-3; Neukirchen-Vluyn: Neukirchener Verlag; Zürich and Düsseldorf: Benziger Verlag, 1991, 1995, 1999), I, p. 150, comments that the primary source of the divisions at Corinth was 'Weisheitsfaszination'.

36. Litfin, *Proclamation*, pp. 3-4. To these should perhaps be added rabbinic wisdom, as advocated by those who stress the importance of the supposed Cephas party (e.g. Goulder, 'Σοφία', pp. 516-34).

37. The view that Paul's opponents, in both 1 and 2 Corinthians, were Gnostics was widely held in the middle of the twentieth century but since then, as James Dunn observes, has been in steady retreat (J.D.G. Dunn, *1 Corinthians* [New Testament Guides; Sheffield: Sheffield Academic Press, 1995], p. 36). The samples of Corinthian γνῶσις that Paul quotes (e.g. 1 Cor. 8.4) have parallels both in Jewish thought and in Greek philosophy. George Caird sees in the word γνῶσις an example of 'indeterminacy'. He means by this word that 'some abstract terms are of such a high degree of generality that on close scrutiny they are found to have no clearly defined referent' (G.B. Caird, *The Language and Imagery of the Bible* [London: Duckworth, 1980], pp. 92-93).

'Since the sophists were in fact disposed to take an interest in what they talked about, the ancient distinction between those who cared only about words and those who cared about ideas breaks down'.[38]

Paul discusses the rhetorical aspect of the Corinthian wisdom in chs. 1–3, and its theological and ethical outworking in chs. 4–16.

The rhetorical aspect has been analysed by Duane Litfin and Bruce Winter.[39] Litfin describes the dominant role of rhetoric in Graeco-Roman education and public life. According to Cicero, 'as soon as our world-empire had been established, and an enduring peace had assured us leisure, there was hardly a youth, athirst for fame, who did not deem it his duty to strive with might and main after eloquence… Our people were fired with a really incredible enthusiasm for eloquence'.[40] This was as true in Corinth as in Rome. For example, the early second-century orator Favorinus so impressed the Corinthians by his excellence in λόγος and σοφία that they put up a bronze statue of him in the city library.[41] Litfin's conclusion is that 'the typical Greco-Roman audiences of the day consisted of people who had been fed with a rich diet of oratory from birth, so that, if they could not produce powerful speeches themselves, they certainly expected it from others'.[42]

Pre-eminent among orators were the sophists, whom W.K.C. Guthrie has defined as 'professional orators who gave instructions to young men, and public displays of eloquence, for fees'.[43] It is on this group that Winter concentrates. He shows how sophists were honoured for their eloquence, but also disliked for their competitive, mercenary lifestyle. According to Philo, sophists were 'winning the admiration of city after city and…drawing well-nigh the whole world to honour them'.[44] But he was also critical of the sophists for selling their words and ideas in the marketplace like any other goods.[45] Dio Chrysostom similarly criticizes the sophists as mer-

---

38. E.A. Judge, 'The Early Christians as a Scholastic Community', *JRH* 1 (1960), pp. 4-15, 125-37 (126).

39. Litfin, *Proclamation*; Bruce Winter, *Philo and Paul among the Sophists* (SNTSMS, 96; Cambridge: Cambridge University Press, 1997).

40. Litfin, *Proclamation*, p. 98; Cicero, *De Oratore* 1.13.

41. Litfin, *Proclamation*, p. 144.

42. Litfin, *Proclamation*, p. 131.

43. Litfin, *Proclamation*, pp. 37-38; W.K.C. Guthrie, *The Sophists* (Cambridge: Cambridge University Press, 1971), p. 38.

44. Philo, *Agr.* 143. This quotation, and the quotations that follow, are drawn from Winter, *Philo and Paul*, pp. 4, 55-57, 95, 128.

45. Philo, *Vit. Mos.* 2.212.

cenary, engaging in rivalry with other sophists, with their pupils contributing to the factionalism.[46] He describes them as like peacocks, lifted aloft as
on wings by their fame and their disciples, and refers to 'crowds of
sophists reviling one another'.[47] But in spite of his criticisms Dio listened
to sophists because of his 'uncontrolled craving' for the spoken word.[48]

The great importance attached to rhetoric and oratory in the Graeco-
Roman world must influence our interpretation of phrases such as 'wisdom of words' (σοφία λόγου) (1.17); 'excess of speech or wisdom' (καθ'
ὑπεροχὴν λόγου ἢ σοφίας) (2.1); 'persuasive words of wisdom' (ἐν
πειθοῖς σοφίας λόγοις) (2.4);[49] and 'words taught by human wisdom'
(ἐν διδακτοῖς ἀνθρωπίνης σοφίας λόγοις) (2.13). In a world in which
rhetoric formed a major part of education, and in which virtuoso orators
had the status accorded in modern culture to football players or pop stars,
'excess of speech' and 'persuasive words' could scarcely denote anything
other than rhetorical skill.

In 2.1 Paul states that, when he came to Corinth, he did not come with
an excess of oratory or wisdom. Twice in this verse he refers to his 'coming' to Corinth. Winter suggests that Paul may have had in mind the conventions governing the initial visit to a city by an orator seeking to
establish a reputation. Favorinus, for example, describes how on his initial
visit to Corinth he gave a sample of his eloquence and thus established a
friendly relationship with the people. Philostratus records initial visits to
Athens by three sophists. Alexander's visit was successful because he
gave a panegyric of the city, flatteringly explained why he had not visited
earlier and spoke for the appropriate length of time. Polemo broke with
convention by failing to give an encomium in honour of the Athenians, nor
did he make the usual oration about his own renown. This neglect was
attributed to his arrogance. Philagrus failed to impress, partly because his
oration was not original but had been published elsewhere—a fact known
to the disciples of a rival sophist Herodes Atticus.[50] Winter's understanding of 1 Cor. 2.1 in the light of sophistic practice is convincing. It suggests

46. Dio Chrysostom, *Or.* 8.9.
47. Dio Chrysostom, *Or.* 8.9, 12.5.
48. Dio Chrysostom, *Or.* 19.3-5.
49. Cf. Timothy H. Lim, ' "Not in Persuasive Words of Wisdom but in the Demonstration of the Spirit and Power" ', *NovT* 29.2 (1987), pp. 137-49 (146-47): 'Taken together as a phrase οὐκ ἐν πειθοῖς σοφίας λόγοις explicitly means the setting aside of
persuasive speech'.
50. Winter, *Philo and Paul*, pp. 150-51.

that Paul was concerned to distance himself from the conventional behaviour of visiting sophists.

Why is it, that in the first two chapters of 1 Corinthians, Paul draws this
contrast between his own style of speaking and the rhetorical style typical
of the sophists? The fact that Apollos had visited Corinth some time
before is not a sufficient explanation. Paul is addressing the current situation at Corinth, and makes it clear in 4.6 that his mention of Apollos is
a form of disguise, to avoid naming the real party leaders. The most
likely answer is that these leaders resembled the sophists, both in their
style of speaking and in their competitive recruitment of rival groups of
disciples.[51] Though this reconstruction of the situation is not accepted
by either Litfin or Winter, it provides the simplest explanation of the
rhetorical and sophistic parallels they have adduced.[52]

The wisdom condemned by Paul was not only a matter of style, it had
also a doctrinal content. In this respect it resembled contemporary rhetoric.
Rhetoric in the Graeco-Roman world involved a lot more than clever use
of words. It was concerned, in S.M. Pogoloff's words, with 'the complete
act of communication'.[53] According to Isocrates, speech was the surest
index of sound understanding and the faculty by which one attains to
wisdom.[54] According to Cicero, 'a knowledge of many matters must be
grasped, without which oratory is but an empty and ridiculous swirl of
verbiage'.[55] Quintilian defined rhetoric as 'the science of speaking well';
this involved character as well as technique, since 'no man can speak well

---

51. Cf. Lim's comment on 1 Cor. 2.1-5 ('Demonstration', pp. 145-46): 'Paul in this
passage employs terminology which traditionally belongs to rhetoric and appears to be
distinguishing himself from the other preachers who were circulating in the Corinthian
church'.

52. According to Winter, 'the recent proposal that Paul opposed other preachers
who had accepted rhetorical devices does not fit well with the text of 1 Corinthians. In
fact, it seems a more plausible scenario for 2 Corinthians, though the description of the
ministry of Apollos in Acts 18.24-8 must be taken into account' (Winter, *Philo and
Paul*, p. 161, commenting on Lim, 'Demonstration', p. 148). Litfin (*Proclamation*, p.
229) argues that chs. 1–4 are addressed largely to the concerns of the Apollos group.

53. S.M. Pogoloff, *Logos and Sophia: The Rhetorical Situation of 1 Corinthians*
(SBLDS, 134; Atlanta, GA: Scholars Press, 1992), p. 10.

54. Isocrates, *Nicocles* 6–9; Pogoloff, *Logos and Sophia*, pp. 43-44; Litfin, *Proclamation*, p. 69.

55. Cicero, *De Or.* 1.17; Pogoloff, *Logos and Sophia*, p. 45; Litfin, *Proclamation*,
p. 96.

who is not good himself'.[56] He resented the fact that the philosophers had claimed for themselves matters relating to ethics and wisdom, matters which 'actually belong to the art of oratory', since 'eloquence has its fountain-head in the most secret springs of wisdom'.[57] Admittedly the background to such statements was the fact that some sophists were mere windbags. But many were not. As Edwin Judge says, 'since versatility was a prime test of rhetorical skill, the sophists needed to be much more learned than their critics have credited them with being'.[58]

The Corinthian party leaders were Christian sophists, who combined rhetorical skill with doctrinal and ethical teaching. Before their arrival the Corinthians had enjoyed the ministry of Apollos, who is described by Luke as a learned (or eloquent) man,[59] powerful in the scriptures (Acts 18.24).[60] After experiencing such a powerful expository ministry, it is unlikely that the Corinthians would be seduced by teachers for whom wisdom meant style without content. And there are clear indicators that for Paul σοφία included theological truth. The opposite of wisdom is not poor speaking but foolishness (1.22-25). The contrast Paul draws between divine and human wisdom centres on content—specifically on the preaching of the cross (1.21-25; 2.1-2).

It is sometimes asserted that 'Paul is not arguing in chapters 1–4 against false doctrine'.[61] The basis of such an assertion seems to be a distinction between theology and ethics. Pogoloff quotes with approval the statement

56. Quintilian, *Inst. Or.* 2.15.34; Litfin, *Proclamation*, p. 102.
57. Quintilian, *Inst. Or.* 12.2.6; Litfin, *Proclamation*, pp. 106-107.
58. Judge, 'Early Christians', p. 126.
59. λόγιος can mean either 'learned' or 'eloquent' and BAGD (sv. λόγιος) recognizes both as possible translations. The fact that a single adjective combines both meanings is in itself significant.
60. It is difficult to justify the often-made assertion that, because the evidence of Acts is 'secondary', it should not be used in discussing the background to Paul's letters. Paul's letters refer to their background only indirectly and allusively, and the reconstruction of that background from the letters alone is largely a matter of conjecture. What this assertion really means is that modern conjectural reconstructions are always to be preferred to the evidence of a first-century historian.
61. J. Munck, *Paul and the Salvation of Mankind* (London: SCM Press, 1959), p. 152, quoted and endorsed by Pogoloff, *Logos and Sophia*, pp. 102-103. Litfin's position (*Proclamation*, p. 172) is similar: 'rather than seeking to correct theological errors among the Corinthians, Paul actually assumes a basic agreement with the Corinthians on theological matters and uses this agreement to defend his modus operandi as a preacher'.

of J. Munck that in chs. 1–4 Paul is not concerned with false doctrine or dogmatic controversy but regards the Corinthians' shortcomings as 'ethical failures'.[62] Similarly, Litfin accepts the distinction made by A.E. Harvey between theological controversies and behavioural improprieties, and declares that Paul is not refuting theological error in chs. 1–4 but 'the problem had to do with the contrast of ὁδοί as seen in 4.6-13'.[63]

The distinction between theology and ethics is not one Paul would have recognized. He was sending Timothy to remind the Corinthians of 'my ways in Christ as I teach them everywhere in every church' (4.17). The Christian lifestyle was an integral part of Paul's teaching. In all his letters ethics is grounded in theology. In Romans, for example, the ethical exhortations of chs. 12–15 are introduced in 12.1 by an appeal to 'the mercies of God'—that is to say, to the gospel of salvation and new life in the Spirit expounded in chs. 1–11. Similarly in 1 Corinthians, as will be shown in the next chapter, the behavioural problems discussed in chs. 5–16 are offshoots of the 'wisdom' being taught in Corinth by the party leaders. That is why Paul deals in chs. 1–4 with the root cause of the problem, and then turns to its practical outworking in chs. 5–16.

EXCURSUS A:
THE MEANING OF μετασχηματίζειν IN 1 CORINTHIANS 4.6

In an article entitled 'Der μετασχηματισμός in 1 Kor 4,6', Johan S. Vos has provided a well-documented critical survey of the history of the interpretation of this verse.[64] He notes the opinion of many interpreters that μετασχηματίζειν indicates a covert allusion: that Paul, when ostensibly referring to himself and Apollos, is really directing his remarks at some other person or persons. Vos rejects the idea of a covert allusion.[65] In

62. Pogoloff, *Logos and Sophia*, p. 103, quoting Munck, *Paul*, p. 152.

63. Litfin, *Proclamation*, p. 182, quoting A.E. Harvey, 'The Opposition to St. Paul', in F.L. Cross (ed.), *Studia Evangelica*, IV (TU, 102; Berlin: Akademie Verlag, 1968), pp. 319-32 (319-21).

64. Vos, 'Μετασχηματισμός'.

65. I shall not comment in detail on Vos's lengthy discussion of the meaning of the word σχῆμα. The meaning of σχῆμα is of no relevance to the exegesis of 1 Cor. 4.6. It is true that the verb μετασχηματίζειν was originally formed from the noun σχῆμα. But to interpret a word in the light of its original formation is to be guilty of what James Barr has called 'the root fallacy'. According to Barr, the etymology of a word is not a statement about its meaning but about its history (J. Barr, *The Semantics of*

his opinion, μετασχηματίζειν denotes exemplification—the transformation of a general statement into a particular statement. Paul's remarks about himself and Apollos, he believes, apply to Christian teachers in general. He finds support for this interpretation in the works of two Church Fathers—Origen and Cyril of Alexandria.

Towards the end of his article Vos suggests that μετασχηματίζειν could also have a second meaning: it could indicate the alternation of roles (*Rollenwechsel*). Paul describes himself in chs. 1–4 as fulfilling several roles, such as those of preacher, parent and steward. Vos thinks that in 4.6 the two ideas of exemplification and of alternation of roles may be combined. He finds support for the latter meaning in the writings of Athanasius.

1. *Origen*

The first authority to which Vos appeals is Origen. In his commentary on 1 Corinthians Origen understood the μετασχηματισμός of 1 Cor. 4.6 to be Paul's transformation of teaching true for all generations into the historical case of himself and Apollos.[66] This interpretation is unlikely to be correct. Origen's exegesis was influenced by his general approach to scripture. He believed scripture should be interpreted at three levels. The 'flesh' of scripture was the obvious interpretation. Those who had made some progress in understanding could appreciate its 'soul'. Those who were perfect could be edified by the 'spiritual law'.[67] The literal, historical understanding of scripture was in Origen's view the lowest form of understanding. It was

---

Biblical Language [Oxford: Oxford University Press, 1961], p. 109). In supporting Barr, Anthony Thiselton commends the distinction drawn by Ferdinand de Saussure between diachronic and synchronic linguistics. Diachrony concentrates on the evolutionary development of a word from its root meaning; synchrony ignores the past and concentrates on the current usage of the word. According to Thiselton (writing in 1977), 'the distinction between synchronic and diachronic perspectives has become an axiom in linguistics' (A.C. Thiselton, 'Semantics and New Testament Interpretation', in I.H. Marshall [ed.], *New Testament Interpretation* [Exeter: Paternoster, 1977], pp. 75-104 [81]). If this is true, attempts to discover the meaning of μετασχηματίζειν should concentrate on the usage of that word rather than on the usage of the root word σχῆμα.

66. The Greek text of Origen's commentary on 1 Cor. 4.6 is to be found in C. Jenkins, 'Origen on 1 Corinthians', *JTS* 9 (1908), pp. 231-47, 353-72, 500-14; *JTS* 10 (1909), pp. 29-51 (357). It is discussed in Vos, 'Μετασχηματισμός', pp. 156, 164.

67. Origen, *De Principiis* 4.2.4; *Philocalia* 1.11, as translated in J. Stevenson, *A New Eusebius* (London: SPCK, 1957), pp. 219-20.

therefore natural for him to think that Paul, under the guise of statements about the historical situation at Corinth, was really making statements that applied to every generation.

Such an approach has rightly been discarded in modern scholarship. Paul's interest was in the situation at Corinth. When in 1 Cor. 4.6 he declared his purpose to be 'that you may learn by our example', 'you' meant the Christians at Corinth to whom he was writing.

It should be noted that Origen fully accepted the element of disguise inherent in the word μετασχηματίζειν. His words read: γέγραπται ταῦτα, φησίν, ἐν μετασχηματισμῷ τῷ κατὰ τὰ τότε πράγματα. 'These things are written, says Paul, in the form of a disguise that corresponds to the situation at that time'. The cryptic element, in Origen's opinion, was Paul's failure to indicate that his teaching applied to all generations. But if we reject Origen's approach as unhistorical, we are left with the question: what is the hidden reference that Paul fails to reveal when talking about himself and Apollos? Is he, as Vos seems to suggest, a systematic theologian, using the relationship between himself and Apollos as a vehicle for propounding general theological truths? Or is the example of himself and Apollos cited because of its relevance to a specific situation at Corinth?

In the final clause of 4.6 Paul states that the reason for his 'disguise' is 'so that you may not be puffed up, each in favour of one person in opposition to another'. Paul's concern here is not general and abstract, but springs directly from the Corinthian situation—from the rivalry between the supporters of different teachers described in 1.12. His argument throughout chs. 1–4 is rooted in its historical context.

2. *Cyril of Alexandria*

The second authority to which Vos appeals is Cyril of Alexandria's commentary on the Psalms. The passage he quotes is a difficult one, which raises more questions than it answers.[68] Cyril is commenting on the words of Ps. 10.1 (LXX) (Ps. 11.1 in Hebrew): 'I am trusting in God. How will you say to my soul, "go off like a sparrow to the mountains"?' According to Cyril, the purpose of the psalm is to teach us how to behave in threatening situations. The psalmist tries to teach this by saying, 'I am trusting in God', and 'transforms the word in his own person' (μετασχηματίσας τὸν λόγον ἐφ᾽ ἑαυτῷ). In Vos's opinion Cyril means by these words that

68. Vos, 'Μετασχηματισμός', pp. 163-64, commenting on Cyril of Alexandria, *Expositio in Psalmos*, MPG 69: 789A-D.

the psalmist is exemplifying a general point (how to react in threatening situations) by means of his own example (I am trusting in God).

In order to evaluate Vos's interpretation we need to look at the whole passage. Cyril's exposition of Ps. 10.1 begins with its literal meaning. The psalmist rebukes (ἐπιπλήττει) those who are advising him, and asks them, 'why do you tell me to flee to the mountains when I am trusting in God?' But then Cyril moves on to another interpretation. The mountains are the holy prophets and just men. To dwell in these mountains means to study the lives of the holy men of old, and to realize that they became famous not in their own strength but by trusting in God. In this sense it is right to say to someone who is trusting in God, 'go off like a bird to the mountains'. There follows yet another good reason for going off to the mountains. The mountains are the virtues, which contain nothing that is earthbound. If we let our thoughts travel to these mountains, we shall be able to get rid of earthly things and win the victory over evil desires.

The words Vos quotes come from the middle of this passage, where Cyril is moving from the literal understanding of the verse to its allegorical meaning. The word μετασχηματίσας probably refers to this change. The psalmist is not only rebuking his advisers, he is trying to teach them the inner significance of their words. By this means what was originally bad advice is transformed into good advice. The psalmist has transformed the meaning of the words spoken by his advisers by virtue of of his own faith and insight.

One problem with Vos's interpretation is that μετασχηματίσας is followed, not by εἰς ἑαυτόν, but by ἐφ᾽ ἑαυτῷ. Vos claims the two phrases have more or less the same meaning, but provides no arguments to support his claim. In the light of these uncertainties, Cyril's words can scarcely be used as evidence to determine the meaning of what Paul wrote several centuries earlier.

3. *Athanasius*

Vos believes that μετασχηματίζειν can also indicate an alternation of roles (*Rollenwechsel*). But the passage from Athanasius's 'Life of Antony' that he cites in support of this meaning in fact supports the theory of a 'covert allusion'.[69]

---

69. Vos, 'μετασχηματισμός', pp. 166, 172, commenting on Athanasius, *Vita Antonii*, MPG 26: 900A-904A.

In this passage Antony is describing his battles with the demons who tried to afflict him, and comments:

> It was not I who stopped them and made them ineffective but the Lord, who said, 'I beheld Satan fall like lightning from heaven'. But I, children, mindful of the words of the apostle, have transformed this into myself (μετεσχημάτισα ταῦτα εἰς ἐμαυτόν), so that you may learn not to give up in your spiritual discipline and not to be afraid of the manifestations of the devil and his demons.

In describing his conflict with the demons, Antony attributes to himself the victory that really belongs to the Lord. He does this so that his followers may learn from his example and copy his ascetic lifestyle. He uses the word μετασχηματίζειν in a sense that is true to Paul's usage in 1 Cor. 4.6: he is saying things about himself which, though true, should really have been said about the Lord, just as Paul was saying things about himself and Apollos which, though true, should really have been said about other people.

Vos recognizes that this is the meaning of Antony's words, but also tries to read into them an additional meaning. Both before and after the passage just quoted Antony states that, in talking about himself, he is playing the part of a fool (ἄφρων), as Paul did in 2 Corinthians. Vos thinks his use of μετασχηματίζειν may be a reference to his adoption of the fool's role.

It is true that the word μετασχηματίζειν could be used, in a context that made this plain, to indicate the adoption of a role. But when it is followed by εἰς, the noun or pronoun governed by εἰς denotes the end product of the transformation. This is true of all Greek verbs compounded with μετα- which denote change from one state into another.[70] In Antony's case, μετεσχημάτισα is followed by εἰς ἐμαυτόν, and this makes it plain that the transformation he has in mind is not transformation from being sensible into being a fool, but the transformation of things that should be said about the Lord into things said about himself. Had he been referring to an exchange of roles, he would have written something like μετεσχημάτισα ἐμαυτὸν εἰς ἄφρονα.

4. General Comments

In his review of Paul's argument in 1 Cor. 3.5–4.5 Vos makes a number of valid observations.[71]

---

70. For examples see Hall, 'Disguise', p. 144.
71. Vos, 'Μετασχηματισμός', pp. 167-71.

i.   He believes that the main theme of this section, which Paul regards as the root cause of the problems in the Corinthian church, is their false evaluation of apostles.

ii.   In 3.10-17 Paul uses indefinite terms such as τις and ἄλλος. Vos notes that many scholars have seen in these indefinite terms a reference either to an individual (such as Apollos or Peter) or to members of the church. In his opinion these terms suggest people on a par with Apollos— namely, incoming missionaries rather than local church members, and there is nothing in the passage to suggest a reference to any one individual apostle.

iii. Vos points out that the problem at Corinth exemplified a problem Paul faced in many other churches—the problem of rival missionaries. His conclusion is that, in referring to himself and Apollos, Paul was giving a particular example of how such a problem should be dealt with in general.

It seems to me that Vos's understanding of this section is correct at every point except the final conclusion. Paul is indeed referring to the evaluation of missionaries. But his concern in chs. 1–4 is with the current situation at Corinth, as reported by Chloe's people. His description of church builders in 3.10-15 is not a generalized depiction of a situation that arose from time to time in the Pauline churches, but a depiction of what was currently happening at Corinth. It is significant that the Church Father whose interpretation Vos commends most warmly is Origen, for whom the general and theoretical understanding of scripture took precedence over the particular and the historical.

Vos objects on two grounds to the idea that there could be a covert allusion to people currently at work in Corinth.[72] His first objection is that in other places Paul does confront people openly, such as the 'puffed-up people' in 1 Cor. 4.18-21, the apostle Peter in Gal. 2.11-14, and the 'false apostles' in 2 Cor. 10–13. This objection fails to appreciate that Paul was a tactician, who chose the right moment to launch a personal attack.[73] His uninhibited language in 2 Cor. 10–13 should not be regarded as normative for his handling of controversies in all circumstances.

Vos's second objection is that, if 4.6 refers to the putting on of a mask, it also takes off the mask; and this procedure is contrary to the nature of figurative language as Quintilian has defined it. This is a half-truth. Paul does not fully take off the mask in 4.6. He still does not name the

---

72. Vos, 'Μετασχηματισμός', p. 170.
73. For a discussion of Paul's tactics in 1 and 2 Corinthians, see Chapter 12.

people concerned, but uses the indefinite terms ὁ εἷς and ὁ ἕτερος. Moreover, Paul does elsewhere use figurative language and then explain it—Rom. 7.1-7 is a good example. Paul's letters are so flawed from a technical literary point of view that it is doubtful if Quintilian would have recognised them as literature even if he had read them. Those who try to make Paul's letters conform to the standards laid down by ancient literary purists are disciples, not of Quintilian or of Aristotle, but of Procrustes.[74]

EXCURSUS B:
THE TRANSLATION OF 1 CORINTHIANS 4.15

1 Cor. 4.15 reads: ἐὰν γὰρ μυρίους παιδαγωγοὺς ἔχητε ἐν Χριστῷ, ἀλλ᾽ οὐ πολλοὺς πατέρας. According to Robertson and Plummer, the present subjunctive in this verse 'implies futurity'. They translate: 'if, as time goes by, ye should have in turn an indefinite number of tutors in Christ, yet ye will never have had but one father'.[75] Fee offers a similar translation: 'Even though you may end up having countless thousands of guardians in Christ, at least you do not have many fathers'. He claims that ἐάν with the present subjunctive has the sense of 'a contemplated future result' and cites Robertson's *Grammar* as his authority.[76] The contention of this note is that ἐάν with the present subjunctive does not imply futurity, and that the present tenses in 1 Cor. 4.15 refer to the current situation at Corinth.

1. ἐάν *with the Present Subjunctive*

The construction of ἐάν with the present subjunctive is common in the New Testament (as it is also common in the papyri). Most commonly this

74. See Chapter 5 for a critique of the attempts that are sometimes made to make Paul's letters conform to ancient rhetorical orthodoxy.

75. A. Robertson and A. Plummer, *A Critical and Exegetical Commentary on the First Epistle of St. Paul to the Corinthians* (ICC; Edinburgh: T. & T. Clark, 2nd edn, 1914), p. 89.

76. Fee, *First Epistle*, p. 185, citing A.T. Robertson, *A Grammar of New Testament Greek in the Light of Historical Research* (London: Hodder & Stoughton, 1914), p. 1018. All the quotations from Robertson in this Excursus are from p. 1018.

Fee describes his translation as 'an attempt to give to ἐάν with the subjunctive the sense of a contemplated future result', without mentioning the tense of the verb. But it is the use of ἐάν with the *present* subjunctive that calls his translation into question. No one disputes the future reference of ἐάν with the aorist subjunctive.

construction denotes a general statement—'a hypothesis which can occur over and over again'.[77] In such cases ἐάν can often be translated 'when' or 'whenever'. The apodosis (where it is not an imperative) can be either in the present or in the future indicative, with little difference in meaning between the two.

In this respect Greek is similar to English. In English you can say either 'if you are well prepared, you feel confident' (present indicative); or 'if you are well prepared, you will feel confident' (future indicative). There is little difference in meaning between these two statements. Similarly in Greek you can say either ἐάν τις περιπατῇ ἐν τῇ ἡμέρᾳ, οὐ προσκόπτει (if anyone walks in daylight, he does not stumble; Jn 11.9) or τυφλὸς δὲ τυφλὸν ἐὰν ὁδηγῇ, ἀμφότεροι εἰς βόθυνον πεσοῦνται (if a blind person leads a blind person, they will both fall into the ditch; Mt. 15.14).

Some of the verses in which ἐάν + present subjunctive in the protasis is combined with an indicative in the apodosis are not general statements but refer to a specific occasion. In such cases it is the tense of the verb in the apodosis that determines whether that occasion is present or future. For example, in Lk. 19.31 the disciples are given instructions for fetching the Palm Sunday donkey: ἐάν τις ὑμᾶς ἐρωτᾷ, Διὰ τί λύετε; οὕτως ἐρεῖτε ὅτι Ὁ κύριος αὐτοῦ χρείαν ἔχει (If anyone asks you why you are untying it, you are to say, 'the master needs it'). In this verse the apodosis is in the future tense, and therefore the whole sentence refers to the future. The element of futurity is not inherent in the construction of ἐάν + present subjunctive, but is determined by the future tense in the apodosis. Other examples of this construction are Mk 14.31; Lk. 13.3 and 1 Cor. 16.4.

Similarly, when ἐάν + present subjunctive is combined with an apodosis in the present indicative, both clauses relate to the same period of time. In most cases these are general statements (Lk. 6.33; Jn 9.31; 11.9, 10; 13.35; 15.14; Rom. 2.25; 14.8; 1 Cor. 6.4; 9.16; 11.14; 13.2, 3; 14.14, 24; 1 Tim. 1.8; 2 Tim. 2.5; Jas 2.14-16; 1 Jn 1.5, 7, plus various verses in which ἐάν μή means 'unless'). In a few instances, however, the reference is to a specific current situation, and in these cases the current reference is common to both clauses.

In Mt. 8.2 a man with leprosy says: Κύριε, ἐὰν θέλῃς δύνασαί με καθαρίσαι. Robertson asserts that ἐὰν θέλῃς 'is future in conception'. But this is not so. The man knows Jesus has the power to heal him, but doubts

---

77. N. Turner, *Syntax* (vol. III of J.H. Moulton, *A Grammar of New Testament Greek*; Edinburgh: T. & T. Clark, 1990), p. 114.

whether he has the will. It is Jesus' present state of mind that the man is concerned about. We should translate: 'if you want to cleanse me, you are able to cleanse me'.

In Jn 5.31 and 8.14 there are two paradoxical statements—ἐὰν ἐγὼ μαρτυρῶ περὶ ἐμαυτοῦ, ἡ μαρτυρία μου οὐκ ἔστιν ἀληθής (if I bear witness about myself, my witness is not true) and κἂν ἐγὼ μαρτυρῶ περὶ ἐμαυτοῦ, ἀληθής ἐστιν ἡ μαρτυρία μου (even if I bear witness about myself, my witness is true). Robertson translates 5.31 'if perchance I bear witness', and thus tries to force a future reference onto these words. But the context of both these verses is criticism by Jesus' opponents of what he is currently saying.

John 5.31 is part of a long discourse running from v. 19 to v. 47. The context of the discourse is given by John in v. 18. The Jewish opponents of Jesus wanted to kill him because he was talking about God as his own father and thus making himself equal with God. Jesus replied, 'the son can do nothing of himself except what he sees the father doing' (v. 19). Verse 30 is an amplification of v. 19: 'I can do nothing of myself; as I hear, I judge', and it is this statement that is commented on in v. 31. Throughout the passage the point at issue is what Jesus is currently saying about his relationship with his Father.

The reference to the present is even clearer in 8.14. In this verse Jesus is replying to a statement of the Pharisees: 'you are bearing witness about yourself; your witness is not true'. This in turn is a comment on the words of Jesus in v. 12: 'I am the light of the world'. A statement of Jesus in the present tense provokes a comment by the Pharisees in the present tense to which Jesus replies in the present tense. The debate is about the claims Jesus is currently making.

The other verses cited by Robertson as parallels to 1 Cor. 4.15 are Acts 5.38 and Mt. 6.22. But neither of these verses is a proper parallel.

Acts 5.38 reads: ὅτι ἐὰν ἦ ἐξ ἀνθρώπων ἡ βουλὴ αὕτη ἢ τὸ ἔργον τοῦτο, καταλυθήσεται (because if the theory and practice of these people is of human origin, it will be demolished). Robertson asserts that 'the supposition is about a present situation, but ἐάν and the subjunctive contemplate the future result (turn out to be)'. This is not the case. The ἐάν-clause relates to the *origin* of the Christian faith, not to its future development. The 'future result' appears only in the apodosis. The sentence as a whole refers to the future because the verb in the apodosis (καταλυθήσεται) is future, not because of any inherent futurity in the ἐάν-clause. This verse is therefore not parallel to 1 Cor. 4.15, which does not have a future verb in the apodosis.

Mt. 6.22 reads: ἐὰν οὖν ᾖ ὁ ὀφθαλμός σου ἁπλοῦς, ὅλον τὸ σῶμά σου φωτεινὸν ἔσται (so if your eye is single, your whole body will be bright). This is a general statement and, as we saw earlier, in such general statements the apodosis can contain either a present or a future indicative with little difference in meaning. In the Lukan parallel (11.34) the apodosis is in the present tense: ὅταν ὁ ὀφθαλμός σου ἁπλοῦς ᾖ, καὶ ὅλον τὸ σῶμά σου φωτεινόν ἐστιν. Mt. 6.22 is a general statement set in the middle of the Sermon of the Mount, which consists of generalized ethical teaching; it is not parallel to 1 Cor. 4.15, which is rooted in the current situation at Corinth.

2. *The Meaning of 1 Corinthians 4.15*

In 1 Cor. 4.15 there is no verb in the apodosis, and a verb has to be understood—either ἀλλ᾽ οὐκ ἔχετε πολλοὺς πατέρας (you do not have many fathers), if the reference is to the present, or ἀλλ᾽ οὐχ ἕξετε πολλοὺς πατέρας (you will not have many fathers), if the reference is to the future. The words in the second half of the verse ἐγὼ ὑμᾶς ἐγέννησα (I have become your father) make it clear that Paul's fatherhood is a present reality, and the verb ἔχετε in the present tense should therefore be understood. But if the apodosis has a present reference, this is likely to be true also of the protasis.

It is Paul's use of ἀλλά in this verse that defines its meaning. 1 Cor. 4.15 is one of six verses in Paul's letters in which a conditional clause is followed by ἀλλά. Examination of the five other cases reveals this is a logical, argumentative idiom. The meaning is: 'even though the statement in the protasis is true, the statement in the apodosis is also true'. In 1 Cor. 8.5 the supposition in the protasis (v. 5a) ('if there are many so-called gods') is specifically stated to be a true supposition in v. 5b. In 1 Cor. 9.2 the supposition 'if others do not regard me as an apostle' relates to a real, not to a hypothetical situation, as is made clear by Paul's allusion to his 'examiners' in the following verse (v. 3). In 2 Cor. 4.16 the words εἰ καὶ ὁ ἔξω ἡμῶν ἄνθρωπος διαφθείρεται (even if our external being is falling into decay) are a summary of what Paul has been saying in the preceding verses (vv. 7-15) about the bodies of the apostles being like fragile clay pots. In 2 Cor. 11.6 the words εἰ δὲ καὶ ἰδιώτης τῷ λόγῳ echo a taunt of Paul's opponents which he accepts: 'yes, I am not a professional orator, but...' The precise meaning of 2 Cor. 5.16 is uncertain because of the dispute about the meaning of 'knowing Christ according to the flesh', but the general sense is clear: 'even if it is true that we know Christ after the flesh, now we know him differently'. In each of these five verses the 'if' clause does not express doubt, but a logical concession, and the ἀλλά clause presents another consideration that should be borne in mind: 'even though *x* is the case, *y* is also the case'.

In all these verses Paul uses εἰ in the protasis, whereas in 1 Cor. 4.15 he uses ἐάν; but this is not of major importance. As J.H. Moulton says, 'the difference between εἰ and ἐάν has been considerably lessened in Hellenistic as compared with earlier Greek'.[78] It is the use of ἀλλά in the apodosis that determines the nature of the idiom, and BAGD is correct in classifying 1 Cor. 4.15 under the same section as the other passages.[79]

The reason why Paul used ἐάν rather than εἰ here can only be conjectured, but two factors may have influenced him. First, the statement in the protasis is an ironic, not a literal statement. The teachers at Corinth did not literally number ten thousand, and the title 'pedagogue' was not one used either by them or by their Corinthian disciples. Second, Paul's knowledge of what was going on at Corinth was by hearsay—from Chloe's people and from Stephanas and party. For both these reasons, he may have wished to express himself somewhat provisionally—'even though you may have thousands of "pedagogues", you have only one father'.

In the light of all these considerations, the present tense of the verbs in 1 Cor. 4.15 should be understood as having a present reference. Paul is commenting on the existing situation at Corinth. The Corinthians have one father (Paul) and many pedagogues (their new teachers). This interpretation is not only grammatically preferable, it also suits the context, since the main subject of vv. 14-21 is the conflict between the ethical teaching and practice of Paul and the ethical teaching and practice of his opponents.

---

78. J.H. Moulton, *A Grammar of New Testament Greek*. I. *Prolegomena* (Edinburgh: T. & T. Clark, 1906), p. 187.

79. BAGD sv. ἀλλά, Section 4.

Chapter 2

THE UNITY OF 1 CORINTHIANS

The thesis of this chapter is that 1 Corinthians is a unity. I shall maintain
that the practical problems dealt with in chs. 5–16 have their roots in the
'wisdom' attacked in chs. 1–4, and that the arguments commonly used by
advocates of the partition of 1 Corinthians are unsound.

In chs. 5–16 Paul deals with a variety of issues, all of them (with the exception of chs. 15 and 16) concerned with day-to-day behaviour—relationships between the sexes (chs. 5–7); the eating of food sacrificed to idols
(chs. 8–10); and the proper conduct of worship and exercise of spiritual
gifts (chs. 11–14). In each case Paul based his advice on theological
principle, and the Corinthian slogans he quoted reveal that they based their
behaviour on theological principle. In ch. 8, for example, their behaviour
was based on γνῶσις, and it is probable that the wisdom teaching of the
party leaders lay behind all the slogans quoted in chs. 5–16. These chapters reveal the ethical principles of the 'wisdom' in vogue at Corinth, and
help to explain why Paul was so vehemently opposed to it.

1. *Unity and Diversity*

Paul recognizes the presence in the Corinthian church of both unity and
diversity. In chs. 5–16 he acknowledges a variety of opinion at Corinth on
many of the issues discussed. But throughout the letter he presupposes
the unity of the church as well as its diversity. Schrage comments on the
fact that, in the attempt to identify the differences between the parties, too
little attention has been paid to what they had in common.[1] Paul regards
the 'wisdom' criticized in chs. 1–4 as a common feature of all the parties,
and when discussing the behavioural problems resulting from that 'wisdom' in chs. 5–16, addresses his remarks to the church as a whole.

---

1.   Schrage, *Der erste Brief*, I, p. 142.

In his analysis of what he calls 'the Corinthian interpretation of Christian faith', John Barclay makes two points. First, there were many different interpretations of Christian faith at Corinth. 'There are libertines and ascetics, rich and poor, weak and strong—not to mention the four parties whose slogans Paul ridicules in 1 Corinthians 1–4'. Second, there was at the same time a 'dominant ethos' in the church—'a consistent theological pattern which is the recognizable target of Paul's critical comments in most sections of the letter'. This dominant ethos centred on two themes: wisdom and knowledge on the one hand (they possessed σοφία and γνῶσις), and possession of the Spirit on the other hand (they were πνευματικοί and τέλειοι).[2]

If the party leaders were Christian sophists, Barclay's analysis makes good sense. They all possessed a 'wisdom' that included both rhetorical skill and theological content. They also shared a common emphasis on the Holy Spirit, expressed in the exercise of spiritual gifts and particularly in prophecy, which gave to their teaching a supernatural authority.[3] At the same time they differed from each other in point of detail. Paul does not attempt to attribute specific views to specific people. Throughout the letter he refuses to name names and refers instead to 'someone' (τις) or 'some people' (τινες). But these Christian sophists were probably the moving force behind the various problems dealt with in chs. 5–16, both by virtue of the 'dominant ethos' they collectively inculcated and also by virtue of their individual emphases.

We do not know how many or how few were the 'some' who denied the resurrection (15.12);[4] the people who were argumentative about the behaviour of women prophets (11.16); the people who claimed to be prophets

2.   J.M.G. Barclay, 'Thessalonica and Corinth: Social Contrasts in Pauline Christianity', *JSNT* 47 (1992), pp. 49-74 (61-62).

3.   For further discussion of the prophetic authority claimed by Paul's opponents see Chapter 7.

4.   A.J.M. Wedderburn ('The Problem of the Denial of the Resurrection in 1 Corinthians XV', *NovT* 23.3 [1981], pp. 229-41 [240]) argues against the opinion that the deniers of the resurrection were a small minority; but he does so on the less than conclusive grounds that most scholars are reluctant to adopt this opinion and that it would be 'more satisfactory' if the denial of the resurrection was in continuity with beliefs reflected elsewhere in the letter. In 1 Cor. 15.33-34 Paul warns the church against being led astray by 'some people' (τινες) who do not know God, and whose company members of the church should avoid. Some members of the church (ἐν ὑμῖν τινες, v. 12) had probably been influenced by these people, but it is unclear who they were or how many people they had influenced.

and opposed Paul's attitude to the conduct of worship (14.37); the people who ate meals in temples, relying on their γνῶσις (8.10); the prophets claiming to possess the Spirit whose views about marriage Paul opposes in 7.40. All these people would have been influenced by the 'dominant ethos' at Corinth; but their views on specific issues would not have been shared by all the members of the church.

2. *Puffed-upness at Corinth*

The clearest indication of the continuity between chs. 1–4 and chs. 5–16 is the verb φυσιοῦσθαι (to be puffed up). This verb occurs six times in 1 Corinthians and only once elsewhere in the Pauline corpus.[5] Thiselton defines it as 'being blown up with self-importance like the frog in Aesop's fables'.[6] It occurs three times in ch. 4 and three times in chs. 5–16. Examination of these six occurrences reveals the continuity between the competitive pursuit of 'wisdom' rebuked in chs. 1–4 and the behavioural problems discussed in chs. 5–16.

In 4.6 Paul states that he has disguised his criticism of the party leaders by using the names of himself and Apollos 'so that you may learn from our example the principle "not beyond what is written",[7] so that you may not be puffed up, each supporting one person in opposition to another' (ἵνα μὴ εἷς ὑπὲρ τοῦ ἑνὸς φυσιοῦσθε κατὰ τοῦ ἑτέρου).[8] The puffed-upness of the Corinthians is here related to the party divisions. By saying 'I support so-and-so' they were boasting of the wisdom of their particular teacher and devaluing the wisdom of other teachers. There is a close parallel to this situation in the rivalries between competing sophists and their disciples, as described by contemporary writers,[9] and this is a strong argument in favour of identifying the party leaders as Christian sophists.

The next three occurrences of φυσιοῦσθαι are in 4.18–5.2. In 4.18 Paul states that some people have become puffed up 'on the grounds that I am not coming to you' (ὡς μὴ ἐρχομένου δέ μου πρὸς ὑμᾶς ἐφυσιώθησαν

5.   The other instance is Col. 2.18: εἰκῇ φυσιούμενος ὑπὸ τοῦ νοὸς τῆς σαρκὸς αὐτοῦ.
6.   Thiselton, *First Epistle*, p. 355.
7.   For discussion of the phrase τὸ μὴ ὑπὲρ ἃ γέγραπται, see Chapter 6.
8.   For the meaning of this phrase, see Chapter 1 n. 11.
9.   Dio Chrysostom, *Or.* 8.9; Plutarch, *Mor.* 131A; Philo, *Rer. Div. Her.* 246–48; *Agr.* 159–64.

τινες).[10] These words follow v. 17, in which Paul talks of sending Timothy to remind them of his 'ways in Christ'—the Christian standards of behaviour that were being challenged at Corinth. The puffed-up people were apparently boasting about 'ways' of a different sort—behaviour of which they knew Paul would disapprove if he were present. This puffed-upness is attributed in v. 18 only to 'some people'—perhaps only a small group; but they were an influential group. The same word φυσιοῦσθαι that is used in 4.18 to describe the attitude of 'some people' is used in 5.2 to describe the attitude of the church as a whole.

In 4.19 Paul asserts that on his next visit he will discover not the words of these puffed-up people but their power. The tone of 4.19-21 is very similar to that of 2 Cor. 13.1-10. In both passages Paul voices his fear that his forthcoming visit will be a power struggle—that he may have to come with a rod (1 Cor. 4.21) and use rigorously the authority the Lord has given him (2 Cor. 13.2, 10). In both cases he hopes that this will not be the case—that he will be able to come not with a rod but in love and a spirit of meekness (1 Cor. 4.21) and will be able to use his authority to build up rather than to destroy (2 Cor. 13.10). It is interesting that the climax of Paul's confrontation with his opponents in 2 Cor. 10–13 consists of a virtual repetition of what he said in 1 Cor. 4.

In 4.18-21 the verb φυσιοῦσθαι denotes an attitude on the part of 'some people' that may require disciplinary action in the future. In 5.2 it denotes the attitude of the church as a whole, in a situation that requires immediate disciplinary action. In spite of these differences, chs. 4 and 5 are closely connected. Kenneth Bailey has drawn attention to the links between 4.17-21 and 5.1-11.[11] Chapter 4 ends with a threat: some people are puffed up

---

10. The force of ὡς is to give the subjective ground of the verb that follows. Their belief that Paul was not coming was the reason for their puffed-upness. BAGD (sv. ὡς) 3b paraphrase: 'as though I were not coming (according to their mistaken idea)'. Their mistaken idea may have been derived from the previous letter mentioned in 5.9. Paul's statement raises the question: why should the belief of 'some people' that he was not coming to Corinth make them puffed up? The most likely reason is that they interpreted his preference for a letter rather than a visit as a sign of timidity—the accusation to which Paul refers explicitly in 2 Cor. 10.10.

11. K.E. Bailey, 'The Structure of 1 Corinthians and Paul's Theological Method with Special Reference to 4.17', *NovT* 25 (1983), pp. 152-81 (160-63). Bailey's contention is that 4.17 marks the beginning of a new section of the letter (what he calls 'the second essay'). But 4.17 is in fact a link verse, referring backwards as well as forwards. The reason why Paul is sending Timothy to remind them of his Christian

on the grounds that Paul is not coming to Corinth; but he will come, if the Lord wills, and will discover not the fine words of these puffed-up people but their power (4.18-19). It is for the Corinthians to choose whether his next visit will be friendly or disciplinary (4.21). This threat is immediately followed by a specific instance of Corinthian puffed-upness (5.1-2). Paul, though physically absent, has already passed judgment on the man's action as though he were present (5.3), and expects the Corinthians to ratify his judgment. As Bailey says, the words ἀπών and παρών in 5.3 echo the discussion in 4.18-19 as to whether Paul is coming to Corinth or not. 'Paul seems to be saying, "Some think I am not coming (4.18) but I am indeed coming (4.19); as a matter of fact, although I am absent in body consider me already present in spirit (5.3)" '.[12]

There is thus a continuity between the puffed-upness of the τινες who were defying Paul's authority in 4.18-19 and the puffed-upness of the church as a whole in 5.2. Thiselton points out that half of the occurrences of φυσιοῦσθαι in 1 Corinthians 'appear as part of a refrain in the fourth chapter which leads naturally towards the thrust of Paul's censure in 5.1ff'.[13] This suggests that the action of the incestuous man was what Schrage calls a 'provocatively ideological act'.[14] His behaviour was related to the puffed-up attitude of 4.18, and was in conscious defiance of Paul's moral teaching. The man was either one of the τινες who were confident that Paul would not come to Corinth to deal with the matter, or was under their influence.

The people referred to as τινες in 4.18 realized that their teaching and behaviour were in conflict with the tradition taught by Paul. But the

lifestyle (v. 17) is the presence at Corinth of a number of 'pedagogues', whose moral guidance of the Corinthians commended an alternative lifestyle (v. 15).

12. Bailey, 'Structure', p. 161.

13. A.C. Thiselton, 'The Meaning of Σάρξ in 1 Cor. 5.5: A Fresh Approach in the Light of Logical and Semantic Factors', *SJT* 26 (1973), pp. 204-28 (212). In his commentary (*First Epistle*, p. 381) Thiselton points out 'various continuities of theme and argument' between chs. 1–4 and the chapters that follow.

14. Schrage, *Der erste Brief*, I, p. 372. Schrage mentions this as a possibility without committing himself. As he says, if the phrase ἐν τῷ ὀνόματι τοῦ κυρίου ἡμῶν Ἰησοῦ is taken with κατεργασάμενον (i.e. the man had acted 'in the name of our Lord Jesus') the case for this interpretation is greatly strengthened. But v. 3 is concerned throughout with judgment, not with the man's motivation, and the phrase should be taken with κέκρικα. The main reason for seeing the man's action as provocatively ideological (*provokativ-ideologisch*) is the puffed-upness of the Corinthians in supporting it.

majority of the church may not have realized this. In 11.2 Paul writes: 'I praise you because you always remember me and keep the traditions as I handed them on to you'. These words are generally recognized to be a quotation of a Corinthian claim to be loyal to Paul's tradition (a claim probably made in their letter to Paul).[15] Most of the Corinthians, it would appear, did not appreciate the inconsistency between the new teaching and the tradition handed down by Paul. It is easy to imagine elements in Paul's tradition that could have led them to think in this way, such as his insistence that Christians were free from the law (Gal. 5.1; Rom. 7.1-6) and that the Spirit should not be quenched (1 Thess. 5.19-20). The church as a whole was still loyal to Paul and in 1 Corinthians he presupposes this basic loyalty, but as a group of relatively recent converts they had been beguiled by their new teachers into believing that the incestuous behaviour of this man involved the exercise of Christian freedom and was therefore something to be proud of.

Those who deny that the puffed-upness of the Corinthians in 5.2 was ideological usually argue that the Corinthians were puffed up *in spite* of what the man had done, not because of it. In other words, the Corinthians were complacent, and Paul was saying to them, 'how can you continue to be puffed up when such behaviour is going on in your community?'[16] But being puffed up is more than complacency. Paul comments in 5.6 that 'your boasting (καύχημα) is not good'. As Thiselton says, 'the words φυσιόω and καύχημα respectively introduce and conclude the rebuke of 5.2-6'.[17] The Corinthians were boasting of the man's action, not just tolerating it.[18]

---

15. Cf. N.A. Dahl, 'Paul and the Church at Corinth according to 1 Cor. 1.10–4.21', in W.R. Farmer, C.F.D. Moule and R.R. Niebuhr (eds.), *Christian History and Interpretation: Studies Presented to John Knox* (Cambridge: Cambridge University Press, 1967), pp. 313-35 (323): 'The official attitude of the congregation seems to have been one of loyalty to the apostle'. For further discussion of 11.2, see Chapter 3.

16. A. Robertson and A. Plummer (*Critical and Exegetical Commentary*, p. 93) paraphrase 5.2: 'And you, with this monstrous crime among you, have gone on in your inflated self-complacency'. Further examples of this interpretation can be found in A.D. Clarke, *Secular and Christian Leadership in Corinth: A Socio-Historical and Exegetical Study of 1 Corinthians 1–6* (AGJU, 18; Leiden: E.J. Brill, 1993), p. 76 n. 12. Thiselton (*First Epistle*, p. 384) translates: 'and you remain complacent!', and discusses various interpretations of this verse on pp. 388-90.

17. Thiselton, 'Σάρξ', p. 213.

18. Clarke (*Leadership*, pp. 72-88) and J.K. Chow (*Patronage and Power: A Study of Social Networks in Corinth* [JSNTSup, 75; Sheffield: Sheffield Academic Press,

The key to the puffed-upness of the church over the case of incest is to be found in the slogans quoted in 6.12-20. Chs. 5 and 6 form a single unit whose subject is πορνεία.[19] Paul begins in 5.1 with a reference to πορνεία in general (ὅλως),[20] and then proceeds to the extreme case of πορνεία represented by the incestuous relationship. After dealing with that case, and after the digression of 6.1-11,[21] he reverts to the subject of πορνεία in general in 6.12-20. By handling the topic in this way Paul reveals his understanding that the particular case dealt with in 5.1-13 is an extreme example of the general Corinthian approval of πορνεία countered in 6.12-20.[22] If this is so, the slogans refuted in 6.12-20, which constitute the

1992], pp. 139-40) speculate that the Corinthians may have taken no action because the man was a rich patron. Dunn (*1 Corinthians*, p. 53) agrees that this view is speculative, but comments: 'Certainly when Paul talks of arrogance in 5.2 we may well envisage a congregation whose quiet acquiescence to such behaviour Paul sees as reflecting the arrogance of a powerful figure able to act in such disregard for established morality'. This suggestion does violence to Paul's language. What he condemns is the arrogance of the Corinthian church as a whole, not the arrogance of one man; and 'puffed-upness' and 'boasting' are almost the opposite of quiet acquiescence.

19. On the meaning of πορνεία see the debate between B. Malina ('Does πορνεία Mean Fornication?', *NovT* 14 [1972], pp. 10-17) and J. Jensen ('Does πορνεία Mean Fornication? A Critique of Bruce Malina', *NovT* 20 (1978), pp. 161-84. The term was comprehensive enough to include both recourse to a prostitute (6.12-20) and an incestuous relationship with a member of one's own family (5.1-13). The common translation 'sexual immorality' may be the best means of conveying this comprehensiveness (cf. Fee, *First Epistle*, pp. 199-200).

20. Of the various meanings of ὅλως given in BAGD (2nd edn), 'generally speaking' suits the context best. ὅλως (sexual immorality in general) is contrasted with καὶ τοιαύτη (and such a case of sexual immorality in particular). The translation 'it is actually reported' is preferred by BAGD (2nd edn) and by Thiselton (*First Epistle*, p. 384). BAGD (3rd edn) offers in addition (as a preferred translation) 'it's bandied about everywhere, it's a matter of general knowledge'. Alternatively, ὅλως can be translated 'at all'—when used with a negative ὅλως means 'not at all' (Mt. 5.34; 1 Cor. 15.29).

21. The trigger for the digression may have been the word πλεονέκτης in the list of vices in 5.11. The Corinthians' pride in their tolerance of sexual immorality seems to Paul to be symptomatic of their proud tolerance of immorality in general, and the case of πλεονεξία that forms the subject of 6.1-11 is a case in point. It is significant that near the end of 6.1-11 (in vv. 9-10) there appears a very similar vice list to that of 5.11.

22. G. Harris ('The Beginnings of Church Discipline: 1 Cor. 5', *NTS* 37 [1991], pp. 1-21 [5]) notes the observation of P.S. Zaas that Paul's argument moves from the condemnation of a specific vice to the condemnation of a general one, and comments: 'It would be better to say that Paul is concerned with the general topic throughout the passage, and that the case of incest is an instance of the general topic'.

theoretical basis of the Corinthian justification of πορνεία, can properly be used to explain the puffed-up pride of the Corinthians in the case of incest.

In 6.12-20 Paul quotes three slogans. The first is πάντα μοι ἔξεστιν (all things are allowable to me). The background to this saying is probably the widespread philosophical idea that the wise man will always make wise decisions and therefore has the right to do whatever he wishes. Examples of this idea can be found, for example, in Dio Chrysostom and in Philo.[23] The slogan is a product of the 'wisdom of this world' that Paul had earlier criticized in 2.6-16.

The second slogan is in 6.13: τὰ βρώματα τῇ κοιλίᾳ καὶ ἡ κοιλία τοῖς βρώμασιν· ὁ δὲ θεὸς καὶ ταύτην καὶ ταῦτα καταργήσει (food is for the belly and the belly for food; and God will put an end to both).[24] This slogan implies a separation between the physical and the spiritual. The belly is regarded as nothing more than a temporary food disposal unit, and has no spiritual or moral significance; therefore it does not matter what you eat. The relevance of this slogan to the discussion of πορνεία is probably that the Corinthians regarded all bodily functions, not just eating and drinking, as morally indifferent, including sexual practices. Paul's reply is that, for a Christian, the body is holy and belongs to the Lord: we are responsible to God for the way we use our bodies, and sexual relationships have a spiritual significance.

The third slogan in 6.18 is of a similar type: πᾶν ἁμάρτημα, ὃ ἐὰν ποιήσῃ ἄνθρωπος, ἐκτὸς τοῦ σώματός ἐστιν (every sin that is committed is external to the body).[25] According to this slogan sin is something spiritual, not something physical, and therefore what you do with your body cannot be regarded as sin. Paul replies that πορνεία is not so much

23. Dio Chrysostom, *Or.* 14.16; Philo, *Omn. Prob. Lib.* 59.

24. See Thiselton, *First Epistle*, pp. 462-63, for arguments in favour of including the words ὁ δὲ θεὸς καὶ ταύτην καὶ ταῦτα καταργήσει within the slogan.

25. For arguments in favour of regarding 6.18a as a Corinthian slogan, see J. Murphy-O'Connor, 'Corinthian Slogans in 1 Cor. 6.12-20', *CBQ* 40 (1978), pp. 391-96. Fee (*First Epistle*, pp. 261-63) does not accept Murphy-O'Connor's arguments but admits that 'this is an attractive option and may well be right'. The main alternative is the view that Paul is distinguishing between sexual sins and other kinds of sin—in other words, πᾶν ἁμάρτημα means 'every other sin apart from sexual sin'. This interpretation raises both grammatical and theological problems. Paul's main argument in vv. 18-20 is that the body is holy, and misuse of the body is like the desecration of a temple. The force of this argument is not limited to sexual sins, but applies to misuse of the body in any form.

sin committed *with* the body as sin committed *against* the body. Because our bodies belong to God and are holy, misuse of the body is like the desecration of a temple.

All these three slogans can be called philosophical or theological.[26] This fact helps to explain the puffed-up attitude of the Corinthians. Their approval of πορνεία was based on their philosophy. They were proud of the wisdom their new teachers had taught them, and of the freedom of action that wisdom gave them.

The four occurrences of φυσιοῦσθαι we have so far examined reveal the following three features of the Corinthian puffed-upness: (a) they were proud of their party leaders; (b) they were proud of their ethical freedom (of which the case of incest was a prime example) and of the 'wisdom' that undergirded it; (c) Paul singles out certain individuals as 'the puffed-up ones', who were in conscious opposition to him and puffed up at the thought that he was not going to come to Corinth to challenge them. It is not difficult to combine these three features. The individuals singled out were the party leaders (or at least some of them), who had inspired their followers with their own inflated pride. The wisdom they taught was not mere empty words, but included the philosophical teaching that the wise were allowed to do anything they wanted, and that sin was purely spiritual and did not affect the body. The case of incest was a source of pride because it was a demonstration of their new wisdom—in J. Murphy-O'Connor's words, 'a graphic illustration, an existential statement, of their freedom from outmoded convention'.[27]

The fifth occurrence (this time of the active verb φυσιοῦν) is in 8.1: περὶ δὲ τῶν εἰδωλοθύτων, οἴδαμεν ὅτι πάντες γνῶσιν ἔχομεν. ἡ γνῶσις φυσιοῖ, ἡ δὲ ἀγάπη οἰκοδομεῖ (now concerning food offered to idols, we know that we all have knowledge. Knowledge puffs up, but love builds up). The phrase 'we all have knowledge' probably echoes a claim

---

26. Clarke (*Leadership*, p. 106) suggests that the theoretical basis of the 6.12 slogan was philosophical *rather than* theological (my italics). But this distinction is difficult to maintain. The teachers at Corinth were propagating philosophical ideas in a Christian context to teach lessons about Christian behaviour. Their terminology may well have been borrowed from contemporary philosophical descriptions of the 'wise man', but both they and their Corinthian disciples believed the wisdom of the truly wise man to be God-given.

27. J. Murphy-O'Connor, 'Sex and Logic in 1 Corinthians 11.2-16', *CBQ* 42 (1980), pp. 482-500 (490).

made by the Corinthians.[28] Their puffed-upness was due to their pride in their knowledge. The content of this knowledge is spelt out in vv. 4-6: there is only one God, idols are nothing, and the 'gods' worshipped by others are of no importance to Christians. On the basis of this 'knowledge' some Corinthians were saying there was nothing wrong in eating food sacrificed to idols.

As in chs. 5 and 6, the puffed-upness of the Corinthians in ch. 8 had a theological basis. It is often argued today that the difference between the 'weak' and the 'strong' was mainly sociological.[29] This may or may not be the case. But the grounds on which the 'strong' justified their behaviour were theological, and it is their claim to possess 'knowledge' (most probably expressed in the Corinthian letter to Paul) that he attacks.

There is a close connection between the γνῶσις of ch. 8 and the σοφία of chs. 1–3. In 2.8 σοφίαν is the object of the verb γινώσκω—'wisdom' in that verse denoting the content of God's plan of salvation and 'knowing' its apprehension (cf. also the use of γινώσκω in 2.11, 16). A similar combination is found in Col. 2.3: οἱ θησαυροὶ τῆς σοφίας καὶ γνώσεως (the treasures of wisdom and knowledge). In that verse the words σοφία and γνῶσις are almost synonymous, used together (as in the English phrase 'part and parcel') to make the statement more emphatic. James Davis points out that this is also true of the use of these words in Sirach.[30] There is no reason to suppose that in 1 Cor. 12.8 Paul regards the λόγος σοφίας and the λόγος γνώσεως as two separate and distinct types of utterance.[31] The Corinthian love of γνῶσις in ch. 8 and their love of

---

28. According to Thiselton (*First Epistle*, p. 620), 'few doubt that Paul is quoting a Corinthian slogan or maxim [in 8.1]'. One indication of this is the fact that v. 7: οὐκ ἐν πᾶσιν ἡ γνῶσις contradicts v. 1. The words πάντες γνῶσιν ἔχομεν would be in inverted commas in a modern text. Paul treats this Corinthian slogan in his usual manner—he quotes it, agrees with it in general terms in vv. 4-6, and then qualifies it in v. 7.

29. For a refutation of the view that Paul is addressing an elite minority in ch. 8 see Chapter 3.

30. Sir. 1.18-20; 21.11-15, quoted in J.A. Davis, *Wisdom and Spirit: An Investigation of 1 Corinthians 1.18–3.20 against the Background of Jewish Sapiential Traditions in the Greco-Roman Period* (Lanham, NY: University Press of America, 1984), p. 24. In Sirach the four words σοφία, γνῶσις, σύνεσις and ἐπιστήμη are virtual synonyms and are used interchangeably for the sake of poetic parallelism.

31. According to Fee (*First Epistle*, p. 593), 'the two should probably be understood as parallel in some way'. J.D.G. Dunn (*Jesus and the Spirit* [London: SCM Press, 1975], p. 220) argues that, for Paul, γνῶσις was a Greek concept and σοφία a

σοφία in chs. 1–3 reveal the same attitude of mind inspired by the same teachers.

It is significant that the slogan πάντα [μοι] ἔξεστιν (6.12; 10.23) is used both in the discussion of πορνεία in chs. 5–6 and in the discussion of food offered to idols in chs. 8–10. In both cases the slogan is not only libertarian but also individualistic—I decide what to do on the basis of my individual rights. In both cases Paul tries to shift the perspective of the Corinthians from rights to relationships—to their relationship with Christ in 6.12-20, and to their relationship with their fellow-believers in 10.23-24. In both cases the Corinthian attitude is described by the verb φυσιοῦν, which denotes their pride in their sexual permissiveness in 5.2 and their pride in the knowledge that frees them from taboos about eating in 8.1-13. In both cases the most probable reason for their pride is the belief that they are wise and possess the ἐξουσία αὐτοπραγίας (right to independent action) ascribed to the wise in popular philosophy.[32]

The sixth occurrence of the verb φυσιοῦσθαι is in 13.4: ἡ ἀγάπη...οὐ φυσιοῦται (love is not puffed up). Chapter 13 lies at the heart of Paul's discussion of spiritual gifts in chs. 12–14, and makes the point that gifts such as prophecy and tongues are of no value without love. By using the word φυσιοῦσθαι Paul relates the issue of spiritual gifts to the general atmosphere of freedom and individualism at Corinth. Some Corinthian prophets seem to have felt they had a right to prophesy even if someone else wanted to prophesy at the same time (14.19-23). Paul replies that Christian ethics is based on love, and love is centred not on the rights of the individual but on the needs of the community.

The essence of the body of Christ, as Paul pictures it in ch. 12, is inter-dependence. As in a human body, the members belong together because God has put them together (v. 24), to enable each member to care about the other members (v. 25). The relevance of this thesis to communal

---

Jewish concept. But the use of σοφία and γνῶσις in Sirach, and the use of γινώσκω in connection with σοφία in 1 Cor. 2, suggest otherwise. Goulder ('Σοφία', p. 534), who sees the problems at Corinth as stemming from a Petrine party, thinks the Christians at Corinth 'invoked rulings on *halakha* drawn from scripture (λόγοι σοφίας) and from angelic vision (λόγοι γνώσεως)'. But Paul's use of γνῶσις in ch. 8 does not support the 'angelic vision' hypothesis. Thiselton (*First Epistle*, p. 941) comments that 'there is no consensus whatever about any clear distinction between (1) λόγος σοφίας...and (2) λόγος γνώσεως'.

32. For the phrase ἐξουσία αὐτοπραγίας see Diogenes Laertius, *Vit. Phil.* 7.121. For the general idea see Epictetus, *Diss.* 2.1.23; Dio Chrysostom, *Or.* 14.16; Philo, *Omn. Prob. Lib.* 59.

worship is worked out in ch. 14. Gifts given to individuals should be used for the benefit of the church as a whole (v. 26). Those speaking in tongues should speak one at a time and remain silent if there is no interpreter (vv. 27-28). Prophets should speak one at a time and give way to each other (vv. 29-31). The whole of chs. 12–14 represents Paul's attempt to swing the Corinthian mind-set from puffed-up individualism to mutual caring.

In 12.24-25 Paul states that God has designed the human body (and, by implication, the body of Christ) to work co-operatively not divisively (ἵνα μὴ ᾖ σχίσμα ἐν τῷ σώματι). By using the word σχίσμα he relates the issue of spiritual gifts to the σχίσματα of 1.10, and reveals that he sees a connection between the individualism of Corinthian spirituality and their party spirit.[33] This is not surprising. The parties were based on competition between individuals—'I support A' and 'I support B'. The party leaders seem to have taught that Christian behaviour was an individual not a corporate matter, and their competitive lifestyle exemplified their teaching. For Paul, by contrast, Christian behaviour consisted of co-operation and interdependence within the body of Christ. Most of ch. 12 is an amplification of Paul's comment on the Corinthian divisions in 1.13: μεμέρισται ὁ Χριστός; (how can Christ be divided?)

3. *Literary Unity*

There have been many theories arguing for the partition of 1 Corinthians, and it is not possible here to examine them all.[34] In this section I shall concentrate on two issues that appear in a large number of those theories —the proposed break between chs. 1–4 and chs. 5–16; and the alleged inconsistency between 8.1-13 and 10.1-22.

---

33. According to S. Pogoloff (*Logos and Sophia*, p. 103), the 'apparent disappearance' of the groups as a concern after the first four chapters of 1 Corinthians 'makes it difficult to read the letter as addressing the same divisions throughout'. He recognizes that the word σχίσμα occurs in 11.18 and 12.25, but argues that 'the divisions in each case are different' (*Logos and Sophia*, p. 101). This is unconvincing. It is difficult to believe that a fairly small church could be split apart in three unrelated ways at the same time, and that Paul could use the same word σχίσμα to refer to all three unrelated splits. The relevance of 11.18 to the general situation at Corinth is discussed in Chapter 3.

34. For an overview of theories of partition of 1 Corinthians, see U. Schnelle, *The History and Theology of the New Testament Writings* (London: SCM Press, 1998), pp. 62-66; H. Merklein, 'Die Einheitlichkeit des ersten Korintherbriefes', *ZNW* 75 (1984), pp. 153-83 (153-56).

a. *The Proposed Break between 4.21 and 5.1*

The theory of a break between 4.21 and 5.1 has recently been championed by Martinus de Boer, and I propose to examine his arguments in some detail.[35] In de Boer's opinion Paul wrote chs. 1–4 on the basis of information from members of Chloe's household, and later added chs. 5–16 after the visit of Stephanas and his party and his receipt of the letter they brought. Thus 1 Corinthians is 'a composite of Paul's own making'.[36]

Most theories of the partition of 1 Corinthians go a lot further than de Boer's modest proposal, but at least one aspect of his article is typical of a large number of partition theories—his reliance on the argument from silence. Partitionists who employ this argument often point out that elements prominent in one section of a letter are not mentioned in another section and deduce from these 'silences' that the sections cannot belong to the same letter.[37] De Boer draws attention to five 'silences' of this sort.[38]

First, a large part of chs. 5–16 is concerned with Paul's replies to questions raised in the letter from Corinth (7.1). De Boer observes that there is no hint of such a letter in chs. 1–4. This is true, but proves nothing. If, as is probable, Paul was aware throughout 1 Corinthians both of the issues raised in the letter from Corinth and of the issues reported by word of mouth, he had a good reason for dealing with the orally reported issues first. The wisdom teaching that lay at the heart of the Corinthian divisions was also the inspiration behind their ethical stance and practical behaviour. It made sense for Paul to consider first (in chs. 1–4) the underlying cause of their ethical stance, and only after that (in chs. 5–16) its practical outworking.

Second, the factions which Paul condemns in chs. 1–4 are, in de Boer's words 'no longer evident, certainly not explicitly' in chs. 5–16. But there is no reason why they should be. For much of chs. 5–16 Paul was replying to points raised in the Corinthian letter. The party divisions do not seem to

35. M.C. de Boer, 'The Composition of 1 Corinthians', *NTS* 40 (1994), pp. 229-45. This is a new presentation of an old theory. Cf. Schnelle, *History*, p. 64: 'Literary criticism has found no reason to question the unity of 1 Cor. 1.1–4.21 as a coherent text. Thus this section is often regarded as an independent letter, for which 1 Cor. 4.14-21 is supposed to form the conclusion'.

36. De Boer, 'Composition', p. 231.

37. For a critique of the widespread use of the argument from silence in New Testament scholarship, see D.R. Hall, *The Seven Pillories of Wisdom* (Macon, GA: Mercer University Press, 1990), pp. 55-64.

38. These five arguments from silence are found in de Boer, 'Composition', pp. 240-42.

have featured in that letter, and therefore Paul did not discuss them in his replies to their questions.

This raises the question: why did the party divisions not feature in the letter from Corinth? Is it because, in the short interval between the visit of 'Chloe's people' and the bringing of the letter from Corinth, these divisions had suddenly disappeared? This seems most unlikely. It is more probable, as Helmut Merklein suggests, that the matters raised in the letter from Corinth were disputed issues, about which they asked Paul to give his judgment; but the party divisions were not disputed issues because the Corinthians did not think they were doing anything wrong.[39] In their eyes competition in rhetorical skills and divisions between the supporters of rival orators were normal features of life at Corinth. Paul saw things differently. In his opinion the matters the Corinthians did not feel the need to raise were more fundamental than the matters they did raise, and this explains why he dealt with the party divisions before anything else.

Third, there is no mention in chs. 1–4 of the case of incest. De Boer asks the question: 'Given the tone of incredulity, disgust and shock that marks 5.1 are we really to think that this information has come to Paul before he wrote chs. 1–4 and that he delayed mentioning it till now?' The answer to this question is 'Yes'. The Corinthians were proud of what had been done (5.2). Their pride was a product of the wisdom teaching they had been given by the party leaders, and Paul felt it necessary to attack the root of the problem before dealing with its practical consequences. Moreover, the rhetorical questions of 1.13 make it clear that Paul felt just as much incredulity, disgust and shock over the competitive divisions in the church as he did over the case of incest.

Fourth, in chs. 1–4 the words λόγος and σοφία are prominent, but in chs. 5–16 they are not.[40] This fact does not justify de Boer's conclusion that these are separate letters. Paul was a contextualist, and his vocabulary in each section of the letter was determined by the subject matter of that section.

39. Cf. Merklein, 'Einheitlichkeit', p. 161: 'Dass "gerade eine so brennende Gemeindefrage, wie sie Kap. 1-4 behandelt, nicht in dem Gemeindebrief gestanden haben sollte", ist nur verwunderlich, wenn man voraussetzt, dass die Korinther in der Parteienfrage ein ähnliches Problembewusstsein hatten wie Paulus'. Merklein is commenting on the words of W. Schenk, 'Der 1 Korintherbrief als Briefsammlung', *ZNW* 60 (1969), pp. 219-43 (237).

40. There are 15 occurrences of σοφία in chs. 1–2, one occurrence in ch. 3 and one occurrence in ch. 12. If de Boer's argument were sound, it would suggest a division at the end of ch. 2 (or possibly at the end of ch. 3) not at the end of ch. 4.

Fifth, according to de Boer, chs. 1–4 focus on the cross, with no mention of the resurrection; but the language of the cross is missing from chs. 5–16, and ch. 15 focuses on the resurrection. This is largely true, but proves nothing. A letter covering many different issues will use many different types of vocabulary. If de Boer's methodology were sound, we should have to conclude that ch. 15 belonged to a separate letter from the rest of chs. 5–16, since the emphasis on resurrection is found almost entirely within that chapter. Taken to its logical conclusion, de Boer's methodology would dissolve 1 Corinthians into a mosaic of fragments. For example, the word πορνεία is peculiar to chs. 5–7, and these chapters would have to be regarded as a separate letter, as would chs. 8–10 because of the incidence of the word εἰδωλόθυτος.

At the heart of de Boer's argument lies a methodological error, which is revealed in the following statement:

> Of course, there are considerable points of continuity between the two sections of the epistle… But such points of continuity are to be expected from a work that presents itself to the reader as a unity. They are not worthy of special notice and certainly need no explanation. The discontinuities or discrepancies, however, do.[41]

This statement is wrong in principle. 1 Corinthians deals with a variety of topics and the vocabulary of each section is geared to the subject matter. In such a letter there will inevitably be points of continuity and points of discontinuity. Both are to be expected, and neither needs special notice. As Merklein says, partition theories tend to be one-sided in that they concentrate on 'criteria of incoherence', and in any literary work if you look for incoherence you will find it. In Merklein's opinion literary criticism should begin with those factors in the text that are coherent.[42]

In addition to his arguments from silence, de Boer makes a number of other points. In his opinion, the verses 4.14-21 contain the characteristic elements of the concluding section of a Pauline letter, and suggest that he is moving towards epistolary closure.[43] Udo Schnelle denies this. 'The elements of a letter conclusion are not found here', he writes, 'but rather the epistolary self commendation'.[44] Many of Paul's letters consist of well-

41. De Boer, 'Composition', p. 242.
42. Merklein, 'Einheitlichkeit', pp. 157-58.
43. De Boer, 'Composition', p. 238. Merklein ('Einheitlichkeit', p. 159 n. 17) lists other scholars who use a similar argument, and opposes them on pp. 159-60.
44. Schnelle, *History*, p. 64.

defined sections and he often ends these sections with conclusory language. There is nothing in 4.14-21 that indicates the end of a letter rather than the ending of a section within a letter.

De Boer also contrasts the words of 1 Cor. 16.10: ἐὰν δὲ ἔλθη Τιμόθεος (if/when Timothy comes) with Paul's earlier statement in 1 Cor. 4.17: ἔπεμψα ὑμῖν Τιμόθεον (I have sent Timothy to you). He suggests that the use of ἐάν (if) rather than ὅταν (when) may imply that Timothy's original mission, to deal with the Corinthian divisions, was no longer necessary.[45] But in fact 16.10 is a follow-up to 4.17. In 4.17 Paul announces Timothy's forthcoming visit, and explains one of the reasons behind it; in 16.10 he asks the Corinthians to give him a good welcome when he comes.

The wording of 4.17 implies that Timothy has not yet arrived at Corinth —he 'will remind you' when he arrives. The word ἔπεμψα could be an epistolary aorist (I am sending Timothy with this letter) or a constative aorist (I have already sent Timothy). The latter translation is supported by the statement in Acts 19.22 that Paul sent Timothy from Ephesus to Macedonia (presumably with a view to his then proceeding from Macedonia to Corinth).

In 16.10 ἐάν can be translated either as 'if' or as 'when'. According to Nigel Turner, ἐάν with the aorist 'is very near the meaning of ὅταν, and is often more than mere probability'.[46] In either case, the most likely source of Paul's doubt would be that Timothy had been sent to Corinth via somewhere else, so that the time of his arrival was uncertain. Doubt as to when or whether Timothy will arrive (which is the only doubt the word ἐάν can convey in 16.10) has nothing to do with doubt as to the purpose of his journey.

According to de Boer, in 4.18-21 Paul 'warns that he will come very soon and implies that he may come in a foul mood'; whereas in 16.5-9 he 'makes definite and matter-of-fact plans to travel to Corinth himself when it is feasible to do so, though this will not be soon'. De Boer explains this difference by supposing that the delegation of Stephanas and party had arrived between the two letters and put Paul's mind at ease.

It is true that in 16.5-9 Paul does not expect to visit Corinth soon. But he does not expect this in 4.18-21 either. The phrase 'I will come quickly if it is the will of the Lord' (v. 19) means 'I will come quickly if the Lord makes it clear to me that my presence is urgently required'. Verse 19 is a threat, not a promise.[47]

---

45. De Boer, 'Composition', p. 241.
46. Turner, *Syntax*, p. 114.
47. Cf. Merklein, 'Einheitlichkeit', p. 160: 'In 4.18-21 deutet Paulus warnend an,

The alternative 'gentleness or a rod' that Paul states in 4.21 offers a choice between two timetables. Either he will pay a hurried disciplinary visit necessitated by circumstances; or (as he hopes and believes will happen) the Corinthians will change their attitude after reading his letter, and he will then be able to pay them a more leisurely visit after some months. It is the latter plan that is outlined in 16.5-9.

b. *The Alleged Inconsistency between 8.1-13 and 10.1-22*
It is often asserted that 8.1-13 and 10.1-22 must belong to different letters because they present two inconsistent points of view. In 8.1-13, it is alleged, Paul treats the eating of food that has been sacrificed to idols as an ἀδιάφορον (something in itself neither good nor bad), only to be avoided if it is a stumbling-block to another Christian; in 10.1-22, on the other hand, eating such food is roundly condemned as disloyalty to Christ.[48]

This would not be a problem if the two chapters referred to two different situations. According to Thiselton, the coherence of these chapters is vulnerable only 'if the varied circumstantial differences between specific cases under review are neglected'.[49] He suggests that 10.1-22 may present a 'worst case' scenario found among an extremist minority, which involved not just eating a meal in the temple precincts but active participation in cultic events.[50] However, 10.21 implies that the eating of meals was a major factor in the background to ch. 10, as it is in 8.10, and it is probable that both chs. 8 and 10 refer to the same scenario.[51]

The key to understanding the section 8.1–11.1 is what Merklein calls Paul's 'text strategy'. He argues that in 8.10 Paul does not dogmatically prohibit the eating of idol-food, but nevertheless clearly implies that it should be avoided, since the 'weak' were a permanent feature of the church at Corinth, and offence could be caused at any time. In 8.11-12 the consequences of eating in temples are starkly portrayed in the present tense: 'you are destroying the "weak" and sinning against Christ'. Such state-

---

dass er seine, wie der Leser dann aus 16.5-9 erfährt, ansonsten schon feststehenden Reisepläne notfalls (wenn der Herr will) auch ändern könnte, um in Korinth nach dem Rechten zu sehen'.

48. Merklein ('Einheitlichkeit', p. 163) traces this assertion back to Johannes Weiss (*Der erste Korintherbrief* [Göttingen: Vandenhoeck & Ruprecht, 2nd rev. edn, 1910], pp. 210-13), and gives a detailed summary of Weiss's argument.

49. Thiselton, *First Epistle*, p. 609.

50. Thiselton, *First Epistle*, p. 718.

51. Cf. Fee, *First Epistle*, p. 359; Merklein, 'Einheitlichkeit', pp. 167-68.

ments, in Merklein's opinion, prepare the way for the stricter language of 10.1-22.[52]

The reason why Paul adopted this 'text strategy' can be found in the situation he faced. It is generally agreed that in 8.1 Paul is quoting a statement made in the letter from Corinth. We have knowledge (γνῶσις), some Corinthians were saying, and this knowledge tells us that idols count for nothing—they are mere human artefacts of wood or stone (8.4). Therefore, it was argued, food that has been offered to idols is no different from any other food, and the Christian is allowed to eat it. It was on this logical argument that Paul was asked to comment.

At the same time he was aware that there were other viewpoints within the church—either because the letter from Corinth mentioned them, or because of his conversations with Chloe's people and with Stephanas and party. Some still felt the power of the idol worship in which they had once participated, and felt unhappy about eating meals in temples when pressurized to do so by the example of their 'strong' fellow-Christians (8.9-13). Others may have openly condemned the 'strong'. This is implied by 10.29-30, which talks about the freedom of action of the 'strong' being condemned, and the 'strong' being abused for doing what they believed to be pleasing to God. Paul would not have mentioned this unless he believed such remarks had already been made, or were likely to be made in the near future.

Throughout these chapters Paul was trying to be fair to all sides. In theory, he had a great deal of sympathy with the 'strong'. The doctrine of Christian freedom they were proclaiming (10.29) was dear to his heart (Gal. 5.1). Insofar as the 'weak' were still afraid of the power of idols, he regarded their weakness as a defect (8.7). It is on the basis of the 'strong' position that he was able to recommend to the Corinthians that they buy meat in the market and eat meat in their friends' houses without scruples (10.25-27). He was also anxious to ensure that the 'weak' did not con-

---

52. Merklein, 'Einheitlichkeit', pp. 164-66: 'Berücksightigt man nun, dass der angesprochene Fall des Gesehenswerdens in der Öffentlichkeit des Tempels eine immer gegebene Möglichkeit war, wird die aüsserst geschickt angelegte Textstrategie der Frage von v.10 offenkundig: Ohne ein (dogmatisch begründetes) Verbot auszusprechen, drängt sie in Verbindung mit v. 9 den Leser selbst zu der Schlussfolgerung, in der Praxis auf die Teilnahme an Mähler im Tempel zu verzichten. Dass Paulus im konkreten Fall von 8.10 kein Adiaphoron mehr erblickt, bestätigen schliesslich die drei folgenden Verse... Der Sache nach ist damit das strikte Verbot von 10.14, 21 vorbereitet'.

demn the 'strong'. He pointed out that the 'strong' had a carefully thought out position and were acting in good faith (10.30).[53] In spite of all this, however, it was the attitude of the 'strong' that caused him the greatest concern. Their way of thinking was individualistic rather than corporate. Their slogan πάντα ἔξεστιν (10.23) may be paraphrased: 'I have the right to do whatever I want to do, and other people's scruples and objections will not stand in my way'.

Paul's most common strategy in such situations (in this and in other letters) was to begin with persuasion. In Fee's words, for Paul the indicative precedes the imperative.[54] His rhetoric is deliberative—the language of debate, not of declamation. This is as true of 10.14-22 as of 8.1-13. The only imperatives in 10.14-22 are the general advice to run away from idolatry (v. 14), a request to the Corinthians to exercise their critical judgment on the logic of his argument (v. 15), and a request that they look carefully at an illustration of that argument (v. 18). The passage is presented as a reasoned argument to intelligent people (v. 15). It points out logical inconsistencies in the 'strong' position, rather than telling them what to do. The word δύνασθε (v. 21) is significant. Paul does not say they *ought not* to eat at both the table of demons and the Lord's table (though, as in 8.10-13, he implies this). He says they *cannot*—there is a logical inconsistency in their attempt to do so.[55]

---

53. For a detailed survey of various approaches to vv. 29-30, see Thiselton, *First Epistle*, pp. 788-92. He dismisses the theory that Paul's comments are addressed to the 'weak' on the grounds that 'this is not the major thrust of the three chapters' (p. 792). But Paul was a pastor as well as a logician. While his main argument in these chapters was directed at the 'strong', he was also concerned about the 'weak'—indeed, his advice in 10.25-27 is probably designed more to allay the scruples of the 'weak' than to confirm the pre-existing opinion of the 'strong'. There is no need to specify which section of the Corinthian church Paul is addressing at which point. He writes to the church as a whole, presenting a balanced opinion and trying to be fair to all sides.

It is significant that in his letter to the Romans Paul warns against two equal and parallel dangers—the 'strong' are tempted to despise the 'weak', and the 'weak' are tempted to condemn the 'strong' (Rom. 14.3). It is true that the point at issue is not identical in the two letters (there is no mention of idolatry in Romans). But it is difficult to believe that, in writing Rom. 14–15, Paul was not influenced by what had happened in the fairly recent past in Corinth. Whatever the specific issue, whenever a church is divided between the strict and the permissive, the temptation to despise and the temptation to judge are inevitable.

54. Fee, *First Epistle*, p. 363 n. 23.

55. Cf. H.L. Goudge, *The First Epistle to the Corinthians* (WC; London: Methuen, 1903), p. 90, commenting on 10.21: 'Ye cannot drink. S. Paul means more than "ye

The thinking behind this strategy is revealed in 2 Cor. 1.24, where Paul declares: 'we do not have sovereignty over your faith' (οὐχ ὅτι κυριεύομεν ὑμῶν τῆς πίστεως). Throughout 1 and 2 Corinthians Paul tries to avoid the charge of being dictatorial. He lays down general principles, in the light of which the Corinthians are free to make up their own minds.

The most explicit statement of Paul's strategy comes in his letter to Philemon. He is sending a runaway slave, Onesimus, back to his master Philemon. Onesimus has become a Christian under Paul's ministry, and Paul would like to retain his services to assist him in his imprisonment (v. 13). The easiest way to ensure this would have been to keep Onesimus with him, and to present Philemon with a *fait accompli*. But Paul is not willing to do this. He wants Philemon's decision to forgive his slave and send him back to Paul to be freely made (v. 14). Though he has the authority to command, he prefers to make a request (vv. 8-9). So he uses persuasive arguments—the change wrought in Onesimus's character by his faith in Christ (vv. 10-11); the fact that he is now not just a slave but a beloved brother (v. 16); Paul's willingness to pay his debts (vv. 18-19); the fact that Philemon owes his life as a Christian to Paul's ministry (v. 19); the joy Philemon would bring to Paul by making this decision (v. 20). Paul is confident Philemon will do what he asks (v. 21), but allows him the freedom to decide otherwise (v. 15).

Paul's belief in persuading rather than commanding, exemplified in the letter to Philemon, explains his approach to the problems of chs. 8–10, and to all the other problems dealt with in 1 Corinthians. Even in 5.1-13, where he exerts maximum pressure on the Corinthians over the case of incest, the only imperatives are allusions to the Old Testament (vv. 7-8, 13). I hope to show later (in Chapter 12) how Paul's belief that the indicative precedes the imperative underlies his pastoral strategy, not just in 1 Corinthians, but in the Corinthian correspondence as a whole.

Having stated his case in ch. 8, Paul illustrates it in ch. 9 from his own

---

ought not". Communion with the Lord and communion with devils are incompatible; to have the one is to forfeit the other'. In other words, though the physical act of eating at both tables is possible, the spiritual meanings of the two acts are incompatible. Thiselton (*First Epistle*, p. 776) sees three meanings in δύνασθε: (i) a logical cannot (the two possibilities logically exclude each other); (ii) an empirical cannot (something will be destroyed if you try to do both); and (iii) an institutional cannot (Christians cannot, and still be counted as Christians).

experience.[56] Then in 10.1-22 he introduces a second argument against participation in meals at temples. This argument was probably not mentioned in the Corinthian letter, and was the fruit of Paul's own thinking. He argues that, although idols are nothing in themselves, there is demonic influence in idolatrous worship. Therefore to participate in such worship is disloyalty to Christ. Such disloyalty makes the people concerned vulnerable to divine punishment, as it did for the children of Israel in the wilderness. Paul's rhetoric in ch. 10 is still deliberative, but he feels able to speak more dogmatically because in ch. 8 he has taken the argument of the 'strong' seriously and sympathetically, and hopefully made them more receptive to another point of view.

In 10.23–11.1 Paul turns to practical advice (though the question of eating in temples is not raised in this section because it has been adequately covered already). His opening statement πάντα ἔξεστιν, ἀλλ᾽ οὐ πάντα συμφέρει ('everything is allowable', but not everything is beneficial) is a summary of his argument throughout 8.1–10.22. In these chapters he has been pointing out to the 'strong' the practical consequences of adhering strictly to their slogan. One consequence is the damage done to other Christians (ch. 8); the other consequence is the spiritual danger to themselves, if they are disloyal to Christ and provoke God to jealousy (10.1-22).

The section 8.1–11.1 is a coherent unity, and follows the pattern a-b-c-a:

(a)   The main principle (8.1-13). In deciding one's attitude to food sacrificed to idols, love for other Christians takes precedence over knowledge of one's rights.

(b)   Illustration of the main principle (9.1-27). Paul has the right to financial support, but has renounced it in order to help other people.

(c)   Ancillary argument (10.1-22). It is spiritually dangerous and logically inconsistent for Christians to associate themselves with idolatry.

(d)   Application of the main principle to a variety of situations (10.23–11.1).

56. For a detailed discussion of 1 Cor. 9, see Chapter 8.

Chapter 3

THE SOCIAL BACKGROUND TO 1 CORINTHIANS

It is widely believed today that social conflict between the rich and the poor was a major factor in the situation Paul faced at Corinth. One of the key figures in the development of this theory has been Gerd Theissen. Theissen's thesis was put forward in a number of articles written in German in the 1970s, which have been collected and published in English translation under the title *The Social Setting of Pauline Christianity*.[1] Other scholars have built on the foundation he laid. As David Horrell says, 'of all the sociological work that has emerged [in New Testament research], Theissen's remains perhaps the most influential'.[2]

In this chapter I shall examine Theissen's thesis in some detail, and indicate what seem to me to be fundamental weaknesses in his argument. I realize that much water has flowed under the bridge since his articles were first published. But it is important, when evaluating any approach to the New Testament, to start with the foundation documents. Otherwise, there is always the danger that, in trying to modify the details of a theory, one may take its presuppositions for granted.

1. *The Upper-Class Minority*

Theissen's theory is that the church at Corinth was dominated by a minority of upper-class members, and that much of what Paul says in 1 Corinthians was directed at this minority. His starting point is Paul's statement in 1 Cor. 1.26: 'Think about the way you were called [to be Christians]. Not many of you were naturally wise, not many of you were powerful, not many of you were noble'. In Theissen's opinion, the words

---

1. G. Theissen, *The Social Setting of Pauline Christianity* (Edinburgh: T. & T. Clark, 1982).
2. D.G. Horrell, *The Social Ethos of the Corinthian Correspondence: Interests and Ideology from 1 Corinthians to 1 Clement* (Edinburgh: T. & T. Clark, 1996), p. 2.

'not many' (οὐ πολλοί) imply that there were a few upper-class members of the church.[3] This judgment seems to me to be sound, despite the efforts of some scholars to interpret the verse in a different way. James Davis, for example, thinks the terms used in 1.26 'are all applicable to those who, because of their possession of wisdom, think of themselves as wise, powerful and well-born', and he cites the use of the word εὐγένεια (nobility) by Philo in such a sense.[4] But the phrase κατὰ σάρκα (at a human level, naturally) in 1.26, and the references in the two following verses (vv. 27-28) to the foolish, weak, ignoble and despised of this world (τοῦ κόσμου) indicate that Paul is talking, not of spiritual or mental wisdom, power and nobility, but of these qualities as normally understood in society.

Those philosophers who thought of nobility in spiritual terms were well aware that society as a whole did not agree with them. For example, Philo censured those who thought people with generations of wealth behind them to be noble, and Dio Chrysostom declared scornfully that the term εὐγενής (noble) was applied to the descendants of families of ancient wealth by 'a certain class'.[5] Such comments reveal that the views attacked by the philosophers were widely held in popular thinking. As Bruce Winter says (commenting on Dio, Philo and Plutarch), 'while all these authors denounce εὐγένεια in one form or another, it remains clear that the term referred to a powerful group in first-century society who possessed "old money" and great prestige'.[6]

Justin Meggitt accepts that the terms 'wise, powerful and noble' in 1.26 are sociological, but argues that their meaning is imprecise. The term εὐγενής was indeed used to signify noble birth by the elite of the Graeco-Roman world, but was also applied in inscriptions to an actor, an athlete and a doctor. It was even used as a name for slaves. Meggitt suggests that these terms could have been applied to those artisans who were literate. He notes that the similar term 'rich' (πλούσιος) was applied by Dio Chrysostom to a village man whose house was far from impressive—he was rich by village standards not by urban ones.[7]

3.   Theissen, *Social Setting*, p. 72.
4.   Davis, *Wisdom and Spirit*, pp. 75-76. The same comparison with Philo is found in B.A. Pearson, *The Pneumatikos-Psychikos Terminology in 1 Corinthians: A Study in the Theology of the Corinthian Opponents of Paul and its Relation to Gnosticism* (SBLDS, 12; Missoula, MT: Scholars Press, 1973), p. 40.
5.   Dio Chrysostom, *Or.* 15.29; Philo, *Virt.* 187.
6.   Winter, *Philo and Paul*, p. 190.
7.   J.J. Meggitt, *Paul, Poverty and Survival* (Edinburgh: T. & T. Clark, 1998), pp. 102-106.

It is true that these words are relative. This means that their meaning is related to the context in which they are used. The context of 1 Cor. 1.26 is the call to follow Christ that came to certain people in the urban society of Corinth. The phrases κατὰ σάρκα and τοῦ κόσμου indicate that Paul is concerned with the common understanding of those terms in that society. Just as the rich man described by Dio was rich in the context of his village society, so also the 'few' implied by 1.26 were regarded as wise, powerful and noble in the context of their urban society. Admittedly we cannot determine precisely how wise, powerful and noble they were, but Paul's words imply a much more significant difference than that between artisans who could read and write and those who could not.

We may accept, then, Theissen's statement that there was a small minority of Christians at Corinth who could in some sense be called upper class. He attempts to identify nine such people, from the data in 1 Corinthians and Acts and the list of names in Rom. 16.[8] Some of these identifications are more convincing than others. According to Rom. 16.23 Gaius was 'host to the whole church'.[9] A house capable of accommodating the whole Corinthian church would need to be of a fair size and belong to a rich man.[10] Crispus and Sosthenes were synagogue leaders (Acts 18.8,

8. Theissen, *Social Setting*, p. 95. The nine are Aquila, Priscilla, Stephanas, Erastus, Sosthenes, Crispus, Phoebe, Gaius and Titius Justus.

9. J. Meggitt (following a suggestion of C.E.B. Cranfield) argues that the words 'host to the whole church' could mean that Gaius gave hospitality to travelling Christians passing through Corinth and thus served the world-wide church (*Paul, Poverty and Survival*, p. 121). But the phrase 'the whole church' in 1 Cor. 14.23 means the whole local church (cf. Acts 5.11; 15.22). Where Paul thinks globally in 1 and 2 Corinthians and Romans he usually refers to 'the churches' or 'all the churches' (1 Cor. 11.16; 14.33; 2 Cor. 8.18; Rom. 16.16). Cranfield, who is undecided between the global and the local meaning of the church in this verse, comments that 'in either case, the implication would probably be that he was, at least, fairly wealthy' (C.E.B. Cranfield, *The Epistle to the Romans* [2 vols.; ICC; Edinburgh: T. & T. Clark, 1975, 1979], II, p. 807).

10. J. Murphy-O'Connor (*St. Paul's Corinth: Texts and Archaeology* [Wilmington, DE: Michael Glazier, 1983], pp. 153-58) specifies the ground plan of a number of rich people's houses from the Graeco-Roman period and estimates that the maximum number of people who could be accommodated in such houses would be fifty. However, Bradley Blue ('Acts and the House Church', in D.W.J. Gill and C. Gempf [eds.], *The Book of Acts in its Graeco-Roman Setting* [Carlisle: Paternoster, 1994], pp. 119-222 [142-43]), after describing a first-century house in Jerusalem, estimates that the reception hall and the rooms opening off it would between them have accommodated some 100 people quite comfortably. He also comments (p. 143 n. 88)

17).[11] In a prosperous city such as Corinth, synagogue leaders would probably be people of some social standing.[12] Erastus is described in Rom. 16.23 as 'city steward' (οἰκονόμος τῆς πόλεως). The meaning of this phrase has been much debated,[13] but the fact that Paul mentions Erastus's civic office suggests that it is significant, and Erastus may well have been one of the upper-class minority.

The status of other people classified by Theissen as elite is less clear. Aquila and Priscilla were artisans (Acts 18.1-3).[14] Phoebe is described in

---

on the proximity of the courtyard and of other rooms opening off the courtyard. This is a significant factor. Whereas in cold Northern countries meals and meetings have to be arranged indoors, in warmer climates meals and meetings can be arranged out of doors, and a house with a garden (or a peristyle court like the house of the Vettii illustrated in Murphy O'Connor, *St. Paul's Corinth*, p. 157) could accommodate a lot more people than a house alone.

11. The Sosthenes whom Paul associates with himself in sending 1 Corinthians (1.1) may well have been the same person as the synagogue leader of Acts 18.17, but this cannot be proved.

12. Theissen argues that synagogue leaders would be men of wealth because they were responsible for the upkeep of the building (*Social Setting*, pp. 73-75). In the opinion of Meggitt, however (*Paul, Poverty and Survival*, pp. 141-43), the fact that inscriptions are normally to do with buildings has distorted the picture, and not all synagogue leaders would be upper class. He cites one example of a synagogue leader who was a yokemaker. The truth lies perhaps between these two extremes. Synagogue leaders were well respected within the Jewish community and often wealthy. Since Corinth was a prosperous city, and 1 Cor. 1.26 implies a small minority of upper-class members, Crispus and Sosthenes probably belonged to this minority.

13. Theissen discusses this title at length and concludes that it could denote high office and elevated social status or could be applied to slaves and freedmen (*Social Setting*, pp. 75-83). There is an inscription referring to an Erastus who held the high office of aedile and paid for the laying of a pavement at Corinth. This may or may not be the Erastus of Rom. 16.23. Meggitt lists 78 occurrences of the name Erastus in inscriptions (*Paul, Poverty and Survival*, p. 139).

14. Theissen (*Social Setting*, pp. 89-91) states that Aquila and Priscilla were 'scarcely insolvent', since they gave hospitality both to Paul and to the visiting preacher Apollos (Acts 18.26) and hosted a house church (1 Cor. 16.19; Rom. 16.3-5). The presupposition of this argument is that Paul received free hospitality in their home. But it is more likely that he paid his way. According to Acts 18.3, 'because Paul had the same trade, he stayed with them and worked'. This suggests a co-operative enterprise, in which all three of them shared both the profits and the expenses. The trade they shared, according to Luke, was tentmaking or leather working, which was scarcely an elite occupation in the Graeco-Roman world. (For the meaning of σκηνοποιός see R.F. Hock, *The Social Context of Paul's Ministry: Tentmaking and Apostleship*

Rom. 16.2 as a προστάτις—a word that sometimes has the technical sense of 'patron'; but it is unlikely that Paul was using the word in its technical sense.[15] Titius Justus, who, according to Acts 18.7, gave hospitality to Paul, may have been the same person as Gaius, his full name being Gaius Titius Justus.[16] Stephanas, Fortunatus and Achaicus are commended in 1 Cor. 16.15 for ministering (διακονία) to the saints.[17] In commending them, Paul urges the Corinthians to submit to the authority of such men and to all who 'work together and work hard' (παντὶ τῷ συνεργοῦντι καὶ κοπιῶντι). His wording suggests that, whatever the original status of these men, they were not behaving as though they were upper class. The aristocratic virtues in the Graeco-Roman world were not co-operation and hard work but a consciousness of one's own superiority to others and the freedom to cultivate a life of leisure.[18] Paul's comment that Stephanas and

[Philadelphia: Fortress Press, 1980], pp. 20-21; Meggitt, *Paul, Poverty and Survival*, p. 76 n. 5; C.J. Hemer, *The Book of Acts in the Setting of Hellenistic History* [Winona Lake: Eisenbrauns, 1990], p. 119 n. 46).

15. It is sometimes alleged that, by using the word προστάτις, 'Paul is acknowledging his social dependence upon Phoebe' (E.A. Judge, 'Cultural Conformity and Innovation in Paul: Some Clues from Contemporary Documents', *TynBul* 35 [1984], pp. 3-24 [21]). But Meggitt makes the point that it was not usual for clients to write letters of recommendation for their patrons, as Paul does for Phoebe in Rom. 16.1-2 (*Paul, Poverty and Survival*, p. 148). The idea of Paul entering a patron/client relationship is difficult to reconcile with his protestations of financial independence in 1 Cor. 9.12-15 and 2 Cor. 11.7-11. Moreover, the grammatical form of Rom. 16.13 is very similar to that of Rom. 16.2. If the statement that Rufus's mother was Paul's mother is not taken literally, there is no need to take literally the statement that Phoebe was Paul's patroness.

16. F.F. Bruce (*Commentary on the Book of Acts* [London: Marshall, Morgan and Scott, 1965], p. 371) traces this suggestion back to William Ramsay in 1910. It is also supported by E.J. Goodspeed, 'Gaius Titius Justus', *JBL* 69 (1950), pp. 382-83; Blue, 'Acts and the House Church', p. 174.

17. The ministry of Stephanas and his companions may, on the analogy of 2 Cor. 8.4, have involved financial help, as Theissen suggests. But he admits that 'we can scarcely infer high social status from catchwords like διακονεῖν and διάκονος' (*Social Setting*, pp. 87-88). David Gill's suggestion that Stephanas may have provided help to other Christians at a time of food shortage could be correct but is incapable of proof (D.W.J. Gill, 'In Search of the Social Elite in the Corinthian Church', *TynBul* 44.2 [1993], pp. 323-37 [336]).

18. Edwin Judge ('Early Christians', p. 130) notes that several people named in Rom. 16 are commended for their hard work (κοπιᾶν) (Rom. 16.6, 12). In his opinion this means that 'they had assumed responsibility for the maintenance of the church'. This interpretation reflects Judge's belief that forty or so people mentioned in Paul's

party were 'making up for what was lacking' in the Corinthians' support of him refers to their physical presence with him, not to money.[19]

Theissen's statement that 'the great majority of the Corinthians known to us by name probably enjoyed high social status' needs some qualification.[20] This was probably true of Gaius, Crispus, Sosthenes and Erastus. It may have been true of Stephanas and Phoebe. It was not true of Aquila and Priscilla, and may or may not have been true of Fortunatus and

letters belonged to the social elite. But Paul's use of κοπιᾶν and κόπος elsewhere does not support this view. In 1 Cor. 15.58 Paul assures the whole church that their labour (κόπος) is not in vain and in 1 Thess. 1.3 he remembers the hard work of the whole church at Thessalonica. When he talks of his own hard work, this includes preaching the gospel (1 Cor. 3.8; 15.10; 2 Cor. 10.15; 1 Thess. 3.5), his labour as a leather worker (1 Cor. 4.12; 1 Thess. 2.9) and general references in hardship catalogues that may include both these ideas (2 Cor. 6.5; 11.23, 27). Hard work was not a notably aristocratic virtue in the Graeco-Roman world, particularly when linked with manual labour.

19. Theissen's comment on this verse is ambivalent. He argues that, since ὑστέρημα is used in connection with the collection in 2 Cor. 8 and 9, 'it is reasonable to assume' that Paul received some financial support from Stephanas. But he then admits that this may not be the case. 'According to 1 Cor. 16.18 Stephanas and his circle refreshed Paul's "spirit"…which doesn't sound much like material gifts' (*Social Setting*, p. 88).

It is true that Paul uses the word ὑστέρημα to denote a shortage of money in a financial context (2 Cor. 8.14; 9.12); but in other contexts it denotes a deficiency in faith (1 Thess. 3.10) or a deficiency in suffering (Col. 1.24). The meaning of Col. 1.24 may be that the church is called to suffer, but not all members suffer to the same degree. Some, such as Paul, are called to endure more than their fair share of suffering as representative persons on behalf of the church as a whole (the prefix ἀντι- in ἀνταναπληροῦν looking forward to ὑπὲρ τοῦ σώματος, cf. 1 Tim. 2.6). This is the interpretation of J.A. Bengel, *Gnomon Novi Testamenti* (Berlin: Schlawitz, 1860), p. 510: 'Fixa est mensura passionum, quas tota exantlare debet ecclesia. Quo plus igitur Paulus exhausit, eo minus et ipsi posthac et ceteris relinquitur'. It is adopted by J.A.T. Robinson, *The Body: A Study in Pauline Theology* (London: SCM Press, 1952), pp. 70-71, and mentioned as a possibility by F.F. Bruce (E.K. Simpson and F.F. Bruce, *The Epistles of Paul to the Ephesians and to the Colossians* [London: Marshall, Morgan and Scott, 1957], pp. 216-17, especially n. 164). If this interpretation is correct, Paul's experience of compensatory suffering is closely parallel to the experience of Epaphroditus, who 'gambled with his life' in order to make up for what was lacking in the service rendered by the Philippians to Paul (Phil. 2.30) (ἵνα ἀναπληρώσῃ τὸ ὑμῶν ὑστέρημα τῆς πρός με λειτουργίας). The whole church would have liked to come and visit Paul, and Epaphroditus did it on their behalf as a representative person. In a similar way Stephanas and party visited Paul and refreshed his spirit as representatives of, and substitutes for, the Corinthian church as a whole.

20. Theissen, *Social Setting*, p. 95.

Achaicus and of other people mentioned in Rom. 16.[21] The evidence does not justify Theissen's assertion that 'in all probability the most active and important members of the congregation belonged to the οὐ πολλοὶ σοφοί, δυνατοί and εὐγενεῖς', and that 'those of the lower strata scarcely appear as individuals in the Corinthian correspondence'.[22]

In Theissen's opinion many of the problems dealt with in 1 Corinthians stemmed from social conflict between the rich minority and the poor majority; and many passages written in the second person plural, and addressed to the church as a whole, were in fact directed at this small minority. A case in point is the party division rebuked in ch. 1. 'In the matter of partisan allegiance', Theissen asserts, 'Paul addresses himself to the few who are wise, powerful and of noble birth'.[23]

This statement is completely unjustified. In broaching the matter of party divisions, the mode of address Paul uses is 'brothers' (ἀδελφοί) (1.10); 'my brothers' (ἀδελφοί μου) (1.11); 'each one of you' (ἕκαστος ὑμῶν) (1.12). These words come immediately after his initial greeting to 'the church of God in Corinth' (1.2) and his thanksgiving for the gifts that the church has received (1.4-9). There is no suggestion that, in using the terms 'my brothers' and 'each one of you', Paul has ceased to address the church as a whole, or that he recognizes as his brothers only those few members of the church who are socially privileged. The words 'each one of you' mean what they say. The party spirit was not limited to a few—it affected the church as a whole.[24]

It is true that sometimes, when Paul addresses the church as a whole, some members of the church are not covered by his remarks. Examples are: 1.26 (where the words 'not many' imply a minority to whom the verse does not apply); 8.1 (where the words 'we all have knowledge' are

---

21. As Theissen says, Chloe's people were probably slaves or dependent workers. They may have been members of the Corinthian church or may have been visitors to Corinth (Theissen, *Social Setting*, pp. 92-94; Merklein, 'Einheitlichkeit', p. 161). Fortunatus and Achaicus may have been slaves or may have been family members (Theissen, *Social Setting*, p. 92).

22. Theissen, *Social Setting*, p. 96.

23. Theissen, *Social Setting*, p. 56.

24. Even if one accepts the hypothesis of 'social groups headed by various prominent members of the congregation' (Horrell, *Social Ethos*, p. 117), it would still be the general membership of the groups, not the leadership only, that Paul was addressing in these verses. Schrage (*Der erste Brief*, I, pp. 151-52) excludes the possibility that Paul could be addressing a small elite, and insists that Paul regarded the party conflict as primarily theological.

followed in 8.7 by the statement: 'not all have this knowledge');[25] 11.22 (where the 'have nots' are referred to in the third person in comments addressed to the church as a whole);[26] and 12.2 (where the words 'when you were Gentiles' are generally agreed not to exclude the possibility that some Corinthian Christians were Jews). The most natural explanation of such passages is that the people excluded were in each case a minority—Paul's statements were generalizations, covering the majority of the church members.

Another passage in which Theissen detects a reference to an elite minority is 4.8-13. In this passage Paul draws an ironical comparison between the royal status of his readers and the lowly status of the apostles.[27] Theissen understands these words in a literal, sociological sense:

> when he [Paul] contrasts his own social situation with that of the Corin-thians—more precisely, with that of the 'wise', the 'strong' and the 'repu-table' (RSV 'held in honor') Corinthians (4.10)—it is not accidental that he mentions working with his hands, suggesting that among those whom he addresses are Christians who do not need to support themselves with their own labor.[28]

These words imply that when Paul says 'you' he really means 'those of you who are socially privileged'. But there is nothing in the passage to suggest this. Paul is referring to the spiritual pretensions of the Corinthian Christians, not to their social origins—they are 'wise in Christ' (v. 10).

David Horrell, while accepting that the phrase 'in Christ' denotes a spiritual dimension, follows Theissen in thinking it likely that 4.8-13 is 'directed primarily at the socially prominent members of the congre-gation'.[29] But it is not easy to see why 'wise in Christ' should imply 'socially prominent'. Even if some Corinthians felt that the wisdom they had received through Christ had raised their standing in the community, it would not affect their social class. As John Barclay says, 'the ironic

25. It may be that the word 'all' in 8.1 is part of a Corinthian slogan Paul is quot-ing. But if so, Paul accepts the statement as true. His normal treatment of Corinthian slogans is the so-called 'Yes, but' approach: yes, your statement is true in a sense, but its practical application must take into account the following considerations.

26. For fuller discussion of 11.22 see Section 3 of this chapter.

27. Cf. Fee, *First Epistle*, p. 82 n. 15: 'The argument in 4.8-11 is filled with so much irony that it is difficult to take it for sober reality'. Fee later criticizes Theissen's literal interpretation of these verses (*First Epistle*, p. 176 n. 57).

28. Theissen, *Social Setting*, p. 56.

29. Horrell, *Social Ethos*, pp. 136, 201.

rebuke is directed at the whole church and may reflect a consciousness among the Christians that, whatever their social origins, their status had been enhanced by their adoption of Christianity'.[30]

The fact that this passage is addressed to the church as a whole is also indicated by the word ἤδη (now) in v. 8.[31] *Now* you are rich and have become kings, Paul is saying, but you were not always so. When you were called you were (with few exceptions) foolish, weak and despised (1.26-29). It is because Christ has become for you the source of divine wisdom that you are now different (1.30). You have nothing that you have not received, but you boast as if you had earned your new status yourselves (4.7). The whole context proclaims the fact that the self-image of the Corinthians, which Paul ironically depicts in 4.8-10, consisted in acquired rather than inherited qualities.

The fact that Paul mentions working with his hands in v. 12 does not imply that some of his addressees 'do not need to support themselves with their own labour'. Paul's determination to be self-supporting was related to his status as an apostle. He had deliberately refused to exercise his apostolic right to be supported by the church and chosen instead to support himself by manual labour (9.14-15). In social terms, he had resolved to become downwardly mobile. His allusion to this policy in 4.12 was probably directed, not at the elite, but at those in Corinth who were seeking to be upwardly mobile—who, to use Edwin Judge's distinction, were seeking a status above their rank.[32]

2. *The Social Background to 1 Corinthians 8–10*

The third chapter of Theissen's book is concerned with the issue of food offered to idols, which Paul discusses in 1 Cor. 8–10.[33] Theissen believes that in these chapters Paul is responding to a Corinthian letter written from the point of view of the 'strong', who probably belonged to the small

---

30. Barclay, 'Thessalonica and Corinth', p. 57.

31. The word ἤδη in 4.8 is often interpreted in terms of realized eschatology, as meaning 'now, rather than at the end time'. But the fact that in this verse ἤδη is correlative with χωρὶς ἡμῶν (independently of us) makes this unlikely. For a full discussion see Excursus C: 'The Meaning of ἤδη in 1 Corinthians 4.8'.

32. Judge, 'Cultural Conformity', pp. 5, 9.

33. Theissen, *Social Setting*, pp. 121-43: 'The Strong and the Weak in Corinth: A Sociological Analysis of a Theological Quarrel'.

group who were wise, powerful and of noble birth.[34] Before considering his argument in detail, questions must be raised about several assumptions on which that argument rests.

The first assumption is that it is possible to identify those sections of 1 Corinthians in which Paul responds to the letter from Corinth rather than to oral information. Such a distinction is normally based on Paul's use of the introductory formula περὶ δέ (now concerning). He uses this formula first in 7.1, with specific reference to the letter from Corinth, and then repeats it when introducing five other sections (7.25; 8.1; 12.1; 16.1; 16.12). Margaret Mitchell makes the point that this formula in itself need not denote anything more than the transition to a new topic.[35] True though this is, what needs to be explained is not the formula as such, but the fact that Paul uses it six times in 1 Corinthians as though he were ticking off a checklist. Other Pauline letters are written quite differently.[36] The simplest explanation of this fact is that a series of questions was raised in the letter from Corinth, and Paul dealt with them one by one. This remains probable though it cannot be proved.

Theissen's second assumption, however, that the letter from Corinth was written from the point of view of the 'strong', is not true to the evidence. In 7.1 (the only verse in 1 Corinthians that specifically mentions the letter from Corinth) Paul quotes an ascetic slogan that is difficult to reconcile with the libertarian slogan of the 'strong' quoted in 10.23.[37] This

34. Theissen, *Social Setting*, pp. 137-38.
35. M.M. Mitchell, 'Concerning περὶ δέ in 1 Corinthians', *NovT* 31 (1989), pp. 229-56.
36. The only parallel is in 1 Thessalonians, where Paul uses the formula περὶ δέ twice (4.9; 5.1). He may be responding in these verses to items raised by the Thessalonians (whether orally or in writing), since Timothy has just reported to him about his recent visit to Thessalonica (3.6).
37. Dale Martin attempts to reconcile these two slogans and regards them both as slogans of the 'strong'. He believes that the 'strong' valued sexual abstinence not from fear of pollution but as a source of strength, and were willing to tolerate the sexual misdemeanours of 'weaker' members of the church (D.B. Martin, *The Corinthian Body* [New Haven: Yale University Press, 1995], pp. 207-208). This interpretation does not do justice either to ch. 6 or to ch. 7. In ch. 7 Paul's repeated assertion that it is not a sin to marry (vv. 28, 36) seems to presuppose the presence in Corinth of people who were saying the opposite—who were opposed to marriage and sexual relations on principle and believed them to be sinful. The asceticism Paul was fighting in this chapter was not just a personal preference but a theological dogma.

As for the slogan of 6.12 (πάντα μοι ἔξεστιν), that slogan is concerned not with permissiveness but with the claiming of rights. Both in 6.12 and in 10.23 Paul is

suggests that the letter from Corinth informed Paul of the variety of opinion within the church on various issues, and asked him to evaluate the different viewpoints.

Theissen's third assumption is that the 'weak' of chs. 8–10 are the same as the 'weak' of 1.27—that is, that they are socially weak.[38] The problem with this assumption is that Paul talks about various kinds of weakness in his epistles, and the precise nuance of the word ἀσθενής is determined by the context of each occurrence.[39] For example, in 9.22 Paul states that he became weak when mixing with the weak (ἐγενόμην τοῖς ἀσθενέσιν ἀσθενής). The context of this verse is Paul's policy of identification with whichever group he happened to be with—in the company of Jews who were 'under law', he observed Jewish practices and ate kosher food; in the company of Gentiles he did not observe Jewish practices and ate whatever he was given. In such a context the word ἀσθενής may have both a theological and a sociological reference.[40]

In ch. 8 Paul talks about a weak conscience (v. 12) and the conscience of a person who is weak (v. 10). This suggests that the weakness referred to in this chapter is mental or spiritual—a failure to grasp the principles laid down in vv. 4-6, which those with 'knowledge' have grasped but the

---

dealing with people who are asserting their rights—their right to consort with a prostitute, and their right to eat food offered to idols. There is no way the rights claimed in 6.12-20 can be reconciled with the theologically-based asceticism that lies behind ch. 7. Martin has been forced into an unnatural exegesis by his belief that all the viewpoints Paul opposed had a single origin.

38. Theissen, *Social Setting*, pp. 124-25.

39. The need to interpret each occurrence of ἀσθενής according to its context is illustrated by 1 Cor. 12, where Paul uses the metaphor of the human body. In vv. 22-24 he states that we clothe the weaker parts of the body with more honour than the stronger parts. Some scholars see in these verses a reference to social divisions at Corinth (Fee, *First Epistle*, p. 612; Horrell, *Social Ethos*, pp. 180-82; Martin, *Body*, pp. 92-96; Thiselton, *First Epistle*, pp. 1006-1007). But the context suggests otherwise. Ch. 12 begins with the words περὶ δὲ τῶν πνευματικῶν. Verses 4-11 describe the variety of spiritual gifts being exercised by the Corinthians. Verses 27-31 also describe the variety of spiritual gifts, but in more hierarchical terms, ending with a reference to 'the greater gifts'. The whole chapter is concerned with the fact that some Corinthians exercised spiritual gifts that were considered greater than those of others, and their spiritual virtuosity gave them higher status. To import into this chapter a reference to socio-economic distinctions is to make it irrelevant to its context.

40. Barrett (*First Epistle*, p. 215) sees the reference as religious. Fee (*First Epistle*, pp. 430-31) sees the reference as primarily sociological. Thiselton (*First Epistle*, p. 705) is comprehensive.

'weak' have not (v. 7). There is a close parallel between 1 Cor. 8–10 and Rom. 14, which begins: τὸν δὲ ἀσθενοῦντα τῇ πίστει προσλαμβάνεσθε (welcome those who are weak in faith). John Barclay suggests that becoming Christians may have involved major social dislocation for some of the higher-status Corinthians, and that some of the 'weak' could have been among the wealthier members of the church.[41]

Theissen's fourth assumption is that the 'strong' formed a homogeneous party at Corinth. This assumption has been challenged by Derek Newton, on the basis of his experiences in the regency of Toraja in Sulawesi in Indonesia. In this area, food offered to idols is a living issue for the church. When Newton asked a wide spectrum of local church leaders for their views on this issue he discovered a considerable variety of opinion. He therefore suggests that, instead of a single 'strong' theology, there could have been 'a web-like maze of viewpoints' among those classifiable as 'strong' at Corinth.[42] It should be remembered that there is no reference in 1 Corinthians to the existence of the 'strong' as a definable group.

In his detailed analysis of chs. 8–10 Theissen provides four arguments in favour of his theory.

a. *The Eating of Meat*
According to Theissen, meat was a rarity for the poorer classes and would only be eaten in connection with special events such as religious festivals, or distributions of meat by a victorious general or a candidate for municipal office. For the poor, he believes, meat was associated with religion and had a 'numinous' character. The rich, by contrast, would eat meat more regularly and it would not have the religious connotation it had for the poor.[43] Justin Meggitt objects to this distinction, on the grounds that cookshops (*popinae* or *ganeae*) were common in Graeco-Roman cities. At these cookshops people from the lower strata of society were able to buy meat, albeit meat of poor quality (blood pudding, tripe etc.).[44]

b. *Attendance at Feasts*
Theissen maintains that the rich would be more likely than the poor to share in feasts, whether socially or professionally.[45] This is true as a

41. Barclay, 'Thessalonica and Corinth', p. 68.
42. Derek Newton, *The Dilemma of Sacrificial Food at Corinth* (JSNTSup, 169; Sheffield: Sheffield Academic Press, 1998), pp. 305-10.
43. Theissen, *Social Setting*, pp. 125-29.
44. Meggitt, *Paul, Poverty and Survival*, pp. 108-12.
45. Theissen, *Social Setting*, pp. 129-32.

generalization, though according to Richard Oster the archaeological evidence suggests a more widespread use of temple dining halls than is sometimes supposed.[46] Feasting in temples was not a habit of the very poor, but would not be confined to the very rich.[47]

c. *The Appeal to Knowledge*

The 'strong' appealed to their 'knowledge' (γνῶσις). Theissen sees in this attitude a parallel to the attitude of second-century Gnostics and suggests that 'the Christian Gnosticism of the second century may have been largely a theology of the upper classes'.[48] However, the Corinthian slogans that Paul quotes in ch. 8 represent the popular philosophy of the marketplace and in Meggitt's opinion 'are no more mentally challenging than an advertising jingle'.[49] It is generally agreed today that references to second-century Gnosticism are of little relevance in determining the background to a first-century literary work.

d. *Paul's Addressees*

In 8.9-12 Paul addresses his remarks to the 'strong' and refers to the weak in the third person. For most of chs. 8–10 it is the attitude of the 'strong' that he is seeking to modify. Theissen makes two deductions from this—that the letter from Corinth to which Paul is replying in this section

46. R.E. Oster, 'Use, Misuse and Neglect of Archaeological Evidence in Some Modern Works on 1 Corinthians (1 Cor. 7.1-5; 8.10; 11.2-16; 12.14-26)', *ZNW* 83 (1992), pp. 52-73 (64-67).

47. There has been much discussion of the identity of the person who objects to eating meat in 10.27-29, whose conscience the meat-eater is asked to respect. Was this person sharing a meal with the meat-eater and of a similar social class? Theissen (*Social Setting*, p. 131) argues that the objector was not a Christian. However, as Barrett says, 'it is not easy to see how a non-Christian's conscience could enter into the matter' (*First Epistle*, p. 242, endorsed by Meggitt, *Paul, Poverty and Survival*, p. 113). The section 10.23–11.1 is a restatement and practical application of the principles laid down in 8.1–10.22 (Horrell, *Social Ethos*, pp. 145-46). It is difficult to believe that, in restating and applying these principles, Paul should use the word 'conscience' (συνείδησις) with a different reference to that which it had in ch. 8. Fee's view (*First Epistle*, p. 484) that the use of the word ἱερόθυτον rather than εἰδωλόθυτον implies a non-Christian informant is opposed by B.N. Fisk, 'Eating Meat Offered to Idols: Corinthian Behaviour and Pauline Response in 1 Corinthians 8–10 (A Response to Gordon Fee)', *TJ* 10 (1989), pp. 49-70 (67 n. 14). For a balanced discussion of this verse see Horrell, *Social Ethos*, pp. 146-47, especially n. 109.

48. Theissen, *Social Setting*, p. 136.

49. Meggitt, *Paul, Poverty and Survival*, p. 114.

represented the point of view of the 'strong'; and that the weak had no position of leadership in the congregation.[50] Both these deductions are questionable. As we saw earlier, the letter from Corinth probably reported the variety of opinion in the church on this issue. And the fact that in ch. 8 Paul addresses his remarks to the 'strong' does not imply anything about their leadership roles, any more than the fact that Paul addresses his remarks to Jews in Rom. 2.17-29 indicates that the leadership of the Roman church lay exclusively in the hands of Jewish Christians.

e. *Conclusion*

In his discussion of chs. 8–10 Theissen has failed to demonstrate his thesis. The picture he paints of a small elite group of strong Christians and a majority of conscience-stricken weak Christians is imposed upon the text, not elicited from it.

3. *The Social Background to 1 Corinthians 11.17-34*

The fourth chapter of *The Social Setting* discusses the problems at the Lord's Supper described in 1 Cor. 11.17-34.[51] Theissen's thesis is that the 'divisions' (σχίσματα) to which Paul refers in v. 18 consisted of a single division between the rich and the poor—the despising of the 'have nots' by the 'haves' (v. 22). 'It can be assumed', he writes, 'that the conflict over the Lord's Supper is a conflict between poor and rich Christians'.[52]

This interpretation is grammatically on shaky ground. If there was a single division between the rich and the poor the word used to denote it should be singular not plural—σχίσμα instead of σχίσματα (cf. Jn 7.40-43; 9.16; 10.19-21). The arguments Theissen uses to support his thesis are equally questionable.

a. *The Absence of Theology*

Theissen points out that Paul is silent about any theological motive for the Corinthian behaviour, and deduces from this silence that the conflict had a social background.[53] This argument, like almost all arguments from silence, is weak. Paul uses the word σχίσματα—the same word as is used

---

50. Theissen, *Social Setting*, p. 137.
51. Theissen, *Social Setting*, pp. 145-74: 'Social Integration and Sacramental Activity: An Analysis of 1 Cor. 11.17-34'.
52. Theissen, *Social Setting*, pp. 147-51 (151).
53. Theissen, *Social Setting*, p. 146.

in 1.10. It is sometimes argued that the divisions of ch. 1 and those of ch. 11 are unrelated, but it is difficult to believe that the church at Corinth should have been split asunder at the same time by two independent sources of division.[54] It is more probable that in ch. 11 Paul presupposes his earlier discussion of the σχίσματα and does not need to repeat what he has already said. In chs. 1–4 he has dealt with the divisions in general; in ch. 11 he deals with one particular manifestation of the divisions, when the whole church gathers together to celebrate the Lord's Supper (v. 18).

It is also unlikely that purely sociological divisions would be described as αἱρέσεις (v. 19). The word αἵρεσις commonly denotes a group sharing the same belief, not the same social status. It is used in Acts of the Sadducees, the Pharisees and the Christians (the sect of the Nazarenes), and in Ignatius of heretical sects.[55]

b. *Paul's Informants*
The word ἀκούω in v. 18 indicates that Paul's information about the divisions at the Lord's Supper came to him by word of mouth. Theissen suggests that the rich appear in a bad light in this passage because Paul's informants were poor (possibly Chloe's people). When Paul says he 'partly believes' the report (μέρος τι πιστεύω), he is, according to Theissen, putting some distance between himself and his informants, and this makes it unlikely that Stephanas was the informant; 'one cannot recommend somebody wholeheartedly (1 Cor. 16.15ff.) and at the same time suggest that one only "partly" believes his reports'.[56]

Theissen here fails to recognize the deep irony of vv. 18-19.[57] In v. 19

---

54. Fee's main argument for regarding the two references to σχίσματα as unrelated is an argument from silence: Paul does not mention in ch. 11 various details that are mentioned in ch. 1 (Fee, *First Epistle*, p. 537). But Paul's reference to σχίσματα in ch. 11 presupposes the earlier discussion, and there was no need for him to repeat everything he had said before.

55. R.A. Campbell ('Does Paul Acquiesce in Divisions at the Lord's Supper?', *NovT* 33 [1991], pp. 61-70 [65-67]) maintains that αἵρεσις in this passage means 'choice'. This is improbable. Certainly the word in itself can have this meaning, but it does not suit the context. The purpose of the αἱρέσεις, according to Paul, was to demonstrate that certain people at Corinth were 'approved'. The fact that they had gathered groups of supporters would demonstrate this more effectively than the existence of undefined 'choices'.

56. Theissen, *Social Setting*, pp. 162-63.

57. R.B. Hays (*First Corinthians* [Interpretation; Louisville, KY: Westminster/John Knox Press, 1997], p. 193) comments on Paul's 'mock disbelief' and adds: 'it is

Paul states that there are bound to be factions within the Corinthian church 'so that it may become clear which of you are approved (δόκιμοι)'. The word δόκιμος and its cognates are discussed more fully in Chapter 9, where I argue that they were favourite words of Paul's opponents at Corinth, and relate particularly to the competitive assessment of preachers.[58] We may paraphrase vv. 18-19 as follows: 'In the first place, I am told that when you meet together as a full assembly there are divisions among you. I am inclined to believe this! After all, if you are determined to engage in a competition to show which preachers are "approved", the church will inevitably be divided into factions supporting the various candidates'. Thus the 'necessity' of the word δεῖ does not indicate 'the basic legitimacy of divisions', as Theissen asserts,[59] but the inevitability of divisions in the current climate of thought at Corinth. In view of the ironical nature of v. 19, v. 18 should also be seen as ironical. The ironical interpretation makes more sense of v. 18 than the literal interpretation. It is unlikely that Paul would literally only 'partly believe' in Corinthian divisions at the Lord's Supper when in earlier chapters he has regarded divisive behaviour as a major characterisic of the Corinthian church (1.10-12; 3.1-4; 4.6). He shows no hesitation in believing the oral report about σχίσματα in ch. 1.

c. *The Humiliation of the 'Have-Nots'*

The key clause for Theissen's exegesis is in v. 22: καὶ καταισχύνετε τοὺς μὴ ἔχοντας (and you humiliate the 'have-nots').[60] The phrase 'the have-nots' (τοὺς μὴ ἔχοντας) can mean 'those who are very poor' (who have nothing), or the object of the verb could be implied from the context—either 'those who do not have houses' or 'those who do not have food'.[61] Whichever translation is adopted, the context seems to be that of a

---

perfectly clear from vv. 20-22 that Paul does in fact believe the reports'. If, as Theissen suggests, Paul's informants were Chloe's people (so also Schrage, *Der erste Brief*, III, p. 19), Paul has no doubts about the accuracy of their report in 1.11.

Schrage's objection (*Der erste Brief*, III, p. 21) that Paul's argument is too serious for the use of irony is groundless. It is in 2 Cor. 10–13, where Paul is in deadly earnest, that he employs irony the most.

58. Alastair Campbell ('Does Paul Acquiesce', pp. 67-69) correctly sees that the word δόκιμος was used by Paul's opponents, and notes the link between 1 Cor. 11.18 and 2 Cor. 13.5-10. However, he thinks the word refers to social status, which is quite alien to its use in 2 Cor. 13.

59. Theissen, *Social Setting*, p. 163.

60. Theissen, *Social Setting*, p. 148.

61. Meggitt (*Paul, Poverty and Survival*, pp. 119-20) discusses the translation of

shared meal (ἔρανος), to which church members brought contributions. Peter Lampe has described how the ἔρανος worked: 'It could be practiced in two ways. Either each participant ate his or her own food, brought along in a basket, or all the provisions were put on a common table, as is done at a potluck dinner'.[62]

Lampe quotes an incident recorded by Xenophon from the life of Socrates. When some of the guests brought more food to a dinner than others, Socrates insisted that all the food should be pooled and shared out equally. This, as Lampe says, is a close parallel to the Corinthian situation.[63] It seems likely that the Corinthians had previously followed the practice of Socrates. But now the party members were gathering in their own groups and eating their own food, while the poorest Christians, who did not belong to these groups, got nothing to eat.

The current practice at Corinth is described in v. 21: ἕκαστος γὰρ τὸ ἴδιον δεῖπνον προλαμβάνει ἐν τῷ φαγεῖν. Theissen (in my opinion correctly) translates this: 'for in eating each one goes ahead with his own meal'.[64] The view that the prefix προ- in προλαμβάνει has a temporal

---

τοὺς μὴ ἔχοντας in some detail. His description of the translation 'the have-nots' (the very poor) as 'thoroughly unsound' is unjustified. For one thing, he admits that there seem to be parallels in Greek literature to justify this translation. For another thing, he ignores the passages from the gospels and from classical literature cited in BAGD sv. ἔχω 1α where ὁ ἔχων (the one who has) is contrasted with ὁ μὴ ἔχων (the one who does not have). In practice, it does not make much difference whether the phrase is used absolutely or whether an object such as 'food' or 'houses' is supplied, since in any case it is the poorest members of the church who are referred to.

The least likely suggestion is Meggitt's own—that the phrase refers to those who do not receive the bread and wine of the eucharist. He questions the assumption that the Corinthians celebrated the Lord's Supper in the context of a full meal rather than a token meal, and argues that when Paul talks about people going hungry and getting drunk, he is using the language of caricature (p. 191). But while it is true, as Meggitt says, that πεινᾶν can be used metaphorically of spiritual hunger, that is clearly not the sense in v. 34. The question as to whether a word is being used literally or metaphorically is decided by the context, and the context of 1 Cor. 11.17-34 points clearly to a literal sense. As Peter Lampe says, δεῖπνον always means a proper meal and 'the blessing of the bread implied the blessing of all foods on the table' (P. Lampe, 'The Eucharist: Identifying with Christ on the Cross', *Int* 48 [1994], pp. 36-49 [42, 49 n. 22]).

62. Lampe, 'Eucharist', p. 38.
63. Lampe, 'Eucharist', p. 39.
64. Theissen, *Social Setting*, p. 147. He takes these words to mean that the people concerned ate their food before the words of institution had been pronounced, on the

force is supported by Paul's exhortation in v. 33: ἀλλήλους ἐκδέχεσθε. This should be translated 'wait for each other'—the meaning of the verb ἐκδέχεσθαι in all its other New Testament occurrences.[65] The poorest members of the church may have been slaves or day labourers with little control over their time, who would often arrive late at church gatherings and could therefore miss their share of the meal.[66]

Theissen correctly regards the phrase τὸ ἴδιον δεῖπνον (his own supper) in v. 21 as a probable indication of food that individual Christians bring with them and eat individually. He then comments: 'If this behavior has certain "individualistic" traits it is nonetheless the individualistic behavior of a particular group which as such, under some circumstances, is class-specific'.[67] The first part of this comment is true. Paul's conjunction of the word ἕκαστος (each individual) with the words σχίσματα and αἱρέσεις (splits and factions) indicates individual behaviour in a group context. But this behaviour was only to a limited extent class-specific. The only people excluded were the 'have-nots' of v. 22—people so poor that they had nothing to contribute. The rest of the church—the great majority—belonged to the various groups and ate their food within them. This is clear from v. 18: 'when you gather together as an ἐκκλησία there are splits among you'. If 'you' means the church as a whole in vv. 18, 19 and 20, it should mean the church as a whole in v. 22.

grounds that only after that was the food consecrated for communal use. This interpretation reads a great deal into Paul's words that is left unsaid. The same is true of
Lampe's theory that there were two stages in the meal—'First Tables' for a few and
'Second Tables' for a larger number (Lampe, 'Eucharist', pp. 37-41). Paul's use of the
word ἕκαστος (each one) does not fit well with this theory.

65. Acts 17.16; 1 Cor. 16.11; Heb. 10.31; 11.10; Jas 5.7 and a variant reading of Jn
5.3.

66. The meaning of both προλαμβάνει and ἐκδέχεσθε is disputed. According
to BAGD, the temporal sense of the prefix προ- in προλαμβάνει is 'felt very little,
if at all' in this verse and the word means '*take, get* of a meal'. Lampe protests that
this translation is based on only one Greek parallel—an inscription in which the use of
προλαμβάνειν for προσλαμβάνειν could be a mistake by the stonemason (Lampe,
'Eucharist', p. 48 n. 13—see also the discussion in MM, p. 542). Moreover, if
προλαμβάνει τὸ ἴδιον δεῖπνον means simply 'eats his own supper', the words ἐν τῷ
φαγεῖν (in his eating) are redundant. With regard to ἐκδέχεσθε, Fee (*First Epistle*,
pp. 567-68) translates it 'receive' or 'welcome'. But if προλαμβάνει has a temporal
sense, it is likely that ἐκδέχεσθε has one also. Thiselton (*First Epistle*, p. 899) comments that the lexicographical evidence for the meaning 'welcome, receive' is not
strong.

67. Theissen, *Social Setting*, pp. 148-50 (150).

It is true, as Theissen points out, that the word ἕκαστος in v. 21 cannot mean literally 'every member of the church', since the 'have-nots' are excluded.[68] At the same time, however, the use of the word ἕκαστος makes it difficult to believe that Paul is addressing a small upper-class minority, and this theory does not suit the corporate context.[69]

The basic error in Theissen's exegesis is that he treats v. 22 as a definition of the nature of the divisions. He writes: 'It is only from 1 Cor. 11.22 that we learn that there are two groups opposed to one another, those who have no food, the μὴ ἔχοντες, and those who can avail themselves of their own meal, ἴδιον δεῖπνον'.[70] But in v. 22 Paul is pointing out the *result* of the divisions, not their cause.[71] Because you are a divided society, Paul declares, you eat what should be a common meal in a divisive way, and the result is that the very poor go hungry and are humiliated. The only thing this tells us about the groups is that the very poorest members did not belong to them. The most probable reason for this is the one given in Chapter 1 of this book: the party leaders were like sophists and charged fees for their teaching, which the very poor could not afford.

d. *The Theory of Different Menus*
Theissen notes the fact that the words of institution (11.23-26) refer only to bread and wine and do not mention meat. He suggests that the 'own supper' the richer Corinthians enjoyed was eaten before the Lord's Supper, and contained delicacies not available to the general membership.[72]

---

68. Theissen, *Social Setting*, p. 148. He compares the use of ἕκαστος in 1 Cor. 14.26, where 'each one' contributes a hymn, lesson, revelation or tongue, and in 1 Cor. 1.12, where 'each one' says, 'I belong to Paul, Apollos, Cephas or Christ'. In all these cases ἕκαστος would be a most unnatural word for Paul to use if he were referring only to a small minority.

69. See the discussion of this passage in A. Lindemann, 'Die paulinische Ekklesiologie angesichts der Lebens-wirklichkeit der christlichen Gemeinde in Korinth', in R. Bieringer (ed.), *The Corinthian Correspondence* (Leuven: Leuven University Press, 1996), pp. 63-86 (71-73). Lindemann criticizes Theissen's theory of separate meals, and points out that Paul stresses the corporate nature of the occasion with the phrases ἐν ἐκκλησίᾳ, ἐπὶ τὸ αὐτό and ἕκαστος.

70. Theissen, *Social Setting*, p. 148.

71. There is no suggestion in the text that the action of those eating their own meal was a deliberate display of status, 'an attempt to dominate by imposing shame', as Stephen Barton asserts ('Paul's Sense of Place: An Anthropological Approach to Community Formation in Corinth', *NTS* 32 [1986], pp. 225-46 [239]).

72. Theissen, *Social Setting*, pp. 155-60.

This theory is improbable. What Paul objects to is not differences in menu, but the fact that the poorest members of the church got nothing and went hungry.

Theissen cites references in Pliny, Juvenal and Martial to meals at which the host provides good quality food to his closest friends and inferior food to other guests.[73] These parallels are of little relevance to 1 Cor. 11. For one thing, these were private banquets provided by individuals for invited guests, whereas the Lord's Supper was celebrated at Corinth by the whole church gathered together (vv. 18, 20). For another thing, the practices described were condemned by the authors concerned and were clearly not standard practice. As Theissen admits, 'it should not be supposed that the Roman (bad) manners just described were widespread in the Corinthian congregation'.[74] The most such parallels can show is that discrimination was practised at private banquets by some Roman hosts and that the Corinthian Christians were not unique in humiliating the poorest members of their company.

e. *The Context of 11.17-34*

One of the drawbacks of Theissen's approach to 11.17-34 is that he fails to consider this passage in the light of its context as part of the section 11.2–14.40. Thiselton (commenting on a later part of this section) emphasizes the unity of the section as a whole:

> Too many writers treat 12.1–14.40 as if it were simply an ad hoc response to questions about spiritual gifts (or spiritual persons) rather than as an address to this topic within the broader theological framework of 11.2–14.40 in deliberate continuity with 8.1–11.1, and indeed ultimately with 1.1–4.21.[75]

The section 11.2–14.40 begins in 11.2 with Paul's commendation of the Corinthians for remembering him and observing the traditions he had taught them. Most probably, as H. Merklein says, he is echoing a Corinthian claim, expressed in their letter to him.[76] A parallel verse is 8.1, where Paul echoes the Corinthian claim 'we all have knowledge' and then proceeds to point out in v. 5 that in fact 'not all have this knowledge'. Similarly in ch. 11 he accepts the Corinthian claim that they observe his

---

73. Theissen, *Social Setting*, pp. 156-58.
74. Theissen, *Social Setting*, p. 158.
75. Thiselton, *First Epistle*, p. 900.
76. Merklein, 'Einheitlichkeit', p. 174. He cites Lietzmann, Hurd and Barrett in support of this view (p. 174 n. 86).

traditions as a generalization, but then proceeds to point out that some of them—in particular the argumentative person or (more probably) persons referred to in v. 16—do not correctly understand what these traditions mean.[77]

The Corinthian claim is more fully discussed in Excursus F, where I suggest that the traditions the Corinthians have in mind could have included both 'in Christ there is no male or female' (Gal. 3.28) and 'do not quench the Spirit; do not despise prophecies' (1 Thess. 5.19-20).[78] The key verse in 11.2-16 is v. 10, where Paul insists that women prophets have the right to keep their heads covered, and are not required to abandon themselves to ecstasy or frenzy.[79] The background to 11.2-16, in my opinion, is the same as the background to chs. 12–14—the clash between two different understandings of prophetic inspiration. Paul believed inspired prophets were still in control of themselves (14.32) and should observe 'decency and good order' (14.40). Some argumentative people at Corinth (11.16) who described themselves as 'spiritual' (14.37) believed in an ecstatic type of inspiration that made self-control impossible.

In v. 17 Paul repeats the motif of commendation. Whereas in v. 2 he commended the Corinthians for their eagerness to be faithful to his traditions, in vv. 17-22 he refuses to commend them for their manner of celebrating the Lord's Supper. 'Shall I commend you for this?' he asks; 'no, I will not' (v. 22). The implication of these words is that the Corinthians were expecting Paul to commend them. This is also implied in v. 17, 'your gatherings for worship have become not better but worse' (οὐκ εἰς τὸ κρεῖσσον ἀλλὰ εἰς τὸ ἧσσον συνέρχεσθε). There seems to be little point in this remark unless the Corinthians were claiming that their gatherings to celebrate the Lord's Supper were now an improvement

---

77. In Merklein's opinion, Paul's commendation of the Corinthians had primarily a rhetorical function ('Einheitlichkeit', p. 174).

78. Excursus F: 'The Interpretation of 1 Corinthians 11.10'.

79. It is sometimes stated that Paul's concern in 11.2-16 was with the dress (or hairstyle) of both men and women. According to Thiselton (*First Epistle*, p. 800) this is 'made clear' by v. 4. The passage as a whole, however, does not suggest this. Paul makes two kinds of statement in this passage: (i) statements involving both sexes and contrasting one with the other (vv. 3-5, 7-9, 11-12, 14-15); and (ii) statements involving one sex only (vv. 6, 10, 13). In each of the latter cases it is women who are involved. This suggests that Paul brings men into his argument by way of contrast, to reveal what he sees as God-given differences between the sexes. The controversial issue concerned only the women.

on the celebrations that took place when Paul was at Corinth. If the sole difference between their present practice and their former practice consisted in eating the meal in separate groups it is difficult to see why they should expect Paul to commend them. However, the words πρῶτον μέν (firstly) in v. 18 suggest that this was not the only factor. Admittedly, we cannot hold strictly to the rule that μέν requires a following δέ— Paul's grammar was so eccentric that there is no difficulty in supposing an anacolouthon. But even if there is an anacolouthon, Paul's use of μέν would still indicate a feeling in his mind—an awareness that the divisive eating habits of the Corinthians were not his only reason for failing to commend them.[80]

H.A.W. Meyer sees the contrast to πρῶτον μέν in the words περὶ δὲ τῶν πνευματικῶν (12.1) that introduce the discussion of spiritual gifts in 12.1–14.40.[81] A strong argument in favour of Meyer's interpretation is the presence of verbal parallels between 11.17-34 and ch. 14:

συνερχομένων ὑμῶν ἐν ἐκκλησίᾳ (when you gather as an assembly) (11.18)

συνερχομένων οὖν ὑμῶν ἐπὶ τὸ αὐτό (when you gather together in one place) (11.20)

συνερχόμενοι εἰς τὸ φαγεῖν (when you gather together to eat) (11.33)

ἐν ἐκκλησίᾳ (in the gathered assembly) (14.19)

ἐὰν οὖν συνέλθῃ ἡ ἐκκλησία ὅλη ἐπὶ τὸ αὐτό (if the whole assembly gathers together in one place) (14.23)

ὅταν συνέρχησθε (when you gather together) (14.26).

All these phrases distinguish the occasions when the whole church gathered together from the worship that took place in private houses. In 11.2-16 (which lacks any such phrase) Paul envisages women prophesying in small groups.[82] In 11.17-34 and ch. 14 he envisages the whole church

80. For various theories as to the complement to πρῶτον μέν, see Fee, *First Epistle*, p. 536 n. 26.

81. Meyer, *Corinthians*, I, p. 333.

82. Two factors suggest that the context of 11.2-16 is small groups.

First, the emphasis on the whole church gathering in one place in 11.17-20 implies a contrast with the preceding section. Paul's reply to the Corinthian claim that they were observing his traditions is in two parts. First, in the case of women prophets, he accepts their claim with reservations. Second, in the case of their behaviour when they all gather together as an ἐκκλησία, he rejects their claim completely. This contrast suggests that the ministry of women prophets did not take place when they gathered

gathering together, possibly in the house and grounds of Gaius (Rom. 16.23). Such gatherings would involve both the sharing of a Christianized passover meal (as described in 11.17-34) and opportunity for free worship and the exercise of spiritual gifts (as described in 14.26).

The conjunction of these two elements explains why the Corinthians believed their new style of celebration to be an improvement on the old style, and expected Paul to commend them. Their emphasis was no longer (as it had been in Paul's day) on the remembrance of Christ's death (11.23-26); it was on speaking in tongues and prophesying. They were, they believed, obeying Paul's injunction not to quench the Spirit. But in Paul's opinion the fact that they were divided into factions was a sign of deterioration, not of progress. This division had two consequences. Because they were not eating all together but in factional groups, the poorest members of the church were ignored and humiliated (11.17-34), and their approach to the exercise of spiritual gifts was now competitive rather than co-operative (14.1-40). Everyone wanted to take part (14.26), there was too much speaking in tongues (14.23, 27-28) and several prophets were speaking at the same time (14.29-30).

The train of thought in 11.2–14.40 can be summarized as follows. Paul was responding to a Corinthian claim that they were faithful to the traditions he had taught them. This claim was probably based mainly on their implementation of Paul's advice not to quench the Spirit.[83] In commend-

---

together as a full ἐκκλησία. That phrase is used in vv. 17-18 to introduce a new, hitherto unexplored situation.

According to Fee (*First Epistle*, p. 703 n. 18) this was the view of most Protestant interpreters before the twentieth century. It is stoutly defended by H.A.W. Meyer (*Corinthians*, I, pp. 320-21). For more recent advocacy see P. Ellingworth, 'Translating 1 Corinthians', *BT* 31 (1980), pp. 234-38 (236); P. Ellingworth and H.A. Hatton, *Paul's First Letter to the Corinthians* (UBS Handbook; New York: United Bible Societies, 1994), pp. 240-42.

The other argument in favour of this interpretation is the prohibition in 14.34-35 of women speaking ἐν ταῖς ἐκκλησίαις—i.e. in the full assemblies. However, discussion of these verses is complicated by the possibility that they are interpolated, and by different scholarly estimates of the likelihood of Paul contradicting himself (cf. Fee, *First Epistle*, pp. 699-708; Thiselton, *First Epistle*, pp. 1146-61). It is the internal evidence of ch. 11 that is exegetically decisive.

83. The spiritual equality of men and women was also part of Paul's tradition (Gal. 3.28) and was relevant to the issue discussed in 11.3-16. But 11.2 introduces the whole section 11.2–14.40, and the exercise of spiritual gifts in worship is the overall theme of the section.

ing them for this, Paul was not just being polite—he had earlier thanked God for enriching them with speech, knowledge and spiritual gifts (1.4-7). But in two areas he believed they had turned away from the approach to worship he had taught them.

The first area concerned the women who prophesied in small groups and house meetings. Some argumentative people were insisting that women prophets should uncover their heads and abandon themselves to the inspiration of the Spirit like Bacchic maenads. Such behaviour, in Paul's opinion, did not recognize the God-given difference between men and women, and it was not recognized as part of the tradition by himself or by any other church. The second area concerned the gathering of the whole church to celebrate the Lord's Supper. The Corinthians, Paul believed, had forgotten the true purpose of the Lord's Supper—the commemoration of the new covenant sealed by the death of Christ. By eating in separate groups they were humiliating those poor church members who did not belong to any group; and their exercise of spiritual gifts was individualistic and competitive rather than seeking the good of the whole church.

This reconstruction confirms the truth of Thiselton's comment that the section 11.2–14.40 is in continuity with 8.1–11.1 and with 1.1–4.21. The whole of 1 Corinthians is an attempt to turn the Corinthian mindset from an individualistic, competitive assertion of one's own gifts and rights into an ethic of consideration for others.

4. *The Criticism of Theissen by Justin Meggitt*

Justin Meggitt has recently painted a picture of the Corinthian situation very different to that of Theissen. He believes that, in the Roman Empire, 'those devoid of political power, the non-elite, over 99% of the Empire's population, could expect little more from life than abject poverty'. In Rome, he asserts, there was mass urban destitution, and 'we can, with some certainty, assume a similar situation in other Graeco-Roman πόλεις'. In his opinion the Christians at Corinth belonged, without exception, to the ranks of the weak and under-privileged and 'shared fully the bleak material existence which was the lot of more than 99% of the inhabitants of the Empire'.[84]

According to Meggitt this view of the situation was generally accepted until the coming of the so-called 'New Consensus', according to which

---

84. Meggitt, *Paul, Poverty and Survival*, pp. 50, 52, 99.

some members of the early churches belonged to the higher strata of society. The New Consensus, Meggitt declares, 'has been most famously articulated for the Pauline epistles by G. Theissen and W. Meeks' and 'has gone almost unchallenged for the last two decades'.[85] In opposing the New Consensus, Meggitt attacks the views of Theissen more than those of anyone else, rightly seeing his contribution as foundational.[86]

Mention has already been made of several of Meggitt's criticisms, in which he provides a valuable corrective to Theissen's sweeping generalizations. However, Meggitt's thesis as a whole is just as implausible as Theissen's. There are two reasons for this. First, much of his argument is based on conditions at Rome, and he has no right to assume 'with some certainty' that conditions at Corinth were similar to those at Rome.[87] The city of Corinth was refounded by Julius Caesar in 44 BCE as a Roman colony, peopled mainly by freedmen. As such it had no continuity in its tradition. Many families were socially ascendant, being originally descended from slaves.[88] It had the reputation, according to Strabo, of being a great and wealthy city, mainly because of its commerce.[89] It was the seat of the governor of Achaia and host to the Isthmian Games. In such a city, lacking as it did the rigid social stratification of Rome, there would be many opportunities for upward mobility.[90]

The second reason for rejecting Meggitt's analysis is the presence in 1 and 2 Corinthians of several indications of a degree of relative affluence at least among some members of the Corinthian church.

First, the criticism of Paul for not accepting support from the church presupposes that other travelling preachers did accept such support (1 Cor. 9.12; 2 Cor. 2.17; 11.12; 12.13). Meggitt claims that 'supporting a missionary is not a sure sign of affluence. It is possible for all except those facing an immediate subsistence crisis'.[91] But support for these missionaries went

---

85. Meggitt, *Paul, Poverty and Survival*, pp. 99-100.

86. For example, in discussing the attribution of high social status to named individuals, Meggitt comments that 'once again Theissen's work has proved perhaps the most influential in this area' (*Paul, Poverty and Survival*, p. 128).

87. Meggitt, *Paul, Poverty and Survival*, p. 52.

88. On the status of freedmen see W.A. Meeks, *The First Urban Christians: The Social World of the Apostle Paul* (New Haven: Yale University Press, 1983), pp. 20-23.

89. Theissen, *Social Setting*, p. 101, quoting Strabo, *Geography* 8.6.20 and 8.6.23.

90. See the description of the city of Corinth in Theissen, *Social Setting*, pp. 99-102; Thiselton, *First Epistle*, pp. 1-12.

91. Meggitt, *Paul, Poverty and Survival*, p. 117.

on for a considerable time and would be difficult for victims of 'urban destitution'. If, as I have argued in this book, the missionaries currently at Corinth were like sophists, they would not have been content with the meagre offerings of the destitute.

Second, Paul assumes in 1 Cor. 16.1-4 that the majority of the Corinthians will support the collection, and urges each member to save up money towards it 'as he prospers' (ὅ τι ἐὰν εὐοδῶται). The language of prosperity would be inappropriate for people engaged in a daily struggle to find enough to eat.[92]

Third, in 2 Cor. 8 and 9 Paul urges the Corinthians to contribute generously to the collection for the poor Christians in Judaea. At the present time, he writes, your surplus can relieve their shortage (8.14). It would not be fitting to talk of a surplus to people who were barely subsisting.[93]

Fourth, Paul pictures a member of the church reclining at a meal-table in a temple (1 Cor. 8.10). While it is true that the sharing of meals in temples was not limited to a small elite, it is equally true that it was not a practice of the destitute.

Fifth, 1 Corinthians 6.1-11 is concerned with members of the church engaging in litigation. In the Graeco-Roman world, litigation was not limited to the elite, but would be beyond the means of the abjectly poor.[94] Paul suggests that the people concerned should let themselves be robbed rather than go to court (1 Cor. 6.7), which implies that they possessed property of enough value to justify a lawsuit.

---

92. According to Meeks (*First Urban Christians*, p. 65), Paul's language implies an 'economy of small people, not destitute, but not commanding capital either'. G. Schöllgen ('Was wissen wir über die Sozialstruktur der Paulinischen Gemeinden?', *NTS* 34 [1988], pp. 71-82 [76-77]) argues that Paul's words imply differences in the financial capability of different church members.

93. Cf. Horrell, *Social Ethos*, p. 95: 'Paul's description of their present abundance (2 Cor. 8.14) in contrast to the poverty of the Macedonian believers (2 Cor. 8.2), in a context which certainly refers to material things, suggests that at least some of the Corinthians seemed quite prosperous'.

94. Although the lawcourts were so weighted in favour of the elite that a lower-status person could not bring a case against them, there is ample evidence in the Graeco-Roman world of lower-status people taking each other to court (see Meggitt, *Paul, Poverty and Survival*, pp. 123-24). Wayne Meeks observes that 'as the papyri show, it was a litigious age, when even small traders or village farmers could and did appear before magistrates to complain about the encroachments of their neighbours' (Meeks, *First Urban Christians*, p. 66).

The problem with both Theissen's thesis and Meggitt's thesis is that the evidence is not sufficient to justify their conclusions. Robin Scroggs believes the data for a sociological analysis of the New Testament to be so scanty and sociologically inaccessible that 'the sociologist must read the text as though it were a palimpsest'.[95] Andreas Lindemann asserts that, apart from 1 Cor. 1.26-29, the social structure of the Corinthian church is never mentioned in the letter, and that this brief statement cannot bear the weight of argument based upon it.[96] Georg Schöllgen criticizes the statement of Meeks that 'a Pauline congregation generally reflected a fair cross-section of urban society' on the grounds that we do not have enough information to say what the social structure of Graeco-Roman cities was.[97] In his view the question of the social structure of early Christian congregations cannot adequately be answered in our present state of ignorance.[98] If these judgments are true, any estimate of the social composition of the Corinthian church, or of the city of Corinth as a whole, whether on the lines of Theissen or on the lines of Meggitt, is bound to be speculative.

1 Corinthians 1.26 implies a small minority of church members who were socially superior, but exactly how socially superior it is impossible to say. 1 Cor. 11.22 refers to some who were poor, but exactly how poor it is impossible to say. In a city such as Corinth neither social class nor poverty were immutable. The pretentious claims of the Corinthian Christians in 1 Cor. 4.8 may reflect the values of a society where status was fluid. But if so, this is a comment on the psychology of the Corinthian Christians, not on their socio-economic circumstances, which are unknown and (at least in detail) unknowable.

5. *Leadership and Spiritual Gifts*

One important factor that the sociological approach tends to overlook is the revolutionary change wrought in the personality and self-image of the Corinthian Christians by the Holy Spirit. It should not be assumed that human behaviour is always and everywhere socially determined.[99] The

95. R. Scroggs, 'The Sociological Interpretation of the New Testament: The Present State of Research', *NTS* 26 (1980), pp. 164-79 (166).

96. Lindemann, 'Ekklesiologie', pp. 69, 73.

97. Schöllgen, 'Was wissen wir?', p. 72, criticizing Meeks, *First Urban Christians*, p. 73.

98. Schöllgen, 'Was wissen wir?', p. 78.

99. Cf. Horrell, *Social Ethos*, p. 19: 'A deterministic view of human behaviour is in no way an ubiquitous feature of social science; indeed, the determinism of some forms

church at Corinth was a charismatic church, in which the gifts of the Holy Spirit were given to 'each one' (1 Cor. 12.7); and in a charismatic church spiritual gifts of prophecy and teaching are bound up with leadership. An example is the church at Antioch, where, according to Acts 13.1-3, the momentous decision to send out Barnabas and Paul as missionaries was taken by a group of prophets and teachers. Within 1 Corinthians itself the influential role played by prophets and 'spiritual people' is shown by verses such as 7.40 and 14.37. The importance attached to spiritual gifts at Corinth can be seen not only from the fact that Paul devotes three chapters to the subject (1 Cor. 12–14) but also from the fact that this is the outstanding feature of the church for which he praises God in his opening thanksgiving (1.4-9).[100] This thanksgiving, coming immediately after his greeting to 'the church in Corinth' (1.2), must apply to all the church members, not just to an elite. As Horrell says, there is no reason to assume that Christian prophets and teachers at Corinth came from any one social group.[101] It was the church as a whole that had found in Christ a new wisdom (1.30)—a statement addressed to the same people who, in the preceding few verses, were described as weak and foolish from a worldly point of view. The problem was that these people, enriched with every spiritual gift (1.4-7), possessors of a wisdom they had previously never had (1.30) and a spiritual status they had never before enjoyed (7.22), had

of social theory is precisely one of the inadequacies which modern attempts to reformulate such theory are seeking to overcome'.

An example of the deterministic approach is L.L. Welborn's article: 'On the Discord in Corinth: 1 Corinthians 1–4 and Ancient Politics', *JBL* 106 (1987), pp. 85-111. Welborn notes the assumption of ancient writers that, where there was discord, opposition between rich and poor lay behind it, and assumes that this was true at Corinth. In his opinion, Paul's attempt to spiritualize the situation was conditioned by 'the nature of his project', and modern commentators have erred in taking Paul's words at face value. Paul knew well enough, Welborn asserts, that, as Aristotle laid down years before, it is feelings of inequality arising from distinctions of wealth, noble birth and higher learning that are the cause of social conflict (p. 96, quoting Aristotle, *Pol.* 5.1.1301b5).

The presupposition of this argument seems to be that, if Aristotle said something must be so, so it must be. This kind of determinism fails to recognize that the Holy Spirit was at work in the Corinthian church changing lives and attitudes, creating new problems but not automatically reproducing the old problems.

100. Paul's statement in 1 Cor. 1.7 that the Corinthian Christians were not lacking in any spiritual gift may, as Bruce Winter suggests (*Philo and Paul*, p. 183), be an attempt to boost the morale of people used to being despised.

101. Horrell, *Social Ethos*, p. 157.

become puffed up, proud of their attainments, self-satisfied and arrogant (4.8). That is why Paul reminds them that everything they enjoyed had come to them as a gift (4.7); they should not boast of their wisdom and spiritual achievements, but only of the Lord who had supplied them (1.31).

6. *Conclusion*

From the above survey the following conclusions can be drawn.

i. In 1 Cor. 1.26-29 Paul describes the social condition of the Corinthian Christians before they were called to follow Christ. Most of them were of low social status but a few were not.

ii. The terms used to describe the Corinthian Christians in 4.8-13 have nothing to do with social class, and relate to spiritual pretensions. Those who now consider themselves wise, powerful and glorious are the people who were originally poor, weak and despised.

iii. There is no evidence that the upper-class minority monopolized the leadership of the Corinthian church, which was a charismatic church with charismatic leadership.

iv. Apart from the small upper-class minority and the very poor of 11.22, most Corinthian Christians had a social status in between these two extremes. Their status was low, but they were not abjectly poor and could afford to contribute to the collection from their surplus.

v. The Corinthian Christians had attained a spiritual status that in most cases belied their social status. Under the influence of the teaching then prevalent in the church they had become puffed up with pride in their own wisdom and it was this fact, not conflict between rich and poor, that had led to the various types of behaviour Paul felt compelled to rebuke.

EXCURSUS C:
THE MEANING OF ἤδη IN 1 CORINTHIANS 4.8

It is widely believed that the word ἤδη in 1 Cor. 4.8 should be translated 'already', and indicates the over-realized eschatology of the Corinthians. Paul is understood to be echoing a claim by the Corinthians that they already enjoy the blessings of the age to come. This theory is sometimes linked with 1 Cor. 15.12, and the people in that verse who say there is no resurrection of the dead are understood to be really saying that the resurrection has already taken place—the opinion attributed to Hymenaeus and Philetus in 2 Tim. 2.18.[102]

Other scholars disagree with this interpretation. Richard Horsley, who translates ἤδη as 'already' and detects in the word a reference to realized eschatology, points out that this word need not necessarily echo the language of the Corinthians. It could represent Paul's sarcastic description of their position.[103] Others see in the word ἤδη a reference to the present rather than a contrast with the future. Findlay translates: 'so soon you have had your fill...so soon you grew rich', and comments, 'the Corinthians reported themselves, in the Church letter (?), so well fed by Paul's successors, so furnished in talent and grace, that they desired nothing more'.[104] Peter Marshall notes the close link between Paul's use in 4.8 of words such as κορέννυμι (be sated or glutted) and the Greek concept of ὕβρις (overweening pride). He paraphrases: 'Now you are sated! Now you are rich! Why, you have become kings, independently and self-indulgently!', and sees the root of the problem in the arrogance of the social elite in the Corinthian church.[105]

The purpose of this note is to examine the word ἤδη in 4.8 and to ask two questions—has the word an eschatological reference, and is 'already' the right translation?

102. A.J.M. Wedderburn traces the use of 2 Tim. 2.18 to interpret 1 Cor. 15.12 back to Thomas Aquinas. He attributes the prevalence of this view in modern times largely to an influential essay by Julius Schniewind (A.J.M. Wedderburn, *Baptism and Resurrection: Studies in Pauline Theology against its Graeco-Roman Background* [WUNT, 44; Tübingen: J.C.B. Mohr, 1987], p. 10, citing J. Schniewind, 'Die Leugnung der Auferstehung in Korinth', in E. Kähler [ed.], *Nachgelassene Reden und Aufsätze* [Berlin: Töpelmann, 1952], pp. 110-39). David Kuck rightly asserts that, in making this link, Schniewind was 'on shaky ground historically and methodologically' (David W. Kuck, *Judgment and Community Conflict: Paul's Use of Apocalyptic Judgment Language in 1 Cor. 3.5–4.5* [Leiden: E.J. Brill, 1992], p. 21). As Wedderburn says, the phrase 'there is no resurrection of the dead' in 1 Cor. 15.12 would have been an odd phrase to use if the people using it believed that there was a resurrection and that it had happened already and had happened to them (Wedderburn, *Baptism*, p. 13).

103. Richard A. Horsley, ' "How can some of you say that there is no resurrection of the dead?": Spiritual Elitism in Corinth', *NovT* 20 (1978), pp. 203-231 (203).

104. G.G. Findlay, 'St. Paul's First Epistle to the Corinthians', in W.R. Nicoll (ed.), *The Expositor's Greek Testament* (London: Hodder & Stoughton, 1900), II, pp. 727-953 (800).

105. Marshall, *Enmity*, pp. 205-209.

LSJ gives four meanings for ἤδη: (1) already, by this time; (2) forth-with, immediately; (3) opposed to the future or the past, actually, now; (4) of logical proximity. BAGD suggests three possible translations: 'now', 'already' and 'by this time'. These various translations reflect the various contexts in which ἤδη occurs, both in secular Greek and in the New Testament. For example, of the occurrences in the papyri cited in Moulton and Milligan, three mean 'now, this very moment'. In two of these occur-rences, in magical papyri, ἤδη is combined with ἄρτι: 'come out, demon, now, now, now' (ἄρτι ἄρτι ἤδη), and 'now, now, quickly, quickly' (ἐν τῇ ἄρτι ὥρᾳ ἤδη ἤδη ταχὺ ταχύ); and once in a papyrus letter someone is ordered to send off 'now' the supplies of aracus[106] he has received. In the other two occurrences cited by Moulton and Milligan, there is a contrast with the past—'the money which Seleucus told you to give to me, "now" give to Cleon'; and 'he ought to be crowned, because the office is "now" secured to the city'.[107]

The majority of occurrences of ἤδη in the New Testament are in the gospels and have a purely temporal sense. In some cases there is an implied contrast with the future and 'already' is an appropriate translation —for example Mk 15.44: 'Pilate was amazed that Jesus was already dead' (ἤδη τέθνηκεν). In other cases there is an implied contrast with the past—for example Jn 21.4: 'it was now early morning' (πρωίας ἤδη γενομένης) after the disciples had been fishing through the night. In many cases there is no clear contrast with either the past or the future. For exam-ple, the statement of the two travellers to Emmaus: 'it is now evening' (κέκλικεν ἤδη ἡ ἡμέρα; Lk. 24.29) could connote either 'it is no longer broad daylight as it was when we started our journey' or 'it is already getting dark and will soon be darker'.

Paul uses ἤδη on several occasions. Three times there is a contrast with the future. In 1 Cor. 5.3 the phrase 'I have already judged (ἤδη κέκρικα) the man who has done this' anticipates a forthcoming judgment by the Corinthians. In 1 Cor. 6.7 Paul says: 'the fact that you are taking each other to court means that you have already lost' (ἤδη...ἥττημα ὑμῖν ἐστιν). In Phil. 3.12 Paul declares: 'it is not that I have already experi-enced the resurrection (οὐχ ὅτι ἤδη ἔλαβον) or am already perfect (ἢ ἤδη

106. Aracus is a transliteration of the Greek ἄρακος which is a leguminous plant, wild chickling, hathyrus annuus.

107. J.H. Moulton and G. Milligan, *The Vocabulary of the Greek Testament Illustrated from the Papyri and other Non-literary Sources* (London: Hodder & Stoughton, 1914–29), p. 278. They also cite two examples of ἤδη ποτέ (now at length).

τετελείωμαι), but I press on, hoping to lay hold of the prize for which Christ laid hold of me'. Of these occurrences the Philippians passage is the only one with an eschatological reference.

In two of the Pauline occurrences there is an implied contrast with the past. In Rom. 4.19 Abraham saw at the age of about 100 that his body was 'now as good as dead' (ἤδη νενεκρωμένον)—he had passed the normal age for fathering a child. In Rom. 13.11 Paul states that 'now (ἤδη) is the time for you to wake from sleep, because now (νῦν) our salvation is nearer than when we first believed'. There are also two instances of the compound phrase ἤδη ποτέ (now at length) in Rom. 1.10 and Phil. 4.10.

The conclusion to be drawn from this survey is that ἤδη means 'now', and can imply a contrast with the past, with the future, with both or with neither. It is only the context of each occurrence that indicates where, if at all, the implied contrast lies.

In 1 Cor. 4.8 Paul makes three parallel statements: 'now you are satisfied, now you have become rich, independently of us you have become kings' (ἤδη κεκορεσμένοι ἐστέ· ἤδη ἐπλουτήσατε· χωρὶς ἡμῶν ἐβασιλεύσατε). The word ἤδη in the first two statements is correlative to the phrase χωρὶς ἡμῶν in the third statement. This suggests that 'now' means 'now that you are separated from us'. In other words, the contrast is between the years when Paul was with them in Corinth and the present time when Paul is in Ephesus.

This verse is a sarcastic description of how the Corinthians were feeling and behaving. It is probably based mainly on the oral information Paul had received about their attitude. They may have been saying something like this: 'When Paul was with us we were confined by his narrow views and strict moral code. But now that he has left us we have discovered a new teaching that has enabled us to become rich, wise and kingly'. It is possible that they had expressed such views in their letter to Paul. In Findlay's opinion, 'Paul was given to understand, by some Corinthians, that they had outgrown his teaching'.[108]

In the two preceding verses (vv. 6-7) the contrast Paul draws is not between the present and the future, but between the present and the past. The purpose of his argument in the previous chapters, he declares, has been to teach the Corinthians not to be puffed up in support of one teacher in opposition to another (v. 6). 'For who makes you different from anyone else? What do you have that you have not received? And if you have received it, why do you boast as if you had not received it?' (v. 7) The

---

108. Findlay, *First Epistle*, p. 801.

purpose of these questions is to remind the Corinthians of the past—they should understand their present situation in the light of what they have earlier received.

What is the point of this emphasis on 'receiving'? It is no doubt true that 'each can stand before God only as one who has received'.[109] But v. 7 should be understood in its context, sandwiched between the reference to partisan support for various teachers in v. 6 and the reference to Paul's absence in v. 8. The point may be not only that the Corinthians had received from God, but also that they had received from Paul and his colleagues. The things the Corinthians had received—the gospel, their faith, their baptism, the tradition, the gift of the Holy Spirit—had come to them both from God and from Paul. Their desire to be independent of Paul was a denial of their roots. If this is so, the phrase χωρὶς ἡμῶν in v. 8 is a continuation of the theme of v. 7. The Corinthians were not only physically separated from Paul by the Aegean Sea; they were also spiritually separated by their willingness to forget all they had received from God through him. We may paraphrase v. 8: 'now that you are separated from us you have declared your independence and forgotten what we taught you. You are now free to follow your new teachers and become, like them, surfeited, rich and kingly'.

1 Corinthians, more than any other of Paul's letters, stresses the tradition his readers had received.[110] He had handed on to them the tradition of the institution of the Lord's Supper (11.23) and of the resurrection of Christ (15.1-3). He reminds them in 14.36 that the word of God did not originate with them or belong to them only. In 11.2 he seems to be quoting their claim to be faithful to his traditions—a claim which, with his characteristic 'yes, but' style of argument, he both accepts and qualifies.[111] Yes, he agrees, you are faithful to some of the teaching I handed on to you, but in other respects you are going against it (11.16, 17, 23). If the 'receiving' of 4.7 refers (at least in part) to the tradition, it provides a link between vv. 6 and 8. The divisive influence of the party leaders at Corinth and the 'puffed-up' attitude they inculcated (v. 6) had led to spiritual

---

109. R. Bultmann, 'καυχάομαι', in *TDNT*, III, pp. 645-54 (649), commenting on 1 Cor. 4.7.

110. On the importance of the tradition in 1 and 2 Corinthians see Chapter 10, section 2a.

111. Cf. Barrett, *First Epistle*, p. 247: 'Later (15.2) Paul will throw some doubt on whether the Corinthians did indeed hold fast the teaching he had given them; here he accepts at its face value their claim to do so'.

arrogance (v. 8); and Paul saw as the underlying cause of all this the fact that they had forgotten their roots (v. 7).

In making the claim that they possessed all they needed, that they were rich and that they were kings, the Corinthians were not necessarily thinking eschatologically. Similar language occurs frequently in the Greek philosophers and in Philo as a description of the wise man who has attained perfection.[112] In Philo and the philosophers this state of perfection is attainable in this life. A.J.M. Wedderburn points out that if the background to 4.8 is to be found in Hellenistic popular philosophical beliefs, the doctrine of resurrection does not belong to that background.[113] In John Barclay's words, 'it would be misleading to describe Philo's theology as "(over-)realized eschatology"; his theological framework is simply non-eschatological. Perhaps this is also true of the Corinthian Christians'.[114]

According to Richard Hays, the non-eschatological attitude is to be found not only in 4.8 but in 1 Corinthians as a whole:

> Certainly the Corinthians (or at least some of them) were suffering from an excess of pride and self-satisfaction, but there are other ways to arrive at such a state besides having an accelerated apocalyptic timetable. Indeed, most of the evidence of the letter suggests that the Corinthian problem was almost exactly the reverse: they lacked any definite eschatology, with the result that they were heedless of God's future judgment of their actions.[115]

The discussion of judgment in ch. 4 (vv. 1-5) bears out Hays's opinion. Paul criticizes the Corinthians for passing judgment purely by this-worldly criteria. He contrasts their this-worldly attitude with his own conviction that the only judgment that matters is the judgment of Christ at his parousia. Similarly, the contrast drawn in 4.9-13 between the glory and honour of the Corinthians and the despised, lowly status of the apostles is all concerned with this life. There is nothing in the context of ch. 4 to suggest that the Corinthians thought of their spiritual status in terms of realized eschatology.

Conclusion

There are several reasons for questioning the view that the word ἤδη in 1 Cor. 4.8 alludes to the over-realized eschatology of the Corinthians.

---

112. Horsley, 'Spiritual Elitism', pp. 207-10; Wedderburn, *Baptism*, pp. 24-26; Wedderburn, 'Problem', pp. 234-35.

   113. Wedderburn, 'Problem', p. 236; Wedderburn, *Baptism*, p. 27.

   114. Barclay, 'Thessalonica and Corinth', p. 64.

   115. Hays, *First Corinthians*, p. 70.

1.   ἤδη means 'now' and can imply a contrast either with the past or with the future. Only if the contrast with the future is clear from the context should it be translated 'already'.

2.   The correlation with the phrase χωρὶς ἡμῶν in v. 8, and the emphasis on what the Corinthians had received in v. 7, suggest that Paul is here contrasting the gospel they received while he was at Corinth with the new teaching they have now welcomed in his absence.

3.   There is nothing in the vocabulary used in v. 8, or in the rest of ch. 4, to suggest that the Corinthians were thinking eschatologically.

4.   Verse 8 can therefore be paraphrased: 'now at last, you claim, you have all you need; now you have become rich; now that you are independent of us you have become kings'.

Chapter 4

THE UNITY OF 2 CORINTHIANS

There is no textual evidence for the partition of 2 Corinthians. The textual evidence suggests that the letter circulated from the beginning in the form we now have. What is less easy to determine is when that circulation began. Clement of Rome, Ignatius and Polycarp quote frequently from 1 Corinthians, but show no clear evidence of acquaintance with 2 Corinthians. The earliest reliable witness to the existence of 2 Corinthians is Marcion.[1] Günther Bornkamm has deduced from these facts that the publication of 2 Corinthians took place in post-apostolic times, and this is seen as a final 'proof' of the hypothesis that 2 Corinthians is a secondary collection of several letters.[2]

Bornkamm's assertion that 2 Corinthians was known at first only within the province of Achaia may well be correct.[3] The most likely reason for this would be that the Corinthians chose to circulate to other churches copies of 1 Corinthians rather than copies of 2 Corinthians. This would be understandable. 1 Corinthians deals for the most part with matters of general interest, and is addressed not only to 'the church of God at Corinth', but also to 'all those everywhere who call on the name of our Lord Jesus Christ, their Lord and ours' (1.2). 2 Corinthians, on the other hand, is a much more personal letter, in which Paul defends himself against personal attacks and vilifies specific people who are at work in Corinth. It would be natural for the Corinthians to limit the circulation of 2 Corinthians to the immediate area.

However, the question of circulation is quite distinct from the question

---

1.   See Furnish, *II Corinthians*, pp. 29-30, and M.E. Thrall, *A Critical and Exegetical Commentary on the Second Epistle to the Corinthians* (ICC; Edinburgh: T. & T. Clark, 1994), pp. 2-3, for details of the external attestation.

2.   G. Bornkamm, 'The History of the Origin of the So-called Second Letter to the Corinthians', *NTS* 8 (1962), pp. 258-64 (263-64).

3.   Bornkamm, 'Origin', p. 264.

of authenticity. We know of at least one genuine Pauline letter to Corinth that has not survived and was probably not circulated (the 'previous letter' of 1 Cor. 5.9) and there could have been many others.[4] If Paul spent two years at Ephesus (Acts 19.10), he is likely to have kept in touch with Corinth throughout that period, through occasional visitors and through letters carried by those visitors. Most of these letters are now lost, and were probably not generally circulated. The fact that 2 Corinthians was not widely circulated in Paul's lifetime proves nothing whatsoever about the nature of its composition.

It is difficult to understand how 2 Corinthians could have been universally accepted in the second century as a genuine Pauline letter if Paul did not write it. Why should a collage of Pauline fragments put together by a compiler be accepted without question, by the Corinthians and by everyone else, as a genuine letter? If the compilation was made during the lifetime of the original recipients, they would surely have been aware of what was happening. And if the compilation was made after the death of the original recipients, one wonders how anyone could suddenly produce a supposedly genuine Pauline letter without arousing any suspicions. Such a course of events cannot be ruled out as impossible, but very strong arguments are needed to overthrow the evidence of the manuscripts and of the early church as to the integrity of the epistle.

This chapter will be concerned with the most widely held and important partition theory, that alleges a discontinuity between chs. 1–9 and chs. 10–13. Other theories will be considered in Chapter 5. Several arguments have been adduced in support of the theory that there is a break between 9.15 and 10.1.

1. *The Psychological Argument*

According to J.-F. Collange the main argument in favour of a break between ch. 9 and ch. 10 is psychological.[5] A doughty supporter of the psychological argument is Alfred Plummer. He objects to the 'psychological maladroitness' of Paul's approach if the epistle is a unity:

4.   There is a theory that 2 Cor. 6.14–7.1 formed part of the 'previous letter' (for details see Furnish, *II Corinthians*, p. 27). But in that case these verses would only be an extract from that letter, not the letter itself.

5.   J.-F. Collange, *Enigmes de la deuxième épître de Paul aux Corinthiens: étude exégétique de 2 Cor. 2.14–7.4* (SNTSMS, 18; Cambridge: Cambridge University Press, 1972), p. 13: 'En fait l'argument majeur en faveur d'une rupture entre 1-9 et 10-13 d'un côté, entre 8 et 9 de l'autre (etc.) est essentiellement d'ordre psychologique'.

When one wishes to re-establish friendly relations with persons, one may begin by stating one's own grievances frankly and finding fault freely, and then pass on to say all that is conciliatory, showing a willingness to forgive and a desire for renewed affection. But here the Apostle does the opposite. Having written in tender language of his intense longing for reconciliation and his intense joy at having been able to establish it, he suddenly bursts out into a torrent of reproaches, sarcastic self-vindication, and stern warnings, which must almost have effaced the pacific effect of the first seven chapters.[6]

J. Murphy-O'Connor writes in similar vein:

It is psychologically impossible that Paul should suddenly switch from a celebration of reconciliation with the Corinthians (1–9) to savage reproach and sarcastic self-vindication (10–13). Such an attack on the Corinthians would have undone everything he had tried to achieve in chapters 1–9.[7]

Such comments can be questioned in three respects.

a. *The Target of Paul's Language*
It is wrong to call chs. 10–13 'an attack on the Corinthians'. Paul's criticisms are mainly directed at the incoming teachers, not at the church. As Werner Kümmel says, 'even in 10–13 Paul assumes that only certain people are attacking him...and the rest of the community is endangered by these people'.[8] Paul's concern is not that the church members may rebel against him, but that they may be beguiled by the smooth talk of his rivals as Eve was beguiled by the serpent (11.3).

The purpose of chs. 10–13 had been well described by Barrett. Paul is preparing for a personal confrontation with his rivals on his next visit, which he announces in 10.11. The Corinthians 'will witness rather than take part in the encounter'. Paul's aim is to bring them into the right frame of mind. 'He is concerned for them, and angry with those who are imperilling their position as Christians'.[9]

Udo Schnelle adopts a similar position:

---

6.   A. Plummer, *A Critical and Exegetical Commentary on the Second Epistle of St. Paul to the Corinthians* (ICC; Edinburgh: T. & T. Clark, 1915), pp. xxix-xxx.

7.   J. Murphy-O'Connor, *The Theology of the Second Letter to the Corinthians* (Cambridge: Cambridge University Press, 1991), pp. 10-11.

8.   W.G. Kümmel, *Introduction to the New Testament* (London: SCM Press, rev. edn, 1975), p. 290.

9.   Barrett, *Second Epistle*, p. 271.

The polemic in 2 Cor. 10–13 is not directed towards the Corinthians, but against the opponents that are seen as a third group (cf. 2 Cor. 10.1-2) that has interposed itself into the relationship between the apostle and the Corinthian church. Thus there exists no fundamental difference in the relationship between apostle and church in the two major parts of the epistle 1–9/10–13. In both sections Paul attempts to persuade uncommitted members of the congregation to his own cause.[10]

b. *The Tone of Paul's Language*

Philip Hughes objects to Plummer's statement that in chs. 10–13 Paul 'suddenly bursts out' into a torrent of reproaches, sarcastic self-vindication and stern warnings. He points out that the section begins in 10.1 not with an outburst but with an entreaty 'by the meekness and gentleness of Christ'. In Hughes's opinion Paul writes throughout this section as a father, moved by love and 'godly jealousy' (11.1-3, 11; 12.14-15); the severe things he has to say, according to Hughes, 'are said in entire conformity with the spirit that animates the earlier chapters of the letter'.[11]

Plummer himself refers to 'the affectionate ἀγαπητοί' in 12.19, and comments that in 12.20 Paul speaks 'with more tenderness than rigour'.[12] It is interesting that, apart from 12.19, the word ἀγαπητοί occurs in 2 Corinthians only at 7.1, in another passage of stern warning. For Paul, straight speaking was a sign of love. The conclusion of the section at 13.11-13 talks of love and peace. In Schnelle's opinion this conclusion 'remains surprisingly positive and unites in itself both parts of the letter'.[13]

c. *The Rhetorical Appropriateness of Paul's Language*

In leaving his fiercest condemnation of his opponents to the end of the letter, Paul was following ancient rhetorical practice. Frederick Danker has highlighted the many parallels between Paul's procedure in 2 Corinthians and the procedure of Demosthenes in his speech *De Corona*—a speech that was highly regarded in the Graeco-Roman world as an oratorical model.[14] In this speech Demosthenes defends his right to receive a crown

10. Schnelle, *History*, p. 87.
11. P.E. Hughes, *Paul's Second Epistle to the Corinthians* (London: Marshall, Morgan and Scott, 1962), p. xxiii.
12. Plummer, *Second Epistle*, p. 368.
13. Schnelle, *History*, p. 87.
14. F.W. Danker, 'Paul's Debt to the *De Corona* of Demosthenes: A Study of Rhetorical Techniques in Second Corinthians', in D.F.Watson (ed.), *Persuasive Artistry* (Sheffield: JSOT Press, 1991), pp. 262-80 (263).

for his services to Athens, and refutes the allegation of his enemy Aischines that he is unworthy of this honour. Self-praise and criticism of his opponent can be found throughout the speech, but especially near the end, where 'Demosthenes begins to proclaim the script for his own award and at the same time give Aischines the *coup de grâce*'.[15]

In the views of Frances Young and David Ford the change of mood at 10.1 conforms to an established rhetorical pattern of forensic speech in epistolary form. According to this pattern the peroration at the end is more passionate than the preceding argument. As an example of this procedure they cite a letter attributed to Demosthenes.[16] This parallel is apposite, though Young and Ford overstate their case when they allege that '2 Corinthians was self-consciously conceived as an apology according to the norms of the day'.[17] It is unlikely that Paul, after all his criticism of 'wisdom of words' in 1 Corinthians, would deliberately force his letter into a preconceived rhetorical mould. It is more likely that he was subconsciously influenced by the rhetorical conventions with which he was familiar.[18]

Frank Hughes illustrates the same rhetorical practice from Cicero:

> In rhetorical theory (and in most of Cicero's own rhetorical practice) the part of the speech in which one conventionally found appeals to the emotions was the ending of the speech, the *peroratio*. In Cicero's time, there was a conventional understanding that the peroratio had two parts: the recapitulation (*recapitulatio*) of the points demonstrated in the speech, and the appeal to the emotions (*adfectus*), which was further subdivided in Latin rhetoric into the arousal of emotions against the opponent (*indignatio*) and the arousal of emotions for the orator and his client's case (*conquestio*). In Cicero's youthful handbook *De Inventione* are listed fifteen topics which

---

15. Danker, '*De Corona*', p. 271.

16. F. Young and D.F. Ford, *Meaning and Truth in 2 Corinthians* (London: SPCK, 1987), pp. 36-44.

17. Young and Ford, *Meaning and Truth*, p. 43.

18. The debate as to how far Paul's use of rhetoric was deliberate can be illustrated by two quotations. According to Georg Strecker ('Die Legitimität des Paulinischen Apostolates nach 2 Korinther 10–13', *NTS* 38 [1992], pp. 566-86 [567]), 'Mit Chr. Forbes mag man davon ausgehen, dass Paulus (in Tarsus?) eine griechisch-rhetorische Ausbildung erhalten und die überlieferten Stilmittel bewusst in seinen Briefen eingesetzt hat'. Duane Litfin (*Proclamation*, pp. 138-39) regards this assumption as possible but unproven: 'We need assume of Paul nothing more than one would expect of an intelligent and literate man who was born a Roman citizen in Tarsus, spoke Greek, and lived and moved perceptively in the Hellenistic world of the first century, a world in which rhetoric and oratory were common'.

could be used in *indignatio* and sixteen topics which could be used in *conquestio*.[19]

These parallels from Graeco-Roman rhetoric do not, of course, demonstrate the unity of 2 Corinthians. Thrall points out that 2 Cor. 1–7 could also be understood as a rhetorical unity following ancient practice. She concludes that 'one can hardly rely on the rhetorical argument to support the unity of 2 Corinthians'.[20] But this is to miss the point. The effect of the arguments of Danker, Young and Ford, and Hughes is not to demonstrate that the unity of 2 Corinthians is a certainty but to refute the view that the unity of 2 Corinthians is an impossibility.

It should be remembered that invective was a normal feature of Graeco-Roman culture. According to Schnelle, 'the invective passages in 2 Cor. 10–13 are not unusual in the context of ancient literature, for invective content is found especially in tragedy, comedy, and in such famous speakers as Cicero'.[21] In the *De Corona*, Demosthenes defines the circumstances in which vehement language would be justified:

> But under what circumstances ought the politician and orator to be vehement? Of course, when the city is in any way imperilled and when the public is faced by adversaries. Such is the obligation of a noble and patriotic citizen.[22]

The danger from adversaries to which Demosthenes appealed as the justification for his invective was also the driving force behind Paul's language in 2 Corinthians (11.1-4).

Parallels to the structure of 2 Corinthians can be found elsewhere in the New Testament. Bornkamm has described what he calls 'a basic rule of early Christian edificatory literature' that the warning against false teachers is very often expressed at the end of writings. He quotes examples from Rom. 16.17-20; Gal. 6.11-16; 1 Cor. 16.22; Heb. 13.9-16; 1 Pet. 4.17; 5.1-4; 2 Pet. 3.3-7; Jude 17-23; Rev. 22.11, 15, 18-19.[23] Bornkamm's thesis is that 2 Corinthians is a compilation, and the compiler placed chs. 10–13 at the end in conformity with current practice. But if a compiler could

19. F.W. Hughes, 'The Rhetoric of Reconciliation: 2 Corinthians 1.1–2.13 and 7.5–8.24', in D.F. Watson (ed.), *Persuasive Artistry* (Sheffield: JSOT Press, 1991), pp. 246-61 (248-49).
20. Thrall, *Second Epistle*, pp. 11-12.
21. Schnelle, *History*, p. 87.
22. Danker, '*De Corona*', p. 273, quoting Demosthenes, *De Corona* 278.
23. Bornkamm, 'Origin', pp. 261-63.

conform to current practice so convincingly as to deceive the early church into regarding 2 Corinthians as a genuine letter, surely Paul himself could have conformed to current practice in the same way.

2. *Internal Inconsistency*

Another argument focuses not so much on the psychological maladroitness of the canonical 2 Corinthians as on its internal inconsistency. Barrett argues that in the earlier chapters Paul expects the Corinthians to accept what he has to say; chs. 10–13, on the other hand, 'suggest his belief that the cause was as good as lost, and that little remained but to make a desperate counter-attack'. There is thus a change from a hopeful to a despairing attitude.[24] Thrall endorses Barrett's judgment. She finds it difficult to believe that Paul could express such joy at Titus's news in ch. 7 if he felt the apprehension reflected in chs. 10–13, and detects a difference in attitude between the two main sections of the letter:

> In chaps. 1–7 he explains his understanding of apostleship in the apparent confidence that he will meet with acceptance on the part of his readers, whilst in chaps. 10–13 he resorts to an aggressive self-defence which betrays his fear that all might be lost.[25]

Furnish highlights this contrast by a comparison between ch. 7 and chs. 10–13. In ch. 7 Paul writes of pride, comfort, joy and confidence and affirms the obedience of the Corinthians. In chs. 10–13 there are no such expressions of confidence. He writes not of their zeal for him but of how little they love him.[26] He is afraid they may be tempted to follow a different gospel, and that he may find division and immorality in the church on his forthcoming visit.[27]

24. Barrett, *Second Epistle*, pp. 243-44.
25. Thrall, *Second Epistle*, pp. 8-9.
26. Furnish, *II Corinthians*, p. 31. Furnish seems to overlook the fact that shortly before ch. 7, in 6.12, Paul expresses a similar doubt about the extent of the Corinthians' love for him.
27. Furnish, *II Corinthians*, p. 31. Furnish's other example of supposed inconsistency between chs. 1–9 and chs. 10–13 is less felicitous. He contrasts 1.24: 'for you stand by faith' with 13.5: 'test youselves, whether you are in the faith'. But this comparison does not take into account the irony of the latter passage. Paul's opponents and their supporters have subjected him to a series of tests. They are seeking proof that he is a genuine apostle and agent of Christ (13.3). In his ironic reply, the word ἑαυτούς is in an emphatic position: 'it is yourselves and your faith that you ought to be testing, not

These arguments, like the ones considered earlier, are essentially psycho-logical. The fact that there is a change of atmosphere between chs. 9 and 10 is not in dispute. The point at issue is this: is it psychologically possible for a man who is afraid about the gullibility (11.3) and the moral be-haviour (12.20-21) of the Corinthian Christians to state in the same letter: 'I rejoice that I have complete confidence in you' (7.16)? On this question several comments can be made.

a. *The Danger of Literalism*
Paul's declaration of complete confidence in the Corinthians in 7.16 should not be taken literally. In his study of Pauline expressions of confidence, S.J. Olson compares Paul's use of such expressions with their use in other Hellenistic letters. He asserts that Paul, like other Hellenistic writers, used expressions of confidence 'to undergird the purpose of his letter, by increasing the likelihood of a favourable hearing'.[28]

An example is 2 Cor. 9.1-2, where Paul writes: 'it is superfluous for me to write to you about the charitable gift for the saints. I know how en-thusiastic you are, and boast about your enthusiasm to the Macedonians'. In the following verses Paul reveals serious doubts about their participa-tion in the collection, and 9.1-5 gives the impression of being his apology for sending emissaries to promote it. The purpose of the opening statement is, in Olson's opinion, not unfeigned praise, but flattery.[29]

In his conclusion, Olson applies his findings to the Corinthian situation as a whole:

> Thus the typical function of confident praise suggests that such expressions must be used with great caution when trying to reconstruct the relationship between the writer and his readers. The caution would apply, for example, to conclusions about the apparent variations in the tone of the relationship between Paul and his addressees in 2 Corinthians. The epistolary expression

mine'. The fact that this is not a straightforward questioning of their faith is shown by the words that follow: 'Surely you recognize that Christ Jesus is in you (unless you fail the test); so I hope you will recognize that we too pass the test'. The form of the question in v. 5b (ἢ οὐκ ἐπιγινώσκετε;) implies a positive answer. An ironical passage such as this should not be used as evidence for the presence of discrepancies, as though it were an affirmation in a book of systematic theology.

For further discussion of the motif of testing in 1 and 2 Corinthians see Chapter 9, Section 2c.

28. S.J. Olson, 'Pauline Expressions of Confidence in his Addressees', *CBQ* 47 (1985), pp. 282-95 (295).

29. Olson, 'Pauline Expressions', pp. 290-92.

of confidence is best interpreted as a persuasive technique rather than as a sincere reflection of the way the writer thinks the addressees will respond to his proposals or to himself.[30]

Olson's thesis is largely true, but exaggerated. The expressions of joy and confidence in 7.13-16 are not simply a persuasive technique; they represent a genuine feeling on the part of Paul. At the same time, as Olson says, they also perform a function within the letter. For one thing, they prepare the way for the discussion of the collection in chs. 8 and 9, which was, in Danker's words, 'a delicate matter'.[31] Furnish comments that 'in conformity with a familiar Hellenistic literary pattern, Paul emphasizes his confidence in those of whom he is about to make a substantial request'.[32]

The danger of excessive literalism can be most clearly seen in the interpretation of the word πᾶς (all), which occurs several times in ch. 7. In v. 13 Titus's spirit was refreshed 'by all of you' (ὑπὸ πάντων ὑμῶν). In v. 15 Titus remembers with affection 'the obedience of all of you' (τὴν πάντων ὑμῶν ὑπακοήν). In v. 16 Paul declares: 'I rejoice that I have confidence in you in every respect' (χαίρω ὅτι ἐν παντὶ θαρρῶ ἐν ὑμῖν). These 'all's are sometimes taken at face value. For example, Plummer comments on v. 15 (τὴν πάντων ὑμῶν ὑπακοήν): 'these words indicate that Titus had very definite demands to make, and that compliance with them was universal'.[33]

Plummer believed that chs. 1–9 were written later than chs. 10–13, and saw in the wording of ch. 7 evidence of Paul's total victory at the end of the conflict. But the 'all's of ch. 7 are also taken literally by scholars who place it earlier than chs. 10–13. Barrett, for example, suggests that Titus may have misread the situation and instilled in Paul a false confidence.[34] Furnish adopts a similar position:

> Significantly, the apostle uses the phrase *all of you* to describe the source of Titus' joy…; whatever questions and complaints continue to be raised about Paul in Corinth are not deemed to be serious, or representative even of a significant minority in the church there. Subsequent events…will show that this was probably a false perception, whether due to Titus' overly optimistic report or to Paul's overly optimistic interpretation of that report.[35]

30. Olson, 'Pauline Expressions', p. 295.
31. Danker, '*De Corona*', p. 269.
32. Furnish, *II Corinthians*, p. 392.
33. Plummer, *Second Epistle*, p. 228.
34. Barrett, *Second Epistle*, p. 214.
35. Furnish, *II Corinthians*, p. 397.

Such a literal understanding of 'all' is not supported by Paul's use of the word πᾶς elsewhere. Within the Corinthian correspondence alone there are several examples of a non-literal use of this word.

i. 1 Cor. 1.8: ἐν παντὶ ἐπλουτίσθητε ἐν αὐτῷ, ἐν παντὶ λόγῳ καὶ πάσῃ γνώσει (you have been enriched in Christ in every respect, with all speech and all knowledge). If these words are taken literally, Paul is promulgating the dogma of the infallibility of the Corinthian Christians.

ii. 1 Cor. 9.22: τοῖς πᾶσιν γέγονα πάντα (I have become all things to all people). Taken literally, these words imply a degree of adaptability beyond the reach of a chameleon. What Paul means is: 'I have adopted a general policy of adapting my lifestyle to that of others'.

iii. 2 Cor. 9.11: ἐν παντὶ πλουτιζόμενοι εἰς πᾶσαν ἁπλότητα ([you will be] enriched in every respect, resulting in every form of generosity). Taken literally, this implies immense wealth and incessant almsgiving.

Upholders of partition theories would not normally wish to be regarded as literalists; but sometimes, in their eagerness to detect contradictions between one section and another, they are tempted to an over-literal interpretation of phrases such as ἐν παντί. This temptation may be particularly acute in countries such as Britain, where there is a deep suspicion of the use of flowery language. While it would not be true to say that the British are all logical positivists, the concern for logical precision in the use of language that characterizes at least an intellectual minority in Britain is not a feature of all cultures, and was not a characteristic of Paul. Goudge does well to remind us that not all Paul's statements should be taken *au pied de la lettre*, that language means what it is understood to mean, that such understanding is culturally conditioned, and that even in Britain the signature 'yours truly' does not signify the devotion of a lifetime.[36]

b. *Paul's Defensiveness in 2 Corinthians 1–7*
There is ample evidence in chs. 1–7 that all is not well in Paul's relationship with the Corinthians. Immediately after his opening thanksgiving he begins to defend himself against the charge that he has behaved with 'the wisdom of the flesh' (1.12) and has made his travel plans 'according to the flesh' (κατὰ σάρκα; 1.17). Chs. 10–13 begin with a very similar reference to 'those who reckon that we behave according to the flesh' (10.2). Abraham Malherbe suggests that Paul's opponents used the phrase κατὰ σάρκα

36. H.L. Goudge, *The Second Epistle to the Corinthians* (WC; London: Methuen, 1927), pp. l-li.

to describe 'his mean, inconsistent, underhanded, conniving conduct'.[37]
His reply to this charge is that he and his colleagues have behaved with
honesty and sincerity—a theme that runs like a thread through all the main
sections of 2 Corinthians (1.12; 2.17; 4.2; 8.20-21; 10.2-4; 12.16-17;
13.8).

Paul's defensiveness also appears in chs. 6 and 7. His declaration of joy
and confidence in 7.4-16 is preceded by verses that suggest a very different picture. In 6.12-13 he accuses them of being constricted in their affection for him, and asks them to open their hearts wide. In 7.2-4 he defends
himself against a series of accusations: 'we have wronged no one, we have
damaged no one, we have taken advantage of no one', and then goes on to
say: 'I do not say this to condemn you; for I have already said that you are
in our hearts to live and die together. I am very frank in speaking to you, I
am very proud in boasting of you, I am full of encouragement, I am overflowing with joy over all we suffer'. Goudge comments on these verses:
'Warm and glowing words indeed—a beautiful revelation of the heart of
S.Paul! Yet how much lies behind them of unrequited affection, and of
generous sacrifice still met with coldness and suspicion!'[38]

Goudge also points out that the Corinthians had proved themselves
guiltless 'in the matter' (τῷ πράγματι; 7.11)—that is, in the matter of
the punishment of the offender. Paul rejoices in the action they have taken
and in the evidence it provides of their loyalty to him; but this does not
mean that he is inconsistent when he finds them guilty of other things.[39]

In 2.6 Paul talks about the punishment[40] inflicted on the offender by 'the
majority'. It is sometimes alleged that the phrase οἱ πλείονες can function
as the equivalent of the Hebrew *ha rabbim* and mean 'the community as a
whole'. But Thrall has demonstrated the weakness of this argument.[41] The
Greek equivalent of *ha rabbim* is οἱ πολλοί, not οἱ πλείονες.[42] In
Pauline usage οἱ πλείονες normally means 'the majority' and implies the
existence of a minority.[43] The view that the minority at Corinth consisted

37. A.J. Malherbe, 'Antisthenes and Odysseus, and Paul at War', *HTR* 76 (1983),
pp. 143-73 (170).
38. Goudge, *Second Epistle*, p. lii.
39. Goudge, *Second Epistle*, p. liii.
40. For the meaning of ἐπιτιμία see Furnish, *II Corinthians*, p. 155; Thrall, *Second
Epistle*, pp. 173-74.
41. Thrall, *Second Epistle*, pp. 174-76.
42. Furnish, *II Corinthians*, p. 155.
43. Thrall (*Second Epistle*, p. 175 n. 317) sees a possible exception in 2 Cor. 4.15,

of rigorists, who wanted a stiffer penalty, is extremely unlikely. Paul refers to 'this punishment inflicted by the majority' (ἡ ἐπιτιμία αὕτη ἡ ὑπὸ τῶν πλειόνων). The implication is that the minority did not inflict, or wish to inflict, this punishment, not that they agreed with the punishment as far as it went but wanted more. Whatever the nature of the offence, the fact that some members of the church did not want the man to be punished suggests that they were opposed to Paul.

Several times in chs. 1–7 a contrast is drawn between Paul and his colleagues on the one hand and other preachers on the other hand. In 2.17 Paul refers to 'the many' who peddle the word of God like merchandise; in 3.1 he refers to 'some' who bring with them letters of recommendation; in 5.12 he states that he is giving the Corinthian Christians grounds for boasting about him to counteract others who boast of external things. The difference between chs. 1–7 and chs. 10–13 is that such criticism is indirect in chs. 1–7 and direct in chs. 10–13. In Furnish's words, there is a 'polemical edge' to chs. 1–7, but 'outright polemic' in chs. 10–13.[44]

The difference between the muted polemic of the earlier chapters and the uninhibited polemic of the later chapters has been explained in two ways. Some attribute it to a change in circumstances. Barrett uses the metaphor of the seed: the situation that is seen in full flower in chs. 10–13 is 'present in germ' in chs. 1–7.[45] Furnish uses the metaphor of the earthquake: the issue of rival apostles is present in the earlier chapters, but 'it has not yet erupted in such a way as to require a full-scale defense of his own motives and actions'.[46] Others attribute the contrast to Paul's rhetorical plan. According to Menzies, the same material burns in both sections; but in chs. 1–7 the fire is kept down and not allowed to burst into flames.[47] E.-B. Allo comments on 5.12 that 'the eagle is beginning to look down from above on the martins and foxes; but he is not yet ready to pounce down on them in vertical descent'.[48] If the latter interpretation is

---

where Paul declares that the purpose of his ministry is to enable grace and thanksgiving to abound (διὰ τῶν πλειόνων). But it may be that here (as in 2.6) Paul is aware (consciously or subconsciously) of divided loyalties at Corinth—not all would wish to give thanks to God for his ministry.

44. Furnish, *II Corinthians*, p. 191.

45. Barrett, *Second Epistle*, p. 165.

46. Furnish, *II Corinthians*, p. 191.

47. A. Menzies, *The Second Epistle of the Apostle Paul to the Corinthians* (London: Macmillan, 1912), p. xlii.

48. Quoted in Barrett, *Second Epistle*, p. 165.

correct, as I believe it to be, Paul is following a procedure recommended by ancient rhetorical theorists and described by Ben Witherington:

> Because Paul is dealing with a complex and interlocking set of problems, he must follow the procedure known as *insinuatio*, the indirect approach. In this rhetorical move one only alludes to the major issue that is under dispute in the early stages of the rhetorical discourse, reserving the real discussion of the major bone of contention for the end of the discourse, where it is attacked, using much *pathos*, in a more direct fashion. Aristotle is very clear on this point. The closing stages of one's forensic argument must include both praise and defense of one's self *and* blame of one's opponent—precisely what one finds in 2 Corinthians 10–13.[49]

c. *Confidence and Fear*

In 11.1-4 Paul expresses his fear that the minds of the Corinthians may be deceived and corrupted because of their openness to the teaching of his rivals. He expresses other fears in 12.20-21. He is afraid of finding a quarrelling and divided church on his next visit (v. 20), and of finding that some of those guilty of sexual immorality in the past have never repented (v. 21). These fears are in formal contradiction with his declaration in 7.16 that he has complete confidence in the Corinthians. There are two possible explanations of this contradiction—the logical and the psychological.

According to the logical explanation, Paul must be presumed to have revealed his state of mind totally and comprehensively in every statement he made. Therefore, it is impossible for two statements representing contradictory moods to occur within the same letter. According to the psychological explanation, Paul was an emotional man, who expressed on any one occasion the emotion he was feeling at that time. When he thought of the Corinthian change of heart reported by Titus, he was filled with a feeling of confidence, and expressed that confidence without qualification. When he thought of the rival teachers, still at work in Corinth and still influential in the congregation, he was filled with foreboding, and expressed that foreboding without qualification.

In his analysis of the 'Fool's Speech' in 2 Cor. 11 and 12, J. Zmijewski reflects on Paul's changing moods and feelings. He points out that Paul was a man with a deep and rich emotional life, and that this personality

---

49. Witherington, *Conflict*, p. 429. Witherington defines πάθος on p. 353: in contrast to Paul's establishment of ἦθος (moral character) in the first part of the letter, πάθος 'is the expression of stronger emotions such as anger, and has a more disturbing and commanding tone'. The Aristotle reference is to *Rhet.* 1419b.

trait, combined with his sense of call to the apostolic ministry, led to the emotional quality of this section.[50] In the 'Fool's Speech' Zmijewski finds examples of a constantly changing variety of moods and feelings—anger, excitement, loving affection, worry, consideration for others, bold determination, antipathy, biting irony, earnestness and joy.[51] This is not surprising, since in 6.8-10 Paul describes the apostolic lifestyle in terms of paradoxes—we are dying and also living, we are sorrowful but always rejoicing. To these could be added the paradox: 'we are fearful, but always confident'.

An illustration of this paradox is 2 Cor. 2.3. Paul states that he wrote his anguished, tearful letter in the confidence that his joy would also be their joy. The implication of these words, as Thrall comments, is that, even at the time when he wrote the tearful letter, his confidence in the Corinthians was fundamentally unshaken. But if so, why did he write in such a state of distress? Thrall suggests that he may have been 'a prey to two conflicting attitudes, both apprehension and confidence'.[52]

The attempt to interpret 2 Corinthians in psychological terms is sometimes criticized. Hans Dieter Betz, for example, regards 'the reliance on psychology to explain changes of tone and subject matter' as a major flaw in modern attempts to defend the unity of 2 Corinthians.[53] But any attempt to understand 2 Corinthians, whether to defend its unity or to deny it, relies on psychology. A good example is Plummer's comment on 2 Cor. 2.12-13:

> It is difficult to believe that the man who had just been freed from an agony of anxiety as to the effect of a severe letter to the Corinthians should forthwith write the severe reproaches and sarcasms contained in x.-xiii.10, and should send them to the Corinthians in the same letter in which he tells them of this agony of anxiety.[54]

Plummer's wording reflects his recognition that this is a psychological judgment—the criterion is what it is easy or difficult for us to believe. Betz himself illustrates the same principle when he surveys the history of the interpretation of 2 Cor. 2.4:

---

50. J. Zmijewski, *Der Stil der paulinischen Narrenrede* (Bonn: Hanstein, 1978), p. 418.

51. Zmijewski, *Stil*, p. 414.

52. Thrall, *Second Epistle*, p. 169.

53. H.D. Betz, *2 Corinthians 8 and 9* (Hermeneia; Philadelphia: Fortress Press, 1985), p. 34.

54. Plummer, *Second Epistle*, p. 67.

Even if we accept that the sinner of 1 Cor. 5.1ff. and the 'offender' (ἀδικήσας) of 2 Cor. 7.12 are one and the same, in view of the critical observations made by earlier scholars, the notion that 1 Corinthians is the letter of tears remains simply too much to swallow.[55]

In other words, the critical judgment as to whether or not 1 Corinthians was written with anguish and tears is decided ultimately by the swallowing capacity of the critic. Critical judgments on this issue are psychological, and are often made by scholars from a different culture and with a different temperament to that of Paul.[56] The same is true of critical assessments of the composition of 2 Corinthians. The reliance on psychology is just as much a feature of theories of partition as it is of theories of unity.

3. *The Inappropriateness of Chs. 8 and 9*

A further objection to the unity of 2 Corinthians is the central place of the appeal for the collection. In opposing the view of Young and Ford that 2 Corinthians has the style of a forensic defence, Murphy-O'Connor protests that 'a plea for money, even for others, has no place in an ἀπολογία'.[57] This is a valid criticism of Young and Ford's statement that Paul 'self-consciously conceived [the epistle] as an apology according to the norms of the day'.[58] But it does not invalidate the view that Paul regarded the letter in broad terms as an apology, but with various other items thrown in.

When composing 2 Corinthians Paul was forced by circumstances to deal in a single letter with a variety of issues: the punishment of the offender and its follow-up; the new accusations reported by Titus (such as the charge of fickleness answered in 1.12–2.4 and the charge of πλεονεξία answered in 7.2 and 12.16-18); the arrangements for the collection (a matter to which Paul was deeply committed, which was now becoming urgent); and the continuing problem of the influence of his rivals at Corinth. There was no way he could combine all these elements into a logical whole. As Goudge says, 'it was very difficult to deal with all these matters together, and the apparent awkwardness of his arrangement reflects the awkwardness of the situation in which he finds himself'.[59]

55. Betz, *2 Corinthians 8 and 9*, p. 35.
56. For a discussion of the cultural criteria used in identifying the tearful letter see Chapter 10.
57. Murphy-O'Connor, *Theology*, p. 11 n. 8.
58. Young and Ford, *Meaning and Truth*, p. 43.
59. Goudge, *Second Epistle*, p. lvii.

R.F. Collins has raised the question whether it is legitimate to expect perfect unity in any letter. He points out that lack of consistency is a feature of many Graeco-Roman letters:

> Many of the extant, and relatively short, papyrus letters combined several purposes and addressed several topics. Many of the longer letters preserved from antiquity contain several virtually complete rhetorico-epistolary arguments, presented one after the other. Is it not the same with the letters which we write even today?

Collins goes on to speak of the 'mixed' type of letter recognized by ancient theorists, and cites examples of such letters by Plato, Isocrates, Cicero, Horace and Seneca.[60]

The general tone of chs. 8 and 9 is in keeping with 2 Corinthians as a whole. In these chapters Paul is just as much on the defensive as in the rest of the letter. When commending Titus and the two brothers in 8.16-24, he goes out of his way to stress that Titus is going of his own free will (v. 17), and that the two brothers are both representing the Macedonian churches (vv. 19, 23). His object, he declares, is that no one should blame him over the matter of the collection (v. 20). The charge of πλεονεξία to which he responds in 12.16-18 demonstrates (even if 12.16-18 and 8.20 are assigned to different letters) that there was good reason for Paul's defensiveness in this matter.[61]

It should also be noted that Paul's explanation in 9.1-5 of his reasons for sending men to facilitate the collection is diplomatically expressed. He is clearly afraid that, when he arrives on his forthcoming visit, the Corinthians will be unprepared (v. 4), and this probably reflects Titus's report on the lack of enthusiasm for the collection in the congregation.

60. R.F. Collins, 'Reflections on 1 Corinthians as a Hellenistic Letter', in R. Bieringer (ed.), *The Corinthian Correspondence* (Leuven: Leuven University Press, 1996), pp. 39-61 (60).

61. The charge of πλεονεξία that Paul rebuts in 7.2 probably does not relate to financial fraud. οὐδένα ἐπλεονεκτήσαμεν means 'we have not taken advantage of any individual'. By contrast, the charge Paul rebuts in 12.17-18 relates to the defrauding of the church as a whole. A closer parallel to 7.2 may be the use of πλεονεκτεῖν in 2.11. That verse refers to Satan 'taking advantage of' Paul and the Corinthians, with reference, not to finance, but to the punishment of the offender. All three accusations in 7.2 may have the offender in mind. His enemies may have accused Paul of misusing his apostolic authority to take advantage of one of his enemies and to destroy him. For a fuller presentation of this exegesis see R.P. Martin, *2 Corinthians* (WBC, 40; Waco, TX: Word Books, 1986), pp. 217-18.

Barrett correctly warns against exaggerating the difference between the end of ch. 9 and the beginning of ch. 10. He points out that in ch. 9 Paul has been describing what he hopes will happen at Corinth, not what is actually happening. He endorses the judgment of Hans Lietzmann that Paul's praise of the Corinthians in ch. 9 seems exaggerated because he is painting a picture of the future.[62]

4. *Arguments from Vocabulary*

It has sometimes been alleged that a number of words and phrases in chs. 1–9 refer back to chs. 10–13, which must therefore have been written earlier.[63] However, as Thrall says, the paired passages need not necessarily be interpreted in this way.[64] Others interpret the same parallels in the opposite sense, as evidence that chs. 1–9 were written before chs. 10–13.[65] The one link between the two sections that merits fuller consideration concerns the travel arrangements for Titus and his colleagues, and this is dealt with in Excursus H.

5. *Singular and Plural*

One of the striking features of 2 Corinthians is the predominant use of the first person plural ('we') in chs. 1–7 and of the first person singular ('I') in chs. 10–13. Furnish states that this kind of shift occurs in no other Pauline letter, and includes this fact in his list of 'apparent discrepancies' that have led many interpreters to the partition of the letter.[66]

It is difficult to understand why this shift should be regarded as a discrepancy. The reason why Paul uses the first person singular in chs. 10–13 is that in these chapters he is replying to accusations brought against him as an individual, whereas for most of chs. 1–7 he discusses the apostolic ministry in general terms. The personal nature of chs. 10–13 is brought out in the opening words αὐτὸς δὲ ἐγὼ Παῦλος. The meaning of this phrase is discussed in Excursus D, where I argue that it means 'I Paul as an

---

62. Barrett, *Second Epistle*, p. 242.
63. Plummer, *Second Epistle*, pp. xxx-xxxiii.
64. Thrall, *Second Epistle*, p. 16.
65. Hughes, *Second Epistle*, p. xxviii, following E.-B. Allo, *Saint Paul: seconde épître aux Corinthiens* (EBib; Paris: Gabalda, 1958), p. lvi; Thrall, *Second Epistle*, p. 16.
66. Furnish, *II Corinthians*, p. 32.

individual'. The use of the first person singular in these chapters reflects the personal nature of the subject matter.

In 2 Corinthians Paul had to defend himself on two fronts. On the one hand, his rivals understood the nature of Christian ministry in a way that was diametrically opposed to Paul's understanding. He wanted the Corinthians to realize the incompatibility of these two approaches to ministry. He therefore began the letter by describing in chs. 1–7 his own style of ministry (with frequent direct or indirect comparisons with the style of ministry of his opponents). In doing so he linked his colleagues Timothy and Silas with himself. This linkage is explicit in 1.19 and implicit elsewhere.

On the other hand, Paul's rivals had also subjected him to a campaign of personal abuse. One can imagine the reason for this. Paul's blunt condemnation in 1 Corinthians of the party rivalry on which their livelihood as Christian sophists depended may have made them realize that this was a struggle to the death, requiring the rhetorical practice of *vituperatio*.[67] Paul replies to these personal attacks in chs. 10–13, and inevitably uses the first person singular to do so.

Barrett argues that chs. 10–13 should not be described as an apology, in the sense of a personal defence. The main subject of these chapters, he believes, is the nature of the apostolic gospel and of apostolic authority.[68] There is a grain of truth in this statement. Paul does discuss the apostolic office in chs. 10–13 as well as in chs. 1–7. But it is discussed in a quite different way in the two sections. In the earlier chapters he describes in general terms the apostolic ministry he shares with his colleagues; but in the last four chapters he defends himself against the charge that he Paul personally is unfit to be an apostle. The accusations rebutted in the latter section are almost all personal—that he is weak (10.1, 10; 11.21); that he is underhand and 'fleshly' (10.2); that he is lacking in eloquence (10.10; 11.6); that he is foolish (11.1); that he is not a paid professional (11.7-12; 12.13); that he lacks spiritual experiences (12.1-5); that he lacks the 'signs of an apostle' (12.11, 12; 13.3); and that he plans to use the collection for his own personal enrichment (12.16-18).

It is sometimes alleged that the personal element is equally prominent in chs. 1–7, and that, when Paul uses the first person plural in these chapters, by 'we' he means 'I'. The question as to how far, if at all, Paul used the so-called 'epistolary' plural has been much discussed.[69] The epistolary

---

67. On the practice of *vituperatio* see Clarke, *Leadership*, pp. 66-67.
68. Barrett, *Second Epistle*, p. 245.
69. See the discussion in C.F.D. Moule, *An Idiom Book of New Testament Greek*

plural was widely used in papyrus letters, but whether Paul conformed to this usage is disputable. In my opinion, W.F. Lofthouse's judgment is sound:

> When Paul wrote 'I', he was thinking of himself as distinct from his companions, his hearers, and the Church in general, and of experiences which others could not share; when he wrote 'we', he was thinking of himself as one of a number, either the little band of his companions, or his readers, or the whole company of believers always in the background of his mind. The circle expands or contracts; but it is always there when the plural is used; never when it is not.[70]

Lofthouse's hypothesis can be tested by examining some verses in 2 Corinthians that are commonly understood to be epistolary.

7.5 is the only verse that Plummer cites as a definite example of plural for singular.[71] In this verse Paul resumes the narrative of his journey from Troas to Macedonia, which was interrupted by the long digression of 2.14–7.4. The earlier part of the narrative (2.12-13) is in the first person singular—I went to Troas, I felt no peace of mind, I said goodbye to the people there and departed to Macedonia. But the second part of the narrative (7.5-6) is all in the plural—we came to Macedonia, we felt no peace of mind, God encouraged us through the arrival of Titus. The simplest explanation of this shift from singular to plural is that Timothy was with Paul in Macedonia, but was not with him in Troas.

According to Acts 19.22, Timothy was sent to Macedonia towards the end of Paul's stay in Ephesus, and he may well never have left Macedonia. He was certainly with Paul when 2 Corinthians was written, since Paul names him as co-author of the letter (2 Cor. 1.1). If Timothy came to meet Paul off the boat from Troas, they would enter Macedonia together, and share together the emotions of restlessness followed by encouragement that Paul describes in ch. 7. The change from singular to plural between chs. 2 and 7 would in that case precisely reflect Paul's feeling of being on his own at Troas and his feeling of shared colleagueship as he arrived in Macedonia with Timothy.

This does not mean that Paul thought carefully about whether to use

(Cambridge: Cambridge University Press, 2nd edn, 1959), pp. 118-19. According to Nigel Turner (*Syntax*, p. 28), 'singular and plural alternate as capriciously in Paul as in contemporary letters'. BDF 280 (pp. 148-49) is more cautious.

70. W.F. Lofthouse, ' "I" and "We" in the Pauline Letters', *BT* 6 (1955), pp. 72-80 (73).

71. Plummer, *Second Epistle*, p. 10.

singular or plural when dictating his letters. He spoke instinctively, re-capturing the mood of the moment he was describing. In Lofthouse's words, 'there is always a discernible reason for the use of "I" or "we" even if the writer himself may not have been conscious of it'.[72]

E. Verhoef regards most occurrences of the first person plural in Paul as relating to more than one person, but in two verses he regards its occur-rence as epistolary. In 2 Cor. 7.14 the singular κεκαύχημαι (I have boasted) is followed by the plural ἡ καύχησις ἡμῶν (our boast); and in 11.6 the singular εἰ δὲ καὶ ἰδιώτης τῷ λόγῳ (even if I am an amateur in rhetoric) is followed by the plural participle φανερώσαντες (we have made clear).[73] But both these verses make good sense if interpreted according to Lofthouse's principle.

In ch. 7 Paul is describing a mixture of individual and shared experi-ences. Some experiences he shared with Timothy (their restlessness [v. 5], their encouragement by Titus [v. 6] and their participation in Titus's joy [v. 13]). But some things were peculiar to himself—especially the writing of the previous letter (vv. 8-12). The boasting to Titus about the Corin-thians will have been done mainly by Paul, but may also have been done by Timothy, who (according to Acts 18.5) had shared with Paul in his Corinthian ministry. It could therefore be referred to either with a first person singular or a first person plural. The clumsy alternation of singular and plural in 7.13-16 reflects this situation—Paul is thinking both in singular and in plural terms at the same time.

In 11.6 Paul quotes in the singular the accusation of being an amateur in oratory, which had been levelled at him as an individual. The meaning of φανερώσαντες is notoriously obscure, since it is a transitive verb with no object; but the comparison Paul is making throughout this passage (11.1-6) between himself and his rivals suggests he may be repeating here one of the main themes of chs. 1–7: the openness of the preaching of his col-leagues and himself (with an implied contrast with the secrecy of his opponents). The verb φανεροῦν is used in this sense in 2.14-17; 3.1-3; 4.1-2. In 2.14 φανεροῦν is associated with γνῶσις, and it may be that the mention of γνῶσις in 11.6 triggered off this association of ideas in Paul's mind. Since in chs. 1–7 the openness of the apostles is described in the plural, Paul may have instinctively reverted to the plural when referring to an aspect of his preaching that he shared with his colleagues. This is, of

72. Lofthouse, ' "I" and "We" ', p. 73.
73. E. Verhoef, 'The Senders of the Letters to the Corinthians and the Use of "I" and "We" ', in Bieringer (ed.), *Corinthian Correspondence*, pp. 417-25 (421-22).

course, conjectural, but no more so than the theory that Paul changed in mid-sentence from singular to epistolary plural for no obvious reason.

There are no clear examples of the epistolary plural in 2 Corinthians. There is, however, as C.F.D. Moule points out, a careful distinction drawn between the singular and the plural in one passage (1.15-24).[74] We should therefore understand the predominance of 'we' in chs. 1–7 and the predominance of 'I' in chs. 10–13 as an indication of the different emphases within the two sections.

Conclusion

None of the arguments commonly used for separating chs. 10–13 from the rest of 2 Corinthians stands up to examination. We should therefore accept the testimony of the manuscripts and of the early church that the letter is a unity.

EXCURSUS D:
THE MEANING OF αὐτὸς ἐγὼ Παῦλος IN 2 CORINTHIANS 10.1

The phrase αὐτὸς ἐγὼ Παῦλος in 2 Cor. 10.1 is unique in Paul's letters, but there are a number of occurrences of its constituent elements, αὐτὸς ἐγώ and ἐγὼ Παῦλος. The contention of this note is that both these phrases mean 'I Paul personally' every time they occur, and that the combination of the two in 2 Cor. 10.1 is even more emphatic: 'I Paul individually and personally'.

The phrases 'αὐτὸς ἐγώ' and 'ἐγὼ Παῦλος' are used in various contexts in the Pauline corpus.[75]

In two passages the phrase ἐγὼ Παῦλος is used to stamp a statement with Paul's personal authority. In Phlm. 19 he uses the phrase as a guarantee of authenticity: 'This is me Paul writing with my own hand—I will pay the money'. This declaration is similar in style to the greetings Paul writes with his own hand at the end of some of his letters—this is me Paul greeting you personally in my own handwriting (1 Cor. 16.21; Col.

---

74. Moule, *Idiom Book*, p. 119.

75. In my opinion Ephesians, Colossians and 2 Thessalonians were all written by Paul, and I have therefore included verses from these epistles in this survey. However, even if these verses are discounted, there are sufficient occurrences of αὐτὸς ἐγώ and ἐγὼ Παῦλος in the less disputed epistles to illustrate Paul's usage of these terms.

4.18; 2 Thess. 3.17). In the 2 Thessalonians passage this personal greeting is described as a sign—that is, a sign of authenticity.

In Gal. 5.2 Paul writes: 'Behold I Paul say to you: if you receive circumcision Christ will be of no help to you'. It is possible that Paul here, as in Phlm. 19, took up the pen and wrote with his own hand. Be that as it may, he stamps the words that follow with his personal authority. There could be two reasons for this. On the one hand, he wants to imbue these words with the authority of an apostle appointed by God (cf. 1.1). On the other hand, he wants to clear up a misunderstanding. It appears from the earlier chapters that Paul had been accused of being a time-server—of adapting his theology to his audience. In this verse he nails his colours to the mast and makes it absolutely clear what his position is by using his name or possibly his own handwriting.

In two passages these phrases serve to distinguish Paul from other people.

In 2 Cor. 12.11-13 Paul contrasts his style of ministry with that of other apostles. He asks in what way the Corinthian church was treated more shabbily than other churches. The only possible way was that he Paul (αὐτὸς ἐγώ), unlike other apostles, did not receive financial support and was not a burden to them, and he asks them ironically to forgive this 'injustice'.[76]

In 1 Thess. 2.18 Paul writes that 'we' very much wanted to come and visit Thessalonica, I Paul (ἐγὼ Παῦλος) on two occasions, but Satan prevented us. 1 Thessalonians was written in the name of Paul, Silvanus and Timothy (1.1), and in this verse Paul is distinguishing between the general desire to visit Thessalonica that was shared by all three of them and the fact that he Paul as an individual had twice planned a visit that had been frustrated.

In both Col. 1.23 and Eph. 3.1 the phrase ἐγὼ Παῦλος indicates a transition from a general statement of the gospel message to a description of Paul's particular role as the gospel messenger. In the case of Colossians, the preceding passage (1.13-22) has portrayed the risen and exalted Christ as the one who through his death has reconciled us to God. In v. 23 the focus shifts to Paul's part in all this: I Paul am God's special agent to reveal to the Gentiles the mystery of their salvation; my sufferings are for your sake, and, though absent in body, I am with you in spirit.

The use of the phrase ἐγὼ Παῦλος in Ephesians is similar. The preced-

---

76. For further discussion of this passage see Chapter 8.

ing two chapters have described how Jew and Gentile share a common salvation within the household of God. 3.1 introduces Paul's part in this: I Paul am a prisoner of Christ on behalf of the Gentiles, and have been commissioned by God to reveal to the Gentiles the mystery of God's purpose.

Thus in both letters the words 'I Paul' personalize the gospel message, as if Paul were saying: 'what I have just written is not abstract theology; God has personally commissioned me to bring you this message, and my current sufferings are a sign that I have been appointed not only to preach to you but also to suffer for you'.

Romans 15.14 comes at the end of a long section of ethical exhortation (12.1–15.13) in which Paul has been speaking in general terms. In this verse he becomes personal: I myself (αὐτὸς ἐγώ) am convinced that you are living good Christian lives; but I have dared to write to you in this way because God has given me this ministry to the Gentiles. Paul then goes on to reassure them that his call is to be a pioneer evangelist. He is not intending to settle down in Rome and take the church over, but to use his visit as a launching pad for an evangelistic mission to Spain. This explanation is understandable in the circumstances. Paul is writing to people he has never met, who may be wondering what his motives are in planning to visit them. He needs to establish his credentials—his divine commission as apostle to the Gentiles which gives him the right to exhort Christians he has never met—and to reassure them as to his intentions. The words αὐτὸς ἐγώ mark the transition from general theology to an account of his personal involvement.

Romans 9.1-3 introduces a new section of the letter. In chs. 1–8 Paul has surveyed God's purpose for both Jew and Gentile as it works out in Christian experience. It is a survey of 'the fairness of God's dealings with the Jews first and also with the Gentiles' (1.16-17).[77] He then turns to consider, in chs. 9–11, how the availability of salvation on equal terms to both Jew and Gentile is consistent with God's covenant promises to the Jewish people. He begins with a passionate statement of his own personal feelings: I myself (αὐτὸς ἐγώ) feel continuous pain about what has happened to my people, and I would pray to be accursed and separated from Christ if they could be saved as a result.

---

77. The aspect of 'fairness' in δικαιοσύνη can be clearly seen in some parts of Romans, e.g. 3.26: 'God is fair (consistent with his covenant promises to the Jews) in making faith in Christ the basis of justification'; 3.5 and 9.19 (in both of which verses God is defended against a charge of unfairness).

Here Paul is not appealing to his apostolic authority but assuring his readers of his personal involvement in the message he preaches. He remains a Jew, deeply hurt by the fact that the same gospel that brings light to many Gentiles brings darkness to many Jews. The force of αὐτὸς ἐγώ in 9.3 is to show that he Paul, the apostle to the Gentiles, is also a devout Jew, who cares more for his fellow Jews than for his own salvation. This personal testimony gives authenticity to his later encouragement of Jewish Christians not to disown their roots (11.1) and to his warning to Gentile Christians not to think of themselves as superior (11.17-24).

Romans 7.25 is the most disputed occurrence of the phrase αὐτὸς ἐγώ in Paul's letters. The meaning of Rom. 7.13-25 (of which this verse forms the climax) has been hotly debated over many centuries. All I can do here is to express my opinion—that the phrase αὐτὸς ἐγώ should be understood here in the same way as in Rom. 9.5. Paul is bringing his own personal experience into a theological discussion. The theme of Rom. 7.13-25 is the conflict between flesh and spirit—between the sinful desires that are natural to us as human beings and the delight in the law of God that is a fruit of the Spirit. The use of the first person singular throughout this passage could be understood as a rhetorical device; but the phrase αὐτὸς ἐγώ in v. 25 shows that this is not the case. Paul is encouraging the Romans by sharing his own experience.

We can paraphrase his argument as follows: 'Don't think that the continued presence in your life of wrong thoughts and actions means that you are not a proper Christian. I Paul your apostle am in the same position as you. I also delight in God's law in my innermost being, but find myself saying and doing things that are contrary to God's law. For example, I told the Corinthians that love is not provoked to anger (1 Cor. 13.5); but I was provoked to anger when Barnabas wanted to bring his cousin Mark on a mission for which he was not suited (Acts 15.39).[78] This kind of inconsistency is not a sign of sub-Christian experience. I am confident that 'there is no condemnation for those who belong to Christ Jesus' (8.1), not because my discipleship is consistent, but because God sent his Son to atone for my sin (8.3), and he is gradually changing me by his Spirit (8.4-11).

Paul's argument here is (among other things) an argument against perfectionism, and can be compared to his argument in Phil. 3. Some Christians at Philippi seem to have been claiming to be perfect. Paul replies by

78. παροξύνεται in 1 Cor. 13.5 is a verbal form of the noun παροξυσμός used in Acts 15.39.

sharing his experience. I do not think of myself as perfect, he writes, but I am pressing on towards the prize (vv. 12-14). In one sense of the word we can claim to be perfect—that is, mature Christians—but we show our maturity by realizing that we are still imperfect (v. 15). Paul's insistence in Philippians that perfection (in the sense of maturity) involves the recognition of one's own imperfection is very close to the argument of Rom. 7 and 8.[79]

We have seen that Paul uses the phrases αὐτὸς ἐγώ and ἐγὼ Παῦλος in two main ways: (a) to stamp a statement with his personal authority; (b) to refer to his individual experience or ministry. In 2 Cor. 10.1 these two phrases are combined into the composite αὐτὸς ἐγὼ Παῦλος. There are two ways of understanding this phrase. One is to classify it under usage (a)—Paul is investing the exhortation that follows with his full apostolic authority. The other is to classify it under usage (b)—Paul wrote 2 Corinthians in the name of himself and Timothy (1.1); but at this point he speaks in his own name as an individual.

Those who adopt the former interpretation find the closest parallel to this verse in Gal. 5.2. But there are significant differences between Gal. 5.2 and 2 Cor. 10.1. In Gal. 5.2 the words ἴδε ἐγὼ Παῦλος λέγω ὑμῖν introduce a pithy statement of his position. It is obvious what he is saying to them. But in 2 Cor. 10.1 this is not obvious. He begins αὐτὸς δὲ ἐγὼ Παῦλος παρακαλῶ ὑμᾶς. The word παρακαλῶ normally expresses a personal request based on official position or on friendship.[80] However, Paul's does not immediately make his request, but precedes it with a statement of one of the charges levelled against him. The request, when it eventually comes in v. 2, is introduced by the word δέομαι—'I beg of you', and is a plea that he should not be forced to take punitive action against his accusers.

This is a very different atmosphere to that in any other Pauline letter, and a far cry from the dogmatic tone of Gal. 5.2. Even though in Galatians Paul is fighting hard against influential teachers, his use of the phrase ἐγὼ

79. Cf. Cranfield, *Romans*, I, p. 356: 'But we are convinced that it is possible to do justice to the text of Paul—and also to the facts of Christian living wherever they are to be observed—only if we resolutely hold chapters 7 and 8 together, in spite of the obvious tension between them, and see in them not two successive stages but two different aspects, two contemporaneous realities, of the Christian life, both of which continue so long as the Christian is in the flesh'.

80. On the meaning of παρακαλῶ see Thiselton, *First Epistle*, pp. 111-14.

Παῦλος in that verse implies that his name still counts for something. He may have been accused of being a time-server, but once he has made his position plain he clearly expects his apostolic authority to carry weight. There is no other Pauline letter that reflects the strength of personal attack against Paul as an individual that we find reflected in 2 Cor. 10–13.

In the light of this, it is difficult to regard the phrase αὐτὸς ἐγὼ Παῦλος as an assertion of Paul's authority. What Paul is saying, on this theory, is: I Paul, who am accused by my opponents of being weak, vacillating and devious, now request you with my full apostolic authority and beg you not to force me to take action against my accusers. This raises the question: is it appropriate to pull rank and assert one's status when it is precisely that rank and status that is under question?

The alternative explanation, on the other hand, makes good sense. Chs. 10–13 contain Paul's response to personal attacks made on him as an individual. Chs. 1–9 were written in the joint names of Paul and Timothy. Though the earlier chapters do contain some passages that relate to Paul as an individual, on the whole they are concerned with the apostolic ministry that he and Timothy shared. The central theological section on the nature of ministry (2.14–7.1) is almost entirely in the plural.

The occasional use of the first person singular in chs. 1–9 and of the first person plural in chs. 10–13 does not alter the fact of the overwhelming 'we-ness' of the earlier chapters and the overwhelming 'I-ness' of the later chapters. In P. Bachmann's words, endorsed by Barrett, 10.1 marks the change from a 'We-epistle' to an 'I-epistle'.[81] The occasional shift in both sections from singular to plural or from plural to singular is characteristic of letters written by one person in the name of more than one person.

Examples of this genre are the circular letters from married couples, of which my wife and I receive a number every Christmas. Though these letters are sent in the name of both parties, they are often written either by the husband or by the wife. Sometimes the plural 'we' is used to describe shared experiences. At other times the writer is clearly writing as an individual and may even refer to his or her spouse in the third person even though the letter is written in the name of both.

2 Corinthians reveals a similar inconsistency. In chs. 1–9 Paul writes mainly in the plural, in the name of himself and Timothy, but from time to time refers in the singular to personal issues where he alone is involved. In chs. 10–13 he writes mainly as an individual in response to personal

---

81. Barrett, *Second Epistle*, p. 244.

attacks, but from time to time raises more general issues which affect his colleagues as well as himself and slips instinctively into the plural. Had he been writing a rhetorical exercise such inconsistency would have been reprehensible. But Paul was not writing a rhetorical exercise, he was dictating a letter extempore. The occasional inconsistency does not alter the fact of the predominant 'we-ness' of chs. 1–9 and the predominant 'I-ness' of chs. 10–13.

The emphatic individualism of 10.1 implies that an earlier section of the letter to which 10.1 belongs was corporate. The introduction 'now I Paul personally' would not have been necessary if the whole letter had been written by Paul in isolation. Even if chs. 10–13 are regarded as part of a separate letter, any attempt to reconstruct that letter would need to postulate a preceding section of more general import for 10.1 to make sense.

Chapter 5

THE INTERNAL UNITY OF 2 CORINTHIANS 1–9

There are three main theories that deny the literary integrity of 2 Cor. 1–9:

1. The theory that the section 6.14–7.1 is an interpolation—either from another Pauline letter or from a non-Pauline source.
2. The theory that chs. 8 and 9 are separate from chs. 1–7, and constitute either one or two independent letters.
3. The theory that the section 2.14–7.4 is an interpolation from another Pauline letter into the letter comprising 1.1–2.13 and 7.5-16.

I shall not comment in detail on 6.14–7.1. This is a much debated passage,[1] and a proper evaluation of all the issues involved is beyond the scope of this book. Moreover, I have nothing significant to add to the balanced treatment of these verses in Margaret Thrall's commentary.[2] There is a similar, equally obscure passage in 1 Cor. 15.33-34, where Paul warns the Corinthians against keeping the wrong company, and refers to certain unnamed people who do not know God. Both passages assume the Corinthians will know who is being talked about, but all we can do today is form conjectures. Fortunately, a correct conjecture as to the background of these passages is not essential to an understanding of 1 and 2 Corinthians as a whole, or to the main thesis of this book.

With regard to the other two theories, it is not possible in this book to examine in detail all that has been written in their support.[3] I have there-

---

1. Christoph Heil, 'Die Sprache der Absonderung in 2 Kor 6,17 und bei Paulus', in R. Bieringer (ed.), *The Corinthian Correspondence* (Leuven: Leuven University Press, 1996), pp. 717-29 (727-29) lists 24 authors under the heading 'Gegen die Integrität und Authentizität von 2 Kor 6,14-7,1' and 30 authors under the heading 'Für die Integrität und Authentizität von 2 Kor 6,14-7,1'.
2. Thrall, *Second Epistle*, pp. 25-36.
3. For details of scholars who have advocated these theories and the variations

fore chosen two representative presentations: H.D. Betz's book *2 Corinthians 8 and 9* (which argues that these chapters comprise two independent letters), and L.L. Welborn's article 'Like Broken Pieces of a Ring' (which argues for the literary independence of 2 Cor. 2.14–7.4).[4]

1. *2 Corinthians 8 and 9*

In his book entitled *2 Corinthians 8 and 9*, Betz maintains that these chapters were originally two independent letters. He begins with a broadly evolutionist survey of the history of research into 2 Corinthians over the last 200 years, noting various scholars who have 'made progress' and 'advanced the debate'. His conclusion is that, despite the progress made, all these studies show 'a complete lack of methodological reflection'. It is rhetorical criticism that, in Betz's opinion, can make the study of 2 Cor. 8 and 9 truly scientific.[5] What is needed, he believes, is analysis of 2 Cor. 8 and 9 'in order to find out whether they in fact can be related to letter categories known from other ancient epistolary literature, that is, whether their literary form, internal composition, argumentative rhetoric, and function can be shown to be that of independent epistolary fragments'; this approach will meet the challenge facing serious students of the New Testament to sustain 'a developed scientific argument'.[6]

It is open to question whether rhetorical criticism is more 'scientific'

---

between them see Schnelle, *History*, pp. 79-87; Martin, *2 Corinthians*, pp. xl-xlvi; Thrall, *Second Epistle*, pp. 20-25 (on 2.14–7.4), pp. 36-43 (on chs. 8 and 9).

4.   H.D. Betz, *2 Corinthians 8 and 9* (Philadelphia: Fortress Press, 1985). L.L. Welborn, 'Like Broken Pieces of a Ring: 2 Cor. 1.1–2.13; 7.5-16 and Ancient Theories of Literary Unity', *NTS* 42 (1996), pp. 559-83.

5.   Betz, *2 Corinthians 8 and 9*, pp. 4-27. Typical of Betz's evolutionism is his comment (p. 14) on those British scholars who, in the second half of the twentieth century, defended the unity of 2 Corinthians: 'Faced by uncertainties and weary of hypotheses, scholars have always been greatly tempted simply to take refuge in the tradition'. It is no doubt arguable that the disease *conservatitis morbosa* is more prevalent in Britain than in other countries (though of the 17 scholars listed by Schnelle [*History*, p. 87 n. 236] who 'vote for the unity of 2 Corinthians' not one is British). It is equally arguable that scholars in other countries are more at risk from the disease *cainophilia atheniensis* (first diagnosed by Luke in Acts 17.21). This would explain why each new partition theory differs in some significant way from all the partition theories previously proposed.

For a general critique of the role of evolutionism in New Testament scholarship see Hall, *Seven Pillories*, pp. 1-19.

6.   Betz, *2 Corinthians 8 and 9*, p. xi.

than the methods of earlier scholars. Crucial to rhetorical criticism is classification—the classification of every New Testament letter, and every section of every letter, as belonging to a particular rhetorical category. Classification is a very important feature of some branches of science such as botany. The question is whether the techniques of botany can be properly applied to literary works. Do literary works exhibit the same degree of uniformity as plants? If they do not, the application of botanical techniques to the books of the New Testament may prove to be, not progress, but regress. It may be a reversion to the pre-critical tendency to interpret a New Testament book by reference to an external criterion, rather than relying on the internal evidence of the book itself.

The type of scholarship against which the modern critical movement rebelled was the attempt to fit Paul's letters into some external category—to show that Paul was a good Catholic, or a good Lutheran, or a good Anglican. The danger today is that the norms of first-century rhetoric may perform the same function as the creeds and confessions of faith did under the old system. Instead of being shown to be a classic Catholic or Protestant, Paul is now shown to be a classic rhetorician.

In his analysis Betz detects, both in ch. 8 and in ch. 9, the following five elements: *exordium* (introduction); *narratio* (statement of facts); *propositio* (thesis to be proved); *probatio* (arguments in favour of the thesis); and *peroratio* (conclusion).[7] The presence of these elements suggests to Betz that these are two independent letters, each with its own rhetorical structure. Two comments can be made on this argument.

First, the Latin names Betz has given to these five elements suggest that Paul was conforming to a specifically Graeco-Roman rhetorical pattern. But in fact these are the basic elements of persuasive speech in any culture. In the words of S.K. Stowers:

> The reason it is so easy to 'find' such divisions is that the logic of discourse for sections and whole documents alike demands numerous beginnings, middles, and conclusions. That does not mean that Paul studied the technical rhetoric of the handbooks.[8]

Second, Betz's analysis has been forced onto the chapters rather than drawn naturally from them. This is particularly true of the *narratio*. In ch. 8 what Betz calls the *narratio* (v. 6) is a subordinate clause. In ch. 9 the

7. Betz, *2 Corinthians 8 and 9*, pp. 38-41 (for ch. 8) and pp. 88-90 (for ch. 9).
8. S.K. Stowers, 'Review of H.D. Betz, *2 Corinthians 8 and 9*', *JBL* 106 (1987), pp. 727-30 (730).

so-called *narratio* (vv. 3-5a) states Paul's reasons for sending the brothers, not the fact of their sending. In the opinion of Stowers, 'it stretches the imagination beyond belief to think of 8.6 or 9.3-5a as a *narratio*'.[9]

The same is true of the verses Betz classifies as *peroratio*. The *peroratio* of ch. 8 (v. 24) he describes as 'concise, perhaps even elliptic', which is not what one would normally expect of a *peroratio*.[10] The *peroratio* of ch. 9 (v. 15) reads more like a prayer than a peroration. Betz thinks the word ἀνεκδιήγητος (indescribable) derives from the rhetoric of hymns, and that Paul was quoting the first line of an early Christian prayer of thanks-giving: when the letter was read in church this verse would be intoned and the Achaians would recite the rest of the hymn from memory. The func-tion of the *peroratio*, on the other hand, according to Betz, is 'to sum up the contents of the letter, to restate its main concerns, and to include what-ever final emphasis the author wishes to give'. He believes that 'verse 15 certainly suffices as a final summary of the letter', but this is a matter of opinion.[11]

Betz's attempt to separate the end of ch. 8 from the beginning of ch. 9 is unconvincing. Ch. 9 begins with the words περὶ μὲν γάρ. According to Betz, 'the presence of the particle μέν means that γάρ ("for") need not refer to anything preceding. Rather it refers to what follows without connection to what has gone before'.[12] This is special pleading. BAGD states that the conjunction γάρ 'is used to express cause, clarification or inference'. There are eight examples of the combination μὲν γάρ cited in BAGD (sv. γάρ 1b) in addition to 2 Cor. 9.1. In each of these cases there is a clear reference back to the preceding verse or verses. Where, as in 2 Cor. 9.1, the μέν is followed by a δέ (Acts 13.36; 23.6; Rom. 2.25; Heb. 7.20; 12.10) the functions of μέν and γάρ are different—the μέν introduces a contrast with the following δέ, and the γάρ establishes a con-nection with the preceding verse or verses. Moreover, Stowers cites three examples of the combination περὶ μὲν γάρ from Josephus, Philo and [Plutarch], in which these words either introduce reasons for something said before or introduce a new topic within a larger discourse. In Stowers's opinion, these parallels do not support Betz's case but 'in fact argue for the unity of the two chapters'.[13]

---

9.   Stowers, 'Review', p. 730.
10. Betz, *2 Corinthians 8 and 9*, p. 82.
11. Betz, *2 Corinthians 8 and 9*, p. 128.
12. Betz, *2 Corinthians 8 and 9*, p. 90.
13. Stowers, 'Review', p. 728.

If we interpret the combination μὲν γάρ in 9.1 in accordance with its use elsewhere it makes excellent sense. In 8.16-24 Paul has stated that Titus will be accompanied by two brothers. In 9.1-5 he explains his reasons for sending these brothers. His argument can be paraphrased as follows: 'The reason why I am sending the brothers (γάρ) is this: while in one sense (μέν) I do not need to remind you about the collection because you have shown last year your enthusiasm for this project, in another sense (δέ) I have to take action by sending these brothers, to ensure that the money is ready by the time the representatives from Macedonia arrive. Otherwise both you and I will feel ashamed'.

A further link between chs. 8 and 9 is Paul's reference in 9.3 to 'the brothers' without any explanation of who these brothers are. On the assumption that chs. 8 and 9 are part of the same letter, this makes good sense. 'The brothers' means 'the brothers I have just commended to you'. But if ch. 9 is an independent letter, it is unclear who these brothers are.

In Betz's opinion ch. 8 and ch. 9 were addressed to two different audiences—ch. 8 to the Corinthians and ch. 9 to the Achaians. Commenting on 9.2 he writes:

> The fact that Paul was able to boast about the Achaians at the moment when the future of the Corinthian collection was in doubt means that the affairs of Achaia must have been regarded as separate from those of Corinth.[14]

The theory that chs. 8 and 9 were addressed to different audiences has had a number of advocates, but it does not stand up to examination.[15] Corinth was the capital city of the province of Achaia, both administratively and commercially, and was related to the rest of Achaia as London today is related to the rest of England. Let us imagine a modern international organization whose English branch has its headquarters in London. If the general secretary of that organization were to write a letter in which he referred to 'our members in England', could anyone possibly think that this meant 'our members in England excluding London'? 'England' includes London in the twenty-first century, and 'Achaia' included Corinth in the first century. 2 Corinthians was addressed to 'the church in Corinth along with all the saints in the whole of Achaia' (1.1). Presumably the letter was taken first to Corinth, with the expectation that its contents would be shared with the other churches in Achaia. Paul's statement in

---

14. Betz, *2 Corinthians 8 and 9*, p. 92.
15. For a full discussion of the view that ch. 9 was addressed to a different (or wider) audience than ch. 8 see Martin, *2 Corinthians*, pp. 249-50.

2 Cor. 11.10 that his boast of being self-supporting applies to 'the whole of Achaia' suggests that 2 Corinthians was distributed throughout the province.

Paul refers to Achaia in 9.2 because the collection was organized on a province-by-province basis. In a similar way he refers in 8.1-5 to 'the churches of Macedonia' rather than specifying Philippi, Thessalonica and so on. Most of the New Testament occurrences of Achaia link it with Macedonia (Acts 19.21; Rom. 15.26; 2 Cor. 11.9-10; 1 Thess. 1.7, 8), and the theme of 9.2 is a comparison between the two provinces. Paul declares that he is boasting to the Macedonians (i.e. to members of all the churches in Macedonia) of the preparations made by the Achaians (i.e. by all the churches in Achaia including Corinth). Similarly in Rom. 15.26 Paul says that 'Macedonia and Achaia' have decided to help the needy Christians in Jerusalem. 'Achaia' here includes Corinth, and would still do so even if the Corinthians had refused to contribute a single denarius.[16]

One of the strongest indications that for Paul Achaia included Corinth is 1 Cor. 16.15, where Stephanas is described as 'the first-fruits [i.e. first convert] of Achaia'. It is clear from what Paul goes on to say about Stephanas in vv. 16-18 (and also from 1.16) that he was a member of the church in Corinth. The reason why Paul refers to Achaia here may be that he thought of his missionary task in terms of provinces. By staying in Corinth he had evangelized the province of Achaia, just as by staying in Ephesus he was evangelizing the province of Asia (cf. Acts 19.10 and the implications of Rom. 15.23a).

Betz's description of the spiritual superiority of the Achaians to the Corinthians has no basis in fact. It is the Achaians—the addressees of ch. 9—who, Paul fears, may not be prepared with ready cash when he and his party arrive (9.4). The situation envisaged in both chs. 8 and 9 is the same: the people addressed had shown great enthusiasm when the project was launched the previous year, but had not translated that enthusiasm into actual money.

The greatest difficulty with Betz's analysis is 8.16-24, in which Paul introduces a new topic—the commendation of Titus and two brothers. Betz himself admits that 'ch. 8 falls into two parts which seem to have little in common with one another from a formal point of view'. His explanation is that the letter which ch. 8 comprises was of 'mixed' type.[17] But

16. A Roman coin (traditionally translated 'penny' in Mt. 22.19. A day's wage in Mt. 20.2).

17. Betz, *2 Corinthians 8 and 9*, pp. 131, 139.

there seems little point in arguing that vv. 1-15 contain all the characteristics of an independent letter if Paul has then added another section to make it a mixed letter. If one is to use Betz's categories, one could say that the second section of the chapter has its own *narratio* (vv. 16-19, 22), its own *propositio* (vv. 20-21), its own *probatio* (v. 23) and its own *peroratio* (v. 24). So ch. 8 becomes, in effect, two letters.

This prompts the question: if Paul was able to combine within the supposed letter of ch. 8 two sections with different subjects and different rhetorical structures, why should this not be true for 2 Corinthians as a whole? 2 Corinthians, in the form in which we now have it, fits perfectly the category of a 'mixed' letter—several sections, each with its own rhetorical structure, combined into a single whole. Such a combination of semi-independent sections could be called a characteristic Pauline technique. 1 Corinthians is the prime example, consisting as it does of a whole series of separate sections, each with its own rhetorical structure, combined like a patchwork quilt into a single letter. Paul also incorporated poetic or hymnic elements into his letters, such as the hymn to love in 1 Cor. 13 or the christological hymn in Phil. 2.5-11. Some of these poetic or hymnic elements may have had a previous existence; if this is so, by incorporating them into a particular letter Paul made them an integral part of that letter. The fact that a section of a letter has its own internal rhetorical structure does not prevent it from belonging to a larger whole.

When I lived in India, I often heard sermons in which the preacher burst into song, singing part of a hymn, and then continued the sermon as if there had been no interruption. Although the hymn had its own poetic structure, by including it in the sermon the preacher made it an integral part of the sermon. This practice is not so common in many Western societies, perhaps because of a more rigid approach to rhetoric—the demarcation of speech and song as two separate entities. Paul was not inhibited in this respect.

Ben Witherington makes a wise comment on the 'mixed' character of 2 Corinthians:

> Both 1 and 2 Corinthians are composed of a variety of arguments and any or all of these arguments may have any of the parts of a rhetorical discourse from an *exordium* to a *peroratio*. Micro-rhetoric should not be confused with macro-rhetoric, and letters are not completely identical with speeches... Paul normally includes all kinds of things in a single letter, including what could be placed in a letter of recommendation—without writing a separate letter to accomplish this (cf. 1 Corinthians 16 and Romans 16), so why should 2 Corinthians 8–9 be any different?[18]

18. Witherington, *Conflict*, p. 413 n.7.

2. *2 Corinthians 2.14–7.4*

In his article 'Like Broken Pieces of a Ring', L.L. Welborn maintains that
the section 2 Cor. 2.14–7.4 belongs to a separate letter from the rest of 2
Cor. 1–7. This theory, which he traces back to Johannes Weiss, has gained
considerable support over the years.[19] Welborn's restatement of the theory
relies on three main arguments.

a. *The Difference in Tone Between the Two Sections*
Welborn (following Weiss) detects in 2.14–7.4 a different atmosphere to
that of the rest of chs. 1–7:

> Here the reconciliation is not apparent, which, in chapters 1–2 and 7, is a
> presupposition of Paul's joy. On the contrary, Paul must still answer
> charges that he has wronged, corrupted and defrauded the Corinthians, and
> must plead with the Corinthians to open their hearts (2.17; 4.1-2; 6.3-13;
> 7.2-4). This passage must have been written at the height of the conflict,
> before the successful conclusion of peace.[20]

The contrast drawn by Welborn is greatly exaggerated. The apologetic
tone of 2.14–7.4 is also to be seen in 1.1–2.13, where Paul defends himself
against charges of employing 'the wisdom of the flesh' (1.12), of behaving
'in a fleshly way' (κατὰ σάρκα) (1.17), and specifically of fickleness in
saying one thing and doing another (1.17). He introduces his defence
against these charges in v. 12 with the conjunction γάρ, which links his
apology to his opening thanksgiving (1.3-11). This probably indicates his
perception that the prayer support he had just been claiming (1.11) was
dependent on their confidence in his integrity, and on the clearing up of
the doubts about his integrity that had been voiced.[21]

Welborn talks of 'the successful conclusion of peace' which led to
the joy of chs. 1–2 and 7. But what Paul does in 1.12–2.4 is to present a
defence of his actions to those who were questioning them. He is as much
on the defensive in these verses as anywhere else in 2 Corinthians.

---

19. Welborn summarizes Weiss's argument at the beginning of his article and then
gives a list of scholars who have adopted Weiss's theory ('Broken Pieces', pp. 559-
60).

20. Welborn, 'Broken Pieces', p. 559.

21. See Excursus E: 'The Connection between 2 Corinthians 1.11 and 1.12'.

b. *The Sequence of Thought between 2.13 and 7.5*

Welborn quotes the assertion of J. Weiss that, if the interpolated section is removed, 2.13 and 7.5 fit together 'like broken pieces of a ring'.[22] This is an example of what I have called elsewhere the criterion of detachability, which is based on the theory that, if a passage is smoothly detachable from its context, it did not originally belong to that context. This criterion has often been used in criticism of authors such as Mark, whose paratactic style means that almost any passage can be more or less smoothly detached from the narrative.[23] But the criterion of detachability is of little value in the present case. Though Welborn has made a reasonable case for 7.5 to follow 2.13, it follows 7.4 much better.

In 7.4 Paul states: 'I am filled with encouragement; I am overflowing with joy in all our affliction'. Verse 5 explains why this is so. When Paul and Timothy arrived in Macedonia they were at first 'afflicted in every way' by external conflicts and internal fears; but then God encouraged them with the news brought by Titus.[24] Not only do vv. 5-7 explain the reason for Paul's emotions in the previous verse, there are also two linguistic echoes; θλιβόμενοι (afflicted) in v. 5 is a verbal form of the noun θλῖψις (affliction) in v. 4, and παρεκάλεσεν (encouraged) in v. 6 is a verbal form of the noun παράκλησις (encouragement) in v. 4.[25]

Welborn attempts to separate v. 4 from v. 5 on the grounds that vv. 5-7 do not logically follow the verses *preceding* v. 4. He asks: 'In what sense does Paul's account of his search for Titus confirm his appeal to the Corinthians to reciprocate his love?'—in other words, how do vv. 5-7 confirm Paul's argument in 6.11-13?[26] But in the text of 2 Corinthians as we have it, v. 5 follows v. 4, not 6.11-13. Welborn's real problem, it seems to me, is that he cannot understand how Paul can follow the defensive and apologetic statements of v. 2 with the confident statement of v. 4. He believes that Paul is defensive in 2.14–7.4 and confident in 7.5-16; but the confidence begins at v. 4, not at v. 5.[27]

22. Welborn, 'Broken Pieces', p. 559.

23. D.R. Hall, *The Gospel Framework: Fiction or Fact? A Critical Evaluation of 'Der Rahmen der Geschichte Jesu' by Karl Ludwig Schmidt* (Carlisle: Paternoster, 1998), pp. 69-73.

24. I have argued in Chapter 4 that Paul's use of the first person plural in 7.5-7 is due to the the presence of Timothy.

25. Thrall, *Second Epistle*, p. 21; Martin, *2 Corinthians*, p. xliii.

26. Welborn, 'Broken Pieces', p. 581.

27. Welborn describes 7.4 as a 'peroration' which 'one could only expect' to lead

Equally unconvincing is Welborn's attempt to prove a break in thought between 2.13 and 2.14. He declares that 'it is difficult to exaggerate the degree of discontinuity between 2.12-13 and 2.14ff'.[28] This is a gross exaggeration. 2.14-17 depicts the apostles as people who, though personally humiliated, are nevertheless taking part in a victory procession. It follows on very appropriately from 2.12-13, where Paul describes what must have been a humiliating experience—his inability to take advantage of a promising evangelistic opportunity in Troas because of the emotional turmoil inside him. The whole passage illustrates one of the main themes of both 1 and 2 Corinthians—that Paul and his colleagues are weak people, both physically and emotionally, but that God uses weak people as the messengers of his gospel.[29]

Admittedly Paul does not explain his train of thought in these verses; but this is a typical feature of his letters. Welborn seems to think that Paul should explain his train of thought at every point in clear logical language, as though he were writing a doctoral dissertation. But Paul's mind did not work like that. He was more like a dog being taken for a walk, who is distracted first by one scent and then by another. We must not project the style of writing of a modern academic work onto Paul's extempore dictation.

c. *The Rhetorical Argument*

Welborn's main argument is that chs. 1–7 do not bear the 'marks of coherence' which a literary work should possess by the standards of classical theorists, and that the section 2.14–7.4 does not contain the features that a digression should have by those standards.[30] This is largely true. What is not clear is the relevance of this fact to the question under discussion. Does the failure of 2 Corinthians to measure up to the literary standards of classical theorists prove that Paul did not write it in its present form? Or should it be regarded as a sign of Pauline authenticity, since failure to conform to the classical model is a consistent feature of all Paul's letters?

---

into an epistolary postscript ('Broken Pieces', p. 577). But Paul's letters are littered with outbursts of praise and thanksgiving similar to 7.4. In Romans, for example, there are four doxologies ending with 'Amen', only one of which comes at the end of the letter (Rom. 1.25; 9.5; 11.36; 16.24). Welborn's wording 'one could only expect' betrays the fact that the basis of his argument is not objective evidence but critical expectation.

    28. Welborn, 'Broken Pieces', p. 575.
    29. For further discussion of 2.12-17 see Chapter 7.
    30. Welborn, 'Broken Pieces', pp. 560-61.

Welborn states that Johannes Weiss (in whose footsteps he treads) was following a model of literary unity that goes back to Aristotle. Aristotle was writing about the narrative genres of epic and drama and, in Welborn's words, 'does not…profess to offer a universally applicable theory of unity'. He was laying down how plots (μῦθοι) should be constructed if a work is to be successful. Similar principles were later applied to the writing of history. Dionysius, for example, criticized Thucydides for leaving the account of earlier events half-finished and embarking upon others; but he commended Herodotus, whose narrative was complete and continuous.[31]

It appears from this that Aristotle and his successors were grading the Greek literature of their day as a modern examiner grades examination papers. To some types of literature they gave full marks, other types they marked down. But there is no reason to assume that Paul followed the example of those writers whom the literary purists endorsed rather than the example of those they criticized. If Paul's faults were those of Thucydides, he was in good company.

This is equally true of Paul's digressions. According to Welborn, ancient theorists permitted digressions, to produce variety and refresh the reader. But they 'required that digressions be related to the subject at hand, and fit smoothly into the context, emerging from it and returning to the point by an intelligible train of thought'.[32] Paul's supposed digression in 2.14–7.4, on the other hand, 'has no point of departure in the text as it stands, but fractures the surface of the text, like a wedge that is inserted by force'.[33]

This argument raises a fundamental question of methodology. How do we decide what was Paul's attitude to digressions? Is it by studying ancient literary theory and deducing from that theory what Paul must have written? Or is it by examining Paul's letters to discover what he actually did write? In other words, should we analyse Paul's style on the basis of internal or external evidence?

It is possible that Paul had received formal rhetorical training, though there is no hard evidence for this hypothesis.[34] What must be rejected, however, is the assumption that no one can be skilled in any area who has not had formal training. It is this assumption that lies behind the question asked about Jesus in Jn 7.15: 'How can this man be a scholar without having had the proper training?' The same feeling may lead people to say

31. Welborn, 'Broken Pieces', pp. 570-71.
32. Welborn, 'Broken Pieces', p. 574.
33. Welborn, 'Broken Pieces', pp. 576-77.
34. On this question see Chapter 8, n. 27.

that Shakespeare's plays were written by Francis Bacon, or that George Stephenson could not have designed his famous 'Rocket' engine without a degree in engineering. Rhetoric was so much a part of Graeco-Roman life that someone such as Paul who kept his eyes and ears open would absorb rhetorical technique as young people today absorb pop music. But this does not mean that Paul would feel himself under any obligation to conform to the rules of the rhetorical theorists, and the evidence of his letters suggests that in fact he did not do so.

Paul was fond of digressions. In 1 Corinthians there are three major digressions: 6.1-11 in the middle of his discussion of πορνεία in chs. 5 and 6; ch. 9 in the middle of his discussion of food offered to idols in chs. 8–10; and ch. 13 in the middle of his discussion of spiritual gifts in chs. 12–14. In none of these cases does he clearly indicate, 'I am now about to digress' or 'I am now returning to my main theme', in a way the theorists would have approved. It is, of course, possible to regard all these digressions as interpolations, using similar arguments to those used by Welborn in this article. To do this is to make literary criticism the servant of literary dogma.

Conclusion

It is impossible to prove or disprove a partition theory. If the arguments used in support of most partition theories are unconvincing, as I believe them to be, that strengthens the case for their rejection, but does not disprove them. The strongest argument against the partition of either 1 or 2 Corinthians has always been their universal acceptance as genuine letters in the early church. Paul's letters were treasured in the churches he founded. The idea that a compiler could rearrange and republish them, without exciting any comment or criticism, is so improbable that only logically watertight arguments would be sufficient to establish it.

EXCURSUS E:
THE CONNECTION BETWEEN 2 CORINTHIANS 1.11 AND 1.12

In 2 Cor. 1.12 Paul moves from his opening thanksgiving to the main body of the letter. He begins with the words ἡ γὰρ καύχησις ἡμῶν αὕτη ἐστίν. In the opinion of Furnish, the word γάρ in this phrase 'has no strictly causal force. Like the δέ used in Phil. 1.12; 2 Thess. 2.1, it is mainly an introductory word here and does not presuppose any specific continuation of the preceding thought'. He accordingly translates it by the neutral word 'now': 'Now we can be proud of this…'[35]

The contention of this note is that Furnish is partly right and partly wrong. He is right to deny that γάρ has a strictly causal force, but wrong to deny any continuation of the thought of the previous verse. I shall consider the three reasons he gives for his interpretation in reverse order.

1. In ancient Near Eastern letters, including those in Hebrew and Aramaic, the body of the letter after the salutation is almost always introduced by 'Now' or 'And now' (Hebrew *we atta* or the equivalent). This observation could help to explain Paul's use of δέ in the two parallel verses Furnish cites (Phil. 1.12 and 2 Thess. 2.1). Δέ is a similarly neutral word to the English word 'now', and in Phil. 1.12 in particular 'now' would be a suitable translation. What this observation does not explain, however, is why Paul in 2 Cor. 1.12 uses γάρ rather than δέ.

The second and third editions of BAGD (though not the original BAG) follow the ancient grammarian Trypho in declaring that γάρ 'under certain circumstances…is one and the same thing as δέ'. In my opinion, the New Testament texts cited do not justify this statement. Admittedly, there are many texts in which either γάρ or δέ would be appropriate, and this is reflected in the variant readings in the manuscripts. Similarly, in books written in English, many clauses could appropriately begin with either 'and' or 'but'. This does not indicate that 'and' and 'but' have one and the same meaning.

2. Furnish cites the article on γάρ in BAGD (2nd edn) in support of his view. The third edition of BAGD classifies 2 Cor. 1.12 in Section 2 under the heading 'marker of clarification, *for, you see*'. After several examples of explanatory clauses, the section continues: 'Akin to the explanatory function is the use of γάρ as a narrative marker to express continuation or connection… Indeed, in many instances γάρ appears to be used adverbially like our 'now' (in which the temporal sense gives way to signal an important point or transition), 'well, then', 'you see'. 2 Cor. 1.12 is one of the verses cited after this comment. This classification agrees with the opinion of Furnish that γάρ here does not have a strictly causal force, but does not deny any connection with the thought of the previous verse.

3. Furnish argues that the neutral use of γάρ is typical of Paul's usage

35. Furnish, *II Corinthians*, p. 126. Many of the translations either use 'now' or leave γάρ untranslated. But words such as γάρ defy translation. Any attempt to reproduce the train of thought in Paul's mind leads to over-translation. Failure to translate, or use of a neutral word such as 'now', involves under-translation.

at the opening of the body of a letter. He cites Gal. 1.11; 1 Thess. 2.1; Rom. 1.16 (if this verse opens the body of the letter) or 1.18 (if it is opened there). But in each of these verses there is a clear connection with the preceding verse.

In Gal. 1.11 it is uncertain whether the correct reading is γάρ or δέ. If it is γάρ, the sequence of thought is clear. Paul has been accused of being a time-server, and his response in vv. 6-9 is to pronounce an anathema against all those who preach a different gospel to his. He then asks rhetorically in v. 10: 'am I now seeking to please other people? If I were still trying to please other people I would not be a servant of Christ'. This declaration is then amplified in v. 11. For Paul to seek other people's favour would be incompatible with being a servant of Christ because the gospel he preached was not a human product, received from other people, but a divine gift, received directly from Jesus Christ by revelation. Thus v. 11 follows directly and logically from v. 10, and the word ἄνθρωπος (human being) used in both v. 11 and v. 12 echoes the use of the same word in v. 10.

In 1 Thess. 1 Paul describes how the conversion and faith of the Thessalonian believers is being talked about not only in Macedonia and Achaea but all over the world. He then states in 2.1 that they themselves know what an impact his coming to Thessalonica had. We may paraphrase the word γάρ: 'and this worldwide report is not surprising because you yourselves know what an effect my ministry had among you'. Again there is a verbal repetition—2.1 repeats the word εἴσοδος ('our coming to you') used in 1.9.

Rom. 1.16 also is closely connected with the previous verses. Paul has revealed in vv. 11-15 his eagerness to preach the gospel in Rome. The reason for this eagerness is explained in v. 16—he is not ashamed of the gospel because it has God-given power to bring salvation. Here also there is a verbal echo—εὐαγγέλιον in v. 16 echoing εὐαγγελίσασθαι in v. 15.[36]

Thus the verses Furnish cites fail to support his contention. In each case there is not only a continuity of thought but also a verbal echo of the preceding section.

The word γάρ normally introduces an ancillary statement that helps to

---

36. The beginning of the main body of the letter is clearly (pace Furnish) at 1.16, where he turns from a personal address to the Romans in the second person plural to a general consideration of the gospel in the third person singular, and then states in v. 17 the main theme of the letter. However, in v. 18, as in v. 16, there is a close connection with the previous verse, evidenced by the repetition of the word ἀποκαλύπτεται.

make the preceding statement more intelligible. In some cases it has a causal force and may be translated 'because'. In other cases, in the words of BAGD, 'the thought to be supported is not expressed, but must be supplied from the context'.[37] In such cases the continuity of thought in the mind of the author is not always immediately apparent to the modern reader, and has to be deduced.

What, then, is the force of γάρ in 2 Cor. 1.12? In vv. 3-11 Paul has been describing the deliverance of his colleagues and himself from a terrible affliction. God has saved us, he declares, and will continue to save us, and you will play a part in this through your prayers which will result in a great chorus of thanksgiving (v. 11). This statement is immediately followed by v. 12. Our boast, Paul continues, the witness of our conscience, is that we have behaved not with worldly wisdom but honestly and sincerely, particularly in our dealings with you. This verse is clearly apologetic—Paul is rebutting charges of worldly wisdom and insincerity that have been levelled against him by some people at Corinth. What is the connection between his rebuttal of these charges in vv. 12-15 and the theme of prayer and thanksgiving in v. 11?

Thrall comments on v. 12 as follows:

> There may be some logical connection with v. 11: Paul can request his readers' assistance in prayer because (γάρ) his boast is that his conscience witnesses to his blameless conduct towards them. Essentially, however, he is leading into the following more specific defence of his integrity in v. 13 and in vv. 15-19, 23-24. This was forced upon him by Corinthian criticism.[38]

Thrall here contrasts two ways of looking at v. 12. Looking backwards, the assertion that his conduct has been blameless justifies his request for prayer support in the previous verse; looking forwards, his conduct has been criticized and he needs to defend it in the rest of the chapter. These two aspects of v. 12 are not antithetical but complementary.

The train of thought in Paul's mind may be this: 'I and my colleagues depend on your prayers, and we are looking forward to being helped by them in the future. But prayer support of this kind is only possible if there is a good relationship between us—if you have confidence in our sincerity. The reason why we look forward with confidence to your continuing prayer and thanksgiving for us is that we are not, as has been alleged, dis-

---

37. BAGD, sv. γάρ, 1e. BAGD does not classify 2 Cor. 1.12 under Section 1e, but the Sections 1e and 2 are very similar, and the comment quoted would, in my opinion, apply to most of the verses cited in Section 2 as well as to those cited in Section 1e.

38. Thrall, *Second Epistle*, p. 129.

honest and devious but have been open and above-board in all our dealings with you'. In other words, Paul believed that Corinthian belief in the personal integrity of himself and his colleagues was the essential precondition of his receiving their prayer backing. That is why the first major theme of the letter is his defence of his personal integrity in the light of criticism recently voiced at Corinth (1.15–2.4).

There are two striking things about Paul's train of thought in these verses. The first is the way in which, right at the start of the letter, he turns to apologetic. The opening chapter of 2 Corinthians illustrates how strongly Paul feels himself to be on the defensive. The second striking thing is the importance Paul attached to his personal relationship with the Corinthians—to their loyalty to him expressed not only in obedience to his teaching but also in thanksgiving and prayer. This father/child relationship was also emphasized in 1 Corinthians (4.14-17); and in 2 Cor. 7.12 Paul reveals that the cementing of this relationship was his main purpose in demanding the punishment of the offender. 2 Corinthians is not a theological tract but a personal letter from a father to members of his family.

Chapter 6

THE BACKGROUND OF PAUL'S OPPONENTS

In 2 Corinthians Paul refers directly to his opponents; in 1 Corinthians only indirectly. I shall therefore concentrate in this chapter on the background of Paul's opponents as revealed in 2 Corinthians, and then look more briefly at such hints as we can pick up about the background of his opponents in 1 Corinthians.

1. *Paul's Opponents: Palestinian or Hellenistic?*

It is clear from 2 Cor. 11.22 that Paul's opponents boasted of their Jewish birth. This has sometimes been taken to mean that they were Judaizers from Palestine. There are, however, strong grounds for questioning this view, and for locating their background in Hellenistic Judaism.

First, there is little trace in 2 Corinthians of the ideas and vocabulary Paul uses to combat Judaizers elsewhere. As Udo Schnelle says, 'circumcision, and therefore the issue of the Law in general, are not the disputed issues in 2 Corinthians; it is characteristic of this that the word νόμος (law) does not occur in 2 Corinthians'.[1]

Second, although in the opinion of Ernst Käsemann, Paul's opponents were officially authorized by the Jerusalem leadership, this theory is not true to the evidence.[2] The letters they brought with them were letters of commendation not of authorization.[3] The decisive argument against regarding them as letters of authorization is the phrase ἢ ἐξ ὑμῶν in 3.1—these

---

1. Schnelle, *History*, pp. 89-90.
2. E. Käsemann, 'Die Legitimität des Apostels. Eine Untersuchung zu II Korinther 10–13', *ZNW* 41 (1942), pp. 33-71.
3. For the distinction between commendation and authorization see C.J.A. Hickling, 'The Sequence of Thought in II Corinthians, Chapter Three', *NTS* 21 (1975), pp. 380-95 (381-82).

were the kind of letters the Corinthian church was as capable of writing as any other.[4]

Third, the phrase οἱ ὑπερλίαν ἀπόστολοι (the super-apostles) in 11.5 and 12.11 has been interpreted in two main ways—as an ironical reference to Paul's opponents at Corinth; or as a reference to the Jerusalem apostles. One argument used in favour of the latter view is that Paul refers to his rivals at Corinth as false apostles and servants of Satan (11.13-15), but simply claims to be 'not inferior' to the super-apostles (11.5; 12.11). According to Barrett, 'it is difficult to resist the force of Dr. Käsemann's argument that to say of men who are described as servants of Satan, "I am not inferior to them" is intolerable'.[5] Barrett fails to appreciate the ironical way in which Paul is echoing the language of his opponents. The words 'not inferior' are an ironical rebuttal of their accusation that he is inferior. Similarly, the phrase 'servants of Christ' (διάκονοι Χριστοῦ) in 11.2 echoes the claim Paul's opponents made for themselves, and does not represent what he believed them to be.[6] In a modern text, phrases of this sort would be placed in inverted commas. The phrase 'right honourable member' in British parliamentary debates can have a similar ironical connotation and be combined with suggestions that the member concerned is in fact far from honourable.

A number of arguments against the Jerusalem origin of the 'super-apostles' have been presented by Bultmann and Furnish.[7] The most telling argument is the contrast drawn between these 'apostles' and Paul with regard to professional rhetorical expertise (11.5-6). This makes it extremely unlikely that Peter the Galilean fisherman should be the object of comparison—unless it is assumed that Peter's rhetorical skills developed over the years, and that 2 Peter represents his mature Greek style.[8]

4.   This point is made by R. Bultmann, *Exegetische Probleme des zweiten Korintherbriefes* (Symbolae Biblicae Uppsalienses, 9; Uppsala, 1947), p. 22; Collange, *Enigmes*, p. 44; D. Georgi, *The Opponents of Paul in Second Corinthians* (Edinburgh: T. & T. Clark, 1987), p. 244; Furnish, *II Corinthians*, p. 193, Schnelle, *History*, p. 88.

5.   Barrett, *Second Epistle*, p. 31, quoting Käsemann, 'Legitimität', p. 42.

6.   Contra Barrett, *Second Epistle*, p. 237: 'we must conclude either that the situation was a complex one, involving at least two groups over against Paul, or that Paul was lashing out blindly, and using language irresponsibly'.

7.   Bultmann, *Probleme*, pp. 26-30; Furnish, *II Corinthians*, pp. 502-505.

8.   Barrett (*Second Epistle*, pp. 277-78) attempts to avoid this difficulty by relating the γάρ of 11.5 not to the preceding v. 4 but to v. 1. However, the sequence γάρ... γάρ...γάρ in vv. 2, 4-5 cannot mean 'firstly because...secondly because...thirdly because'. The γάρ in v. 4 follows on from v. 3. Paul is afraid the minds of the Corin-

Fourth, it has been argued that the term ῾Εβραῖος (Hebrew) indicates Palestinian origin.[9] But this is not so. BAGD gives two meanings for ῾Εβραῖος—(a) ethnic name for an Israelite, *Hebrew* in contrast to other nations; (b) Hebrew- /Aramaic-speaking Israelite in contrast to a Greek-speaking Israelite. BAGD also points out that Eusebius applied the term to Hellenistic Jews such as Philo and Aristobulus.[10] Moreover, Paul replies to the claim of his opponents to be Hebrews with the word κἀγώ (I am too; 11.22). He could not have said this if the word meant 'Palestinian', since he was a Hellenistic Jew from Tarsus.

Fifth, Jerry Sumney notes the tendency of advocates of the Judaistic hypothesis to appeal to other Pauline letters.[11] F.C. Baur did this because he believed that in all his letters Paul faced a similar type of opposition.[12] Others, while rejecting Baur's position, nevertheless see parallels to the 2 Corinthians situation in Galatians, especially in the Jerusalem concordat described in Gal. 2.1-10. There is nothing in 2 Corinthians to suggest such parallels.[13] The nature of the opposition in 2 Corinthians must be determined solely by the internal evidence of the letter itself. And the features of that letter we have already noted—the lack of any reference to observance of the law; the suggestion that the Corinthians themselves would be competent to recommend their teachers to other churches; and the emphasis on rhetorical expertise—all point to a Hellenistic rather than a Palestinian provenance.[14]

---

thians may be corrupted (v. 3) because of the welcome they give to preachers of a different gospel (v. 4). Similarly, the γάρ of v. 5 follows on from v. 4, since the 'super-apostles' of v. 5 are the same as the preachers of a different gospel of v. 4. The phrase ὁ ἐρχόμενος in v. 4 is generic and means 'anyone who comes'—see the discussion of this phrase in Chapter 7.

9. E.g. Barrett, *Second Epistle*, p. 294.

10. Eusebius, *Hist. Eccl.* 2.4.2 (for Philo); *Praep. Ev.* 8.8.34 (for Aristobulus).

11. J.L. Sumney, *Identifying Paul's Opponents: The Question of Method in 2 Corinthians* (JSNTSup, 4; Sheffield: Sheffield Academic Press, 1990), pp. 40-42, summarizing his discussion of five leading advocates of the Judaistic hypothesis.

12. F.C. Baur, *Paul the Apostle of Jesus Christ, His Life and Work, His Epistles and His Doctrine* (2 vols.; London: Williams and Norgate, 1876). For a perceptive analysis of Baur's approach see Sumney, *Opponents*, pp. 15-22.

13. For a discussion of the supposed parallels between 2 Cor. 10.12-18 and Gal. 2 see Chapter 9.

14. According to Schnelle, *History*, p. 91, 'on the issue of the identity of Paul's opponents a consensus is emerging, inasmuch as the opponents are mostly described as Hellenistic Jewish Christians (Furnish, Lang, Wolff), while most scholars have rejected the θεῖος ἀνήρ ("divine man") model of D. Georgi'.

2. *Scripture Exposition in Hellenistic Judaism*

If the background of Paul's opponents lay in Hellenistic Judaism, it is probable that the interpretation of Scripture played a large part in their preaching. Dieter Georgi has indicated the importance of scripture exposition in Hellenistic Jewish propaganda. He states that 'since the days of Jesus ben Sirach the Jewish sage (the actual charismatic) was essentially an interpreter of scripture',[15] and argues that Philo and Josephus were not only exegetes themselves, but depended on an established exegetical tradition.[16] In the case of Philo, James Davis estimates that almost three-quarters of Philo's work is exposition of the Torah.[17] Sirach exalts the role of the man who meditates on the law of the Most High as follows: 'if the great Lord wills, he will be filled with the spirit of understanding...he will show forth the instruction which he has been taught, and will glory in the law of the covenant of the Lord'.[18]

Scripture exposition was available in the synagogue services to both Jews and Gentiles. Philo boasts that 'each seventh day there stand wide open in every city innumerable schools of good sense, sobriety, courage, justice and the other virtues'.[19] He describes how, in the synagogue service, 'some priest who is present or one of the elders reads the holy laws to them and expounds them point by point till about the late afternoon, when they depart, having gained both expert knowledge of the holy laws and considerable advance in piety'.[20] In addition, there were travelling preachers, like the Jewess mockingly described by Juvenal:

> No sooner has that fellow departed than a palsied Jewess, leaving her basket and her truss of hay, comes begging to her secret ear; she is an interpreter of the laws of Jerusalem, a high priestess of the tree, a trusty go-between of highest heaven. She too fills her palm, but more sparingly, for a Jew will tell you dreams of any kind you please for the minutest of coins.[21]

By describing this woman as an 'interpreter of the laws of Jerusalem', Juvenal reveals how closely Judaism was associated with exposition of the law in the popular mind.

15. Georgi, *Opponents*, p. 114.
16. Georgi, *Opponents*, p. 89.
17. Davis, *Wisdom and Spirit*, p. 51.
18. Sirach 39.1, 6, 8, 10 (RV translation slightly adapted).
19. Philo, *Spec. Leg.* 2.62-63 as translated in Georgi, *Opponents*, p. 85.
20. Philo, *Hypothetica* 7.13 as translated in Georgi, *Opponents*, p. 178 n. 23.
21. Juvenal 6.542-47 as translated in Georgi, *Opponents*, p. 96.

There are three noteworthy features of the type of Hellenistic–Jewish exposition of scripture exemplified by Philo and Sirach.

a. *It was Prophetic*
Philo on four occasions depicts his exegetical activity as prophetically inspired.[22] Sirach says, 'I will pour out teaching like prophecy',[23] and describes the expositor of the Law as 'filled with the spirit of understanding'.[24]

b. *It was Syncretistic*
Aristobulus is described in 2 Macc. 1.10 as a Jew of priestly descent who was King Ptolemy's teacher. According to Eusebius, he combined Aristotelian and Jewish philosophy, and believed the law of Moses had been studied by Plato.[25] His attempt to prove the unity of Greek and Hebrew thought was continued and developed by Philo.

c. *It was Allegorical*
The literal understanding of scripture was in Hellenistic Judaism often compared unfavourably with its deeper spiritual meaning. Aristobulus, for example, commented on the fact that the Law attributes to God hands, feet and a face. When it says that God 'descended' to a mountain this is not literal because God is everywhere. In Aristobulus's view the Jewish nation was divided into two sections—the majority who followed the Law literally and those who grasped a more divine philosophy beyond the reach of the majority.[26] A development of this approach can be seen in Philo, whose attempt to show the unity of Greek and Mosaic thought relies on an allegorical interpretation of scriptural texts.[27] Philo defines various stages of understanding, ranging from the beginner (ὁ ἀρχόμενος) via the one who is making progress (ὁ προκόπτων) to the perfect wise man (ὁ τέλειος).[28] The right way to expound the Law, according to Philo, was 'to seek the hidden meaning rather than the obvious' and 'to unfold and reveal what is not known to the multitude'.[29]

22. Georgi, *Opponents*, p. 111, citing Philo, *Migr. Abr.* 34–35; *Cher.* 27; *Somn.* 2.252; *Spec. Leg.* 3.1-6.
23. Sirach 39.6.
24. Sirach 24.33.
25. Eusebius, *Praep. Ev.* 8.9; 13.11.
26. Eusebius, *Praep. Ev.* 8.9.38–8.10.18.
27. See Georgi, *Opponents*, p. 142.
28. Philo, *Leg. All.* 3.159; *Agr.* 159, 160.
29. Philo, *Dec.* 1; *Spec. Leg.* 3.6 as quoted by Davis, *Wisdom and Spirit*, pp. 50-51.

These ideas—the exposition of the Law as a Spirit-inspired, prophetic activity; the compatibility of the Mosaic law and Greek philosophy; and the deeper, spiritual meaning of the Law available to those who are 'perfect' in wisdom—would not necessarily be shared equally by all Hellenistic Jews. Nor, of course, would they necessarily be taken over *en bloc* by all Christians who came from a Hellenistic–Jewish background. A case in point is Apollos, whose warm commendation by Paul in 1 Cor. 3.5-9 makes it unlikely that he was a syncretizer in the Philonic mould. However, the exposition of the Law was of such significance in Hellenistic Judaism as a whole that it would almost inevitably have been a significant element in the ministry of Paul's opponents in 2 Corinthians. It is in 2 Cor. 3 that this becomes most obvious.[30]

3. *The Interpretation of 2 Corinthians 3*

The literature on 2 Cor. 3 is enormous and it is not possible here to consider in detail all the views that have been put forward.[31] Rather, I shall propose some general guidelines for approaching this chapter and then comment on particular points that Paul seems to be making.

a. *General Guidelines for the Interpretation of 2 Corinthians 3*
This chapter should be seen in its context. It is not an independent unit, but part of a longer section that runs from 2.14 to 4.6.[32] The section begins in 2.14-16 with the depiction of the apostolic ministry as one of humiliation and glory—the humiliation of being led like a captive in a triumphal procession and the glory of diffusing the sweet scent of God's salvation.[33] Paul then asks the question: 'Who is adequate for such a ministry?', and

30. In discussing 2 Cor. 3 I shall assume that Paul has the same opponents in mind as in chs. 10–13. Reasons for this assumption can be found in Chapter 4 (which argues for the unity of 2 Corinthians), and also in the writings of scholars such as Georgi and Furnish who believe 2 Corinthians to be composite (Georgi, *Opponents*, pp. 9-14; Furnish, *II Corinthians*, pp. 50-51).

31. A careful and balanced survey can be found in Thrall, *Second Epistle*, pp. 217-97. Her conclusions are on pp. 296-97.

32. This is emphasized by T.E. Provence, ' "Who is sufficient for these things?" An Exegesis of 2 Corinthians ii.15–iii.18', *NovT* 24 (1982), pp. 54-81 (57). He points out that 4.1-6 picks up the themes of 2.16-17 and of ch. 3, and quotes the comment of Plummer (*Second Epistle*, p. 109) that the division of chapters between 3 and 4 was 'unintelligently made'.

33. For further discussion of this passage see Chapter 7.

offers two possible answers. Is it the majority (οἱ πολλοί), who preach for money and adulterate the word of God?[34] Or is it himself and his colleagues, whose ministry is sincere and God-centred? (2.16-18).[35]

The comparison between two types of ministry is continued in ch. 3. The chapter begins with a reference to τινες (some people—Paul's favourite way of referring to his opponents), who carried with them letters of commendation from other churches, and seem to have criticized Paul for not having such letters. In reply, Paul affirms the credentials of himself and his colleagues as people equipped and blessed by God (vv. 1-5). He then contrasts their ministry (a ministry of the Spirit and of the new covenant) with another type of ministry that brings death and condemnation (vv. 6-11). Given the argumentative nature of the context, it is probable that the ministry of death and condemnation does not only denote the ministry of Moses, but also has in mind the ministry of Paul's opponents—of the people alluded to in v. 1 as τινες, and in 2.17 as οἱ πολλοί.

The various allusions to two styles of ministry in 2.14–3.11 may be combined into a single picture. On the one hand there were Paul and his colleagues. On the other hand there were preachers who had come from elsewhere bearing letters of commendation. These preachers, like the sophists, charged fees to their disciples; the 'word of God' which, in Paul's view, they both marketed and adulterated was the Mosaic Torah; and it was their exposition of the Torah which, Paul believed, led their hearers into death and condemnation.

In the latter half of ch. 3 (vv. 12-17) Paul uses the veil worn by Moses as a symbol of the deficiencies of the ministry of Moses and, by implication, of the 'Mosaic' ministry of the incomers. The implied contrast is between the hiddenness, impermanence and blindness characteristic of 'Mosaic' ministry and the brightness and ever-increasing glory of the ministry of Paul and his colleagues. This comparison is continued in 4.1-6, where the openness and sincerity of the ministry of Paul and his colleagues is implicitly contrasted with the hiddenness and deceitfulness of the ministry of his opponents.[36]

---

34. Καπηλεύω in 2.17 is closely related in meaning to δολόω in 4.2 (see H. Windisch in *TDNT*, III [1965], pp. 603-605; Barrett, *Second Epistle*, pp. 103, 128; Provence, 'Exegesis', pp. 58-59). But in the case of καπηλεύω the implication of adulteration is attached to the basic meaning of trading for profit.

35. In my opinion 'we' in 2 Corinthians usually means 'I and my apostolic colleagues'. For arguments in favour of this opinion see Chapter 4.

36. It is arguable that the negatives of 4.2 are purely apologetic—i.e. that Paul is

As can be seen from this summary, the whole section 2.14–4.6 is controversial. It combines apologetic and polemic. It is apologetic in that Paul's style of ministry was being attacked and he had to defend it. It is polemical in that attack is often the best form of defence, and from time to time Paul makes thinly veiled criticism of his opponents as mercenary and deceitful.[37]

One cannot distinguish between apologetic and polemic in such a situation. A prominent feature of the ministry of Paul's opponents was σύγκρισις —comparing themselves with others (10.12). Their comparison of their own ministry with that of Paul and his colleagues involved both the claim that they were adequate (equipped for the job) and the claim that Paul and his colleagues were inadequate. Correspondingly, Paul's reply combines both a statement of the adequacy of his colleagues and himself and allusions to the inadequacy of his opponents. In addition, this section is didactic, since Paul believed that exposition of the glory of the apostolic ministry was the best antidote to rival conceptions of ministry.

Attempts are sometimes made to categorize this passage too narrowly as either apologetic or polemical or didactic. Sumney, for example, argues that 3.7-18 is didactic, in that 'it springs from comments of Paul rather than from accusations or teaching of opponents'.[38] Similarly, C.J.A. Hickling comments that 'we frustrate Paul's intention in writing [2 Cor. 3] when we read into such superb expository theology a limited aim of locally directed polemic'.[39] Such statements are only partially true. Hickling is right to condemn the view of Georgi and others that Paul is here replying point by

simply defending himself against the charge of being deceitful. But two factors make this improbable. One is the close similarity of thought between 4.2 and 2.17 (which is clearly polemical). The other is the contrast running throughout 2.17–3.18 between two groups of people (οἱ πολλοί and τινες on the one hand; Paul and his colleagues on the other hand) and between two types of ministry (of the letter and of condemnation on the one hand; of the Spirit and of justification on the other hand). These two factors make it probable that in 4.2 also Paul is contrasting the openness of the ministry of his colleagues and himself with the secrecy and deceitfulness of the ministry of his opponents.

37. Furnish (*II Corinthians*, p. 243) describes 3.7-18 as 'theological exposition with a polemical edge'.

38. Sumney, *Opponents*, p. 142. Thrall (*Second Epistle*, p. 239) comments on 3.7-18 that 'Paul's aim is apologetic rather than polemical'.

39. C.J.A. Hickling, 'Is the Second Epistle to the Corinthians a Source for Early Church History?', *ZNW* 66 (1975), pp. 284-87 (286).

point to a document produced by his opponents.[40] But in a broader sense most of 2 Corinthians is 'locally directed polemic'. One of Paul's greatest gifts was his ability to relate his 'superb expository theology' to the needs of a local church. As v. 18 illustrates, he could see the glory of God shining in the midst of the confusions and competing ideologies of the Corinthian situation.

The figure of Moses appears in this chapter purely as the mediator of the Law. There is no suggestion that Moses was seen as a 'divine man' (θεῖος ἀνήρ). Dieter Georgi regards the concept of the 'divine man' as crucial to the understanding of this chapter, but his theory has rightly been called into question by other scholars.[41] In Morna Hooker's words, 'it has been well said that there are far more references to the figure of a "divine man" in the pages of modern scholarship than in all the pages of antiquity'.[42] A decisive argument against understanding Moses as a 'divine man' is the reference in v. 15 to Moses being read aloud. One cannot talk about a divine man being read aloud. Moses is a personification of the Law of which he was the mediator. The contrast Paul is drawing is between the ministers of the old covenant (Moses and his later disciples) on the one hand and the ministers of the new covenant (Paul and his colleagues) on the other hand.

Paul's argument is not systematic. This is true both of his attempt to combine the metaphors of writing a letter and of writing on stone in vv. 1-3 and of his exposition of Moses' veil in vv. 12-18. In the latter passage his argument resembles a modern sermon based on a biblical text which elicits from the text three points, all related to the text, but not closely related to each other. Paul takes as his text the account in Exod. 34 of the veil with which Moses covered his face. He uses this account to make a series of points, each of which has its own independent validity. Morna Hooker has commented on the unsystematic nature of Paul's procedure:

> From our point of view, his exposition is inconsistent. His arguments do not
> stand up logically, and he juxtaposes conflicting images and interpretations

---

40. Georgi, *Opponents*, pp. 258-82. Arguments against Georgi's theory can be found in Furnish, *II Corinthians*, pp. 242-45; Martin, *2 Corinthians*, p. 58; Thrall, *Second Epistle*, pp. 258-61, 296.

41. Georgi, *Opponents*, passim. The most important critique of Georgi's position can be found in C.R. Holladay, *Theios Aner in Hellenistic Judaism: A Critique of the Use of this Category in New Testament Christology* (SBLDS, 40; Missoula, MT: Scholars Press, 1977).

42. M.D. Hooker, *Pauline Pieces* (London: Epworth, 1979), p. 59.

of the biblical text. Yet I have no doubt whatever that from his point of view, Paul's argument seemed proper and acceptable. He is, after all, using a well-known method of biblical exegesis [sc. *midrash pesher*]... The fact that in a single passage he can develop a clear line of argument and at the same time apparently tie himself in knots, can combine several images into a mixed metaphor, and apply one image in several different ways, is a salutary reminder that one should not try to force Paul into the straitjacket of a systematic theologian.[43]

b. *Particular Emphases in 2 Cor. 3*

i. *Letter and Spirit.* As we have seen, the theory that Paul's opponents were legalists does not stand up to examination. The question therefore arises, in what way could they have been teaching the law that was different from the kind of legalism combatted in Galatians?

The phrase τὸ γράμμα ἀποκτείνει (the written text kills; 3.6) resembles the reference in Romans 7 to the commandment that leads to death (v. 10), and the contrast in that chapter between 'newness of the Spirit' (καινότης πνεύματος) and 'oldness of the letter' (παλαιότης γράμματος) (v. 6). In the interpretation of both passages it is often stated that, for Paul, γράμμα does not mean the Law itself but a particular way of interpreting the Law. Käsemann argues that in 2 Cor. 3.6 γράμμα does not mean the Mosaic Torah but law as it has been perverted by Jewish interpretation into a demand for good works.[44] In similar vein Cranfield maintains that in Rom. 7 τὸ γράμμα is what the legalist is left with as a result of his misunderstanding and misuse of the law: it is the letter of the law in separation from the Spirit.[45] There are two reasons why this view should be rejected.

First, the fact that, in Paul's thinking, the Law is spiritual and holy (Rom.

43. M.D. Hooker, 'Beyond the Things that are Written? St. Paul's Use of Scripture', *NTS* 27 (1980–81), pp. 295-309 (304-305). Cf. Thrall's comment (*Second Epistle*, p. 268) on Paul's use of the imagery of the veil: 'There is no reason why Paul himself should not have employed one basic image in various ways'.

44. E. Käsemann, 'The Spirit and the Letter', in *idem* (ed.), *Perspectives on Paul* (Philadelphia: Fortress Press, 1971), pp. 138-66. Furnish (*II Corinthians*, p. 200) follows Käsemann, and states that Paul rejects not the law itself, but 'that way of using the law which presumes that the "letter" provides a sure way to righteousness and life'. Cf. Collange, *Enigmes*, p. 64: 'Γράμμα désigne l'Ecriture prise comme objet religieux, si l'on veut, péjorativement, la Thora petrifié'.

45. Cranfield, *Romans*, I, pp. 339-40, followed by Martin, *2 Corinthians*, p. 55.

7.12, 14) does not mean, as is often asserted,[46] that it cannot also be a letter that kills. In Rom. 7 the same ἐντολή (commandment) that leads people to death in v. 10 is described in v. 12 as 'holy and just and good'. This is the dilemma that Paul faces in v. 13: how can something good lead people into death? His solution is that the Law is the agent of death but not its cause (which is sin).

Second, the argument of Rom. 7 is not concerned with legalism. Paul describes himself in that chapter not as self-righteous but as defeated and despairing. The theme of Rom. 7.14-25 is summarized in 8.3: 'the power-lessness of the Law, because human nature made it ineffective' (τὸ... ἀδύνατον τοῦ νόμου, ἐν ᾧ ἠσθένει διὰ τῆς σαρκός). Paul illustrates this powerlessness not from the commands that a legalist could claim to have kept but from the tenth commandment: 'you shall not desire what belongs to your neighbour'. This commandment does not have the power to produce the behaviour it demands. As a result, devoted believers, delighting in the law of God in their innermost being (v. 22), are led into self-condemnation and despair. But 'those who are in Christ Jesus' have found the antidote to this experience. Because of the cross they know they are not condemned (8.1-3); and the Holy Spirit gives them a new attitude of mind (φρόνημα) that enables them to please God (8.6-9).

There is no trace in all this of the battle with legalism and salvation by works that has featured so largely in Protestant theology. The point at issue is not whether the Law brings salvation, but whether it can empower the believer who is already saved to do what it commands. The ability to please God, according to Paul, cannot come from external commands but only through the internal working of the Holy Spirit. Similarly, in 2 Cor. 3 it is the external, objective nature of the Law that Paul emphasizes by calling it γράμμα and by referring in v. 3 to tablets of stone. As Stephen Westerholm says, γράμμα denotes 'the law of God in its written form, made up of concrete commands'.[47]

In 2 Cor. 3.3-11 Paul contrasts two covenants and the ministers of those covenants. Moses was the minister of a covenant based on a written code, that was 'powerless to produce the behaviour it enjoined'.[48] Paul and his

---

46. Provence, 'Exegesis', p. 64; Cranfield, *Romans*, I, p. 339; Furnish, *II Corinthians*, p. 200.

47. S. Westerholm, 'Letter and Spirit: The Foundation of Pauline Ethics', *NTS* 30 (1984), pp. 229-48 (241).

48. Thrall, *Second Epistle*, p. 235, following E. Kamlah, 'Buchstabe und Geist', *EvT* 14 (1954), pp. 276-82 (278).

colleagues are ministers of a new covenant, a 'ministry of the Spirit' (v. 8). In drawing this contrast, Paul uses language drawn from Old Testament prophecy. Verse 3 echoes Ezek. 11.19; 36.26, where God promises to remove from the people their heart of stone and give them a heart of flesh. Verse 6 echoes the words of Jer. 31.33, where God promises to replace the old covenant, which the people broke, with a new covenant in which God's law will be written on the heart. The difference between the ministers of the two covenants is then portrayed as a logical consequence of the difference between the covenants themselves. The ministry of the old covenant was glorious, and made the face of Moses shine with a fading splendour; but the ministry of the new covenant is even more glorious, and its ministers shine with a permanent and greater splendour.

Why did Paul draw this contrast? His concern was that the 'adequacy' (ἱκανότης) of his colleagues and himself had been called into question by practitioners of a rival style of ministry, whose main emphasis lay on exposition of the Law. Their exposition cannot have demanded literal obedience to the Law, such as observation of circumcision and the food laws. If it had, Paul's reply would have been very different, and more similar to his argument in Galatians. Their exposition must have demanded obedience to the Law in a non-literal and allegorical sense, such as one would expect from Christians with a Hellenistic–Jewish background.[49] Such teaching would lead to death and condemnation just as much as a literal understanding of the Law, since in both cases pressure would be put on the believer to conform to an external code, as interpreted by the pressurizer.[50]

Little can be deduced from this chapter about the doctrinal and ethical content of the opponents' teaching. Allegorical exegesis can be used to justify virtually any interpretation of the text. All we can gather from 2 Cor. 3 is that Paul's opponents were claiming the authority of Moses for their exegesis of the Mosaic Torah. The details of that exegesis must be deduced from the Corinthian correspondence as a whole.

ii. *Veiled and Unveiled.* In 3.12-18 Paul interprets the image of the veil in three ways. First, the veil is a symbol of secrecy. By using a veil Moses hid the divine glory from the people. In v. 12 Paul contrasts this secrecy

49. Sumney (*Opponents*, p. 155) asserts that Jews could claim a special competence as teachers whatever the nature of their teaching, and that the reference to Jewishness in 2 Cor. 11.21-23 does not imply Paul's opponents were Judaizers.

50. Cf. the examples in 1 Corinthians of pressure (ἀνάγκη) by Paul's opponents, discussed in Chapter 7.

with the openness (παρρησία) of himself and his colleagues.[51] The same theme is made explicit in 4.2: 'We have renounced shameful secrecy (τὰ κρυπτὰ τῆς αἰσχύνης). We do not behave craftily or adulterate the word of God, but by revealing the truth openly (τῇ φανερώσει τῆς ἀληθείας) we commend ourselves to everyone's sense of right and wrong in the presence of God'.[52] The adulteration of the word of God is here associated with secrecy, whereas in 2.17 it was associated with commercialism. This combination of secrecy and commercialism suggests that Paul's opponents were like sophists, revealing their message only to those who could afford to pay.

Second, the veil is a symbol of blindness. The person who is veiled is unable to see. It is in this sense that Paul talks of a veil lying on the minds and hearts of contemporary Jewish people when the law is read aloud in their synagogues (v. 15). The veil symbolizes their inability to see Christ, in whom the law finds its fulfilment. This idea is made explicit in 4.4: 'In their case the god of this world has blinded their unbelieving minds, so that they are not illuminated by the shining of the gospel of the glory of Christ, who is the image of God'.

Why does Paul single out the Jews in 3.15 as the ones who are unable to see the glory of Christ?[53] The explanation may perhaps be found in Paul's

51. The word παρρησία has three meanings in the New Testament according to BAGD: (i) outspokenness, frankness; (ii) openness to the public; (iii) courage, confidence, fearlessness. The context of 2 Cor. 3.12 suggests that the emphasis here lies on the openness of Paul's preaching.

52. The word συνείδησις is sometimes translated more generally as 'consciousness' or 'self-awareness'. But Paul seems to use the word specifically to refer to moral consciousness—to a sense of right and wrong. A revealing verse is 1 Cor. 4.4 οὐδὲν γὰρ ἐμαυτῷ σύνοιδα (σύνοιδα being the verbal form of συνείδησις). This does not mean 'I am not aware of myself', but 'I know nothing against myself'. For an overview of the various interpretations of συνείδησις in Paul see Thiselton, *First Epistle*, pp. 640-44.

53. Hickling ('Sequence of Thought', p. 393) offers two explanations for Paul's emphasis on Jewish unbelief. First, he states that this issue was of such importance to Paul that he would be bound to think of it in any discussion of the Mosaic covenant. This is not a sufficient explanation. Although Paul was fond of digressions, his digressions usually consisted of matters he wanted to raise anyway. The question must still be asked, why did he wish to raise this issue at this point? If he was engaged in a battle for the minds of the Corinthians against opponents who regarded their Jewish birth as a guarantee of orthodoxy, this would explain his introduction of this issue more convincingly than an appeal to automatic reflexes.

Second, Hickling suggests that Paul's failure to convert a significant number of his

statement that the veiling of the minds of the Jewish people occurs 'when Moses is read aloud' (v. 15). Such a statement would have added significance if Paul's opponents were claiming that, because they were 'Hebrews', they were especially competent to expound the scriptures. Paul would then be replying to this claim by asserting that the Jews of his day were in fact not able to see the true meaning of scripture; it was those who had seen 'the glory of God in the face of Jesus Christ' (4.6), whether Jews or Gentiles, for whom the veil had been taken away. They alone could see the glory of the Lord and reflect it in their own lives (3.18).

Third, Paul sees in the veil a pointer to the impermanence of the old dispensation. The glory that Moses concealed from the people was a fading glory.[54] Paul sees the fading glory on Moses' face as symbolic of the fading away of the Mosaic covenant.[55]

There is no suggestion in Paul's exposition that Moses was being deceitful in trying to hide his fading glory from the people. According to v. 7 the giving of the law was accompanied by radiance, ὥστε μὴ δύνασθαι ἀτενίσαι τοὺς υἱοὺς Ἰσραὴλ εἰς τὸ πρόσωπον Μωϋσέως διὰ τὴν

---

fellow Jews may have been used by his opponents to attack his reputation. This is possible, though hypothetical. In 4.3 Paul does seem to be conceding to the opposition the point that his gospel is 'veiled' to some people. However, in 4.3-4 the people from whom his preaching is veiled are not Jews in particular, but unbelievers in general.

54. According to S.J. Hafemann ('Paul's Argument from the Old Testament and Christology in 2 Cor. 1–9', in R. Bieringer [ed.], *The Corinthian Correspondence* [Leuven: Leuven University Press, 1996], pp. 277-303 [288]), καταργεῖσθαι cannot mean 'to fade', but in Paul's letters always means 'to be rendered inoperative, to be nullified'. But the purpose of δόξα is to shine and it becomes inoperative when it ceases to shine—i.e. when it fades. In other words, the word καταργεῖσθαι implies fading when used with a noun that refers to shining, but not when used with a noun such as νόμος.

55. It is sometimes stated that Paul was misinterpreting the Exodus narrative, in that there is no mention in that narrative of a fading glory. Furnish, for example, asserts that 'there is no basis for this in the text of Exod. 34' (*II Corinthians*, p. 227). But vv. 34-35 of Exod. 34 state that, whenever Moses returned from speaking with the Lord, the children of Israel saw that his face was shining. The implication is that it was the time spent with the Lord that caused the shining, and that this experience was renewed on each occasion. If the radiance had been permanent, as some Jewish commentators have maintained, there would have been no need for its renewal. The fading of the radiance during the time of veiling is thus implicit in the narrative, and is not, as Thrall says, an idea that it is 'just possible to detect' with 'some degree of ingenuity' (Thrall, *Second Epistle*, p. 243). For details of Jewish commentaries see Thrall, *Second Epistle*, p. 244 n. 365.

δόξαν τοῦ προσώπου αὐτοῦ τὴν καταργουμένην (so that it was impossible for the sons of Israel to gaze on the face of Moses because of the brightness of his face that was fading away). In this clause, the reason why the children of Israel could not gaze at the face of Moses was that his face was too bright, not that the brightness was fading. The words τὴν καταργουμένην were added by Paul as a kind of footnote, and can be paraphrased 'even though it was a fading glory'.[56] These words are a *comment* on the inability of the people to gaze, not an explanation.[57] It is therefore reasonable to interpret v. 13 in the same way. The words τὸ τέλος τοῦ καταργουμένου (the end of something that was ceasing to be effective) are a *comment* on the brightness of Moses' face, not an explanation of Moses' psychology. The clause may be paraphrased: 'Moses put a veil over his face, so that the Israelites should not gaze at what was in fact the tail-end of a fading glory'.

Exodus 34 does not supply any reason for Moses' action. If Paul thought about the matter at all, he may, as Hickling suggests, have thought of Moses' motive as reverential.[58] Be that as it may, his concern in 2 Cor. 3 is not with Moses' psychology, but with the inferiority of the old covenant, of which the fading glory was a symbol.

Why does Paul emphasize the impermanence and fading glory of the old covenant? His description of his opponents in chs. 10–13 probably provides the answer to this question. These opponents boasted of their Jewish birth (11.22). As we have seen, this boast probably involved a claim to expertise in expounding the Law, which they did in such a way as to preach what in Paul's view was a different Jesus and a different gospel (11.4). In reply to their claim, Paul insists that the old covenant with its written code was temporary and impermanent and has been superseded by the new covenant of the Spirit. It is only those who have seen the glory of

---

56. NIV: 'fading though it was' is better than NEB: 'though it was soon to fade'. καραργουμένην is a *present* participle. Paul's point is that the radiance on the face of Moses was already beginning to lose its effectiveness, though it was still too bright to be gazed at.

57. Furnish translates v. 7: 'the Israelites could not bear to gaze at Moses' face— because the splendor of his face was being annulled' (*II Corinthians*, p. 201). But δύνασθαι means 'were not able to', not 'could not bear to'. The impermanence of the splendour cannot be the factor that made it impossible to gaze at.

58. Hickling, 'Sequence of Thought', p. 390, following H. Windisch, *Der zweite Korintherbrief* (MeyerK, 6; Göttingen: Vandenhoeck & Ruprecht, 9th edn, 1924), p. 119: 'die δόξα nicht zu profanieren'.

God in the face of Jesus Christ, whether they be Jews or Gentiles, who can properly understand and expound it.

4. *Paul's Opponents in 1 Corinthians*

In 1 Corinthians Paul does not refer directly to his opponents but uses impersonal terms such as τις and τινες (3.12-15; 4.18; 11.16; 14.37-38; 15.34). The only way to determine the background of these opponents is to look for clues in the ideas Paul attacks. Throughout the letter he is combatting the 'wisdom' taught by the party leaders. He pictures them as builders, erecting a superstructure of wood, hay and stubble on the foundation he laid, and as pedagogues, self-appointed ethical guides to their Corinthian pupils. It is therefore reasonable to deduce from the ideas currently in vogue in the Corinthian church the nature of the wisdom imparted by their new teachers, and its probable background.

A number of scholars have attributed the ideas current at Corinth to the influence of Hellenistic Judaism. Richard Horsley, for example, describes how Philo and the Hellenistic Jewish tradition he represented had assimilated Greek philosophical ideas and understood them as 'expressions of the true (Jewish) relation to God, as taught in the sacred writings of Moses'.[59] He believes many words appearing in 1 Corinthians, such as τέλειος (perfect or mature), νήπιος (a small child), εὐγενής (noble), βασιλεύς (king) and πλούσιος (rich), to be terms common in popular philosophy which Hellenistic Jews such as Philo had appropriated.[60] James Davis has emphasized the many parallels between Philo and Sirach on the one hand and Paul's arguments (and the situation at Corinth his arguments presuppose) on the other hand.[61]

Not everyone agrees in seeing Hellenistic Judaism as the primary source of the beliefs of the Corinthian Christians. Fee points out that in 1.22 Paul regards the quest for wisdom as a Greek quest, contrasting it with the Jewish demand for miraculous signs. He argues that 'if Paul is attacking a

59. R.A. Horsley, 'Consciousness and Freedom among the Corinthians: 1 Corinthians 8–10', *CBQ* 40 (1978), pp. 574-89 (581).

60. R.A. Horsley, 'Wisdom of Word and Words of Wisdom in Corinth', *CBQ* 39 (1977), pp. 224-39 (233-34), esp. 234 n. 23. Horsley points out that Philo uses such language both in a literal, social sense and also in a spiritual sense. Thus both Paul's use of εὐγενής in its literal, social sense in 1 Cor. 1.26 and his use of βασιλεύω and πλουτέω in a spiritual sense in 1 Cor. 4.8 have parallels in Philo.

61. Davis, *Wisdom and Spirit*, passim.

form of Hellenized Judaism, it is most perceptible as Hellenism, not Judaism'.[62] Similarly, John Barclay asserts that many of the Philonic parallels to 1 Corinthians are in passages that borrow from Stoic or Platonic philosophy and are not unique to Hellenistic Judaism. He also thinks that the 'Jewish' features of Corinthian theology, such as the oneness of God and the nothingness of idols, could have been derived equally well from Paul's teaching or study of the Septuagint, and that the Corinthian reliance on the inspiration of the Spirit could have led to the forging of new language not derived from anywhere.[63]

What these objections show is that the link with Hellenistic Judaism is not proven, and that each element in the Corinthian beliefs, taken by itself, could be derived from another source. However, the combination of ideas at Corinth is so closely paralleled in Philo that Hellenistic Judaism remains a very probable background, particularly if this is confirmed by other factors. If the thesis of this book is correct, and the opponents Paul attacks in 2 Cor. 10–13 were already at work in Corinth at the time of the writing of 1 Corinthians, the influence of Hellenistic Judaism becomes very probable. Those opponents were certainly Jews (2 Cor. 11.22) and probably came from a Hellenistic background. Though the evidence of 1 Corinthians does not conclusively demonstrate the Hellenistic–Jewish background of these opponents, it fits in well with that hypothesis.

Evidence of the influence of Greek philosophy is easy to find in 1 Corinthians. A good example is the word ἀπερισπάστως (without distraction) in 7.35, a word that was frequently used in philosophical discussions about the comparative advantages of marriage and celibacy.[64] But there are also two verses that may suggest a Jewish element in the background to that letter—1.20 and 4.6.

In 1.20 Paul writes: ποῦ σοφός; ποῦ γραμματεύς; ποῦ συζητητὴς τοῦ κόσμου τούτου; (Where is the wise man? Where is the scribe? Where is the debater of this world?). It has often been pointed out that the meaning of γραμματεύς in Hellenistic Greek was 'secretary' or 'clerk'—a meaning that is not appropriate to the context of this verse.[65] In first-

---

62. Fee, *First Epistle*, p. 14 n. 36.

63. Barclay, 'Thessalonica and Corinth', pp. 64-65.

64. D.L. Balch, '1 Cor. 7.32-35 and Stoic Debates about Marriage, Anxiety and Distraction', *JBL* 102/3 (1983), pp. 429-39.

65. Thiselton (*First Epistle*, pp. 163-64) tries to combine the Jewish and the Greek meanings with the translation 'person of letters' or 'expert'. But this does justice to neither culture. A secretary or clerk is not normally regarded as a teacher of wisdom,

century Judaism, on the other hand, γραμματεύς denoted an expert in, or teacher of, the Mosaic law, who would be regarded as a wise man in Jewish circles.⁶⁶ The rare word συζητητής probably denotes a debater—one who engages in the philosophical and rhetorical debates which were a popular feature of Hellenistic culture. In combining these two words, Paul's aim seems to be to bring all forms of human wisdom under God's judgment, including both Jewish exposition of the law and Greek philosophy and rhetoric.⁶⁷

It is possible that, in combining these two forms of wisdom, Paul was making an abstract generalization; but it may well be that his words reflected the Corinthian situation. Their relevance becomes obvious if the teachers he was opposing were Hellenistic–Jewish Christians, who claimed for themselves both expertise in expounding the law and expertise in rhetoric.

The other verse that may suggest a Jewish background is 4.6. In this verse Paul explains why he has alluded to the party leaders only indirectly, through the example of himself and Apollos. He has done this 'so that you may learn through our example the meaning of the saying "not beyond what is written"' (ἵνα ἐν ἡμῖν μάθητε τὸ μὴ ὑπὲρ ἃ γέγραπται). There has been much debate about the interpretation of the phrase 'not beyond what is written', and its origin remains a mystery.⁶⁸ It could be a phrase

and the Jewish teacher of the law had a much more specific role than the generalized 'person of letters'.

66. See BAGD sv. γραμματεύς; Fee, *First Epistle*, p. 71; Thiselton, *First Epistle*, p. 164.

67. Fee (*First Epistle*, pp. 70-71) regards σοφός as a reference to Greek philosophers, and thinks that in the two terms σοφός and γραμματεύς Paul 'is anticipating the distinctions of v. 22, where the Jews demand signs and the Greeks ask for wisdom'. He does, however, recognize the possibility that σοφός could be a general term, and γραμματεύς and συζητητής more specific.

The fact that in v. 22 the Greeks are singled out as seekers after wisdom does not necessarily mean that the word σοφός in v. 20 should be limited to Greeks. Verse 20 is a comment on the Old Testament quotation in v. 19, in which Isaiah is probably referring to the Jewish wise men at the court of Hezekiah (see Thiselton, *First Epistle*, pp. 159-62 on the background to v. 19).

68. The fact that the origin of a saying is unknown to us does not mean it was unknown to the Corinthians. There is no justification for the astonishing statement of J. Murphy-O'Connor that J. Strugnell 'has raised the hypothesis of a gloss [in 1 Cor. 4.6] to the level of certitude' (J. Murphy-O'Connor, 'Interpolations in 1 Corinthians', *CBQ* 48 [1986], pp. 81-94 [85], following J. Strugnell, 'A Plea for Conjectural Emendation in the NT, with a Coda on 1 Cor. 4.6', *CBQ* 36 [1974], pp. 543-58 [555-58]).

used by Paul to characterize his preaching (cf. Acts 26.22-23), or a phrase used by his opponents to characterize their preaching, or a Pauline saying adopted by the Corinthians to indicate that they were being faithful to his teaching (cf. 1 Cor. 11.2).[69] Whichever of these possibilities is correct, the phrase must have been well known to the Corinthians—τό is a definite article, referring to a known entity.[70]

The meaning of γέγραπται is easier to determine. In all its 30 other Pauline occurrences it refers to the Old Testament. As Schrage says, 'it is generally agreed today that this is a reference to the Old Testament scriptures, to which γέγραπται refers in all its other occurrences'.[71] The plural ἅ suggests that it is scripture in general Paul has in mind, not any one particular text.[72] He seems to be drawing a contrast between partisan

Strugnell's theory is that τὸ μὴ ὑπὲρ ἃ γέγραπται is a comment by a scribe who has emended the manuscript, and means: 'the μή [that I have just added] is beyond what is written [in the manuscript]'. This is implausible. Scribes do not make that sort of comment; and the use of τό with whole sentences and clauses is a well-documented Greek idiom (see the examples cited in BAGD sv. ὁ, 2h and LSJ sv. ὁ, B5).

69. 1 Cor. 11.2 is commonly, and probably rightly, understood to be a quotation of a Corinthian claim that they were being faithful to Paul's tradition. For further discussion of this verse see Excursus F.

70. Contra Barrett (*First Epistle*, p. 106), who suggests that the saying quoted 'was not necessarily current at Corinth'.

71. Schrage, *Der erste Brief*, I, pp. 334-35.

72. Marshall (*Enmity*, p. 202) sees in τὸ μὴ ὑπὲρ ἃ γέγραπται a counsel for moderation, a warning against behaving excessively or being a ὑβριστής. But 'the scriptures' (ἃ γέγραπται) denote a lot more than the teaching of moderation. It is the attitude of his opponents to scripture as a whole that Paul rejects.

The same objection applies to the attempt of J.R. Wagner ('Not Beyond the Things that are Written: A Call to Boast Only in the Lord', *NTS* 44 [1998], pp. 279-87) to limit the application of 'what is written' to one quotation only: 'let him who boasts boast of the Lord'. The word ἃ is plural—ἃ γέγραπται is not the same as τὸ γεγραμμένον.

Welborn ('Discord', p. 109) thinks the phrase refers to the need to be law-abiding, and cites the appeals to abide by the law made by ancient Greek opponents of civil strife. For γέγραπται in this sense he quotes an inscription in which the newly reconciled inhabitants of Magnesia and Smyrna swear as follows: 'I will not transgress the agreement nor will I change for the worse the things that are written in it...and I will live in concord and without faction' (καὶ οὐθὲν παραβήσομαι κατὰ τὴν ὁμολογίαν οὐδὲ μεταθήσω ἐπὶ τὸ χεῖρον τὰ γεγραμμένα ἐν αὐτῇ...καὶ πολιτεύσομαι μεθ' ὁμονοίας ἀστασιάστως) (OGIS, p. 229). But in that inscription the words ἐν αὐτῇ specify the particular 'scripture' that is to be obeyed. Where the phrase ἃ γέγραπται is used absolutely, as in 1 Cor. 4.6, it can only denote the Old Testament scripture in general.

support of rival preachers on the one hand and faithfulness to the scriptures on the other hand. If the preachers concerned were Hellenistic–Jewish Christian expositors of scripture, the relevance of the saying becomes clear. Paul considered them to be, not exegetes, but eisegetes, who were introducing under the guise of allegorical exposition ideas that went beyond the plain meaning of the text. In his opinion the eloquence of these eisegetes had beguiled the Corinthians and led to the kind of sophistic competition that he deplored in 1.10-17. This interpretation is conjectural, like all the other interpretations.[73] But it makes good sense of the verse in its context.

---

73. For example, Hooker ('Scripture', pp. 295-96) understands the element of eisegesis to be philosophical notions, while Goulder ('Σοφία', p. 526) understands it to be Jewish words of wisdom. Hellenistic–Jewish Christian teaching could combine both these elements.

Chapter 7

THE TEACHING OF PAUL'S OPPONENTS

The key verse for understanding the teaching of Paul's opponents is 2 Cor. 11.4: εἰ μὲν γὰρ ὁ ἐρχόμενος ἄλλον Ἰησοῦν κηρύσσει, ὃν οὐκ ἐκηρύξαμεν, ἢ πνεῦμα ἕτερον λαμβάνετε ὃ οὐκ ἐλάβετε, ἢ εὐαγγέλιον ἕτερον ὃ οὐκ ἐδέξασθε, καλῶς ἀνέχεσθε (for if someone comes and preaches a different Jesus whom we did not preach, or you receive a different Spirit which you did not receive or a different gospel which you did not accept, you put up with it in fine style).[1] R.P. Martin describes this verse as 'arguably...the most important, explicit—and discussed—verse in the entire four chapter section (10–13)', and quotes E. Käsemann's judgment that this verse is a key to understanding Paul's opponents in those chapters.[2]

In the opinion of Martin and Käsemann, Paul is here facing a new situation, brought about by people who had only recently arrived in Corinth. In this chapter I shall seek to show that this opinion is mistaken: Paul refers in 11.4 to some of the main themes of 1 Corinthians, and his words could almost be regarded as a summary of his argument in the earlier letter.

Before examining the three phrases 'another Jesus', 'another Spirit' and 'another gospel', three points need to be made about the context in which they occur.

The first point is the meaning of the phrase ὁ ἐρχόμενος. Barrett (followed by Martin) takes the fact that this phrase is in the singular to indicate an individual, the ringleader of the intruders.[3] But throughout 1 and 2 Corinthians Paul regularly refers to his opponents collectively with words and phrases in the singular. The most striking example is 2 Cor. 11.21-22: ἐν ᾧ δ' ἄν τις τολμᾷ...τολμῶ κἀγώ. Ἑβραῖοί εἰσιν; κἀγώ.

---

1. As Martin says (*2 Corinthians*, p. 336), citing Turner, *Syntax*, p. 197, there is no vital distinction between ἄλλος and ἕτερος; both adjectives mean 'different'.
2. Martin, *2 Corinthians*, p. 334, quoting Käsemann, 'Legitimität', p. 37.
3. Barrett, *Second Epistle*, p. 275; Martin, *2 Corinthians*, p. 335.

Ἰσραηλῖταί εἰσιν; κἀγώ (Whatever gives someone confidence gives me confidence too. Are they Hebrews? So am I. Are they Israelites? So am I). Here the singular τις (someone) clearly refers to the same people as the plurals Ἑβραῖοι and Ἰσραηλῖται. A similar case is 1 Cor. 3.10: θεμέλιον ἔθηκα, ἄλλος δὲ ἐποικοδομεῖ. ἕκαστος δὲ βλεπέτω πῶς ἐποικοδομεῖ (I laid a foundation and someone else is building on it. But each one should be careful how he builds). Here ἕκαστος (each one) indicates that Paul has a number of builders in mind, and the preceding ἄλλος, though singular, cannot denote a single individual. We should therefore follow the judgment of Furnish and most commentators that ὁ ἐρχόμενος should be interpreted generically to mean 'anyone who comes'.[4]

The second point is the aorist tense of ἐκηρύξαμεν, ἐλάβετε and ἐδέξασθε. As J. Murphy-O'Connor says, these aorists refer to the time when Paul converted the Corinthians.[5] Paul is contrasting the teaching of the incomers with his own teaching during his initial visit to Corinth. There is a close parallel to this verse in 1 Corinthians 1–2, where he draws a similar contrast. He declares that Christ commissioned him to preach the gospel (εὐαγγελίζεσθαι), and to avoid wisdom of words, so that the cross should not be robbed of its effectiveness (1.17). Therefore, when he visited Corinth, he did not use 'persuasive words of wisdom' but con-centrated on 'Jesus Christ and him crucified' (2.1-5). I have argued earlier that the reason why Paul drew this contrast was most probably the pres-ence in Corinth of rival wisdom-teachers, whose style was influenced by the sophistic movement,[6] and this is also the most probable background to 2 Cor. 11.4.

The third point is the briefness of the allusion to a different Jesus, a different Spirit and a different gospel. Paul does not feel the need to explain what he means by these phrases. This does not indicate that these subjects are not important to him. Rather, it indicates that he assumes the Corinthians will understand what he is talking about because these are subjects he has already dealt with in his earlier letter. As we try to understand Paul's words in the twenty-first century, it is legitimate to fill out his brief allusions with the help of 1 Corinthians, because it was Paul's earlier treatment of these issues in 1 Corinthians that enabled the church members to understand what he meant.

4.   Furnish, *II Corinthians*, p. 448.
5.   J. Murphy-O'Connor, 'Another Jesus (2 Cor. 11.4)', *RB* 97 (1990), pp. 238-51 (239), following Plummer, *Second Epistle*, p. 297.
6.   See Chapter 1.

According to Furnish, there is no direct information about the doctrinal stance of Paul's opponents in 2 Corinthians, not even in 11.4:

> Whatever doctrinal basis the actions and attitudes of Paul's rivals may have had, the actions and attitudes themselves are what Paul attacks, so the personal dimensions of the conflict are much more apparent than the doctrinal aspects of it.[7]

This statement is at best a half-truth. It is true that in 11.4 the content of the incomers' preaching is so concisely described that it can be interpreted by modern scholars in many different ways.[8] But Paul expected the Corinthians to understand the reference, and to realize that he was criticizing his opponents for the content of their message as well as on personal grounds. The fact that the three subjects mentioned in 11.4 were all prominent subjects in 1 Corinthians cannot be ignored. Those who drive a wedge between 1 and 2 Corinthians, and regard the 2 Corinthians situation as almost totally distinct from the 1 Corinthians situation, may dismiss this fact as an irrelevance; but there are too many links between the two letters to make this approach plausible. Paul's earlier discussion of the topics raised in 11.4 would be in his mind when he referred to them, and he would expect the Corinthians to understand his words because of the earlier discussion.

Käsemann makes much of Paul's silence in 2 Cor. 10–13 about the main issues of 1 Corinthians, and deduces from this silence that the situation had radically changed.[9] This argument from silence has been rightly rejected by R. Bultmann, who points out that in 2 Corinthians Paul is responding to attacks on his apostolic legitimacy. In such circumstances, he asks, why should we expect him to repeat the themes of 1 Corinthians? The most one can expect is that these themes should occur 'occasionally and unthematically' (*gelegentlich und unthematisch*).[10] Bultmann's argument is sound.[11] There would be no point in Paul sending two separate letters to the church in Corinth and repeating in the second letter what he had already said in the first. We should rather expect in the second letter occasional echoes of what was said in the first, and 2 Cor. 11.4 provides such an echo.

Although Käsemann's argument from silence, like most arguments from

7. Furnish, *II Corinthians*, p. 53.
8. For a survey of various opinions see Furnish, *II Corinthians*, pp. 500-502.
9. Käsemann, 'Legitimität', p. 40.
10. Bultmann, *Probleme*, pp. 23-24.
11. The soundness of Bultmann's argument is not dependent on his belief in a Gnostic background to 1 and 2 Corinthians.

silence,[12] is unsound, it has often been used. Barrett, for example, lists four subjects dealt with in 1 Corinthians that he claims are not dealt with in 2 Corinthians, and concludes that 'the second epistle must not be interpreted in terms of the situation presupposed by the first'.[13] This statement needs some qualification. It is true that the conflict between Paul and his opponents developed between the two letters, and some of the accusations Paul rebuts in 2 Corinthians are new. But the underlying source of the conflict was unchanged, and all the issues Barrett mentions as lacking in 2 Corinthians are in fact either mentioned or presupposed in that letter.

First, two of the items that Barrett claims are not dealt with in 2 Corinthians are the tendency to division and libertinism. But according to 2 Cor. 12.20-21, division and libertinism are precisely the things Paul is afraid he may find at Corinth on his next visit. Though he does not repeat what he said about these problems in his earlier letter, he is still aware of their presence at Corinth and concerned about their persistence.[14]

Second, as Barrett says, 2 Corinthians is not characterized by 'the free use of the terms wisdom and gnosis'. But if the comparative absence of these words in 2 Corinthians has the significance Barrett claims, this must also be true within 1 Corinthians. Of 17 occurrences of the word σοφία in 1 Corinthians, 15 are in chs. 1 and 2, one is in ch. 3 and one is in ch. 12. In other words, the free use of the term σοφία is a characteristic of chs. 1–2, but not of chs. 3–16. This would suggest, if Barrett's statistical argument were sound, not only that 1 Corinthians consisted of two separate letters, but also that the break between these separate letters came at the end of ch. 2.[15]

Within 1 Cor. 5–16, though the actual word σοφία occurs only once, the content of the Corinthian wisdom is presupposed. The arguments used by the Corinthians to justify their behaviour with regard to sexual relationships, eating meals in temples and so on, were products of the 'wisdom' Paul attacks in general terms in the first two chapters. And what is true of 1 Cor. 5–16 is also true of 2 Corinthians. Though Paul uses the actual word

12. For a critique of the widespread use of the argument from silence in New Testament study see Hall, *Seven Pillories*, pp. 55-64, where I maintain that the argument from silence fails to appreciate the reasons (practical and stylistic) why authors often make a deliberate choice to be brief.

13. C.K. Barrett, 'Paul's Opponents in 2 Corinthians', *NTS* 17 (1971), pp. 233-54 (236). This article is reprinted in C.K. Barrett, *Essays in Paul* (London: SCM Press, 1982), pp. 60-86.

14. For further discussion of 2 Cor. 12.20-21 see Chapter 11.

15. Those who advocate the partition of 1 Corinthians commonly make a division at the end of ch. 4. See Chapter 2 n. 35.

σοφία only once in 2 Corinthians,[16] he presupposes his earlier treatment of the topic. For example, in 2 Cor. 11.6 he contrasts his lack of expertise in rhetoric with his expertise in knowledge (γνῶσις). This statement could be described as a one-sentence summary of his argument in 1 Cor. 2, where he contrasts his avoidance of flowery rhetoric (ὑπεροχὴ λόγου ἢ σοφίας) with his teaching of a divine wisdom (θεοῦ σοφία), which only spiritual people are able to know (γνῶναι, v. 14).

Third, Barrett can find no discussion in 2 Corinthians of 'the misunderstanding of the resurrection'. Admittedly, in 2 Corinthians Paul does not refute once again the specific opinion quoted in 1 Cor. 15.12. But 2 Cor. 5.1-10 both amplifies and presupposes the teaching of 1 Cor. 15.

The theme of 2 Cor. 5.1-10 is sometimes taken to be eschatological chronology. The state of nakedness (v. 3) is thought to be the state of the soul between death and the parousia, from which Paul shrinks. But the passage is not concerned with the question of *when* we receive our new bodies, but with the certainty that one day we *shall* receive them. This certainty is expressed by the emphatic words οἴδαμεν (v. 1), εἴ γε (v. 3) and the ἀρραβών metaphor in v. 5.[17] Margaret Thrall, in her examination of Greek particles in the New Testament, has argued convincingly that εἴ γε in v. 3 expresses confidence, not doubt.[18] She concludes that the interpretation of εἴ γε as expressing assurance would seem to remove from v. 3, at

16. The phrase οὐκ ἐν σοφίᾳ σαρκικῇ in 2 Cor. 1.12 comes at the beginning of Paul's defence against the charge of deceit and trickery in 1.12–2.4, and σοφία σαρκικῇ means something like 'worldly cunning'. The idea that Paul behaved 'according to the flesh' occurs several times in 2 Corinthians (2.17; 4.1-2; 10.2-4; 12.16) and must represent an accusation of his enemies. It is possible that the phrase σοφία σαρκική was used by Paul's opponents as part of their counter-attack against Paul's criticism of σοφία in 1 Corinthians. They may have said: 'you accuse us of overreliance on σοφία, but you have a σοφία of your own—a skill in manipulative cunning and deceitfulness'.

17. This paragraph is largely quoted from my earlier article 'Pauline Church Discipline', *TynBul* 20 (1969), pp. 3-26 (10 n. 15).

18. M. Thrall, *Greek Particles in the New Testament: Linguistic and Exegetical Studies* (NTTS, 3; Leiden: E.J. Brill, 1962), pp. 82-91. The only questionable element in her argument is the statement that in Gal. 3.4 (εἴ γε καὶ εἰκῇ) the words εἴ γε introduce 'a clause which is of doubtful validity' (p. 86). This is not necessarily the case. The meaning of this clause, in my opinion, is: 'since, if you follow the Judaizers, your suffering will indeed have been in vain'. This gives to καί its proper force of emphasizing the word that follows it. As Thrall says (*Particles*, p. 90): 'The use of καί to emphasize a word repeated from the previous sentence is a common Pauline idiom and is by no means restricted to clauses introduced by εἴ γε (see 1 Cor. 4.7; 7.11; Phil. 3.12; 4.10)'.

any rate, the suggestion that Paul fears he may have to endure a period of disembodiment, and indeed to turn the verse into a positive assertion that the Christian believer will not be disembodied.[19] In other words, v. 3 (and the whole of vv. 1-11) is a reaffirmation of Paul's assertion in 1 Cor. 15 that the Christian hope involves, not nakedness, but being clothed with a new body.

The contention of this chapter is that in 2 Cor. 11.4 Paul refers in brief and summary fashion to two issues he has discussed in detail in 1 Corinthians. I shall maintain that the 'different Jesus' and 'different gospel' of 2 Cor. 11.4 relate to the triumphalist message of Paul's opponents that is contrasted in 1 Corinthians with the gospel of Christ crucified; and that the 'different Spirit' of 2 Cor. 11.4 relates to the conflict evident in 1 Corinthians between Paul's conception of the inspiration of the Holy Spirit and that of his opponents.

1. *A Different Jesus and a Different Gospel*

The two phrases 'a different Jesus' and 'a different gospel' can be considered together. In Paul's view the content of the gospel was 'Jesus Christ and him crucified' (1 Cor. 1.17-18; 2.1-2). Therefore the preaching of a different Jesus inevitably meant for him the preaching of a different gospel and vice versa. There are two elements in Paul's preaching about the cross, both of which are common to 1 and 2 Corinthians.

On the one hand, the death of Christ was God's chosen means of salvation, of effecting reconciliation between human beings and God. Paul had handed down to the Corinthians the tradition that Christ died for our sins according to the scriptures (1 Cor. 15.3), and that the cup of wine at the Lord's Supper signified a new covenant sealed by his blood (1 Cor. 11.23-26). Similar ideas are found in 2 Corinthians. Christ died for all people in a representative capacity, so that all people died with him (2 Cor. 5.14). Through his death God was reconciling the world to himself, not reckoning their sins against them (2 Cor. 5.19). It was this gospel of reconciliation and forgiveness through the death of Christ that the apostles had been commissioned to proclaim (2 Cor. 5.18-21).

On the other hand, the death of Christ was also a model for his followers

19. Thrall, *Particles*, p. 91. Cf. Thrall, *Second Epistle*, p. 379 (commenting on 2 Cor. 5.3): 'Paul underlines his assurance, indeed his insistence, that the final state of the believer is not one of disembodiment: having received the σῶμα πνευματικόν, he will never be found in a bodiless state'.

(and particularly his apostles) to follow. This theme, like the previous one, is common to both letters. In 1 Corinthians, Paul describes how his message of a crucified Saviour was accompanied by weakness, fear and trembling (2.1-5).[20] If that message had been delivered in flowery oratory, the preaching of the cross would have been ineffective (1.17). In Paul's view, God had deliberately made the apostles a laughing-stock, despised and rejected by the world (4.9-13). Christ saved the world through suffering and humiliation, and his messengers were called to share his humiliation as well as his salvation.

In 2 Corinthians the connection between the suffering of Christ and the suffering of the apostles becomes even more prominent. Paul describes his recent near-death experience in 1.3-11 and comments: 'as the sufferings of Christ abound to us, so also through Christ our encouragement abounds' (v. 5). These words depict the sufferings of the apostles as a sharing in the sufferings of Christ. In 4.7-18 the apostles are compared to clay pots that are easily broken. They are persecuted, depressed and at their wits' end. They carry about in their bodies the dying of Jesus, so that the life of Jesus can also be revealed (v. 10). The phrase τὴν νέκρωσιν τοῦ Ἰησοῦ (the being-put-to-death of Jesus) is a clear reference to the crucifixion and to the identification of the apostles with the crucifixion experience. The death of Jesus brought the promise of life, and the being-put-to-death of the apostles reveals that life to the world.

In both 1 and 2 Corinthians the theme of apostolic weakness and suffering has its background in controversy. Three of the elements in this controversy are: (a) Paul's defence against the accusation of weakness; (b) his response to the alleged strength of his opponents; and (c) his assertion of the positive value of weakness.

a. *Paul's Defence against the Accusation of Weakness*

The accusation of weakness appears most prominently in 2 Cor. 10–13. According to Paul's opponents his physical appearance was weak and his speech contemptible (10.10).[21] He was also socially weak, in that his insis-

---

20. Weakness in Paul's writings can be physical, emotional, theological or sociological, and the nuance in each case must be determined by the context. The association with fear and trembling in 1 Cor. 2.3 indicates that in this verse the emotional aspect is uppermost in Paul's mind.

21. Mockery of the physical defects of other orators was a common feature of ancient rhetoric. For examples see Marshall, *Enmity*, pp. 64-66. Dale Martin (*Body*, p.

tence on self-support through manual labour led to humiliation (11.7).[22] Above all, he was weak in standing up to his opponents. In 11.21 he contrasts his weakness with their boldness (τολμᾶν). The words ὡς ὅτι ἡμεῖς ἠσθενήκαμεν are probably an echo of their accusation. Martin quotes the judgment of Plummer that 'what is introduced by ὅτι is given as the thought of another, for the correctness of which the speaker does not vouch', and comments: 'Paul seems consciously to be reflecting on what they have rumored about him: he is weak'.[23]

This accusation was probably already in the air at the time of 1 Corinthians. In 1 Cor. 4.8 Paul declares that 'some people' have become puffed up with pride on the grounds that he is not coming to Corinth. This probably means that they believed he was afraid to confront them.[24] If so, this verse anticipates the accusation to which Paul replies in 2 Cor. 10.9-11— that he is weak when meeting people face to face but bold when writing letters at a distance. I shall discuss in Chapter 11 the historical circumstances that led to this accusation.

b. *Paul's Response to the Alleged Strength of his Opponents*
Paul's opponents in 2 Corinthians did not only pour scorn on his weakness, they also emphasized their own strength. Their boasting (11.18) included a claim to possess the sophistic virtue of τόλμα (boldness) (11.21).[25] This boldness stemmed partly from their pride in their Jewish birth and partly from the fact that they were 'ministers of Christ' (διάκονοι Χριστοῦ; vv. 22-23). So far as Jewish descent was concerned, Paul claimed equality with his rivals—he opposed strength to strength. But his response to their claim to be ministers of Christ is a catalogue of his sufferings.

35) cites Polemo's attack on the rival orator Favorinus, in which Polemo alleges that weakness of body proves weakness of character.

22. On manual labour as humiliation (ταπείνωσις) see Hock, *Social Context*, p. 64; Furnish, *II Corinthians*, pp. 456, 506-507; Martin, *2 Corinthians*, p. 225. Lucian contrasts the sublime words and dignified appearance of the great teacher with the filthy clothes and unkempt appearance of the craftsman, who clutches his tools, 'bent back over his work;…altogether demeaned (ταπεινός)' (Lucian, *The Dream* 13, quoted in Furnish, *II Corinthians*, p. 479).

23. Martin, *2 Corinthians*, p. 361; Plummer, *Second Epistle*, p. 317.

24. See Chapter 2 n. 10.

25. Litfin (*Proclamation*, p. 154) quotes the statement of Isocrates that he did not deliver speeches in public because he lacked the assurance to deal with hecklers, and comments: 'Isocrates's reference to a lack of assurance (τόλμα) is striking and should be noted. He repeats it elsewhere (*Panath.* 9-10; *Epist.* 8.7) and states at one point that τόλμα is the one thing without which no speaker can succeed (*Antid.* 192)'.

The climax of these sufferings is 'the worry of all the churches': 'Who is weak without me being weak? Whose faith is at risk without me being on fire?[26] If it is necessary to boast, I will boast of the things that make me weak' (vv. 29-30). This statement is polemical, and scarcely makes sense unless his opponents were boasting of their strength.[27]

Hardship catalogues were a common feature of philosophical thought in the Graeco-Roman world, and were normally intended to show how the wise man was able to overcome all his hardships.[28] By contrast, Paul emphasizes that his hardships made him weak. In particular, he was emo-tionally weak—sharing the weakness of his fellow-Christians and set on fire when they fell into sin. This is a far cry from the philosophical virtue of ἀπάθεια (remaining untroubled by outward circumstances).[29] Paul's emphasis on his emotional vulnerability probably indicates that his oppo-nents had been influenced by Stoic or Cynic thought. They believed 're-maining untroubled' to be a virtue, whereas in Paul's eyes it was a vice.[30]

The contrast Paul draws in 2 Corinthians between his weakness and other people's strength appears in 1 Corinthians in a different form. In 1 Cor. 4 the contrast is not between Paul and his opponents, but between

---

26. Paul's 'being on fire' (πυροῦσθαι) was one aspect of his μέριμνα—his worry about the churches. It should therefore be understood in psychological terms, as a description of Paul's feelings. Those who detect a reference to 'the great eschatological trial' are not interpreting the word according to its context in 2 Cor. 11 but importing into this passage Paul's use of the metaphor of fire in the very different context of 1 Cor. 3 (contra C. Forbes, 'Comparison, Self-Praise and Irony: Paul's Boasting and the Conventions of Hellenistic Rhetoric', *NTS* 32 [1986], pp. 1-30 [20]).

Πυροῦσθαι has a similar psychological meaning in 1 Cor. 7.9—see the discussion of this verse in Fee, *First Epistle*, pp. 288-89 and Thiselton, *First Epistle*, pp. 516-17.

27. Cf. Sumney, *Opponents*, p. 155: 'Verse 30 shows that Paul is not giving the proof the Corinthians expect. From what we have seen of the opponents, we may infer that they claim powerful, glorious lives as evidence of their apostleship'.

28. See especially the section entitled 'The Serene and Steadfast Sage' in Fitz-gerald, *Cracks*, pp. 59-65.

29. According to Fitzgerald (*Cracks*, p. 66) the virtue of ἀπάθεια was extolled by Stoics and Cynics, who believed the wise man was not susceptible to grief or fear. Other philosophers advocated μετριοπάθεια. In their opinion it was acceptable for a wise man to shed tears at the loss of a friend.

30. Thiselton (*First Epistle*, pp. 365-68) points out that the background to the so-called 'περίστασις catalogues' can be found not only in Greek philosophy but also in Jewish apocalyptic. These backgrounds, as he says, are complementary. Both Paul's opponents and Paul lived in a syncretistic world. The combination of ideas from these two sources fits in well with the theory that the background of Paul's opponents lay in Hellenistic Judaism.

the apostles and the church.[31] It is the Corinthians who are self-satisfied, who are rich, who have become independent of Paul and his colleagues, who behave like kings (v. 8). It is Paul and his colleagues who are despised and weak and are treated like refuse (vv. 9-13). The difference is summarized in v. 10: 'we are foolish for Christ's sake, you are wise in Christ; we are weak, you are strong; you are held in honour, we are despised'.

At first sight the 'strength' of the Corinthian church in 1 Cor. 4 and the 'boldness' of incoming missionaries in 2 Cor. 11 may appear to be related to two different situations. But the context of both these passages reveals their interconnection. In the case of 1 Cor. 4, the comparison between the apostles and the Corinthians in vv. 8-13 is immediately followed by a comparison between Paul and rival teachers: 'Though you may have thousands of pedagogues, only I am your father' (v. 15). Paul sees the arrogant, self-satisfied attitude of the Corinthian church as a consequence of the example and teaching of their 'pedagogues'. The difference between Paul and the 'pedagogues' was a difference between two lifestyles. The 'pedagogues' taught and exemplified a triumphalist lifestyle, which was reflected in the triumphalism of their disciples. Paul and his colleagues taught and exemplified the lifestyle of the cross.

A similar situation is implied in 2 Cor. 11.3-4. Even though much of 2 Cor. 10–13 consists of Paul's personal reply to an attempted character assassination by his opponents, he is also worried about the influence these opponents are exerting on the church. He is afraid that the minds of the Corinthians may be so corrupted by the new teaching (v. 3) that they gladly accept the 'different gospel' their teachers are proclaiming (v. 4).

The reason why Paul concentrated his attack on the members of the church in 1 Cor. 4, and on the incoming missionaries in 2 Cor. 11, can be found in the different circumstances of the two letters. His aim in 1 Corinthians was to change the attitude of the Corinthians—to undermine their adherence to the new teaching and to correct the pattern of behaviour this teaching had led them into. By the time 2 Corinthians was written that battle had been largely won. The news Titus brought to Paul in Macedonia was of a church that had repented and had demonstrated its repentance by the punishment of the most extreme offender. But Paul's opponents, seeing their influence waning, seem to have changed their tactics. Instead of attacking Paul's teaching they resorted to abuse of Paul as a person, and to casting doubt on his apostolic authority. This reconstruction of the situa-

31. In the opinion of some scholars 1 Cor. 4.8 is addressed, not to the church as a whole, but to an elite minority. For a refutation of this view see Chapter 3.

tion would explain the apologetic emphasis of 2 Corinthians. It would explain why the main theme of chs. 10–13 is Paul's reply to personal attacks, even though the 'other gospel' of his opponents and their influence on the church is still on his mind.

c. *Paul's Assertion of the Positive Value of Weakness*
Another factor that is common to 1 and 2 Corinthians is the positive value Paul ascribes to his weakness and suffering. A.E. Harvey disputes this, and sees a great difference between the two letters in this respect. In his opinion Paul viewed suffering in 1 Corinthians as a purely negative experience, but in 2 Corinthians as something positive. Harvey believes the reason for this change to be the near-death experience described in 2 Cor. 1.3-11, which revolutionized Paul's attitude to suffering.[32]

Harvey is right to stress the importance of this experience for Paul, but misunderstands its significance. The effect of Paul's near-death experience was not to revolutionize his thinking, but to reinforce ideas already expressed in 1 Corinthians. In his catalogue of apostolic sufferings in 1 Cor. 4.9-13 Paul makes it clear that these sufferings were sent by God. It was God who had put the apostles on display as men condemned to death (v. 9).[33] Their foolishness, weakness and disgrace were διὰ Χριστόν (v. 10)—objectively in the sense that they were a consequence of preaching the gospel of Christ, and subjectively in the sense that they accepted their low status gladly as servants of Christ.[34] Elsewhere in the letter Paul explains the reason why God had made them weak, and the positive benefits resulting from that weakness.

---

32. A.E. Harvey, *Renewal through Suffering* (Edinburgh: T. & T. Clark, 1996), p. 31.

33. The imagery of 1 Cor. 4.9 may be taken both from the gladiatorial games (Robertson and Plummer, *Critical and Exegetical Commentary*, p. 85; Fitzgerald, *Cracks*, pp. 146-47; Barrett, *First Epistle*, p. 110; Thiselton, *First Epistle*, p. 359) and also from the triumphal procession (P.E. Hughes, *Second Epistle*, p. 78 n. 10; Fee, *First Epistle*, pp. 174-75).

34. For the objective sense see Robertson and Plummer, *Critical and Exegetical Commentary*, p. 86: 'The apostles were "fools on account of Christ" (2 Cor. 4.11; Phil. 3.7), because it was owing to their preaching Christ that the world regarded them as crazy (1.23; Acts 26.24)'. The parallel they cite from 2 Cor. 4.11 is a particularly strong argument in favour of the objective interpretation. For the subjective sense see Meyer, *Corinthians*, I, p. 126: 'because we concern ourselves about nothing else save Christ the crucified, are bent on knowing Him only, and on having nothing to do with the world's wisdom (comp. 2.2), we are foolish, weak-minded men, for Christ's sake'. The two senses are compatible. Paul accepts gladly the foolishness and weakness which the gospel of the cross forces upon him.

The main benefit was evangelistic effectiveness. In 2.1-5 Paul contrasts two types of preaching. His own preaching was characterized by weakness, fear and trembling. The preaching of his opponents was characterized by 'persuasive words of wisdom'—by the confident rhetorical display typical of sophists. The reason why Paul avoided such rhetorical display was 'lest the cross of Christ be emptied of its power' (1.17 NIV). These words imply that when the gospel of the cross was preached in Paul's way it was effective, but when preached in a rhetorical way it was ineffective.

Part of the reason for this appears in 9.19-23. Though Paul was a free man, he had become like a slave. When bringing the gospel to weak people he became weak himself. He did this for the sake of the gospel, in order to save people. The context of these words in ch. 9 is Paul's defence of his policy of self-support. Had he come to Corinth like a sophist and relied on the financial support of those who could afford to pay him, the gospel would have reached only an upper-class minority. By sharing the back-breaking labour and financial struggles of most of the population he brought the gospel to the whole city.[35] The result of this policy was the Corinthian church as Paul describes it in 1.26, a church with a few upper-class members but a majority of people who were socially and economically—and because of their poverty often also physically—weak.

Paul's comments on his near-death experience in 2 Cor. 1.3-11 resemble the argument of 1 Cor. 9.19-23. In both passages he sees his identification with the weakness of others as the key to his effectiveness. In 2 Cor. 1 it is his suffering, and the strength he has received from God in that suffering, that enables him to help others who suffer. He has become identified with their experience just as they (through their prayers and concern) are identified with his (vv. 3-7, 11). It is true, of course, that he has also learnt a lesson for his own life—a renewed confidence in the God who brings the dead to life (vv. 8-10). But the main benefit gained from his recent sufferings was the ability it gave him to encourage other sufferers through their shared experience.

---

35. Cf. Hock's comment (*Social Context*, p. 64) on Paul's boasting about his policy of self-support: 'Another cost that Paul had to absorb, if he wanted to keep his boast, was the personal cost. Tentmaking involved wearisome toil (6.5; 11.27); sleeplessness, hunger and thirst (11.27); and, in general, a life of having nothing, of being poor (6.10). Such is what Paul meant when he said he would gladly spend and be physically spent (ἐκδαπανᾶσθαι) for the sake of the Corinthians' souls (12.15). When the physical exhaustion and the social humiliation that came from Paul's tentmaking are kept clearly in mind, it is easy to see that his boast of offering the gospel free of charge was truly a boast in his "weakness" as an artisan'.

The link between the weakness of the apostles and their effectiveness is expressed in a vivid metaphor in 2 Cor. 2.12-17. The passage begins with a description of Paul's visit to Troas. There was a great opportunity for preaching the gospel in Troas—'a door was open in the Lord'—but he had no rest in his spirit, because he was worrying about the Corinthian response to his recent letter. So instead of seizing this opportunity he moved on to Macedonia, in the hope of meeting Titus there and discovering what had happened.

Paul then breaks off his account of his movements with a metaphor taken from the Roman triumphal procession. There is widespread agreement today that the verb θριαμβεύω means 'to parade in a triumphal procession'.[36] Part of the Roman triumph was a procession incorporating some of the emperor's captives.[37] Paul sees himself and his colleagues as resembling those captives—led in procession for the glory of God as the captives were led in procession for the glory of the emperor.[38] As Paul develops the metaphor, the sweet-smelling spices that accompanied the procession are used as a picture of the fragrance of Christ being spread among the people.[39] However, it is through the weakness of the triumphal

36. Furnish, *II Corinthians*, pp. 174-75; Martin, *2 Corinthians*, pp. 46-48; P. Marshall, 'A Metaphor of Social Shame: ΘΡΙΑΜΒΕΥΕΙΝ in 2 Cor. 2.14', *NovT* 25 (1983), pp. 302-317; J. Lambrecht, *Second Corinthians* (Sacra Pagina, 8; Collegeville, MN: The Liturgical Press, 1999), pp. 37-39; J.M. Scott, 'The Triumph of God in 2 Cor. 4.14: Additional Evidence of Merkabah Mysticism in Paul', *NTS* 42 (1996), pp. 260-81 (262).

37. According to T.E. Schmidt, 'Mark 15.16-32: The Crucifixion Narrative and the Roman Triumphal Procession', *NTS* 41 (1995), pp. 1-18 (3-4), from 20 BCE onwards the triumph became the exclusive privilege of the emperor.

38. Fitzgerald (*Cracks*, p. 147) quotes parallels from Epictetus (*Diss.* 3.22.59, 113-14) to the idea of God making a spectacle of the sufferings of his servants. Marshall ('Social Shame', p. 305) quotes a passage from Seneca in which a man complains that his benefactor never lets him forget the help he gave: 'How long will you parade (*circumducis*) me? How long will you refuse to let me forget my misfortune? In a triumph, I should have had to march but once (*semel in triumpho ductus essem*)'. (Seneca, *De Ben.* 2.11.1). Marshall rightly concludes that the image of the triumphal procession was used as 'a metaphor of social shame'.

39. There are several passages in ancient authors that associate sweet-smelling spices with the triumphal procession. Appian (*Pun.* 66) writes, 'next came a number of incense-bearers, and after them the general himself' (for the Greek text see Thrall, *Second Epistle*, p. 197 n. 61). Cf. also Horace, *Odes* 4.2.50:

Tuque dum procedis, Io Triumphe!
Non semel dicemus, Io Triumphe!
Civitas omnis, dabimusque Divis
Tura benignis.

captives that this takes place, not through their strength.

It is easy to see why this picture sprung to Paul's mind at this time. Fresh in his mind was the humiliation of having to admit to his friends at Troas that he was not capable of preaching the gospel there. This humiliation will have hurt him deeply, since, despite his pursuit of humility, Paul was by nature a proud man. The Troas incident was a vivid illustration of 2 Cor. 11.28-30, where Paul's 'worry about all the churches' comes as a climax to the catalogue of his weaknesses. His ministry was a yo-yo of emotional ups and downs, of joys and sorrows, in which his own state of mind was at the mercy of other people. In the words of Frances Young and David Ford:

> He was on tenterhooks waiting for Titus' news, and his concern for them actually took priority over a possible opening for mission. But this pain and concern for the churches is part of the agony of apostleship (11.28). It is God who determines where he will go, and he is like a captive dragged around helpless in a victory procession.[40]

At first sight it seems strange for Paul to talk about his revealing the fragrance of Christ 'in every place' (v. 14) immediately after describing his abandonment of a promising mission-field at Troas.[41] But the time spent at Troas was not a total failure. A door for the gospel had been opened. His preaching at Troas had produced results in spite of his human weakness, and his time there exemplified the paradoxical combination of strength and weakness that is one of the major themes of the Corinthian correspondence.

(While you go in procession, we, the whole community, will repeat 'Io triumphe' and offer incense to the gracious gods).

Thrall (*Second Epistle*, p. 197) calls these parallels into question on the grounds that 'the supporting hellenistic texts…are somewhat sparse'. But the question has to be asked, why the image of fragrance came into Paul's mind when he was talking about a triumphal procession, and these texts explain his train of thought. The use he makes of the theme of fragrance once it has occurred to him does, of course, go beyond the triumph metaphor.

40. Young and Ford, *Meaning and Truth*, p. 19. M.E. Thrall ('A Second Thanksgiving Period in II Corinthians', *JSNT* 16 [1982], pp. 101-124) describes 2.14-17 as an 'introductory thanksgiving period' leading into chs. 3–5, and minimizes the connection with 2.12-13. However, one of the main themes of chs. 3–5 is the coexistence of divine strength and human weakness—a theme to which 2.12-13 is directly relevant. 2.14-17 is indeed an introductory passage, but it is also a link passage.

41. This point is made by Thrall in 'Second Thanksgiving', pp. 105-106, and in *Second Epistle*, p. 22.

Conclusion

In both 1 and 2 Corinthians a contrast is drawn between two gospels and two lifestyles. Central to Paul's gospel was the crucifixion of Jesus, which he regarded both as a means of salvation and as a model for all Christians to follow. Apostles in particular were called to share the weakness and humiliation of their crucified Lord. Paul's opponents, by contrast, boasted of their strength, and had taught their disciples at Corinth to do the same. For them, the cross was an event of the past, leading on to the experience of resurrection power in the present; for Paul both crucifixion and resurrection were present realities, lived out in daily experience.

2. *A Different Spirit*

When Paul accuses his opponents of proclaiming 'a different Spirit', he is reminding the Corinthians of his lengthy discussion of spiritual inspiration in 1 Corinthians. This discussion is found mainly in chs. 12–14, but there are also other places, such as 7.40, where Paul seems to be in conflict with people who claimed the authority of the Spirit for their opinions. There seem to have been two main areas in which Paul disagreed with the 'spiritual' people at Corinth—the nature of inspiration, and the authority of prophetic utterances.

a. *The Nature of Inspiration*
One of the questions underlying 1 Cor. 14 is this: are Christian prophets in control of their actions, or are they totally taken over by the Holy Spirit? Paul recognizes that the essence of prophecy is divine revelation—in 14.26 ἀποκάλυψις seems to denote specifically a prophetic revelation.[42]

---

42. Thiselton (*First Epistle*, pp. 1075-77, 1091-93) argues that, for Paul, prophecy was not always spontaneous. This thesis requires strained exegesis. He comments on 1 Cor. 14.30 (ἐὰν δὲ ἄλλω ἀποκαλυφθῇ): 'what is at issue in this "disclosure" other than the insight of another, given by God, that the first speaker has begun to indulge in self-deception, distraction, or sheer error, or a fertile integration with resources of wisdom or scriptural knowledge which enables the second speaker to take the theme forward more imaginatively, accurately, or deeply than the first?' (p. 1092). This interpretation reads an enormous unexpressed content into the verb. The phrase means 'if someone else receives a revelation', and the apparent use of ἀποκάλυψις as an equivalent to προφητεία in 14.26 suggests that this denotes prophetic revelation in general.

Equally strained is Thiselton's exegesis of v. 19: ἀλλ' ἐν ἐκκλησίᾳ θέλω πέντε

But he also insists that 'the spirits of prophets are subject to the prophets' (v. 32)—that is, that prophets are not taken over by the Holy Spirit but are still in control of their behaviour. In v. 31 the word δύνασθε (you are able) is in an emphatic position. 'You have the ability to speak one at a time', Paul is saying; 'divine inspiration does not make self-control impossible'.[43] In Fee's words, 'there is no seizure here, no loss of control; the speaker is neither frenzied nor a babbler'.[44]

Paul's words imply that some Corinthians held an opposite opinion. They seem to have thought that the words and actions of an inspired prophet could not and should not be controlled. By contrast, Paul tried to instil 'decency and good order' (v. 40), by asking prophets to speak one at a time and give way to each other (vv. 29-33). These two approaches stem from two different understandings of prophetic inspiration.

The nature of inspiration was a much discussed topic in the Graeco-Roman world. Both Paul's view and the view he opposes can be illustrated from the pages of Philo. An often quoted parallel is *Rer. Div. Her.* 249–66. Philo is commenting on the words of Gen. 15.12 (LXX) that an ecstasy fell upon Abraham at sunset. He regards the sun as a symbol of the human mind or reason. When the mind comes to its setting, 'there falls upon us in all likelihood an ecstasy, a divine possession, a madness'. This regularly happens to prophets, 'for the mind is evicted from us at the arrival of the divine Spirit'. When we read in the following verse that 'it was said to

---

λόγους τῷ νοΐ μου λαλῆσαι, ἵνα καὶ ἄλλους κατηχήσω, ἢ μυρίους λόγους ἐν γλώσσῃ (But in the full assembly I would rather speak five words with my mind, so as to instruct others, than ten thousand words in a tongue). He talks about 'five intelligible words carefully thought out' and goes on: 'So strong is Paul's emphasis on the use of mental reflection and control that it is inconceivable (in our view) that most writers are correct to assume that prophecy is necessarily or uniformly "spontaneous"' (pp. 1076-77). But it is unlikely that τῷ νοΐ μου should refer to 'mental reflection' or to 'words carefully thought through'. In the context the contrast is between unintelligible speech and rational speech. Paul was not like a modern preacher who spends long hours sitting at a desk preparing a written sermon. His extempore preaching was, of course, informed by his many years of study and reflection in the past, but this is not the point he is making in 1 Cor. 14.

43. Cf. E. Schweizer, 'The Service of Worship: An Exposition of 1 Corinthians 14', *Int* 13 (1959), pp. 400-408 (405): 'Contrary to statements in the Apostolic Fathers, Paul declares that the Spirit of God is never a Spirit bursting out in such a way that the speaker is unable to regulate his speech'. Schweizer cites Hermas, *Mandatum* 11.8 and the statement in *Martyrium Polycarpi* 7 that 'for two hours he was unable to get silent'.

44. Fee, *First Epistle*, p. 696.

Abraham', this means that 'the prophet, even when he seems to be speaking, is actually silent, while Another makes use of his organs of speech'.[45] It is probable that in 1 Cor. 14.31-32 Paul is opposing a view of inspiration similar to that expressed in this passage from Philo.[46]

Elsewhere, however, Philo presents a different approach to inspiration, more similar to Paul's. Terrance Callan has analysed Philo's description of Moses, the supreme prophet. According to Philo, on some occasions Moses is 'possessed by God and carried out of himself'; but on other occasions God speaks through Moses as his interpreter. Statements in the Law that are not literally true, such as anthropomorphisms, can be explained by Moses' role as interpreter. For example, 'talk about the wrath of God is used by the lawgiver as far as it serves for an elementary lesson, to admonish those who could not otherwise be brought to their senses'.[47]

The main subject of 1 Cor. 12–14 is the exercise of spiritual gifts, especially prophecy and tongues. In Paul's consideration of this subject, the nature of divine inspiration is one of the key issues. It is significant that, after introducing the subject περὶ δὲ τῶν πνευματικῶν, he moves immediately to the topic of inspiration (12.1-3), and draws a contrast between the kind of inspiration experienced by Christians and that experienced in the worship of idols.[48] These introductory verses do not relate closely to

45. Philo, *Rer. Div. Her.* 264–66, as translated in B.A. Pearson, *Pneumatikos-Psychikos Terminology*, pp. 45-46.

46. The fact that there are parallels in Philo to the supposed views of Paul's opponents does not, of course, necessarily mean that these opponents must have come from a Hellenistic–Jewish background. Similar views were widely held in the ancient world and can be found, for example, in Plato's discussion of the Delphic oracle in *Phaedr.* 244-53 (see A.R. Hunt, *The Inspired Body: Paul, the Corinthians, and Divine Inspiration* [Macon, GA: Mercer University Press, 1996], pp. 18-23). What can be said is that, if the thesis of a Hellenistic–Jewish background for Paul's opponents commends itself on other grounds, an enthusiastic approach to prophecy would be appropriate to that background.

47. T. Callan, 'Prophecy and Ecstasy in Greco-Roman Religion and in 1 Corinthians', *NovT* 27.2 (1985), pp. 125-40 (133-35), citing Philo, *Vit. Mos.* 2.188 and *Deus Imm.* 52. This approach was not confined to Philo. Callan quotes Plutarch's opinion about the Delphic oracle: 'the voice is not that of a god, nor the utterance of it, nor the diction, nor the metre, but all these are the woman's; he provides only the visions and puts the light in her soul in regard to the future' ('Prophecy and Ecstasy', p. 130, quoting Plutarch, *De Phythiae Oraculis* 397C as translated by F.C. Babbitt in Plutarch's *Moralia* (LCL 5 [1936]).

48. For a detailed discussion of 12.2 see Thiselton, *First Epistle*, pp. 911-16. According to what Thiselton calls 'the standard modern view', Paul was challenging

the rest of ch. 12, and may represent Paul's initial response to a question raised by the Corinthians in their letter. They may have asked whether the inspiration of Christian prophets was similar in nature to the kind of spirit-possession some of them had experienced before their conversion.

Having raised this question in 12.1-3, Paul does not return to it until ch. 14. The rest of ch. 12, and the whole of ch. 13, is devoted to the laying down of general principles about the purpose and use of spiritual gifts. Then in ch. 14 he applies these principles to the specific problems that had arisen in Corinthian worship, and deals with the nature of prophetic inspiration in that context.

In ch. 14 Paul makes three points. First, prophecy and speaking in tongues are valuable gifts from God, inspired by the Holy Spirit (vv. 2-5, 18). Second, those exercising these gifts are still in control of themselves, and are able to practise discrimination in the way they exercise them (vv. 31-33). Third, the principle to be employed in this discrimination is 'the building up of the church' (v. 12). What is said in a context of public worship should be understandable, which means that prophecy is more suited to public worship than tongues (vv. 1-25); and those exercising their gifts should do so in moderation, so as to allow other members of the church to exercise their gifts as well (vv. 26-30).

b. *The Authority of Prophetic Utterances*
One of the problems Paul faced at Corinth was prophetic dogmatism. In 1 Cor. 14.37 he pitted his own authority against that of certain people who thought of themselves as 'prophets' or 'spiritual'. These people were probably seeking to impose their will on the congregation on the grounds that, as prophetic mouthpieces of the Spirit of God, their words must be obeyed. This prophetic dogmatism may be the reason for Paul's advice that, when a prophet is prophesying, the rest of the church should exercise their critical faculties on what was being said (14.29). Similarly, in his list of gifts of the Spirit in ch. 12, he names the critical assessment of spiritual utterances as a gift on a par with prophecy itself (12.10).[49] It is probable

---

the assumption that divine inspiration involved the suspension of rational thought. This view seems to me to be sound. The strongest argument in its favour is the phrase ὡς ἂν ἤγεσθε (however you were led), which implies being led by an external power in whatever direction that power determines.

49. Dunn (*Jesus and the Spirit*, pp. 233-36) argues convincingly that διακρίσεις πνευμάτων in 12.10 should be understood in the light of διακρινέτωσαν in 14.29 to signify 'an evaluation, an investigation, a testing, a weighing of the prophetic utterance'.

that the 'prophets' and 'spiritual people' of 14.37 disagreed with this, and thought the role of listeners to prophecy to be implicit obedience to the divine will revealed through the words of the prophet.

It is in ch. 7 that the clash between these two approaches comes to a head. The final verse of ch. 7 (v. 40) reads: δοκῶ δὲ κἀγὼ πνεῦμα θεοῦ ἔχειν (and I too think that I have the Spirit of God). The word κἀγώ (I too) implies the existence at Corinth of other people who thought they possessed the Spirit.[50] Paul has just given his advice on the remarriage of widows. These others presumably disagreed with Paul and used their 'spiritual' status as prophets to browbeat widows into accepting their pronouncements as words from the Lord.[51]

The only pronouncements to which Paul grants the status of 'words from the Lord' are sayings of Jesus handed down in the tradition. Twice in ch. 7 he draws a careful distinction between what the Lord said (vv. 10, 25) and his own teaching (vv. 12, 25). His own pronouncements are matters of opinion (γνώμη in vv. 25, 40; νομίζω in v. 26). They are worthy of respect, because by the Lord's mercy he is a reliable person (v. 25) and he is guided by the Spirit of God (v. 40). But they are the words of Paul, not the words of the Lord. The repeated emphasis on this point in vv. 12 and 25, and the polemical conclusion to the chapter in v. 40, strongly suggest that Paul is opposing people at Corinth who thought otherwise, and who gave to their prophetic pronouncements the status of dominical oracles.

The browbeating approach implied by v. 40 would not be limited to the question of the remarriage of widows. The whole of ch. 7 makes sense as Paul's response to the dogmatism of prophets at Corinth who were trying to impose their views on other Christians. In opposing this dogmatism, Paul appeals throughout the chapter to reason and common sense.[52] Again

50. My discussion of ch. 7 is based on, and in part quotes directly from, my article 'A Problem of Authority', *ExpTim* 102 (1990), pp. 39-42. W. Deming (*Paul on Marriage and Celibacy* [Cambridge: Cambridge University Press, 1995], p. 210) denies that Paul is battling 'pneumatics' in ch. 7. He translates v. 40: 'And I, for my part, think that I have the Spirit of God'. 'I, for my part' could be a possible translation of κἀγώ when it comes as the first word in a sentence, as a word of transition. But when it comes later in a sentence, it must mean 'I, too' and imply others who think the same.

51. Since Paul is opposing an ascetic viewpoint in the rest of ch. 7, the objection of these people may have been to Paul's advice in the whole of vv. 39-40—to his assertion of the freedom of widows to remarry, and to his treatment of his advice against remarriage as a personal opinion rather than as a dogma.

52. Cf. Hays, *First Corinthians*, p. 130 (commenting on 7.25): 'He offers them not

and again he insists that more than one course of action is allowable: this is good, but the other is better (v. 38); this is good but it is not a sin to do the other (vv. 8-9, 28, 36); this is good, but the other is in most cases more practicable (vv. 1-2).[53] One gets the impression that Paul's opponents were not so broad-minded.[54] They had not heard of situation ethics. They thought in terms, not of possibilities, but of absolutes.[55] In their view moral decision-making did not consist of weighing up pros and cons in a complicated situation, but of absolute surrender to the will of God, revealed through prophetic utterances.

It is against this background that we should interpret v. 37: ὃς δὲ ἕστηκεν ἐν τῇ καρδίᾳ αὐτοῦ ἑδραῖος μὴ ἔχων ἀνάγκην, ἐξουσίαν δὲ ἔχει περὶ τοῦ ἰδίου θελήματος, καὶ τοῦτο κέκρικεν ἐν τῇ ἰδίᾳ καρδίᾳ, τηρεῖν τὴν ἑαυτοῦ παρθένον, καλῶς ποιήσει (but if anyone stands firm in his own mind and is not under pressure but has authority with regard to his own will, and has made a decision in his own mind to keep his girl a virgin, he will do well). Paul is here advising a man (variously understood to be a parent or guardian, fiancé or lover) who has to decide for or against marriage. He advises that, if a decision is taken against marriage, the man must make the decision out of a settled conviction in his own mind, not

a packaged pronouncement but an invitation to reflection'. Thiselton (*First Epistle*, pp. 381-82) comments that Paul expounds an absolutist ethic in chs. 5–6, and a situational ethic in 7.1–11.1.

53. The word καλόν in 7.1 is often translated 'it is better' (e.g. H. Conzelmann, *A Commentary on the First Epistle to the Corinthians* [Hermeneia; Philadelphia: Fortress Press, 1975], p. 115), and taken to be a recommendation of celibacy. This ignores the contrast between καλῶς (well) and κρεῖσσον (better) in 7.38. Paul insists throughout the chapter that the choice between marriage and celibacy is not a choice between good and bad but between two goods. Both celibacy and marriage are good and involve the exercise of a divine charisma (v. 7). Thiselton (*First Epistle*, p. 606) endorses the comment of Schrage (*Der erste Brief*, II, pp. 156-57) that Paul views both marriage and celibacy as 'good' (καλόν).

54. W.E. Phipps ('Is Paul's Attitude toward Sexual Relations Contained in 1 Cor. 7.1?', *NTS* 28 [1982], pp. 125-31 [125]) cites the comment of Tertullian on 7.1: 'It follows that it is evil to have contact with a woman; for nothing is contrary to good except evil' (Tertullian, *On Monogamy* 3). Paul's repeated assertion that it is not a sin to marry (vv. 28, 36) suggests the presence in Corinth of a viewpoint similar to Tertullian's.

55. L.T. Johnson (*The Writings of the New Testament: An Interpretation* [Philadelphia: Fortress Press; London: SCM Press, 1986], p. 280) comments on ch. 7 that 'In Paul's treatment of the community's questions, he must do what the sloganeers least want: he must make distinctions'.

under pressure, but being in control of his own will. The emphasis is on independent, rational decision-making.

What, then, is the pressure (ἀνάγκη) Paul has in mind? The man's own emotions, or his concern for the well-being of the girl, have been suggested.[56] But the chapter as a whole, and Paul's repeated use of ἴδιος (his own mind and will, not someone else's), suggest rather the external pressure of 'spiritual' Christian prophets.[57] The man concerned, under pressure from those who claimed the authority of the Spirit for their pronouncements, could be forced into an action that his own will and reason did not approve.[58] You could not say of such a man that he 'has authority with regard to his own will' because he has given up the power of individual decision-making under pressure from his 'spiritual' friends.[59]

This interpretation gains support from Paul's use of the word ἀνάγκη elsewhere. In Phlm. 14 he hints that he would like Philemon to send Onesimus back to him; but if Philemon does this, it must be of his own free will, not under pressure (ἀνάγκη) from Paul. In 2 Cor. 9.7 Paul insists that individual Christians must determine their contribution to the relief fund of their own free choice, not under pressure (ἀνάγκη) from Paul or from anyone else. In 1 Cor. 7.37 Paul is drawing the same distinction between a free, independent decision and a decision made under pressure from other people; and v. 40 suggests that it is 'spiritual' people who are applying the pressure—probably through prophetic utterances.

56. Cf. the reference in Epictetus, *Diss.* 4.1.147 to τὸν ὑπ' ἔρωτος ἀναγκαζόμενον (the man who is compelled by passionate love).

57. Fee (*First Epistle*, p. 327) suggests that the παρθένοι and their fiancés were being 'pressurized by the pneumatics'. Thiselton, commenting on v. 37, regards the ἀνάγκη as referring to 'the constraints imposed by other people's beliefs, expectations and pressures' (*First Epistle*, p. 599), and sees in the words τοῦ ἰδίου θελήματος a contrast with 'the pressures imposed by others' (pp. 600-601).

58. H. Chadwick, ' "All Things to All Men" (1 Cor. ix.22)', *NTS* 1 (1954–55), pp. 261-75 (267), comments that the phrase καὶ οὕτως ὀφείλει γίνεσθαι in v. 36 suggests 'the usages of society'. The man concerned recognizes that marriage is the 'right' thing in the circumstances, but has come under the influence of the ascetic teaching at Corinth.

59. According to Thiselton (*First Epistle*, p. 600) the word ἐξουσία here denotes possession of the legal right to make the decision. This is improbable. In the phrase ἐξουσίαν δὲ ἔχει περὶ τοῦ ἰδίου θελήματος, the authority is related to the man's own will, not to his legal status.

Conclusion

Consideration of the views about prophetic inspiration Paul was combatting in 1 Corinthians can help us to understand what he meant by 'a different Spirit' in 2 Cor. 11.4. His words can be paraphrased as follows: 'You
are happy when your teachers tell you that the Holy Spirit works in an
ecstatic, individualistic and authoritarian manner. But the Spirit you
received at the beginning is the Spirit of love, unity and consideration for
others'.

EXCURSUS F:
THE INTERPRETATION OF 1 CORINTHIANS 11.10

I have maintained in Chapter 7 that in 1 Corinthians Paul is combatting
two opinions about the work of the Spirit—the view that prophetic inspiration means a total abandonment to the influence of the Spirit, with loss
of self-control; and the view that prophetic utterances are words from the
Lord that must be obeyed without question. Both these views may form
part of the background to one of the most difficult verses in the letter—
11.10.[60]

In that verse, Paul declares that a woman prophet ought to have authority
over her head (ὀφείλει ἡ γυνὴ ἐξουσίαν ἔχειν ἐπὶ τῆς κεφαλῆς). In
the context he is arguing that women prophets should keep their heads
covered.[61] It has often been assumed that the word ἐξουσία (authority)
must be an oblique reference to a head-covering. The word has been translated accordingly not as 'authority' but as 'sign of authority', and the
head-covering has been regarded as a sign either of the woman prophet's
own authority or of the authority of her husband.

The main difficulty with this interpretation is that the word ἐξουσία is
part of a phrase ἐξουσίαν ἔχειν. This phrase occurs 29 times in the New
Testament, and on all its 28 other occurrences it has a similar meaning to
its literal English translation—'have authority'. The need to translate this
phrase in accordance with normal Greek usage is increasingly being

60. This Excursus is largely based on my article 'A Problem of Authority', pp. 39-
42.
61. For a balanced survey of different opinions about what the covering of the head
means, see Thiselton, *First Epistle*, pp. 823-26.

recognized.[62] But what does it mean to say that someone should have authority over her own head?

Some scholars translate ἐξουσίαν ἔχειν as 'exercise authority' or 'exercise control'.[63] But there is a difference between having authority and exercising authority. In ch. 9 Paul states that he has the authority (or right) to claim support from the church (v. 4: ἔχομεν ἐξουσίαν); but he has not exercised that authority (v. 12: οὐκ ἐχρησάμεθα τῇ ἐξουσίᾳ ταύτῃ). Paul is not exhorting women prophets to exercise their authority, but asserting that they should have this authority in the first place.

The word ὀφείλειν refers to what is right and fitting, and can be used with either a subjective or an objective emphasis. When the emphasis is subjective, the fact that an action is right and fitting implies a moral obligation on the part of the person concerned to perform it (e.g. Rom. 15.1, 27; Jn 13.14). When the emphasis is objective, it relates to a situation that ought to exist rather than to the moral obligation of the subject (e.g. 1 Cor. 9.10; Jn 19.7). In 1 Cor. 11.10, ὀφείλειν is related to the possession of authority, which is something conferred rather than something performed, and the objective sense is appropriate.

There are two passages elsewhere in the epistle that may provide clues to the background of this verse. The first is 14.31-33; here Paul maintains that the spirits of prophets are subject to the prophets—in other words, that prophets are still in control of their minds and are not totally taken over by

---

62. J. Winandy, 'Un Curieux "Casus Pendens": 1 Corinthiens 11.10 et son inter-prétation', *NTS* 38 (1992), pp. 621-29 (625-26): 'La femme doit avoir autorité sur la tête; c'est à dire qu'on doit lui reconnaître le droit d'en disposer comme elle juge convenable de la faire, et, en l'occurrence, de la dissimuler sous un voile'. A.C. Perriman, *Speaking of Women: Interpreting Paul* (Leicester: Apollos, 1998), p. 97: 'it may be that Paul's intention in verse 10 was principally to endorse the woman's right to choose to remain covered'. Fee (*First Epistle*, pp. 520-21) translates: 'For this reason the woman ought to have the freedom over her head to do as she wishes', but begs ignorance as to the situation that caused Paul to say this. Schrage (*Der erste Brief*, II, p. 514) recognizes that ἐπί when used with ἐξουσία signifies the object over which authority is exercised, and sees the authority of the Corinthian women prophets as expressed in the decency of their hairstyle.

63. E.g. J. Delobel, '1 Cor. 11.2-16: Towards a Coherent Interpretation', in A. Vanhoye (ed.), *L'Apôtre Paul* (Leuven: Leuven University Press, 1986), pp. 369-89 (387). Thiselton (*First Epistle*, p. 839) translates 'keep control', and argues that ἔχειν can mean 'keep' as well as 'have'. But the important thing is not what ἔχειν means in other combinations, but what it means when combined with ἐξουσίαν, with which it stands in a syntagmatic relationship.

the Spirit. They are therefore capable of keeping quiet when another prophet is speaking, and of avoiding disorderly behaviour. 11.10 may illustrate the same principle. A woman prophet is not ecstatic and out of control. The Spirit does not deprive her of the right to do what she thinks fit with her own head—in this case, to keep it covered. If this is a correct interpretation, Paul is not trying to force women prophets to cover their heads against their will. Rather, he is defending the right of those who wish to cover their heads to do so.

There may also be a parallel with the use of ἐξουσία in 7.37. I have argued in Chapter 7 that, in that verse, the obstacle to a man having 'authority with regard to his own will' was probably the pressure being exerted by 'spiritual' people. The same may be true in 11.10. Paul may be opposing 'spiritual' people who believed that any form of self-control (whether in speech or in dress) was a denial of true prophetic inspiration, and were trying to pressurize women who were prophets into conformity with their stereotype.

This interpretation makes sense of the two verses within which the passage is framed: 11.2 'I commend you for always remembering me and observing the traditions as I handed them on to you' and 11.16: 'if anyone wants to be quarrelsome (φιλόνεικος), we do not have such a custom, nor do the churches of God'.[64] Both verses seem to echo a claim by some Corinthians that their advocacy of bare-headedness for women prophets was in accordance with Paul's tradition.[65] There are at least two elements

---

64. Mitchell (*Reconciliation*, p. 150) points out that the word φιλόνεικος in 11.16 was a word often used in Greek literature to refer to party strife, and sees here a link with the divisions condemned elsewhere in 1 Corinthians. It is indeed quite possible that one or more of the party leaders was orchestrating the campaign for bare-headedness. However, it is going too far to say that Paul advises women prophets to cover their heads 'to avoid φιλονεικία in the church' (Mitchell, *Reconciliation*, p. 263). Verse 16 is an *ad hominem* remark addressed to the person(s) concerned, not the theological basis of Paul's argument.

65. Thiselton (*First Epistle*, p. 810), following Hays (*First Corinthians*, pp. 181-84), rightly rejects the view that 11.2 is ironic. It is a quotation of a Corinthian claim, and Paul deals with it in the same way as he deals with most such claims—he agrees with it in principle, but modifies it in detail. In v. 17, on the other hand, he moves away from his partial acceptance of the Corinthian claim in respect of women prophets to a total rejection of their claim in respect of the Lord's Supper. This difference is made clear by the verbal repetition of ἐπαινῶ (v. 2) and οὐκ ἐπαινῶ (v. 17). With regard to the Lord's Supper, Paul declares, they are rejecting the tradition he received from the Lord (v. 23) by not discerning the Lord's body (v. 29). The contrast between ἐπαινῶ

in that tradition to which they could have been appealing.[66]

The first element is Paul's emphasis on equality: 'there is no male or female; all are one in Christ Jesus' (Gal. 3.28). Some people at Corinth may have been asserting, on the basis of this teaching, that the behaviour of male and female prophets should be identical. This would explain why Paul insists in 1 Cor. 11.4-9, 11-15 that there are natural, God-given distinctions between the sexes. But the motif of equality does not adequately explain v. 10.

It is probable that some Corinthians were appealing to another element in Paul's tradition—the importance of prophecy—as expressed in 1 Thess. 5.19-20: 'do not quench the Spirit; do not despise prophecies'. They may have understood prophecy in terms of ecstasy, and applied pressure to women prophets to abandon themselves to the control of the Spirit. In such a situation, Paul's concern (as in ch. 14) would be to hold together in creative tension the prophetic fervour of the Corinthians and the need for 'decency and good order'. It was right and proper, in his view, that women prophets should possess the right to cover their heads. This was neither a denial of their spiritual equality nor a stifling of the inspiration of the Spirit.[67]

and οὐκ ἐπαινῶ suggests that, in Paul's view, the Corinthians were not contravening the tradition over the matter of women prophets in the way that they were contravening it when celebrating the Lord's Supper.

66. E.S. Fiorenza (*In Memory of Her: A Feminist Theological Reconstruction of Christian Origins* [London: SCM Press, 1983], pp. 228-29) appreciates the multiple nature of the 'traditions' of 11.2 when she defines them 'as those of liberation, freedom, equality and spirit-empowering in Christ or in the Lord'. However, she does not appreciate the link between v. 2 and v. 16, and regards v. 16 as an authoritarian appeal, probably made because Paul 'himself senses that his reasoning is not very convincing'.

67. On the phrase διὰ τοὺς ἀγγέλους see Thiselton, *First Epistle*, pp. 839-41. This phrase probably refers to angels present at Christian worship, both as fellow-worshippers and as guardians of good order. Paul's abrupt introduction of the angels without any explanation suggests that their presence at worship had been put forward as an argument in the debate at Corinth over this issue. Possibly the women prophets had expressed their unhappiness at being pressurized to behave in an unseemly way in the presence of the angels.

Chapter 8

THE QUESTION OF SELF-SUPPORT

One of the issues that is common to both 1 and 2 Corinthians is Paul's policy of self-support. He defends this policy in ch. 9 of 1 Corinthians and in two passages in 2 Corinthians—11.5-15 and 12.11-18. In both letters the receipt or refusal of financial support is linked to apostleship. Paul's opponents seem to have regarded an apostle who received such support as a professional, and an apostle who was self-supporting as an amateur.

I shall consider first the question, 'What exactly was involved in Paul's refusal of material support?', and then examine his treatment of this issue in the two letters.

1. *The Nature of Paul's Policy*

At first sight, Paul's statements in both letters seem to be clear and un-equivocal. In 1 Cor. 9 he argues that preachers of the gospel have the right (both by virtue of natural justice and by virtue of the teaching of Jesus) to earn their living by their preaching; but he has not exercised this right, and would rather die than allow this boast of his to be nullified (v. 15). In 2 Cor. 11.9 he asserts that he has consistently avoided being a burden to the Corinthians and will continue to do so. These statements imply a system-atic refusal to accept any remuneration for his preaching and a determi-nation to continue that policy in the future.

However, it is sometimes alleged that Paul was not as consistent as his words suggest. David Horrell, for example, maintains that it would not be true to imply that Paul rejected all material support from the Corinthians, and cites three passages to prove his case.[1] In my opinion, these passages do not establish Horrell's theory, and do not contradict Paul's explicit statement that he had refused to be a burden to the Corinthians.

---

1. Horrell, *Social Ethos*, pp. 212-13.

i.   In Rom. 16.23 Paul writes: 'Greetings from Gaius, who has been host to me and to the whole church'. The hospitality of Gaius was enjoyed not only by Paul but by all the church members. Paul's enjoyment of that hospitality, whatever form it took,[2] could not be construed as a burden laid on the church as a whole.

ii.   In 1 Cor. 16.17 Paul states that Stephanas and company 'made up for what was lacking' on the part of the Corinthians (τὸ ὑμῶν ὑστέρημα οὗτοι ἀνεπλήρωσαν). He uses a similar expression with regard to Epaphroditus in Phil. 2.30: 'he risked his life in order to make up for what was lacking in your service to me' (παραβολευσάμενος τῇ ψυχῇ ἵνα ἀναπληρώσῃ τὸ ὑμῶν ὑστέρημα τῆς πρός με λειτουργίας). Horrell suggests that in both passages 'making up for what was lacking' may relate to material aid. If this is so, it can only mean that the gifts of the Philippians and the Corinthians were less than Paul was expecting, and Epaphroditus and Stephanas respectively made up the deficiency out of their own pockets. This would be an unlikely sentiment in Philippians, a letter of thanks that is full of joy and gratitude. It would be an even more unlikely sentiment in 1 Corinthians, after Paul has boasted in ch. 9 of the fact that he is self-supporting. Nor does this idea suit the context in either letter. In 1 Cor. 16.17-18 Paul rejoices in the presence (παρουσία) of Stephanas and his party, and in their refreshment of his spirit, not in their money. In the case of Epaphroditus, he risked his life by travelling, not by topping up the Philippians' gift. Stephanas and Epaphroditus differed from the churches they represented in their physical presence with Paul. By their presence they made up for the inability of the other church members to visit him.[3]

iii. In 1 Cor. 16.6 Paul looks forward to the Corinthians' sending him on his way (ἵνα ὑμεῖς με προπέμψητε) after his next visit. Horrell argues that Paul's use of the term προπέμπω implies a request for personal assistance. Fee is of a similar opinion, and believes the word προπέμπω to be a technical term for 'providing a person with food, money and travelling companions so as to ensure a safe and successful arrival at his or

---

2.   Gaius may well have been the same person as Titius Justus (see Chapter 3 n. 16). In Acts 18.7 Luke states that Paul moved from the synagogue to the house of Titius Justus. In other words, he changed the venue of his preaching and teaching (Acts 18.5-6), not his place of residence, which was the home of Aquila and Priscilla (Acts 18.1-3).

3.   For further discussion of the meaning of ὑστέρημα see Chapter 3 n. 19.

her destination'.[4] But this is not correct. In the New Testament προπέμπω means 'give someone a good send-off', and only in a few cases is material provision a major factor in this send-off.[5]

Two instances in Acts make this clear. In Acts 20.38 the Ephesian elders accompanied Paul on his journey as far as the ship (προέπεμπον δὲ αὐτὸν εἰς τὸ πλοῖον). In Acts 21.5 the Christians in Tyre, including women and children, accompanied Paul to the edge of the town (προπεμπόντων ἡμᾶς πάντων σὺν γυναιξὶ καὶ τέκνοις ἕως ἔξω τῆς πόλεως). The send-off consisted of their physical accompaniment of Paul on the first stage of his journey.

During my years as a presbyter in India I learned to value the importance attached there to a good send-off. If I cycled to a village church, on my departure a number of people would accompany me to the edge of the village. If I travelled by train, they would accompany me to the station. In the Telugu language there is a special word for this custom—*saganampu* —translated in C.P. Brown's dictionary as 'to set a traveller on his way, to convey or accompany one for a little distance'.[6] In Western societies we are often too busy to observe such customs or to appreciate their signifi-

---

4.   Fee, *First Epistle*, p. 819. So also BAGD sv. προπέμπω. Fee detects a similar idea in the words ἵνα δευτέραν χάριν σχῆτε in 2 Cor. 1.15. He understands these words to denote a double opportunity for the Corinthians to show kindness by helping Paul on his way, and regards the traditional interpretation (that the Corinthians would receive grace through his visit) as implying 'latent egotism and condescension' (G.D. Fee, 'ΧΑΡΙΣ in 2 Cor. 1.15: Apostolic Parousia and Paul-Corinth Chronology', *NTS* 24 [1978], pp. 533-38). But Christian humility does not mean undervaluing one's own gifts; it means having confidence in them because they are gifts from God. A parallel verse is Rom. 1.11, where Paul longs to visit the church at Rome so that he can impart to them some spiritual gift. The fact that, as an afterthought, he mentions both giving and receiving in the following verse (v. 12) does not affect his primary perception of himself as an agent of God's blessing.

5.   Fee gives a list of passages in the New Testament and Apocrypha where, in his opinion, προπέμπω refers to the provision of practical assistance (*First Epistle*, p. 819 n. 12). Of these, Acts 15.3, Rom. 15.24 and 2 Cor. 1.16 simply refer to a good send-off, without specifying what that would consist of. In 1 Esdras 4.47 and 1 Macc. 12.4 the primary reference is to ensuring a safe journey, as is shown by the words μετ' εἰρήνης in the latter passage. The only passages linking προπέμπω to material provision are Tit. 3.13 and 3 Jn 6-8. The material aspects of travel between the churches may well have grown in importance as the church expanded, but such an emphasis should not necessarily be read back into the time of 1 Corinthians.

6.   C.P. Brown, *A Telugu-English Dictionary* (Madras: SPCK, 2nd edn, 1903), p. 1327.

cance. This may explain the tendency among Western scholars to understand προπέμπω in material terms.

In 1 Cor. 16.11 Paul asks the Corinthians to send Timothy on his way in peace (προπέμψατε δὲ αὐτὸν ἐν εἰρήνῃ), so that he may travel back to join Paul in Ephesus. The addition of the words 'in peace' does not suit a reference to material assistance. Paul's concern in vv. 10-11 is that the Corinthians, in their present obstreperous mood, may give Timothy a hard time. He therefore makes three requests—for Timothy to arrive without fear, for him not to be despised during his stay, and for him to leave them in peace. The first two requests do not relate to money, nor does the third.

In the case of 1 Cor. 16.6, the interpretation of Fee and Horrell does not only give a false meaning to προπέμπω, it also runs contrary to the context. Paul mentions his send-off from Corinth in a subordinate clause, and sees it as a consequence of his having spent several weeks or months there. If προπέμπω denotes primarily material assistance, this presumably means that it would take that length of time to accumulate the money required. It is most unlikely that Paul should have suggested this in a letter in which he had boasted of his financial independence. As he looked forward to his next visit to Corinth money was the least of his concerns. His frame of mind could have been expressed in the words he used later in 2 Cor. 12.14: 'what I am looking for is not your money but yourselves' (οὐ γὰρ ζητῶ τὰ ὑμῶν ἀλλὰ ὑμᾶς). His hope was that his next visit would restore the relationship of love and trust he had once enjoyed with the Corinthian church. If that happened, he would be able to move on to his next assignment with their encouragement and blessing.[7]

There is, therefore, no reason to doubt Paul's explicit statement that he refused to receive material help from the Corinthians during his stay at Corinth. But this raises the question: why did he accept a gift from

---

7.   Thrall (*Second Epistle*, pp. 74, 128, 139-40) argues that δι' ὑμῶν διελθεῖν εἰς Μακεδονίαν in 2 Cor. 1.16 means 'with your assistance to travel through to Macedonia', the preposition διά being instrumental. She claims that προπεμφθῆναι in the same verse means 'be helped on my journey', with financial assistance, help with travel arrangements, and the like, and that consequently δι' ὑμῶν διελθεῖν will mean the same. But the conjunction of διά plus genitive with the verb διέρχεσθαι is found 11 times in the New Testament, and in the other 10 occurrences the preposition has a spatial sense. One could perhaps turn Thrall's theory on its head and argue that, since διά τινος διέρχεσθαι normally has a spatial reference, the word προπεμφθῆναι must have a spatial reference as well.

Macedonia at a time when he was refusing to accept such gifts from the Corinthians? (2 Cor. 11.8-9)

Paul's reason for mentioning this gift has often been misunderstood. According to Peter Marshall, 'the only reason he gives for his refusal of the Corinthian offer is his acceptance of aid from other churches'.[8] But this is a misinterpretation. Verse 9 reads: καὶ παρὼν πρὸς ὑμᾶς καὶ ὑστερηθεὶς οὐ κατενάρκησα οὐθενός· τὸ γὰρ ὑστέρημά μου προσανεπλήρωσαν οἱ ἀδελφοὶ ἐλθόντες ἀπὸ Μακεδονίας (and when I was with you and was in need, I did not prey on anyone; for the brothers coming from Macedonia helped me out). In this verse the reference to help from Macedonia provides an *illustration* of his policy, not the *reason* for it.[9] He was so determined to receive no financial support from the Corinthians that, even when he was in need, he did not ask for help from Corinth but survived on handouts from another church. There is no suggestion in the text that the Corinthians were angered by his acceptance of this gift,[10] and the casual way in which Paul mentions it makes this theory improbable.

A hint as to the probable explanation of Paul's behaviour is provided by P.D. Gardner:

> There is no evidence that Paul took financial help from any group while preaching in their centre. When he did involve people in his support it was after they were established as a church and it was designed to help him in his missionary work in other centres (2 Cor. 11.8). In this way Paul allowed churches to share with him in his work of proclamation and to benefit from the 'increase in fruit' (Phil. 4.7).[11]

Gardner's explanation is on the right lines, but does not answer one question. Why did Paul insist that he would not be a burden to the Corinthians for the indefinite future, despite his acceptance of aid from Macedonia? (2 Cor. 11.9-10). The answer to this question depends on what Paul

8.   Marshall, *Enmity*, p. 176.

9.   The γάρ of v. 9 can be paraphrased: 'as evidence for the statement I have just made (that I did not prey on anyone at Corinth) I adduce the fact that...' The use of γάρ in such a sense is attested by BAGD sv. γάρ 1.d, under the heading 'the general is confirmed by the specific'.

10.   Contra Marshall, *Enmity*, p. 240. Furnish (*II Corinthians*, p. 507) thinks it 'probable' that the Corinthians were distressed by this inconsistency.

11.   P.D. Gardner, *The Gifts of God and the Authentication of a Christian: An Exegetical Study of 1 Corinthians 8–11.1* (Lanham, NY: University Press of America, 1994), p. 81.

meant by being a burden. In his letter to the Philippians he made it clear that the gift he had just received was a spontaneous act of generosity on the part of the Philippian church, not a response to a request for help (Phil. 4.10, 17). When Gardner says that Paul 'involved people in his support', this implies an organized support group. But nothing in Philippians suggests this. The Philippian gift was unsolicited and spontaneous. Paul's policy of self-support did not mean that he never accepted anything from anyone—that if he was invited for a meal he would refuse to go, or that he would not accept hospitality from a friend when visiting one of the churches (Phlm. 22), or that if the church at Philippi spontaneously decided to send him a love-gift he would refuse it. It meant that he never asked for money, and avoided any gift that could be construed as payment for his preaching.

2. *Paul's Justification of his Policy in 1 Corinthians*

1 Corinthians 9 has a dual purpose. Within its context in chs. 8–10 it deals with the renunciation of rights. Paul presents his renunciation of his apostolic right to be financially supported as a model for the Corinthians to follow (compare 9.12 with 8.9, 13).[12] However, before making this point, his first task was to prove that he possessed the right he was renouncing. He had to do this because 'others' were denying that he was an apostle (v. 2), and under their influence his 'examiners' were calling into question his apostolic status and disputing his apostolic rights (vv. 3, 4). Paul needed to defend himself against these examiners at some point in the letter, and probably felt that the discussion of food offered to idols, which was largely concerned with the claiming of rights (8.9; 10.23), was an appropriate place to do so. Thus he was able, in Richard Hays's words, to kill two birds with one stone.[13]

The idea that Paul's apostleship was under attack at the time of 1 Corinthians has been disputed. For example, Wendell Willis (following Johannes Weiss) points out that the form of the question in 9.2: οὐκ εἰμὶ ἀπόστολος; (am I not an apostle?) implies a positive answer. The Corinthians believed Paul was an apostle. Therefore, Willis concludes, Paul's ἀπολογία cannot

---

12. The continuity between chs. 8 and 9 is emphasized by Horrell, *Social Ethos*, p. 205: 'The first person singular forms of 8.13 provide a clear link with the personal example which follows.'

13. Hays, *First Corinthians*, p. 146. On the dual function of ch. 9 as both an example and a self-defence see Horrell, *Social Ethos*, pp. 204-205 and the references he cites in nn. 28-32.

be a defence of his apostolic office in Corinth.[14] This argument ignores the distinction Paul draws in v. 2 between the view of the church (that he was an apostle) and the view of 'others' (that he was not). It is unlikely that he would refer in this way to unnamed 'others' unless these were people known to the Corinthians—that is, a group who were (or had been) at work in Corinth. Nor is it likely that the examiners of v. 3 were unrelated to the 'others' of v. 2. Paul's argument is continuous, and if a line is drawn between v. 2 and v. 3, vv. 1 and 2 are left hanging in mid-air, unconnected to their context. The examiners either included the 'others' or were influenced by their teaching; and Paul's defence was conducted against the examiners, not against the church as a whole.[15]

Margaret Mitchell denies that Paul was on the defensive at all. In her opinion Paul uses the word ἀπολογία 'to justify rhetorically his use of himself as the example for imitation'.[16] She finds a parallel to this procedure in a passage from Isocrates, in which he adopted the fiction of a trial and cast his speech in the form of an ἀπολογία. Presumably, on this theory, not only is Paul's use of the word ἀπολογία a rhetorical fiction but also his reference to his examiners and to 'others' who dispute his apostleship. In other words, v. 3 means: 'this is the defence I would make against my examiners if such people existed'. This is a strange way to understand Paul's use of the present participle ἀνακρίνουσιν.

One reason for Mitchell's exegesis is that she cannot find any charge in 1 Cor. 9 against which Paul would need to defend himself except what she calls the 'historically implausible' charge that he did not take the Corinthians' money. That such an accusation would ever have been made is, she asserts, 'scarcely possible'. The problem with this assertion is that Paul does respond to such an accusation in 2 Corinthians. 'Did I commit a sin in preaching the gospel to you free of charge?' he asks (2 Cor. 11.7). Such a question is meaningless unless his policy of self-support had been criticized at Corinth. Of course, if a wedge is driven between 1 and 2 Corinthians and they are assigned to two different backgrounds, it is possible to claim that the arguments of 2 Corinthians are irrelevant to 1 Corinthians. But even if this were so, 2 Corinthians would still demonstrate that such an accusation is not historically implausible.[17]

14. Willis, 'Apologia', p. 34.
15. I have argued in Chapter 1 Section 4 that the 'others' were probably the Christian sophists who were responsible for the divisions in the church.
16. Mitchell, *Reconciliation*, p. 246.
17. For further critical comments on Mitchell's argument see Horrell, *Social Ethos*, pp. 205-206.

Horrell accepts that ch. 9 is dual-purpose—Paul offers both an example for the Corinthians to follow and a defence against his critics. What the critics were criticizing, in Horrell's view, was his failure to accept material support.[18] This is true, but not the whole truth. His policy of self-support is indeed the theme of the latter half of the chapter (vv. 15-27); but the connection of thought between v. 3 and v. 4 indicates that there was also another accusation. What Paul defends in vv. 4-14 is his right to receive support, not his practice of refusing it. Since v. 4 is the first item in this ἀπολογία,[19] his critics must have been claiming that he did not have this right. In the light of vv. 1-2 (and on the assumption that vv. 1-2 are relevant to their context) their argument must have been that he did not have this right because he was not a genuine apostle.

We should therefore conclude that in the earlier part of 1 Cor. 9 Paul was defending himself against the accusations of his critics. The fact that he was self-supporting meant, in their eyes, that he was not a professional apostle: he did not accept financial support because he was not entitled to it. In Fee's words:

> Paul's response…is not first of all to defend his renunciation of his rights, but to establish that he has such rights. This must be done because they have questioned his authority altogether. From their point of view his activity would not have been the renunciation of assumed rights; rather, he must have worked with his hands because he lacked such rights.[20]

In the latter half of the chapter Paul explains the reasons for his insistence on self-support. In v. 12 he writes: 'we have not exercised this right [to support], but we put up with everything, so as not to cause any hindrance to the gospel of Christ'. There are several ways in which this statement can be interpreted.

First, it can be understood in the light of the rest of the chapter. Paul's aim was to adapt his lifestyle to that of other people—to become 'all things to all people' in order to save them (vv. 19-22). Most of the inhabitants of Corinth had to work hard in comparative poverty and economic insecurity, and Paul wished to share their way of life. He did this for the sake of the gospel (v. 23). Just as sharing the lifestyle of others promoted the gospel, so also distancing himself from the lifestyle of others

18. Horrell, *Social Ethos*, pp. 204-206.
19. The word αὕτη in v. 3 may be translated 'as follows', and introduces the argument beginning at v. 4. This is convincingly argued by Fee, *First Epistle*, p. 401 n. 21.
20. Fee, *First Epistle*, p. 400.

would have been a hindrance to the gospel.[21]

Second, Paul may have wished to avoid being in a patron–client relationship with upper-class financial supporters. This may have been one factor in Paul's decision, but does not provide a complete explanation. He could have received offers of help from many members of the church, few of whom belonged to the same social class as patrons. This is suggested by his insistence in 2 Cor. 11.9 that he would not be a burden to the Corinthians. Such language would not have been appropriate if he had had rich patrons in mind, who were well able to support him and would have gained in prestige by so doing.[22]

Third, Paul may have wished to avoid being regarded as a sophist. In chs. 1 and 2 (especially in 2.1-3) he distances himself from the rhetorical style of the sophists. Sophists were often criticized for their love of money,[23] and Paul could have been as anxious to avoid the mercenary practices of the sophists as to avoid their rhetorical practices. This is especially likely if his opponents at Corinth were behaving like sophists (as chs. 1–4 imply they were). However, Paul does not mention sophistic practice in ch. 9, and it is probably wiser to interpret v. 12b primarily in the light of his policy of identification with all classes of society, as described in the rest of the chapter.

Paul gives another reason for his insistence on self-support in vv. 15-19.[24] This policy is for him a source of personal pride—it is something to boast about. Ironically he declares that it also gives him his wages. The payment he receives for his unpaid ministry is the self-satisfaction of receiving no payment. By these statements Paul personalizes the issue and treats it as a matter of individual preference. One can only guess at his reasons for doing this. Possibly he hoped that the Corinthians would accept this aspect of his ministry as a personal idiosyncrasy and resist the pressure being put upon them by their new teachers to condemn it. If he did think that, the escalation of the conflict evidenced in 2 Corinthians shows that he was over-optimistic.

21. Cf. Dale Martin, *Slavery as Salvation: The Metaphor of Slavery in Pauline Christianity* (New Haven: Yale University Press, 1990), p. 124; Horrell, *Social Ethos*, pp. 215-16.

22. On the general question of patronage, and the description of Phoebe as a προστάτις in Rom. 16.2, see Chapter 3 n. 15.

23. Winter (*Philo and Paul*, pp. 95-97) quotes examples of such criticism from Plato, Philo, Dio Chrysostom and the Cynic epistles.

24. For further discussion of these verses see Excursus G 'The Interpretation of 1 Corinthians 9.17'.

3. *Paul's Justification of his Policy in 2 Corinthians*

In 2 Cor. 11.5-15 and 12.11-18 Paul defends his policy of self-support against four criticisms. The first criticism (that he is not a professional apostle) is a further development of the charge laid by his 'examiners', to which he has already replied in 1 Cor. 9. The other three criticisms are new, and appear for the first time in 2 Corinthians. They had probably been voiced after the time of writing of 1 Corinthians (partly as a response to Paul's argument in 1 Cor. 9), and had been reported to Paul by Titus.

a. *Paul is not a Professional Apostle*
In both 11.5-15 and 12.11-18 the question of payment is included within a comparison between Paul and the 'super-apostles' (ὑπερλίαν ἀπόστολοι) —a term that is best understood as Paul's ironic description of his opponents.[25] These opponents saw themselves as professional apostles whose status, like that of other professionals, was in proportion to the payment they received. They saw Paul, who refused to receive any payment, as inferior to them and not a proper apostle. In 2 Cor. 11.5-7 Paul declares that he is in no way inferior to these 'super-apostles': he may be unprofessional in respect of rhetorical skill (ἰδιώτης τῷ λόγῳ), but not in respect of knowledge. He then asks: 'Or did I commit a sin in preaching the gospel to you free of charge and thus demeaning myself so that your status could be lifted?' (ἢ ἁμαρτίαν ἐποίησα ἐμαυτὸν ταπεινῶν ἵνα ὑμεῖς ὑψωθῆτε, ὅτι δωρεὰν τὸ τοῦ θεοῦ εὐαγγέλιον εὐηγγελισάμην ὑμῖν;). This reference to his 'sin' in not charging for his preaching immediately follows his reply to the accusation that he is inferior to the 'super-apostles', and lacks the rhetorical skills that apostolic status requires. The word ἤ in v. 7 can be paraphrased: 'or (to quote another example of my alleged inferiority to the super-apostles) did I sin by not charging for my preaching?'

The whole passage is about professionalism. The word ἰδιώτης here means a non-professional.[26] The 'super-apostles' were paid, professional

---

25. On the meaning of the phrase οἱ ὑπερλίαν ἀπόστολοι see Chapter 6, Section 1.

26. The word ἰδιώτης means a private person as opposed to an official, or an unskilled person as opposed to a skilled person. The expert or official with whom the ἰδιώτης is compared can be a king, a doctor, a professional soldier, a craftsman, an orator, a poet, a musician or a philosopher (see the references in LSJ and BAGD sv. ἰδιώτης). In 2 Cor. 11.6 the addition of τῷ λόγῳ indicates that Paul has been accused of lacking the rhetorical skills of the professional orator.

preachers, whereas the unpaid Paul was an amateur. They were full-time preachers, whereas Paul preached in his spare time. Their rhetorical skill was part of their professionalism, just as Paul's lack of rhetorical skill was part of his amateurism.[27] Thus Paul's failure to be paid and his lack of rhetorical skill were intimately connected—they were both evidence of his amateur status.[28]

In 2 Cor. 12.11-18 the link between payment and apostleship is equally clear. Paul begins by repeating the assertion that he is not inferior to the 'super-apostles'. This assertion is then justified by two pieces of evidence. On the one hand (μέν), his ministry was characterized by 'the signs of an apostle'—that is, by miracles. The μέν of v. 12 is followed, not by a δέ, but by an ironical question: τί γάρ ἐστιν ὃ ἡσσώθητε ὑπὲρ τὰς λοιπὰς ἐκκλησίας, εἰ μὴ ὅτι αὐτὸς ἐγὼ οὐ κατενάρκησα ὑμῶν; χαρίσασθέ μοι τὴν ἀδικίαν ταύτην (for in what respect were you made inferior to the other churches except that I [unlike others] did not prey on you? Forgive me for this injustice!).[29] Here, as in ch. 11, the injustice (or sin) of his failure to charge for his preaching is linked to the accusation that he was inferior to the 'super-apostles' who did charge. Because of this, it was alleged, the Corinthian church had become inferior to other churches that had paid, professional leaders.

This passage is concerned with the authentication of apostles. One of the evidences that authenticated a true apostle, in the eyes of Paul's opponents, was the performance of 'signs and wonders and mighty works'. That is why Paul insists that he has performed miracles as much as any of

27. The fact that Paul was regarded as an amateur in rhetoric does not decide the insoluble question as to whether he had had any rhetorical training. Isocrates commented that, of all the students in the rhetorical schools, only a limited number became ἀγωνισταί (men who engaged in rhetorical competition) or teachers of rhetoric; the others became ἰδιῶται, using the skills they had learnt in a non-professional way (Isocrates, *Antidosis* 201-204) (cf. Martin, *Body*, p. 48). If Paul had studied rhetoric under Gamaliel (as he could have done—see E.A. Judge, 'Paul's Boasting in Relation to Contemporary Professional Practice', *AusBR* 16 [1968], pp. 37-50 [40]), he would still have been an ἰδιώτης when compared with professional orators.

28. Thiselton (*First Epistle*, p. 24) endorses the comment of Pogoloff (*Logos and Sophia*, pp. 191, 203) that many Corinthians would have liked Paul to imitate the sophists and turn 'professional'. Lim ('Demonstration', pp. 143-44) gives examples of the willingness of students of the sophists to pay fees, and even of their insistence on doing so.

29. On the translation of αὐτὸς ἐγώ see Excursus D 'The Meaning of αὐτὸς ἐγώ Παῦλος in 2 Corinthians 10.1'.

his opponents. However, he continues ironically, there is one evidence that is lacking to authenticate my ministry—my opponents have extorted money from the church, and I have not. The implication of this statement is that, in the eyes of Paul's opponents, professional remuneration was just as much a 'sign of an apostle' as the performance of miracles.

b. *Paul's Refusal of Support is a Sign of Lack of Love*
In 11.11, after declaring his determination to continue his policy of self-support in the future, Paul asks the question: 'Why is this? Is it because I do not love you? God knows the answer to that!' These words imply that his opponents were interpreting his refusal of support as a sign of lack of love. What is the background to such a judgment?

Peter Marshall has shown how, in the Graeco-Roman world, the refusal of a gift could change friendship into enmity, and 11.11 illustrates this principle.[30] Clearly some of the Corinthians were feeling badly about Paul's refusal of their help. But in one respect Marshall goes beyond the evidence. He argues that the offer of help was made by the more wealthy Corinthians and was 'an attempt to get Paul over to their side and thus obligated to them'.[31] Such a cynical assessment of the motives of the Corinthian Christians is not justified. It is an example of the modern tendency to explain everything that happened within the Corinthian church in terms of the social customs of upper-class Graeco-Roman society. There are several drawbacks to the attempt to use this approach to explain 2 Cor. 11.11.

First, only a few members of the Corinthian church belonged to the upper classes (1 Cor. 1.26). Paul may have received offers of help from people of all classes. Generosity and poverty often go together, as is illustrated by the churches in Macedonia (2 Cor. 8.1-2).

Second, the fact that a certain procedure is commonly observed does not mean that everyone without exception is bound to conform to it. In modern Western societies there is a standard procedure for borrowing money, by calculating the APR (Annual Percentage Rate). But it is still possible for a friend to lend money to a friend without interest, ignoring the standard procedure. Friendship is not always subservient to self-interest.

Third, the influence of the Holy Spirit should not be discounted. On the

---

30. This is the main theme of Peter Marshall's book: *Enmity at Corinth: Social Conventions in Paul's Relations with the Corinthians* (WUNT [2nd Series] 23; Tübingen: J.C.B. Mohr, 1987).
31. Marshall, *Enmity*, p. 232.

one hand, it is wrong to assume that the Corinthian Christians were always pure in their motives simply because they were Christians. The Corinthian church, of all the Pauline churches, was the most integrated with secular society, and the most likely to adopt the values of that society.[32] But they were also people whose lives and attitudes had been changed by the Holy Spirit (1 Cor. 6.9-11). They would not necessarily be as calculating as Marshall assumes.

Fourth, the accusation of lack of love only surfaces in 2 Corinthians and does not appear in 1 Corinthians. It probably represents an attempt by Paul's rivals, in the interval between the two letters, to poison the minds of Paul's friends at Corinth. The offers of help were most likely made originally in good faith; it was Paul's opponents who were trying to inspire feelings of enmity in a situation where they were inappropriate.

c. By his Policy of Self-Support Paul has made the Corinthian Church Inferior to Other Churches
In 12.13 Paul asks the question: 'in what respect were you made inferior to the other churches, except for the fact that I did not prey on you?' The background to this verse is often misunderstood. The other churches are taken to be the churches of Macedonia, from whom Paul received support (in cash or in kind)[33] at a time when he was refusing support from the Corinthians.[34] But Paul's wording makes this interpretation unlikely. In the phrase αὐτὸς ἐγὼ οὐ κατενάρκησα ὑμῶν, the force of αὐτός is to throw all the emphasis on ἐγώ. It was I, Paul, who refused to prey on you. The contrast is not between Paul's attitude to the Corinthians and his attitude to the Macedonians; it is between the church at Corinth (evangelized by the unpaid Paul) and other churches (evangelized by paid professionals).

Paul's opponents had come to Corinth with letters of recommendation from other (probably non-Pauline) churches (3.1), and would be aware that the common practice was for apostles to receive material support. Paul himself acknowledges the widespread adoption of this practice (1 Cor. 9.6). 2 Corinthians 12.13 is therefore best understood as Paul's reply

32. Barclay, 'Thessalonica and Corinth', pp. 57-58.
33. C.C. Caragounis (ΟΨΩΝΙΟΝ: A Reconsideration of its Meaning', *NovT* 16 [1974], pp. 35-57) has shown that the word ὀψώνιον (used in 11.8) refers to provisions which were often in kind but could also be in cash (so also Fee, *First Epistle*, p. 405 n. 44; Hock, *Social Context*, p. 92).
34. Barrett, *Second Epistle*, p. 322; Furnish, *II Corinthians*, p. 556; Marshall, *Enmity*, p. 177.

to the charge that, by working with his hands to support himself, he had made the Corinthian church inferior to other churches which had paid, professional leaders. This accusation first appears in 2 Corinthians, and is an example of the escalation of the conflict since the time of writing of 1 Corinthians.

d. *Paul's Refusal of Support is a Blind; He is Wanting Your Money all the Time*

In 12.16 Paul is accused of dishonesty: ἔστω δέ, ἐγὼ οὐ κατεβάρησα ὑμᾶς· ἀλλὰ ὑπάρχων πανοῦργος δόλῳ ὑμᾶς ἔλαβον (all right, you say, I did not burden you; but I was cunning and trapped you). In the style of the diatribe Paul puts words into the mouths of his opponents. His refusal to accept support during his time in Corinth, they were saying, was a cunning ploy, by which he hoped to win their confidence and then proceed to swindle them. The following verses (vv. 17-18) refer to Titus and an unnamed brother to whom the responsibility of raising the collection for the church in Judaea had been given. Clearly the accusation of dishonesty was related to the arrangements for the collection.

This accusation, like the two previous ones, does not surface in 1 Corinthians. At the same time, it should be noted how careful Paul is in 1 Cor. 16.3 to insist that the money raised will be taken to Judaea by representatives of the Corinthian church appointed in writing, not by himself. These words could be purely precautionary; or it may be that the first rumblings of the accusation of dishonesty had already been heard when he wrote them.

e. *Paul's Reply to his Critics*

In replying to these accusations Paul makes two points. First, his aim was not to be a burden to the church. This idea is expressed by two words—ἀβαρής (not burdensome) in 11.9 and καταναρκᾶν in 11.9 and 12.13-14. The precise meaning of the rare word καταναρκᾶν is uncertain. BAGD takes the meaning to be either 'weigh down, burden' (on the grounds that the word is so understood by several early church fathers and by the Latin and Syriac versions), or a satirical equivalent to the modern colloquial 'Knock out' (on the basis of two passages in Hippocrates).[35] Christopher Wordsworth sees a connection between καταναρκᾶν and νάρκη—the torpedo or electric eel. This fish attaches itself to other fish, numbs them, and then derives nourishment from them. Wordsworth paraphrases 11.9:

---

35. BAGD (3rd edn), sv. καταναρκάω.

'I did not attach myself to any for the purpose of first rendering him torpid by my touch, and then sucking nourishment from him and preying upon him'.[36] This interpretation is attractive, though Wordsworth does not provide the evidence to establish it. Whether we follow BAGD or Wordsworth, the two words ἀβαρής and καταναρκᾶν taken together suggest that Paul believed he could have become a burden to the Corinthians had he expected them to support him throughout his stay in Corinth.

Second, Paul wished to avoid a financial competition. He writes in 11.12: ὃ δὲ ποιῶ καὶ ποιήσω, ἵνα ἐκκόψω τὴν ἀφορμὴν τῶν θελόντων ἀφορμήν, ἵνα ἐν ᾧ καυχῶνται εὑρεθῶσιν καθὼς καὶ ἡμεῖς (What I do I shall continue to do, so as to deprive those who wish for it of the opportunity of saying, 'in the matter we are boasting about we are in the same position as Paul and his colleagues'). Paul's opponents were boasting of the amount they received and wanted a straightforward competition in this respect between themselves and Paul. They wanted to be able to say, 'we and Paul are competing on the same terms, but we are doing better'. But to their disgust Paul had withdrawn from the competition. In his view the quality of someone's apostleship should not be assessed in terms of financial remuneration, but in terms of service and suffering. One of the benefits of his policy of self-support was that his ministry could not be compared with theirs on the basis of income and financial status.

4. *Conclusion*

A comparison of Paul's discussion of his policy of self-support in 1 Corinthians with the discussion in 2 Corinthians reveals both similarities and differences. Among the similarities are the following:

i.   In both letters Paul is on the defensive. This is explicitly stated in 1 Cor. 9.3, where he uses the word ἀπολογία. In 2 Corinthians, the sarcastic tone of 11.7 and 11.11 indicates a response to criticism, and the phrase ἔστω δέ in 12.16 introduces a statement made by his critics in the style of the diatribe.

---

36.   C. Wordsworth, *The New Testament of our Lord and Saviour Jesus Christ, in the Original Greek: With Introduction and Notes*, II (2 vols.; London: Rivington, 1872), p. 175. He cites the description of the νάρκη in Athenaeus, *Deipnosophistae* 7.314C: νάρκη θηρεύει εἰς τροφὴν ἑαυτῆς τὰ ἰχθύδια, προσαπτομένη καὶ ναρκᾶν ποιοῦσα (the electric eel hunts little fish for food by attaching itself to them and making them numb).

ii.   In both letters the implied criticism came not only from members of the church, but also from other unnamed people. In 1 Cor. 9.2 Paul refers to 'others' who denied that he was an apostle. He distinguishes these 'others' from the members of the church, who had experienced the benefits of his ministry in their own lives. In 2 Cor. 11.12-15 he contrasts his policy of self-support with the policy of the 'false apostles', who wanted to compete with him on equal terms.

iii.   In both letters Paul treats his policy of self-support as a source of pride and boasting. In 1 Cor. 9.15-18 he declares that no one will in-validate this boast—he would rather die than preach the gospel for money. In 2 Cor. 11.9-10 he describes his policy of not being a burden to the Corinthians, and goes on: 'no one will put a stop to this boast of mine in the Achaean area'.

iv.   In both letters Paul asserts that, despite his unpaid status, he is a true apostle. In 1 Cor. 9.1-14 he insists on the genuineness of his apostleship (vv. 1-2), and claims that he has the same right as other apostles to be supported by the church (v. 5), even though he has not exercised this right (v. 12). The connection between apostolic status and apostolic payment is equally clear in 2 Cor. 12.11-14, where Paul's defence of his policy of self-support forms part of a defence against the accusation that he is inferior to the 'super-apostles'.

The most natural explanation of these four similarities is that 1 and 2 Corinthians represent different stages of a single conflict—that is, the 'false apostles' of 2 Corinthians were already at work in Corinth at the time of 1 Corinthians.

The differences between the letters in their treatment of this issue are twofold. On the one hand, Paul does not repeat in 2 Corinthians two of the main themes of 1 Cor. 9—the right of those who preach the gospel to be paid, and the opportunity his policy gave him to identify with all classes of society. On the other hand, he responds in 2 Corinthians to three new accusations—that his refusal of their help indicates a lack of love; that his amateur status has made the Corinthian church inferior to other churches; and that his initial refusal of their money was a cunning ploy to enable him to steal their money later through the collection. These differences suggest that Paul's opponents, having lost the first round of the argument, had resorted to character assassination. The contemptuous way in which he dismissed these new accusations with a single phrase (2 Cor. 11.11; 12.13) or with a series of rhetorical questions (12.16-18) suggests that he realized the serious argument had been already won.

EXCURSUS G:
THE INTERPRETATION OF 1 CORINTHIANS 9.17

1 Corinthians 9.17 is a notoriously difficult verse. One of the most influential contributions to the attempt to understand it has been Ernst Käsemann's article 'A Pauline Version of the "Amor Fati"'.[37] Käsemann begins by considering the words εἰ γὰρ ἑκὼν τοῦτο πράσσω, μισθὸν ἔχω, which can be literally translated, 'for if I do this willingly, I have a reward'. For many centuries these words were understood in the light of the doctrine of works of supererogation: Paul's preaching was a necessity, a duty laid upon him, not a service for which he could claim a reward; but by refusing to accept any payment for his preaching he went beyond the claim of duty and was therefore rewarded.

Käsemann rightly rejects this interpretation. He translates v. 17a: 'if I did this on my own initiative, I should expect reward', and comments that, in spite of objections to this translation by earlier scholars, '17a is universally regarded today as an unfulfilled conditional'.[38] Paul, on this interpretation, did not preach on his own initiative (ἑκών), but under a divine compulsion (ἀνάγκη). Käsemann describes this compulsion as 'the power of the divine will which radically and successfully challenges man and makes its servant its instrument'.[39] It is indeed possible to resist this power; but anyone who does so will experience it as a curse which 'smites man like a consuming sickness, penetrates his very being and destroys him from within'. This power of God drives Paul 'like a slave' through the Mediterranean.[40] Verse 17, in Käsemann's opinion, draws out the implications of this situation. If Paul were preaching of his own free will, he could expect a reward. But as it is he is preaching ἄκων 'under a sense of compulsion', and is thus simply discharging a trust.[41]

This understanding of v. 17a, which Käsemann described in the 1960s as the universal view of his contemporaries, has continued to hold sway since that time.[42] But there are four reasons why it should be rejected.

37. In E. Käsemann, *New Testament Questions of Today* (London: SCM Press, 1969), pp. 217-35.
38. Käsemann, *Questions*, pp. 217, 231 n. 81.
39. Käsemann, *Questions*, p. 230.
40. Käsemann, *Questions*, p. 231.
41. Käsemann, *Questions*, p. 217.
42. For advocacy of this interpretation see Barrett, *First Epistle*, pp. 209-10; Fee,

The first problem with Käsemann's interpretation is his translation of the words ἑκών and ἄκων as 'on my own initiative' and 'under a sense of compulsion'. The words ἑκών and ἄκων are psychological terms, and signify, not the external conditions under which an action is performed, but the internal willingness of the person concerned to perform it. This is particularly true of Stoic thought, according to which the wise man is able to do willingly (ἑκών) what God ordains. For example, Epictetus wants to be able to say to God when he dies: 'have I ever found any fault with Thee? Have I blamed Thy governance at all? I fell sick, when it was Thy will; so did other men, but I willingly (ἑκών). I became poor, it being Thy will, but with joy'.[43]

In this passage the word ἑκών denotes the willing acceptance of an involuntary situation. The task of the wise man, according to Epictetus, is to distinguish the things that are under our control (our desires, thoughts and choices) from things that are not under our control (our property, reputation, public offices). If you realize that the only things that really belong to you are the things under your control, then 'no one will ever be able to exert compulsion upon you, no one will hinder you, you will blame no one, you will find fault with no one, you will do absolutely nothing against your will' (ἄκων πράξεις οὐδὲ ἕν).[44] In another passage Epictetus describes a man persuading himself 'to accept willingly the inevitable' (ἑκόντα δέχεσθαι τὰ ἀναγκαῖα).[45] As F. Hauck says, 'the Stoic ideal is that the wise man should willingly accept his divinely imposed lot'.[46] Accordingly, Hauck translates ἑκών as 'willingly' in 1 Cor. 9.17.[47]

First Epistle, pp. 419-20; Schrage, *Der erste Brief*, II, pp. 324-25, who adds 'so heute die meisten' (n. 274). Conzelmann does not translate v. 17a as an unfulfilled conditional, but as 'for if I do it willingly', and comments 'now we have a real case' (*First Epistle*, p. 156 n. 9). But he regards the words 'if willingly' as 'simply a foil for the real case for Paul, for the fact that he "unwillingly" has a charge of stewardship laid upon him' (p. 158). Thiselton (*First Epistle*, p. 696) comments that 'Paul makes a logical point that only acts carried out from self-motivation or self-initiative belong to the logical order of "reward"; and thereby his own irresistible commission excludes such logic'. This interpretation does not regard v. 17a as an unfulfilled conditional from a grammatical point of view, but nevertheless regards it as referring to an unreal situation.

43. Epictetus, *Diss.* 3.5.8-9 (Loeb translation).
44. Epictetus, *Ench.* 1-3.
45. Epictetus, *Fr.* 9.
46. F. Hauck, 'ἑκών (ἄκων), ἑκούσιος', in *TDNT*, II, pp. 469-70 (469) sv. ἑκών.
47. Hauck, 'ἑκών', p. 470.

Paul's use of the words ἑκών and ἄκων was not borrowed directly from Stoicism, nor, of course, was he a Stoic. But the use of these words in this way by Stoic philosophers was only possible because that was the way the words were commonly understood by the Greek speakers they were addressing. It is true that, in many texts, the word ἄκων is associated with external compulsion or with slavery.[48] This is because most people, not being Stoics, are unwilling to do things they are forced to do, and therefore the ideas of unwillingness and external compulsion are related ideas. But this does not affect the fact that both ἑκών and ἄκων refer to the subjective reaction of people to the circumstances of freedom, compulsion or slavery which they encounter, rather than to the circumstances themselves.

Käsemann attacks those scholars who interpret the passage psychologically in terms of Paul's attitudes and emotions.[49] But Paul's attitudes and emotions are the theme of the whole passage. He is describing his boast (καύχημα)—the thing he is proud of, that makes him feel good. My boast, says Paul, is not that I am an evangelist (because that has been forced on me), but that I preach the gospel free of charge. In referring to his policy of self-support in this way Paul is deliberately psychologizing—discussing an economic and sociological issue in terms of his own personal motivation.

Moreover, ch. 9 as a whole is psychological. Paul is illustrating the point made in 8.9-13—that insistence on one's personal rights can prove hurtful to other Christians, and thus be a sin against Christ. He illustrates this by describing his approach to his own rights. As an apostle, he has the right to claim support from the church, but has chosen not to exercise that right for fear it should become a hindrance to the gospel (v. 12). Indeed, he is prepared to sacrifice his social status and his whole way of life in order

48. See the passages cited in Marshall, *Enmity*, pp. 295-306 and Gardner, *Gifts*, pp. 91-95. Dale Martin (*Slavery*, p. 71) claims that in Philo, *Omn. Prob. Lib.* 60–61 ἄκων is equivalent to ἀναγκάζεσθαι (being compelled). But Philo's statement is 'if one is compelled he clearly acts against his will' (εἰ ἀναγκάζεται, δῆλον ὅτι ἄκων τι ποιεῖ). Philo is here relating to each other two different ideas, and stating that one logically follows from the other. If the two ideas were identical, his statement would be tautologous and not worth making. The theme of *Omn. Prob. Lib.* 59–61 is that the good man is never compelled to do anything, because he only does what is right and therefore always wants to do what he does. The meaning of the phrase quoted by Martin is explained in the next sentence: 'He performs his virtuous actions not under compulsion but willingly, since all the things that he does are things he chooses to do' (τὰ μὲν οὖν ἀπ᾽ ἀρετῆς οὐ βιασθεὶς ἀλλ᾽ ἑκών, αἱρετὰ γάρ ἐστιν αὐτῷ πάνθ᾽ ἃ δρᾷ).

49. Käsemann, *Questions*, pp. 228-29.

to identify with other people and win them for Christ (vv. 19-23). He is like an athlete, willing to make any sacrifice to achieve his objective (vv. 24-27). It is within the context of this intensely personal chapter that v. 17 must be understood.[50]

The second problem with Käsemann's interpretation is the question Paul asks in v. 18: τίς οὖν μού ἐστιν ὁ μισθός; (what, then, is my payment?)[51] This question follows on from v. 17. Paul says in v. 17, 'I receive a payment' and asks in v. 18, 'what, then, is my payment?' This makes good sense if the words μισθὸν ἔχω in v. 17 are a statement of fact; but on Käsemann's view they are not a statement of fact. He regards v. 17a as an unreal conditional: 'I have a payment' means 'I would receive a payment if I were acting on my own initiative, but in fact I do not receive one'. This makes the train of thought in vv. 17-18 difficult to follow. How can Paul say, 'what, then, is my payment?' if he has just implied that he does not receive a payment?[52]

The third problem is that if Käsemann's interpretation is adopted, the two clauses in v. 17 do not form a proper antithesis: in the first clause the words in the apodosis μισθὸν ἔχω describe the *result* of the action in the protasis—the payment would be a reward for Paul's preaching on his own initiative; but in the second clause the words in the apodosis οἰκονομίαν

---

50. The subjective emphasis of ch. 9 is not unique in Paul's letters. In Rom. 15.20-23 he explains his future plans to travel via Rome to Spain in terms of personal ambition (φιλοτιμούμενον, v. 20) and personal desire (ἐπιποθία, v. 23). Similarly in ch. 9 he reduces the question of self-support to a matter of personal boasting and motivation. By doing so, he avoids having to explain in detail his reasons for not claiming support. Even in 2 Corinthians, when forced by pressure from his opponents to justify his policy of self-support in more detail, he continues to talk in terms of personal pride and boasting (2 Cor. 12.10). He understood the fact that people respond more positively to a personal and emotional appeal than to an abstract statement of theological principle.

51. The word μισθός often means 'payment' or 'wages', and in the context of Paul's policy of self-support this may be a better translation than the more general 'reward'. There is also a textual variant in v. 18—μοι instead of μου—but both give more or less the same meaning.

I am assuming that v. 18a is a separate sentence, and is not (as is sometimes suggested) the apodosis for v. 17b. Fee points out that οὖν is not an appropriate word for an apodosis, and that elsewhere in such sentences Paul uses ἄρα (Fee, *First Epistle*, p. 420 n. 39).

52. The belief that v. 18 did not make sense as a follow-up to v. 17 (as on his interpretation it did not) was one of the reasons why Johannes Weiss (*Der erste Korintherbrief*, p. 240) deleted v. 17 as a gloss.

πεπίστευμαι describe the *cause* of the action in the protasis—it is because God has laid this duty upon him that he acts under compulsion. Thus the two clauses are not, according to Käsemann's theory, strictly parallel. I shall return to this matter later.

The fourth problem is that v. 17a does not have the normal Greek construction for an unfulfilled conditional. The attempts that have been made to get round this difficulty are not totally convincing.[53]

In the light of these problems the interpretation of v. 17a as an unfulfilled conditional should be rejected. Paul is referring to a genuine possibility. He suggests two possible ways in which he could respond to the divine pressure to be an evangelist. He cannot refuse, because the consequences would be unthinkable (v. 16); but in accepting the divine call, he can do so either willingly or unwillingly.

Some commentators have rejected the idea that Paul could ever preach the gospel unwillingly.[54] But there are various considerations that make this idea understandable.

1.   The experience of some of the Old Testament prophets, particularly of Jeremiah, was similar to Paul's. Jeremiah had a strong sense of call—an awareness that he had been divinely appointed from his mother's womb to be a prophet (Jer. 1.5). But in 20.7-18 he complains to God that all day long he is mocked and insulted, and wishes he had never been born. This feeling of despair did not prevent him from fulfilling his ministry—the word of God was like a fire in his bones and he could not keep it to himself. He continued to be obedient to the divine ἀνάγκη, but did so (at least in part) unwillingly.

2.   Part of the pressure on Paul stemmed from the fact that he was in a caring profession (2 Cor. 11.28-29), and his experience has been shared through the ages by people in other caring professions, such as nurses and mothers. However strongly a nurse feels called to be a carer, however much a mother may see her child as a gift from God, there are times when caring for refractory patients or for endlessly demanding infants becomes a duty rather than a joy.

3.   When Paul first came to Corinth he came in 'fear and trembling' (1

53. For a discussion of the grammatical issue see Robertson and Plummer, *Critical and Exegetical Commentary*, pp. 189-90; Fee, *First Epistle*, p. 419 n. 35; Thiselton, *First Epistle*, p. 696.

54. Gardner (*Gifts*, p. 93 n. 153) comments on ἄκων: 'Surely not "unwillingly"!... The anacolouthon, and emotion of v. 15 speak against the view that Paul could ever have been an "unwilling" recipient of God's ἀνάγκη'.

Cor. 2.3). Part of him wanted to preach the gospel and part of him dreaded it. This is very similar to the state of mind described in 9.17—he was fulfilling the duties of the office entrusted to him half willingly and half unwillingly.

If this is so, how should we interpret v. 17a: 'if I preach willingly, I have a reward'? Are we forced into a doctrine of 'works of supererogation'? To answer this question, we must look at the grammatical construction. Both v. 17a and v. 17b consist of a conditional clause with the indicative mood in both the protasis and the apodosis. In his letters Paul uses this construction in the following six ways.[55]

a.   The apodosis consists of a logical inference from the protasis, and uses the present (or perfect) tense—if X is true, Y is also true. This is what Johannes Weiss calls the theoretical-logical way of speaking, and is the commonest use of this construction in Paul.[56]

b.   The apodosis consists of a logical inference from the protasis in the future tense—if X is true, Y will follow as a consequence.[57]

c.   The apodosis contains the word μᾶλλον—even though X is true, Y is much more true.[58]

d.   An unfulfilled conditional, with imperfect or aorist in the protasis and usually with ἄν in the apodosis—if X had been true, Y would also have been true.[59]

e.   An adversative statement—even though X is true, Y is also true. This is often, though not invariably, signalled by καί in the protasis and/or

---

55.   In this survey I have excluded the following categories:

i.   verses in which the apodosis is imperative or interrogative.
ii.   verses in which εἰ in the protasis is compounded with another word—εἴπερ, εἴγε etc.
iii.   verses in which εἰ is followed by τις (usually meaning 'anyone who').
iv.   phrases such as εἰ τύχοι with no apodosis.
v.   verses in which εἰ is followed by μή, usually meaning 'unless' or 'except'.

I have, however, included a few verses in which the verb 'to be' is understood but not expressed, such as Rom. 8.17.

56.   Weiss, *Der erste Korintherbrief*, p. 240: 'εἰ mit Ind. erklärt sich so, dass hier rein theoretisch-logisch geredet wird: wenn der Fall "a" vorliegt, so folgt "A", im Falle "b" muss man auf "B" schliessen'. Examples of this construction in Paul are: Rom. 4.2; 4.14; 7.16, 20; 8.10, 17, 25; 11.16; 14.15; 15.27; 1 Cor. 15.13, 14, 16, 17, 19; Gal. 2.18, 21; 3.18, 29; 4.7; 5.18.

57.   Rom. 6.5, 8; 8.10, 13; 11.21; 1 Cor. 8.13; 15.29; 2 Cor. 11.30; 1 Thess. 4.14.

58.   Rom. 5.10, 15, 17; 11.12, 24; 2 Cor. 3.7, 9, 11.

59.   Rom. 9.29; 1 Cor. 2.8; 11.31; Gal. 1.10; 3.21; 4.15.

ἀλλά in the apodosis.[60]

    f.   'If' in the protasis is equivalent to 'when'—if or when X happens, Y also happens.[61]

Of the above, only (a) and (f) are possible in 1 Cor. 9.17. (f) would yield the meaning: 'if (or when) I preach willingly, I receive payment'. It is hard to give a satisfactory meaning to such a statement, apart from the doctrine of works of supererogation. But the idea that God rewards people, not for their obedience in fulfilling his commission, but for their state of mind when doing so, is not an idea Paul is likely to have adopted. As he says in 1 Cor. 4.2, what is required in a servant entrusted with a commission is faithfulness, not a certain state of mind. It is therefore best to understand v. 17a and v. 17b as two examples of (a), the logical conditional.

In Pauline logical conditionals, the relationship between the protasis and the apodosis may be of two kinds. Most commonly the apodosis represents the logical *consequence* of the protasis. This is the case, for example, in the verses listed earlier under category (b), where the apodosis is in the future tense, for example Rom. 6.5: 'if we have died like Christ, we shall also be raised like Christ'. It is also often the case when the apodosis is in the present tense, for example Rom. 15.27: 'if the Jews have shared their spiritual blessings with the Gentiles, the Gentiles are under an obligation to help the Jews materially'. But in one instance the apodosis represents the logical *presupposition* of the protasis. In Rom. 7.16 Paul writes: εἰ δὲ ὃ οὐ θέλω τοῦτο ποιῶ, σύμφημι τῷ νόμῳ ὅτι καλός (if I am doing what I do not want to do, I am agreeing with the law and saying it is good). In other words, the fact that I disapprove of what I am doing presupposes that I am in favour of the law—otherwise I would not bother whether what I did was right or wrong.

In the case of 1 Cor. 9.17, the apodosis μισθὸν ἔχω (I have a payment) has usually been regarded as the logical *consequence* of the protasis—if I preach the gospel willingly, it follows that I get a reward. But if the apodosis is regarded as the logical *presupposition* of the protasis, a different sense emerges—if I preach the gospel willingly, it must be because I get a reward. In other words, Paul's reward is not the *result* of his eagerness to preach, but its *motivation*. The assumption is that no one does anything willingly without the prospect of being rewarded (either materially or spiritually). In Paul's case his reward is the privilege of preaching the gospel free of charge, and it is this reward that motivates him to perform

---

    60. Rom. 11.18; 1 Cor. 9.2; 2 Cor. 4.3, 16; 5.16; 7.8, 12; 11.6; Phil. 2.17; Col. 2.5.
    61. 2 Cor. 11.4.

willingly what could otherwise become an unwilling duty.

A strong argument in favour of this interpretation is the parallel statement in v. 17b: εἰ δὲ ἄκων, οἰκονομίαν πεπίστευμαι. The perfect tense of the apodosis in this clause, and the general sense, indicate that the apodosis is not a consequence of the protasis but its presupposition—the fact that I act unwillingly presupposes that I am fulfilling an external commission. If this is true of the logical structure of v. 17b, it is likely to be true also of the logical structure of v. 17a.

This interpretation fits the context. Verse 17 is a continuation of the boasting theme of v. 16. There is nothing to boast about in my being a preacher of the gospel, Paul declares, because I have been forced into it. If I preach willingly, that is nothing to boast about because I am doing it for payment. If I preach unwillingly, that is also nothing to boast about, because I am performing a duty that has been laid upon me.

In these verses Paul is speaking ironically—like other preachers he boasts of what he is paid, but in his case the payment is the privilege of getting no pay. The ironic nature of this argument explains the exaggerated nature of what he is saying. The ability to preach the gospel free of charge was indeed one of the factors that made Paul willing and enthusiastic in his ministry, but it was not the only factor. There were many other encouraging aspects to his work (compare, for example, 1 Thess. 2.19-20). The treatment of this one factor as though it were the sole reward that motivated his preaching is exaggerated; but it is equally exaggerated to describe this one factor as his boast, since there were many other things he boasted about (cf. 1 Cor. 15.31; 2 Cor. 1.12; 7.4, 14 and the 'fool's speech' in 2 Cor. 11–12). His argument here is *ad hominem*, with an implicit challenge to his opponents whose motivation and source of pride was the money they received.[62]

In conclusion, I offer a paraphrase of Paul's argument in 1 Cor. 9.16-18.

---

62. Weiss (*Der erste Korintherbrief*, p. 240) rejects this interpretation on the grounds that the passage is too '*temperamentvoll*' for such a logical construction. But this is a misunderstanding of Paul's nature. It is true that this construction is common in Romans, which is the most logical and theoretical of Paul's letters. But it is also common in Galatians, a letter in which Paul is passionately involved. A logical thinker does not cease to be logical when he or she gets excited.

Thiselton's translation ('if I do this entirely by personal choice, I am in the realm of reward') recognizes the logical nature of the construction, but proceeds from the false premiss that ἑκών refers to 'self-motivation or self-initiative' (Thiselton, *First Epistle*, pp. 676, 696).

I have not exercised my right to receive payment as an apostle, and my insistence that I have this right does not mean that I want to exercise it in future. I would rather die than allow this boast of mine (that I am financially independent) to be nullified. This boast is important to me because my preaching of the gospel is not something I can boast about—it is a necessity laid upon me. If I fail to preach the gospel, I am done for. Whichever way I preach I have nothing to boast about. If I preach willingly, that is because I am getting paid for doing so. If I preach unwillingly, that is because preaching is a responsibility God has entrusted to me, which I cannot avoid. What do I mean by saying I get paid for preaching? My payment is the privilege of preaching the gospel free of charge, and of waiving my right to be financially rewarded.

Chapter 9

THE VOCABULARY OF PAUL'S OPPONENTS

In this chapter I shall discuss some of the words used by Paul's opponents which he quotes (directly or indirectly) in 1 and 2 Corinthians. I shall use the phrase 'Paul's opponents' to refer to those people at Corinth (whether local or visitors) whose opinion Paul was opposing or whose criticism he was answering in the passage under discussion. For example, in 1 Cor. 15 Paul's opponents were the people (whoever they were) who said there was no resurrection (v. 12). In 2 Cor. 10–13 his opponents included both the rival apostles and those members of the church who were criticizing Paul at their instigation.

The attempt is sometimes made to distinguish between words used by the rival apostles and words used by the Corinthians. Barrett, for example, objects to the attribution of the phrase 'the signs of an apostle' (τὰ σημεῖα τοῦ ἀποστόλου) to the rival apostles, and argues that this was a phrase used by the Corinthians, who looked for appropriate signs in those who approached them as missionaries. 'They were the judges, who put others to the test'.[1] This is a misunderstanding of the situation. The background to 2 Cor. 10–13 is the comparison being drawn between Paul's credentials and those of his rivals. In drawing this comparison the Corinthians were not independent arbiters comparing different people's credentials in a spirit of disinterested inquiry. They were under the influence of the rival apostles (11.4, 20) who had taught them their own standards of judgment (10.12). Thus, when Paul says in 13.3: 'you are seeking proof that Christ speaks through me', 'you' includes both the rival apostles and those Corinthians who were under their influence and were evaluating Paul by their criteria.

It is the thesis of this book that the rival apostles of 2 Cor. 10–13 were already present at Corinth at the time of writing of 1 Corinthians. But even

---

1. Barrett, *Second Epistle*, pp. 320-21.

if this thesis is rejected there is ample evidence in 1 Corinthians of an anti-Pauline element in the church. In 9.3 Paul writes: 'this is my defence against those who are examining me'. These words suggest that there was a group at Corinth who had set themselves up as judges of Paul, but who did not represent the church as a whole. In such circumstances it is fair to talk about 'Paul's opponents' in 1 Corinthians as well as in 2 Corinthians.

The attempt has often been made to build up a picture of Paul's opponents and what they were saying by mirror-reading from his response. A pioneer of this approach was Ernst Käsemann, who sought to discover what accusations were made by Paul's opponents in 2 Cor. 10–13 by listing some of the words and phrases used in those chapters. He did not, however, lay down formal criteria for deciding which words and phrases should be attributed to the opponents.[2]

Richard Horsley, in attempting a similar task for 1 Corinthians, did lay down two criteria. First, the language of the Corinthians can be delineated 'by noting those aspects to which Paul reacts negatively'. Second, a comparison can be drawn with Paul's usage elsewhere. 'The absence or relative insignificance of this language in Paul's other letters confirms that this language is that of the Corinthians'. For example, the contrasts drawn in 1 Cor. 2.6–3.3 between πνευματικός (spiritual) and ψυχικός (soulish or natural), between τέλειος (mature) and νήπιος (childish), and between γάλα (milk) and βρῶμα (solid food) are attributed by Horsley to the Corinthians, and this 'is confirmed by the fact that most of these words occur exclusively in 1 Corinthians'.[3]

In some cases the exegesis is not greatly affected by the question of whether or not Paul is using Corinthian language. For example, in 2 Cor. 3.4-6 he uses the three words ἱκανός (adequate), ἱκανότης (adequacy) and ἱκανοῦν (make adequate). Many commentators see here a response to the claims of Paul's opponents that they were adequate (or qualified) for their ministry.[4] This may well be the case, though others deny it.[5] Whichever view is adopted, it does not greatly affect the meaning of Paul's positive statement that he and his colleagues are divinely equipped for their ministry. In other cases, however, the exegesis of a word or of a whole passage can depend on whether or not Paul is quoting the words of his opponents.

2.   Käsemann, 'Legitimität', pp. 34-36.
3.   Horsley, 'Spiritual Elitism', pp. 203-206.
4.   Notably Georgi, *Opponents*, pp. 231-34.
5.   E.g., Hickling, 'Source', p. 286.

I wish to propose some criteria that can be used for the detection of language used by Paul's opponents, and then to look at some passages whose exegesis depends on deciding whether or not this is the case. One factor to be borne in mind in this exercise is that Paul, when using the words of the Corinthians, did not necessarily use them in the same sense as they did. For example, the word πνευματικός (spiritual) seems to have been a self-description of some (or most) of the Corinthian Christians (1 Cor. 14.37), and in 1 Cor. 2.6-16 Paul seems to go along with that. But then suddenly in 3.1-3 he gives to the word a moral connotation, by virtue of which the Corinthians do not qualify as spiritual people.[6] In such cases he may be speaking 'tongue-in-cheek', as J. Murphy-O'Connor suggests.[7] A modern writer can use inverted commas to indicate words used by someone else or words used in a non-literal sense. For letter-writers in Paul's day inverted commas were not available, and modern readers have to work out as best they can those Pauline usages for which inverted commas would have been appropriate.

1. *Criteria for the Detection of Corinthian Language*

a. *Quoted Statements*
The clearest cases are those in which Paul specifically attributes words or phrases to people at Corinth. Several times in 1 Corinthians opinions or statements are attributed to 'some people' (τις or τινες)—people who said 'I am a disciple of such-and-such a teacher' (3.4); people who claimed to be wise (3.18); people who claimed to have knowledge (8.2); people who called themselves prophets and spiritual (14.37); people who denied the resurrection (15.12). This suggests that the frequency of some of the key words of 1 Corinthians, such as σοφία, γνῶσις, πνευματικός and

---

6.   Another example may be Paul's use of ἀπόδειξις in 1 Cor. 2.4. This was a technical term in rhetoric, but Lim ('Demonstration', p. 147) suggests that 'by employing it with πνεύματος and δυνάμεως, Paul uses ἀπόδειξις in a way which is different from and counter to the rhetorical meaning of the term'.

7.   Murphy-O'Connor, 'Interpolations', p. 83. The phrase 'servants of Christ' (διάκονοι Χριστοῦ) in 2 Cor. 11.23 is a case in point. Barrett ('Opponents', p. 237) asserts that 'Paul does not dispute that the persons of whom he is speaking are διάκονοι Χριστοῦ', and that if they are the same people as the 'servants of Satan' in 11.13-15, Paul is 'lashing out blindly, and using language irresponsibly'. He does not realize that the phrase διάκονοι Χριστοῦ is an ironical quotation of what his opponents claimed to be, which would be in inverted commas in a modern text.

ἀνάστασις, reflects the prominence given to these words by people at Corinth.

b. *Modified Statements*
J.C. Hurd suggests that, when Paul makes a statement and immediately modifies it, this indicates a Corinthian slogan. Examples in 1 Corinthians are 6.12; 7.1; 8.1; 10.23 and possibly 8.3-4 (modified after expansion and qualification in 8.7).[8] This suggestion seems sound as a generalization. The main uncertainty is whether Paul quotes these slogans word for word or paraphrases them. For example, 1 Cor. 7.1 reads: 'now concerning what you wrote, it is good for someone not to touch a woman'. Paul here refers to an issue raised in the Corinthian letter; but he does not necessarily quote their letter word for word. The word καλόν (good) could be quoted from their letter, or could equally well be Paul's judgment on one of the points of view expressed in the letter. The same is true of 8.1: 'now concerning food offered to idols, we know that we all have knowledge'. The word γνῶσις (knowledge) was part of the Corinthian vocabulary; but the word πάντες (all) could be either a literal quotation of a Corinthian slogan or Paul's ironic paraphrase of their claims.

c. *Untypical Language*
If a word or phrase that is not typical of Paul's usage in other letters is a key word or phrase in one section of 1 or 2 Corinthians, it is probably an echo of Corinthian language.[9] This is particularly the case when it is repeated several times. A good example is the noun λύπη (sorrow, pain) and its cognate verb λυπεῖν (to cause sorrow or pain to). Of the eight occurrences of the noun in the Pauline corpus six are in 2 Corinthians, and of fourteen occurrences of the verb eleven are in 2 Corinthians. The occurrences in 2 Corinthians are almost all found in two passages—2.1-7 (three noun and three verb) and 7.8-11 (two noun and six verb). Both passages refer to the same situation: Paul had written a letter demanding the punish-

---

8.   J.C. Hurd, *The Origin of 1 Corinthians* (Macon, GA: Mercer University Press, 2nd edn, 1983), pp. 120-23.

9.   This is one of the criteria recognized by Richard Horsley. John Barclay ('Mirror-Reading a Polemical Letter: Galatians as a Test Case', *JSNT* 31 [1987], pp. 73-93 [85]) cautiously recognizes the criterion of unfamiliarity: 'While taking into account our limited knowledge of Paul's theology, we may be entitled to consider the presence of an unfamiliar motif in Paul's letter as a reflection of a particular feature in the situation he is responding to'.

ment of an offender and this letter had hurt the Corinthians. Since Paul's information about the Corinthian reaction came from Titus, it is probable that the words λύπη and λυπεῖν represent their description of how they felt, expressed to Titus and reported by him to Paul.

The antithesis to λύπη is the noun χαρά (joy) and its cognate verb χαίρειν (rejoice). These are also key words in the two passages, occurring twice in 2.1-7 and six times in ch. 7. But these are words Paul uses frequently throughout his letters. While it is possible that the contrast between sorrow and joy was drawn by the Corinthians, it is more probable that Paul counterbalanced the Corinthian emphasis on their sorrow with his own emphasis on the joyful consequences.

d. *Unexplained Ideas*
If Paul suddenly introduces a word or phrase that is not obviously relevant to the context and is not explained, that word or phrase probably echoes something said by the Corinthians. This is particularly the case with negative statements.[10] The unexplained assertion 'I (or we) do not do a certain thing' probably means 'your allegation that I do this is not true'.

For example, in 2 Cor. 7.2 Paul declares, 'we have wronged no one, damaged no one, taken advantage of no one'. Why does he say this? The obvious answer is that these were charges his opponents had laid against him.[11] Similarly, in 2 Cor. 6.12, why should Paul say, 'you are not con-stricted in [or by] us but in your own hearts' (οὐ στενοχωρεῖσθε ἐν ἡμῖν, στενοχωρεῖσθε δὲ ἐν τοῖς σπλάγχνοις ὑμῶν)? The fact that he has just spoken of his heart being enlarged does not explain this. The enlargement of Paul's heart does not logically imply any constriction of the Corin-thians. The likeliest explanation is that the Corinthians had complained of being constricted by Paul.

This complaint may have been brought about by 1 Corinthians, where Paul opposed the Corinthian slogan πάντα ἔξεστιν (all things are allow-able) and indicated a number of things that were not allowable. It would be natural for the advocates of this slogan to complain that Paul was con-stricting them and denying them the freedom that, according to his own teaching, Christians should enjoy. If this was the case, Paul's declaration

---

10. This is one of Richard Horsley's criteria. But negative statements per se are not evidence of catchwords. Paul was capable of making negative statements about himself without any apologetic motive, such as his statement in Rom. 1.16: 'I am not ashamed of the gospel'.

11. On the meaning of πλεονεξία in 2 Cor. 7.2 see Chapter 4 n. 61.

that his heart was enlarged in 2 Cor. 6.11 could be his response to the allegation by certain people in Corinth that he was narrow-minded and restrictive.[12]

e. *An Apologetic Context*

If the context is apologetic, the likelihood increases of words or phrases being echoes of Corinthian criticism. 1 Corinthians is not on the whole apologetic, but does contain apologetic sections. In 4.1-5 Paul implies that there are those at Corinth who are sitting in judgment on him. In 9.3 he states: 'this is my defence against my judicial examiners', and the rest of ch. 9 contains that defence. In most of 1 Corinthians, however, Paul is responding to information received, or to questions asked in their letter, not to direct criticism.

2 Corinthians, by contrast, is very largely apologetic. In chs. 1 and 2 Paul defends himself against a charge of fickleness in changing his travel plans (1.17) and is forced to explain in some detail the reason for this change. The description of the apostolic ministry of Paul and his colleagues in 2.14–6.10 is also largely apologetic—a defence of Paul's style of ministry against advocates of another style of ministry.[13] This makes it probable that many words and phrases within this section reflect the criticism of Paul's style of ministry which Titus had reported.

In interpreting a controversial section such as this, a balance must be struck. On the one hand, we should not search for a hidden background to every single word or phrase within this section.[14] Paul's aim was not just to refute what he regarded as false approaches to ministry but also to put forward a positive approach to ministry in its place. In 3.4-18, for example, there is not only apologetic and polemic but also what C.J.A. Hickling calls 'superb expository theology'.[15] On the other hand, Hickling's reference

---

12. Στενοχωρεῖν means to crowd or cramp. It could be used metaphorically of causing someone difficulties, but the literal sense was still alive—cf. the man in Epictetus, *Diss.* 1.25.26 who 'cramped himself' in the amphitheatre because he wanted to sit where the senators sat—σὺ σαυτῷ στενοχωρίαν παρέχεις, σὺ σαυτὸν θλίβεις.

13. See Chapter 4 Section 2b.

14. Cf. John Barclay's cautionary words about attempts at mirror-reading in Galatians (Barclay, 'Mirror-Reading', pp. 81-82).

15. Hickling, 'Source', p. 286. Cf. Hickling's more detailed study of 2 Cor. 3 in which he insists that the ideas of the chapter 'develop one out of another in an essentially unsystematic and spontaneous manner which itself belies any suggestion of premeditated doctrinal polemic' (Hickling, 'Sequence of Thought', p. 384). Jerry

to 'exposition of the truth for its own sake' fails to place 2 Corinthians in its context. Paul was not writing a theological treatise for the general public. He was engaged in a spiritual struggle for the minds and allegiance of the Corinthian Christians (10.3-6) and in one sense almost everything in 2 Corinthians was either apologetic or polemic.

In chs. 8 and 9 Paul's main concern is to encourage the Corinthians to give generously to the collection; but in the central section commending Titus and two brothers one of his aims is to forestall criticism of his motives in raising the money (8.20-21). Even in an appeal for charitable giving Paul is on the defensive.[16] Chs. 10–13 are almost throughout apologetic. Paul explicitly quotes several personal criticisms of himself as an individual (10.1, 9, 10; 12.16) and describes his boasting as something forced upon him by the critical comparisons of his opponents (11.18; 12.11-13). In such an apologetic context almost every new word or phrase that is introduced is likely to echo their critical comments. A good example is the phrase 'the signs of an apostle' in 12.12, which is listed as a catchword by Käsemann.[17] It does not qualify as a Corinthian phrase under criteria (a) (b) (c) and (d). It is not attributed to the opponents, it occurs only once and its meaning is explained by the following words 'with signs and wonders and mighty works'. But the context is so apologetic that Käsemann was justified in seeing in this phrase an echo of the opponents' language.

2. *Four Passages in which the Presence of Corinthian Language is of Exegetical Significance*

a. *Freedom in 1 Corinthians 9.1*
The rhetorical question 'am I not free?' (οὐκ εἰμὶ ἐλεύθερος;) in 1 Cor. 9.1 is probably Paul's response to an accusation of his opponents. It is introduced suddenly without explanation and it stands at the head of 9.1-14, one of the few apologetic sections in 1 Corinthians.[18] It is linked to the word ἀπόστολος which is similarly brought in abruptly without any explanation of its relevance. Moreover, by introducing the question with

Sumney (*Opponents*, p. 99) comments that 'methodologically we must allow for a counterattack which approaches the general issue from a direction other than that of the opponents'.

16. See Chapter 4, Section 3.
17. Käsemann, 'Legitimität', p. 35.
18. For discussion of the place of 9.1-14 within its context see Chapter 8, Section 2.

οὐ (am I not free?) Paul uses an argumentative formula. All this suggests that Paul had been accused of not being free and of not being an apostle. Since the rest of the chapter is concerned with his policy of self-support, it is reasonable to suppose that the questions introducing the chapter have the same reference. It was his policy of working with his hands to support himself that made him, in the eyes of his critics, not free and not an apostle.

If ἐλεύθερος was a word used by Paul's critics, what kind of freedom did they have in mind? The idea of freedom was used with various emphases in Graeco-Roman philosophy. One emphasis was on psychological freedom. Epictetus defined freedom as 'the right to live as we wish'. It is the educated who have this freedom because they have learnt only to wish for the things that are in their power. They do not wish for external things such as wealth or property and are therefore not at the mercy of those who can deny them such things.[19] Freedom in this sense is a state of mind, a detachment from the bondage to material things that enslaves other people. Philo argues that the wise man cannot be the victim of external compulsion. He only desires to do what is right, and cannot be prevented from attaining this desire. Since what he does is voluntarily chosen, he cannot be compelled.[20]

In similar vein Dio Chrysostom argues that the wise man knows what is right and what is wrong, what is allowable and what is not allowable. It follows that the wise are free to do whatever they wish. Dio defines freedom as the knowledge of what is allowable and what is forbidden.[21] This passage provides a close parallel to the Corinthian slogan 'all things are allowable' quoted in 6.12 and 10.24 and to Paul's use of the word ἐλευθερία in that context in 10.29.[22]

Other philosophers emphasized practical freedom. According to Martin Hengel, one of the attractions of the early Academy and the Cynic philosophy was the motif of radical freedom from the ties of possessions. Crates, for example, publicly declared himself free of his enslavement to property, using the appropriate form for the emancipation of a slave, and either turned his property into cash and gave it away or threw it into the sea.[23] In

19. Epictetus, *Diss.* 2.1.21-24; *Ench.* 1.1-5.
20. Philo, *Omn. Prob. Lib.* 58–61.
21. Dio Chrysostom, *Or.* 14.16.
22. For further examples of the philosophical link between ἐλευθερία and ἐξουσία see Conzelmann, *First Epistle*, p. 109 n. 5.
23. M. Hengel, *The Charismatic Leader and his Followers* (Edinburgh: T. & T. Clark, 1981), pp. 28-29.

an often-quoted passage, Epictetus describes the practical freedom enjoyed
by the true Cynic philosopher:

> Look at me, I have no house or city, property or slave; I sleep on the
> ground, I have no wife or children, no miserable palace, but only earth and
> sky and one poor cloak. Yet what do I lack? Am I not without pain and fear,
> am I not free?[24]

Gerd Theissen suggests that it may have been Paul's insistence on working with his own hands to support himself that caused him to be re-
proached for not being free.[25] Certainly the drudgery of his trade, which
Ronald Hock has vividly described, would prevent him from devoting
his whole time to the pursuit of philosophy, or to the preaching of the
gospel.[26]

The relevance of the philosophical ideas just outlined to Paul's question
in 9.1 is disputed. Some commentators find the key to Paul's reference to
freedom in the preceding chapter. In the verse immediately preceding 9.1
(8.13), Paul sums up the argument of ch. 8 by means of a statement in the
first person: 'if food causes my brother to stumble, I will never eat meat
again'. Fee suggests that it is this shift to the first person in 8.13 that sets
off Paul's impassioned defence of his actions in ch. 9.[27]

Barrett's interpretation is similar: Paul was willing, and by implication
invited his readers, to impose a serious limitation on their Christian
liberty; but he suspected that such a limitation of freedom would not
please the Corinthians and would lead to questioning of his own authority.
The Corinthians would say: 'if Paul were a true apostle, he would not
allow himself to be restricted in this way'. Accordingly Barrett paraphrases Paul's question: 'do you suppose that because I limit my freedom
out of love my freedom does not exist?'[28]

The main difficulty with this interpretation is the style of Paul's question
in 9.1. οὐκ εἰμὶ ἐλεύθερος; is a rhetorical question to which Paul provides
no answer. By contrast, the following question οὐκ εἰμὶ ἀπόστολος; is
followed by a reasoned answer in v. 3. The simplest explanation of this
difference is that Paul's freedom was one aspect of his apostleship, so that
in defending the latter he was also defending the former. In other words,

---

24. Epictetus, *Diss.* 3.22.46-48, as translated in Theissen, *Social Setting*, p. 44.
25. Theissen, *Social Setting*, p. 44.
26. Hock, *Social Context*, pp. 31-37.
27. Fee, *First Epistle*, p. 394.
28. Barrett, *First Epistle*, pp. 199-200.

the 'others' of v. 2 who questioned his apostolic status were also questioning his apostolic freedom, and it is to their criticisms that the two rhetorical questions were addressed.

Moreover, the link between freedom and apostleship that Barrett posits is somewhat forced. The issue discussed in ch. 8 has nothing to do with apostleship—it concerns the behaviour incumbent on every Christian. There is a sharp break between 8.13 and 9.1, both in style and in subject matter. Paul breaks off at a tangent (as he often does in his letters) and introduces a new topic, triggered off in his mind no doubt by what he has just said, but nevertheless having its own logical train of thought.

The argument of ch. 9 as a whole follows on from the argument of ch. 8 as an illustration of the principle that love takes precedence over the claiming of rights. But ch. 9 has also its own internal consistency.[29] It deals specifically with Paul's renunciation of his right to receive material support. It was this policy that led to his apostolic status being questioned, on the grounds that proper apostles do not work with their hands to support themselves.

If this is so, Paul's critics probably used the word ἐλεύθερος with the second of the two emphases listed above—the emphasis on practical freedom. Their objection would be that, by devoting so much time to manual labour, Paul was not free to devote himself to the work of the gospel as a genuine apostle should. When Paul answers similar criticism of his lifestyle in 2 Cor. 11.7-12, he does so in the context of a comparison with other people who had come to Corinth claiming to be apostles. This strongly suggests that these 'apostles' were already present in Corinth at the time of 1 Corinthians, and comparisons between their lifestyle and Paul's were already being drawn.

These 'apostles' were not Cynics who lived a life of poverty. They accepted hospitality and financial rewards from their Corinthian hosts and were in Paul's eyes 'hawkers of the word of God' (2 Cor. 2.17). But they did enjoy the same freedom from the necessity to toil for their daily bread as the Cynic beggars and were thus free to devote themselves to the pursuit of wisdom and to teaching that wisdom to others. They had apparently suggested to the Corinthian Christians that Paul did not enjoy this freedom because, not being a proper apostle, he did not have the right to claim it. Such a reconstruction explains not only the rhetorical questions of 9.1 but also the reference in 9.3 to Paul's defence against his judicial examiners,

29. For further discussion of the way in which, in ch. 9, Paul tries to 'kill two birds with one stone' see Chapter 8, Section 2.

and the necessity he obviously feels to establish his right to receive support, before coming to the main point of the chapter—his reasons for refusing it.

b. *Foolishness in 2 Corinthians 11–12*
The words ἀφροσύνη (foolishness) and ἄφρων (fool) qualify as words used by the Corinthians according to three criteria. Eight of the ten Pauline instances of these words are in 2 Cor. 11 and 12. The discussion of Paul's foolishness is introduced abruptly in 11.1 without explanation. Most decisively of all, the word ὄφελον in 11.1 is equivalent to a positive statement that the charge of ἀφροσύνη had already been levelled against him.

In that verse Paul writes: 'I wish you were willing to put up a little with my foolishness' (ὄφελον ἀνείχεσθέ μου μικρόν τι ἀφροσύνης). According to Plummer the word ὄφελον can have either of two meanings. It can express either 'a wish as to what might happen, but is almost too good to come true' or 'what might have been the case, but was not'. In the former case (which Plummer prefers) it denotes a wistful wish for the future; in the latter case it denotes an unfulfilled wish in the present.[30]

Many translators and commentators follow Plummer in seeing here a wish as to what might happen, for example NIV: 'I hope you will put up with a little of my foolishness'. But there are strong grammatical reasons for regarding Paul's words as an unfulfilled wish in the present. J.H. Moulton refers to 'the familiar fact that the imperfect in all "unreal" indicatives generally denotes present time: cf. the use with ὄφελον in Rev. 3.15 and 2 Cor. 11.1'.[31] BAGD states that ὄφελον functions as 'a particle to introduce unattainable wishes… *O that, would that* with the imperfect to express present time…'[32] The only other occurrence of ὄφελον with the imperfect indicative in the New Testament (Rev. 3.15) clearly relates to present time: 'I wish you were hot or cold, but in fact you are lukewarm'.

This grammatical question has an important bearing on the background to 2 Corinthians. If the verse expresses an unfulfilled wish in present time, that wish implies a negative statement: 'You are not willing to put up with my foolishness, but I wish you were'. In other words, Paul is responding

30. Plummer, *Second Epistle*, p. 292.
31. Moulton, *Prolegomena*, p. 200.
32. BAGD, sv. ὄφελον. So also Bultmann, *Der zweite Brief*, p. 201: 'ὄφελον….zur Bezeichnung des unerfüllbaren Wunsches'.

to a criticism of his foolishness that the Corinthians had recently made.
E.H. Plumptre's comment makes this clear:

> It is impossible to resist the inference that here also we have the echo of
> something which Titus had reported to him as said by his opponents at
> Corinth. Their words, we must believe, had taken some such form as this:
> 'We really can bear with him no longer; his folly has become altogether
> intolerable'.[33]

The most probable reason for Paul to be accused of foolishness lies in
three passages in 1 Corinthians—2.1-5 (where he talks of his weakness,
fear and trembling); 4.7-13 (where he boasts of the fact that the apostles
are treated like dirt); and 9.15-27 (where he boasts of his status as a self-
supporting artisan). In these passages he contrasts (directly or by implication) his own lowly status with the pretensions of his rivals and their
supporters. By insisting in 2 Corinthians that, if it was necessary to boast,
he would boast of his weakness (2 Cor. 11.30; 12.9) he was continuing the
practice exemplified in 1 Corinthians, a practice that his detractors had
already branded as a sign of mental infirmity.

It is possible that the same accusation lies behind the difficult verse 2
Cor. 5.13 which reads: εἴτε γὰρ ἐξέστημεν, θεῷ· εἴτε σωφρονοῦμεν,
ὑμῖν (for if we are out of our mind, it is for God; if we are in our right
mind, it is for you). The reference to Paul being out of his mind is introduced abruptly without explanation and bears the marks of a Corinthian
accusation. It is often taken to be an allusion to ecstatic experiences such
as the one described in 12.1-4. But such a reference would be irrelevant to
the context of ch. 5. Commentators struggle hard to imagine why there
should be a reference to ecstatic experiences at this point.[34] It is better to
give to the verb ἐξίστασθαι the meaning it bears in Mk 3.21, where Jesus
is accused of being out of his mind. Since the reference to sober judgment
(σωφρονοῦμεν) is also introduced abruptly and not explained, it is likely
that 5.13 as a whole represents a Corinthian accusation. What was being
commented on at Corinth was not only Paul's madness but the inconsistency between his occasional madness and his sober judgment at other
times.

Here again, the most likely grounds for such a comment are to be found

33. E.H. Plumptre, 'The Second Epistle to the Corinthians', in C.J. Ellicott (ed.), *A
New Testament Commentary for English Readers* (London and Edinburgh: Marshall
Brothers, n.d.), VII, pp. 359-417 (400), commenting on 2 Cor. 11.1.

34. See, for example, the lengthy speculation in Thrall, *Second Epistle*, pp. 406-
407.

in 1 Corinthians. That letter consists for the most part of deliberative rhetoric.[35] Paul considers a range of issues with a calm, reasoned approach: 'I speak to you as intelligent people; judge for yourselves what I say' (10.15). But from time to time he speaks in a very emotional and personal tone, especially when describing his own lifestyle of suffering and hard labour (4.7-21; 9.14-27). His enemies at Corinth may well have commented on this contrast: 'why does Paul write most of the letter sanely and sensibly, but occasionally take leave of his senses and start to boast about his low status in a way no reasonable person would do?' If such comments were being made, 2 Cor. 5.13 can be seen as Paul's explanation of his inconsistency. The sober, deliberative style of most of 1 Corinthians was 'for your sake', because it was what the church needed at that time. The emotional outbursts expressed his relationship with God, his sense of having been crucified with Christ and sharing in the sufferings of Christ.

This interpretation suits the context. Paul has been describing in 2 Cor. 4.7–5.10 the paradox of apostolic existence. The apostles are physically weak, fragile as clay pots, yet spiritually they are daily strengthened by God and will one day be renewed in body and spirit. 5.11-13 continues the theme of two levels of apostolic existence: outwardly and superficially Paul and his colleagues are persuaders, seeking, like the sophists, to win people over to their point of view; but inwardly they are motivated by their relationship with God, who sees their innermost being and will reward them according to their integrity (v. 11). Paul's purpose in emphasizing this two-fold aspect of apostolic ministry is to enable the Corinthians to resist the pressure from rival apostles, whose attitude is different—they concentrate on the superficial qualities of voice, carriage and eloquence beloved of the sophists rather than on the inner motivation which is what matters to God (v. 12).

The paradoxical lifestyle of the apostles is then summarized in v. 13. Sometimes they are sober and sensible, seeking by the use of reason and deliberative rhetoric to bring people to knowledge of the truth. Sometimes the inner fire of their love for God erupts in passionate outbursts that seem to their worldly-wise opponents to be signs of madness.

The verses that follow explain this in more detail. On the one hand, the apostolic ministry is based on intellectual study and conviction: we have formed a judgment (κρίναντας, v. 14) as to the significance of the death of Christ. On the other hand, our ministry is emotional—the love of Christ constrains us (v. 14), and we therefore plead with people to be reconciled

35. Mitchell, *Reconciliation*, pp. 12-13.

to God (v. 20). It is no wonder that the Corinthians, who had been beguiled by the charms of wisdom and knowledge, could not understand
this combination of sober reasoning in some parts of Paul's letters and
emotionalism in other parts.

c. *Testing and Approval*
The words δόκιμος, ἀδόκιμος, δοκιμή and δοκιμάζειν refer to testing
and approval. Δοκιμάζειν means 'to put to the test', δόκιμος describes
someone who has passed the test and is approved, ἀδόκιμος describes
someone who has failed the test and is not approved, and δοκιμή means
'proof'. The most striking use of these words is in 2 Cor. 13.3-7, where
they occur six times within the space of five verses. In v. 3 Paul states
that δοκιμή is something the Corinthians are looking for—an indication
that the whole passage is his response to what they have said. The 'proof'
they demand is evidence that Christ speaks through him—in other words,
that he is a genuine apostle. His opponents are dividing apostles into two
groups—approved (δόκιμοι) and not approved (ἀδόκιμοι)—and want to
assign Paul to the latter group.

The particular aspect of apostleship under discussion in 13.1-10 is
power and the exercise of discipline. Paul has been accused of writing
powerful letters in his absence but of being physically weak and a poor
speaker when present face to face (10.10). His threats of disciplinary
action, it is implied, are mere paper threats. In 13.1-4, 10 he denies this
and asserts that on his next visit he will be armed with the power of God
and with apostolic authority.

Elsewhere in 2 Corinthians other criteria appear for the genuineness of
apostles. The 'signs of an apostle' mentioned in 12.12 constitute one such
criterion. The reference to letters of recommendation in 3.1 suggests that
such letters could be used as proof of genuineness. Rhetorical ability,
which Paul lacked, was also regarded as a sign of a true apostle (11.5-6).[36]
Professional remuneration was another.[37]

In response to the Corinthian demand for proof of his apostleship, Paul
mounts a counterattack. Instead of testing the genuineness of my calling,
he declares, you should be testing the genuineness of your own Christian
faith—whether Christ dwells within you. If he does not, you are the ones

36. It is immediately after his claim to be not inferior to the super-apostles that Paul
concedes he may be lacking in rhetorical skill.
37. On the remuneration of apostles as a sign of their professional status see
Chapter 8.

who are ἀδόκιμοι—who have failed the test and been shown to be bogus (13.5). I hope you will recognize that we are genuine apostles; but our main concern is not that we should pass the test and be proved to be genuine, but that you should do the right thing. If your conduct is right, we should be happy to be thought bogus (ὡς ἀδόκιμοι; v. 7). We want to build up your strength, not our own. But if the worst comes to the worst, I Paul will exercise the apostolic authority the Lord has given me (vv. 9-10).[38]

In this passage Paul does not reply directly to the demand of his opponents for proof of his apostolic calling. He does not accept their criteria and is not concerned to satisfy them. His concern, he declares ironically, is that the faith of the Corinthians could be so damaged by the influence of their teachers that they might fail the test themselves, not as apostles, but as Christians.

The fact that δόκιμος and its cognates were words used at Corinth for the evaluation of apostles may help to explain two passages in 1 Corinthians. In ch. 11 Paul mentions the divisions that are present at Corinth when they celebrate the Lord's Supper, and comments: 'there must be rival groups among you, so that those who are approved (δόκιμοι) among you may be revealed' (v. 19). He introduces the word δόκιμος without explanation, expecting the Corinthians to understand it because it is one of their catchwords. A Corinthian catchword is unlikely to bear a different meaning in 1 Corinthians from that it bears in 2 Corinthians, and the incidental unexplained allusion in 1 Cor. 11.19 should be interpreted in the light of the fuller discussion in 2 Cor. 13.1-10.

In 1 Cor. 11.19 Paul is speaking ironically. The reason for the divisions at the Lord's Supper, he declares, is the presence at Corinth of rival preachers, each claiming to qualify as a genuine apostle and each gathering a group of adherents. In such a situation, divisions are inevitable. The word δεῖ does not indicate a divine decree but the inevitable result of competitive preaching. The word δόκιμοι could refer to the party leaders alone or could refer also to the party members who were approved by those leaders. In either case, Paul's ironic use of this word is an indication of the common background shared by 1 and 2 Corinthians.

This background may also help to explain 1 Cor. 9.27. Paul has been

38. It is interesting to note how Paul instinctively uses the first person plural when talking about apostolic policy in general (as shared by himself and his colleagues) but the first person singular when issuing a personal threat about his forthcoming visit. For further discussion of Paul's use of singular and plural see Chapter 4, Section 5.

comparing himself to an athlete in the games. He disciplines his body in order that, after having preached to others, he himself should not fail the test (be ἀδόκιμος). Here again, he introduces the word ἀδόκιμος without explanation, assuming his audience will know what he means. In the context of the athletic metaphor, ἀδόκιμος seems to mean 'proved unfit to receive the prize'. But this raises the question: what is the prize?

There are two possibilities. One is that the prize is eternal salvation.[39] This interpretation would provide a good link with ch. 10, but not such a good link with the rest of ch. 9, of which v. 27 is the climax. Ch. 9 is concerned with Paul's policy of working at a trade and identifying himself with the weak rather than enjoying the perks of a professional apostle. In such a context, v. 27 would more naturally refer to Paul's unfitness to be an apostle than to his unfitness to be a Christian.

When Paul thinks in other places of the eschatological prize, he includes in that idea rewards and punishments as well as salvation. For example, in 1 Cor. 3 he talks of various preachers whose work will be tested by fire (δοκιμάζειν) on the day of judgment. If their work is good, they will receive a reward; but even if their work is burnt up, they themselves will be saved (3.10-15). Paul's attitude in 2 Cor. 5.9-10 is very similar—his aim is to please the Lord in everything, because at the judgment we shall be rewarded or punished in the light of what we have done in this life. Equally revealing are his words to the Thessalonians; 'you are our hope, our joy and our crown at the coming of the Lord' (1 Thess. 2.19). On the day of the Lord Paul expects to wear a crown—a symbol of victory— because he will be sharing that day with the Thessalonians who had become Christians through his ministry.

It is likely that the background to Paul's use of ἀδόκιμος in 1 Cor. 9.27 is the argument about apostolic qualification that lies behind 2 Cor. 13.1-10. Paul is saying that, in order to qualify for an eschatological reward an apostle should not, like his opponents, take life easy and enjoy the social and financial perks of apostleship, but should live a life of hardship and self-discipline.

d. *Measurement in 2 Corinthians 10.12-18*

The words κανών and μέτρον in 2 Cor. 10.12-18 should be classified as words used by Paul's opponents by virtue of several criteria. Three of the four Pauline occurrences of κανών are in these verses. Μέτρον, μετρεῖν and ἄμετρος occur between them five times in this passage, and else-

39. Barrett, *First Epistle*, p. 218.

where in the Pauline corpus only once in Romans and three times in Ephesians. Although these words are not obviously related to the context, Paul uses them repeatedly without explanation. As Martin says: 'with his opponents' terms no doubt in his sights, he does not bother to explain all that his words imply'.[40]

Moreover, the context is apologetic. Immediately before this passage comes Paul's defence against the charge of being physically weak and a poor speaker (vv. 10-11). Immediately after this passage, in 11.1, he quotes their complaint of his foolishness. The fact that Paul is directly (v. 12) and indirectly (vv. 15-16) critical of his opponents at some points in these verses exemplifies the principle that the best form of defence is attack, but does not alter the apologetic emphasis of the section as a whole.

The realization that these words were being used by Paul's opponents determines their exegesis. Paul's primary aim is not to lay charges against his opponents but to refute the charges they have laid against him. For example, when he declares in v. 14: 'we are not overstretching ourselves', he is replying to their accusation that he *is* overstretching himself by interfering in Corinth. This apologetic orientation must be constantly borne in mind as we turn to the details of exegesis.

The first thing to notice is the overwhelming emphasis on measurement of geographical distance. Paul talks of reaching as far as Corinth (vv. 13-14), of having come as far as Corinth in the past (v. 14) and of hoping to travel beyond Corinth in the future (v. 16). Whatever the precise meaning of κανών and μέτρον, they must have something to do with this major emphasis. In Lambrecht's words, 'the geographical overtones present in the context must be taken into account'.[41] Similarly Barrett thinks the primary meaning of κανών to be 'measuring-rod', with reference to the measurement of lengths and areas, and states that Paul 'was aware of and did not forget this primary meaning, which appears quite clearly in v. 16'.[42] Paul's main concern in this section is not to defend his apostleship in general terms, but to reply to the specific accusation that he is overstretching himself by regarding Corinth as part of his field of ministry. As Scott Hafemann says, Paul does discuss apostolic legitimacy per se at a later stage, but at this point his concern is with his authority over the Corinthians.[43]

---

40. Martin, *2 Corinthians*, pp. 317-18.
41. Lambrecht, *Second Corinthians*, p. 170.
42. Barrett, *Second Epistle*, pp. 264-65.
43. S.J. Hafemann, ' "Self-Commendation" and Apostolic Legitimacy in 2 Corin-

It is often alleged that in this paragraph Paul 'is directly and specifically critical of his opponents for having overstepped the limits of their commission',[44] and that his words in v. 14 'we are not overstretching ourselves' imply that his opponents were overstretching themselves.[45] Such statements go beyond the evidence. When Paul criticizes his opponents, it is for their boasting, not for their presence at Corinth. He nowhere suggests that they have no right to be there (though he objects to their boasting of the church as though it belonged to them, and to their claiming the credit for the fruit of other people's labours). The point at issue in v. 14 is not whether his opponents were interlopers, but whether Paul was an interloper.

The second thing to note is that the verbs ἐφικνούμενοι (reach) and ὑπερεκτείνομεν (overstretch) in v. 14 are in the present tense. It is Paul's right to interfere in the affairs of the church *at the present time* that is disputed. The one reference to the past (in v. 14b: 'we have come as far as Corinth with the gospel') is introduced by the word γάρ (for) to provide a historical justification for his present involvement. He had, as a matter of historical fact, brought the gospel to Corinth and become a spiritual father to the Corinthian church. This relationship could not be broken by the fact that he was currently working in another area.

It is easy to imagine how the accusation of 'over-stretching' could have arisen. When Paul's opponents came to Corinth, the church may have seemed to them to be leaderless. Paul had departed and was living in Ephesus. They may have regarded themselves as sent by God to take over the leadership of the church, and the welcome they received from the church may have encouraged them in this belief. However, some members of the church continued to correspond with Paul, who made critical comments about what was going on. One can understand their reasons for objecting to this: Paul had no doubt done good work while he was at Corinth, but he had now moved to a new area. His sphere of influence, in their view, was now the province of Asia and extended westwards only as far as the Aegean Sea; he had no right to overstretch himself by interfering in the ongoing life of one of his previous churches. This reconstruction of what Paul's opponents were saying is, of course, conjectural, but it makes sense of Paul's response.

A more commonly accepted theory today, however, relates this section

thians: A Pauline Dialectic', *NTS* 36 (1990), pp. 66-88 (77).
   44. Furnish, *II Corinthians*, p. 480.
   45. Barrett, *Second Epistle*, p. 266; Bultmann, *Probleme*, pp. 21-22.

to the Jerusalem agreement described in Gal. 2.9—the agreement that Peter, James and John should go to the Jews, and Paul and Barnabas to the Gentiles.[46] The link with Gal. 2 is stressed especially by those who believe Paul's opponents to be upholders of the authority of the Jerusalem apostles—of the 'pillars' of Gal. 2.9. There are, however, several difficulties with the linkage of these two passages.

First, if the disputed issue in 2 Cor. 10 is whether or not Corinth is part of Paul's allotted territory, it is Paul's original visit to Corinth several years earlier that is under question. Héring's comment is revealing: 'Instead of "huperekteinomen" it would be preferable to read "huperekteinamen" [*sic*] = "we have not overstretched", etc. But no witness supports this variant. The present tense is also justified, however'.[47] Héring is aware that Paul's use of the present tense does not sit easily with the theory that what is being criticized is Paul's initial decision to visit Corinth rather than his continuing involvement.

In v. 14 Paul argues from the past to the present. The reason why he is not overstretching himself by reaching out to Corinth at the present time is that he has already been to Corinth in the past. But if the objection was to his coming to Corinth in the first place, this argument would be meaningless.

One way to make v. 14 fit in with the supposed reference to the Jerusalem agreement is to translate ἐφθάσαμεν as 'we came first' rather than simply as 'we came'.[48] If this translation is adopted, Paul's point is that he has more right to be involved in affairs at Corinth than his opponents because he got there first and thus established it as his own mission field. But in the only New Testament parallel adduced for this translation (1 Thess. 4.15) the verb φθάνειν is transitive and governs an object: οὐ μὴ

---

46. Käsemann ('Legitimität', p. 51) calls Gal. 1–2 'eine unübersehbare Parallele'. Barrett ('Christianity at Corinth', *BJRL* 46 [1964], pp. 269-97 [294]) lists the questions raised in 2 Cor. 10.12-18 and asserts that 'it is impossible to state these questions without calling to mind Gal. 2.1-10'. In the opinion of Martin (*2 Corinthians*, p. lviii) Paul is here asserting 'that his apostolic writ did run to those Gentile areas which God had given him—and which the "pillar" men had earlier accepted (Gal. 2.7-9)—as his bailiwick'. So also Georg Strecker, 'Legitimität', p. 574: 'Erst mit dem sogenannten Apostelkonvent erfolgte die Aufteilung der Arbeitsgebiete, die 2 Kor. 10.13 mit dem Ausdruck μέτρον τοῦ κανόνος reflektiert ist'.

47. J. Héring, *The Second Epistle of Saint Paul to the Corinthians* (London: Epworth, 1967).

48. Barrett, *Second Epistle*, p. 267; Martin, *2 Corinthians*, p. 322 contra Bultmann, *Der zweite Brief*, p. 197; Furnish, *II Corinthians*, p. 472.

φθάσωμεν τοὺς κοιμηθέντας (we shall not precede those who have died). In all the other New Testament instances the verb is intransitive, and when it is intransitive it means simply 'come' or 'arrive' (Mt. 12.28; Lk. 11.20; Rom. 9.31; Phil. 3.16; 1 Thess. 2.16). Moreover, the word καί before ὑμῶν in v. 14 affects the balance of the whole sentence. The purpose of καί is to throw the emphasis onto the word that immediately follows (the word ὑμῶν). Though we are at present working in Asia, Paul is saying, our ministry is not limited to Asia—we have come as far as *you*. The emphasis is on space not on time—on reaching as far as Corinth not on reaching there before other people.

Second, the division of labour in Gal. 2.9 was not a geographical but a theological division. In every major city in the Eastern part of the Roman Empire there lived both Gentiles and Jews. It would have been impossible for either Paul or Peter to limit their mission to a Jewish or Gentile geographical area. What the Jerusalem accord recognized was that God had entrusted Paul with a gospel for Gentiles and Peter with a gospel for Jews (Gal. 2.7). God had equipped them to share the good news with different groups of people, whichever geographical area they were in.

Günther Bornkamm has pointed out the difficulties in taking the accord of Gal. 2.9 either in a purely geographical or in a purely ethnographical sense. He concludes that the words refer to 'the basic character of the missionary preaching of the two groups'.[49] The point at issue in 2 Cor. 10, by contrast, was geographical, as is shown by the spatial language Paul uses.

Third, the theory of a reference to the Jerusalem agreement has been imported into this passage without any allusion in the text. Furnish's comment is justified: 'Nothing here suggests that Paul is thinking of the agreement with the Jerusalem apostles'.[50]

What, then, did Paul's opponents mean when they used the words μέτρου and κανών? As we have seen, the overwhelmingly geographical nature of the passage requires us to interpret them in a spatial sense. Furnish translates κανών as 'jurisdiction' and thinks it combines the two meanings of 'rule, norm, standard' and 'the extent or area which has been measured or which is governed by the rule or norm'.[51] However, the possibility of the latter meaning is disputed. It is true that, in an inscription from Pisidia,

49. G. Bornkamm, *Paul* (London: Hodder & Stoughton, 1971), pp. 39-40.
50. Furnish, *II Corinthians*, p. 481.
51. Furnish, *II Corinthians*, p. 471.

κανών is the translation of the Latin *formula*, and denotes the schedule of services to be provided by local communities to officially approved travellers.[52] But Scott Hafemann argues that, although the inscription refers to a territorial commitment, this meaning is not 'part of the semantic range of κανών itself'.[53] In my opinion, the decisive argument in favour of Hafemann's view is the phrase 'in accordance with our κανών' (κατὰ τὸν κανόνα ἡμῶν) in v. 15, which suggests that the κανών is a factor in accordance with which an area is demarcated rather than the area itself.

Μέτρον can mean 'measurement', 'a space that is measured' or 'limit' and its meaning in this passage must be determined by the context. In v. 13 it is governed by the verb μερίζειν (to apportion).[54] There is a close parallel to this verse in Rom. 12.3, which talks of God apportioning to each Christian a measure of faith (ἑκάστῳ ὡς ὁ θεὸς ἐμέρισεν μέτρον πίστεως). This is commonly taken to mean that God assigns to each person a measured quantity of faith—that Christians receive from God not only gifts and ministries but also the confidence to believe that they can exercise them.[55] 2 Cor. 10.13 contains a similar idea. God allocates to each

52. E.A. Judge ('A Regional κανών for Requisitioned Transport', in G.H.R. Horsley [ed.], *New Documents Illustrating Early Christianity* [5 vols.; North Ryde: Macquarrie University, 1981–89], I, pp. 36-45 [44-45]) comments: 'The κανών in itself is not a geographical concept; but the services it formulates are in this case geographically partitioned'. He believes that Paul and his colleagues, as they travelled the Roman roads, would be familiar with κανόνες of this sort, and made use of this word which expressed 'their understanding of the way God had measured out their respective territorial commitments'. See also J.F. Strange, '2 Corinthians 10.13-16 Illuminated by a Recently Published Inscription', *BA* 46 (1983), pp. 167-68.

53. Hafemann, ' "Self-Commendation" ', p. 78 n. 41.

54. The grammatical construction of v. 13 is not altogether clear (for one probable interpretation see n. 59). What is clear, on any construction, is that the μέτρον is something apportioned.

55. Charles Cranfield (*Romans*, II, pp. 613-16) objects to this interpretation on the grounds that it would imply that Christians with a greater quantity of faith should think of themselves more highly than they think of fellow-Christians with less faith. But this objection is not valid. Later in the same letter (14.2-3) Paul writes: 'one person has the faith to eat anything, but the person whose faith is weak eats vegetables. The eater should not despise the non-eater; and the non-eater should not condemn the eater, since God has accepted him'. Here Paul recognizes different degrees of faith and insists that both those with strong faith and those with weak faith are accepted by God and should respect each other's position. Commenting on this passage (*Romans*, II, p. 697), Cranfield wonders whether 'confidence' might be a better translation of πίστις here

apostle a measured area, a sphere of influence. This is an idea put forward by Paul's opponents, which he accepts. The disagreement lies in the question of how the measurement has been made, and in whose measured area or sphere of influence Corinth should be included.[56]

The best translation of κανών in v. 13, following H.A.W. Meyer, is 'measuring-line'.[57] The word does not refer to a fixed criterion valid for all, a 'principle of legitimacy' (*Legitimitätsprinzip*).[58] Each apostle has a different sphere of influence and will therefore have a different κανών. This is implied by the contrast Paul draws between 'our κανών' (v. 15) and 'someone else's κανών' (v. 16). The line measuring out one person's sphere of influence will be different from the line measuring out another's.

In v. 13 the phrase κατὰ τὸ μέτρον τοῦ κανόνος follows on from the preceding statement, 'we shall not boast beyond measure' and refers to the limits within which it is allowable for Paul to boast. These limits are assigned by God's measuring-line and reach as far as Corinth. The phrase οὗ ἐμέρισεν ἡμῖν ὁ θεὸς μέτρου is a further comment on this idea—our boasting is in accordance with the measurement of the divine measuring-line that marks out the measured area allotted to us.[59] The idea is similar to that of Rom. 12, but expressed in territorial terms. Just as God allots to each Christian specific gifts and ministries and the confidence to exercise them (Rom. 12.3), so also he allots to each apostle a sphere of ministry measured out by the divine measuring-line.

than 'faith', and states that πίστις in Paul can sometimes mean 'the assurance that one is permitted by one's faith…to do some particular thing'. 'Confidence' would also be a possible translation of πίστις in Rom. 12.3.

56. Cranfield thinks that μέτρον, like κανών, refers to a means of measurement or standard ('Μέτρον πίστεως in Romans 12.3', in C.E.B. Cranfield, *The Bible and Christian Life* [Edinburgh: T. & T. Clark, 1985], pp. 203-14 [211]—an article first published in *NTS* 8 [1961–62], pp. 345-51). But Hafemann rightly objects that giving the two words the same meaning makes them tautologous (Hafemann, ' "Self-Commendation" ', p. 78).

57. Meyer, *Corinthians*, II, pp. 409-10.

58. This is the term used by Käsemann ('Legitimität', p. 50). Hafemann has similarly tried to interpret κανών as a universally valid criterion, and sees the 'norm' of Paul's legitimacy as lying in the fact that he was the one through whom the gospel first came to Corinth. 'This "founding function" is the only appropriate, divinely appointed "canon" according to which apostolic authority over a particular church can be determined' (Hafemann, ' "Self-Commendation" ', p. 80).

59. On the phrase οὗ ἐμέρισεν ἡμῖν ὁ θεὸς μέτρου see BDF 294.5: 'οὗ is probably attracted from ὅ (referring to μέτρον) to κανόνος and then μέτρου repeated, lest οὗ be referred to κανόνος'.

Paul uses the idea of measurement in this passage to refer to two distinct but related issues. In v. 12 the verb μετρεῖν denotes the practice of Paul's opponents of measuring themselves against each other—the established rhetorical practice of σύγκρισις.⁶⁰ Their criteria of measurement would presumably include the usual rhetorical virtues such as linguistic ability and an imposing physical presence.⁶¹ Verse 12 thus follows on from the description of Paul as physically weak and a poor speaker in v. 10. He admits ironically that in a sophistic competition he would not be likely to win and that he is not 'bold' enough to enter such a competition (v. 12a). He then goes on to criticize the rules of the competition. It is an internal competition—a group of people comparing themselves with each other within a narrow ingrown circle with no understanding of what is really important.⁶² Moreover, in their boasting they are exaggerating, going beyond what can be measured (εἰς τὰ ἄμετρα).⁶³

Having made these general comments, Paul moves on in v. 13 to the geographical aspect of measurement that dominates vv. 13-16. Presumably

60. See the discussion of σύγκρισις in Marshall, *Enmity*, pp. 53-55. I follow Furnish (*II Corinthians*, pp. 470-71) in preferring the longer reading of the text in vv. 12-13. According to the longer reading, the σύγκρισις is engaged in by Paul's rivals and is something he condemns. According to the shorter reading, it is engaged in by Paul, or by Paul and his colleagues, and is something he approves.

Bultmann, defending the shorter reading, assumes that the first person plural refers to Paul as an individual (*Probleme*, pp. 21-22). But the idea of Paul comparing himself with himself is a strange one. Moreover, I have given reasons earlier for questioning the assumption that Paul treats the first person singular and first person plural as interchangeable (see Chapter 4, Section 5). If the plural of 10.12 is a genuine plural, the idea of Paul and his colleagues comparing themselves with each other is as unlikely as the idea of Paul comparing himself with himself. 1 Cor. 4.3-5 makes it clear that Paul does not believe in the critical assessment of apostles, whether by other people or by themselves.

61. On the importance attached to physique in ancient rhetorical invective see Marshall, *Enmity*, pp. 64-67.

62. The phrase οὐ συνιᾶσιν can be interpreted in either of two ways. It may mean 'they are without understanding', or it may mean 'they do not realize what they are doing' (see the discussion in Barrett, *Second Epistle*, pp. 262-63).

63. The phrase εἰς τὰ ἄμετρα may have been used by the Corinthians. Paul had been accused of self-commendation (2 Cor. 3.1; 5.12) and his opponents may have argued that his boasting was 'over the top' because it did not recognize the generally accepted standards of measurement of apostolic competence. If this is so, Paul uses their language in v. 15 as a stick with which to beat them—it is your boasting that is 'over the top', he implies, because it claims the credit for work done by others.

he was able to combine these two aspects of measurement because they had already been linked together by his opponents. In their view, the criteria of measurement of apostolic competence included both possession of the rhetorical skills and physical attributes generally valued in sophistic circles and recognition as leaders in a particular local area which (they believed) had been assigned to them by God.

3. *Conclusion*

The four groups of words that we have been considering are all related to the same background situation. Paul ends the section 2 Cor. 10.12-18 (whose main theme is measurement) with the statement: 'it is not those who commend themselves who are approved (δόκιμοι) but those whom the Lord commends'. He thus relates the theme of measurement (expressed by the words μέτρον and κανών) to the theme of testing and approval (expressed by the δόκιμος wordgroup). Both themes have to do with apostleship. A true apostle can be defined either as one who fits the required measurements or as one who passes the required tests.

1 Corinthians 9 has a similar background. Paul's opponents were claiming that he was not free and was not a proper apostle because he did not receive financial support. In other words, he did not satisfy one of the criteria for deciding who was a genuine apostle. At the end of the chapter he declares his ambition not to be ἀδόκιμος (v. 27). He believes he will pass the test and qualify as a true apostle by living a life of physical hardship and self-discipline rather than by enjoying the flesh-pots of Corinth like his opponents.

The accusation that Paul was foolish or mad was probably related to his description of the apostolic lifestyle in 1 Corinthians. His opponents assessed both Paul and themselves by normally accepted sophistic standards, but he boasted of his weakness, of his unpopularity and of his artisan status, and thus, in their opinion, revealed himself to be mentally unbalanced.

What emerges from this analysis is the pervasive presence of the theme of the assessment of apostles in both 1 and 2 Corinthians. The conflict may be sharper in 2 Corinthians, but the battleground is the same.

Chapter 10

The Tearful Letter

In chs. 2 and 7 of 2 Corinthians, Paul refers to an earlier letter, written 'out of great distress and anguish of heart and with many tears' (2.4 NIV). Traditionally (and, I believe, correctly) this letter has been identified as 1 Corinthians. But the majority view today is that this letter was written subsequently to 1 Corinthians and is either now wholly lost, or partially lost with part preserved in 2 Cor. 10–13.[1] There are two main objections raised against identifying this letter as 1 Corinthians—that Paul's description of a distressed, tearful letter does not suit 1 Corinthians; and that there is no mention in 1 Corinthians of the disciplinary action against an offender which the 'tearful letter' demanded.

1. *The Tearfulness of the Letter*

It is often stated that 1 Corinthians was not written in distress and anguish with many tears but, in the words of Allan Menzies, 'with a calm and even flow of reason and argument'.[2] Menzies' description of 1 Corinthians may be quoted as an example of the reasoning behind this objection:

> The Epistle as a whole is a statesmanlike document, in which there are few outbursts of feeling; it is the most objective of the Epistles we have from the Apostle. He is on good terms with his first Greek Church, and has great

---

1. Niels Hyldahl ('Die Frage nach der literarischen Einheit des zweiten Korintherbriefes', *ZNW* 64 [1973], pp. 289-306 [290-91]) wrote in 1973 of the 'tearful letter': 'Dieser Brief wurde von der älteren Exegese für identisch mit 1 Kor gehalten,—eine Auffassung, die m.W. keine Fürsprecher mehr unter den Auslegern findet'. This statement is too sweeping—for a list of advocates of this identification see Kruse, *Second Epistle*, p. 26 n. 2. Hyldahl himself strongly defends the traditional theory, and argues that the tearful letter was written 'at the same time, in the same place and in the same circumstances' as 1 Corinthians ('Einheit', p. 299).
2. Menzies, *Second Epistle*, p. xviii.

sympathy with their liberal tendencies, though inflexibly on his guard against any moral laxity, and he guides them, as one in full possession of the truth, to a reasonable application of it to their problems.[3]

Paul is here pictured as like a Scottish professor, enjoying the kind of civilized and reasoned debate that would be appropriate to a university seminar. There is, to be sure, a grain of truth in this picture. Most of 1 Corinthians consists of deliberative rhetoric, in which Paul provides logical arguments for the views he advocates. As he says in 10.15: 'I am writing to you as thinking people; judge for yourselves what I say'. The question is: why did he adopt this logical approach? Was it because he was not emotionally involved and was therefore able to examine the issues calmly in the light of pure reason? Or was it because he believed the logical approach to be necessary in the circumstances, and therefore kept under control the fire that was burning within him? The latter view seems to me to be much more in keeping with Paul's personality.

Paul was an emotional man and his ministry is described elsewhere in very emotional terms. In Philippians, which is one of his calmer epistles, written to a church with which he had a good relationship, he declares: 'there are many people going about, as I have often told you and weep as I tell you now, who are enemies of the cross of Christ' (Phil. 3.18). And in 2 Cor. 11.28-29 he brings his catalogue of afflictions to a climax with 'the worry of all the churches'. 'Who is weak', he asks, 'without me feeling weak? Who is made to stumble without me burning?'[4] The impression these words create is of an emotional man to whom tears came easily—a man who was especially stirred by any sign that the churches for which he felt responsible were being led astray by other people and were too weak to stand up to the pressure.

There were many issues discussed in 1 Corinthians that could have triggered such an emotional response[5]—the party spirit (1.10-12), which

---

3. Menzies, *Second Epistle*, p. xvi.

4. Plummer's comment on this verse (*Second Epistle*, p. 330) is perceptive: 'The intercourse between the chief centres was fairly constant, he was frequently receiving information which gave him plenty to think about (1 Cor. 1.11; 16.17), and anxiety about people generated care for them, when care is possible. This was specially the case with so sensitive a nature as that of St. Paul. What he experienced went deep and moved him strongly'. It is surprising that, after perceiving Paul's sensitive nature so clearly, Plummer should have found it difficult to believe that 1 Corinthians was written in anguish of heart with many tears (*Second Epistle*, p. 50).

5. For similar lists see Hughes, *Second Epistle*, p. 57 and Udo Borse, ' "Tränen-

Paul saw as a sign that their whole way of thinking was unspiritual (3.1-3);
their behaving like kings in his absence (4.8), puffed up with a pride that
might require his coming with a rod (4.18-21); the case of incest of which
they were boasting (5.2, 6), which required the excommunication of the
offender (5.3-5), and which, if left unpunished, could corrupt the whole
church (5.2, 6-8); members of the church taking other members to court
(6.1-11) and consorting with prostitutes (6.12-20); church members who
were so proud of their knowledge that they were leading other members to
destruction (8.1-11); divisions at the Lord's table that made it impossible
to celebrate the Lord's Supper properly, with the result that a number of
people had become ill and some had died (11.20-22, 27-30); an individualism in the use of spiritual gifts in worship that led to competitive-
ness and chaos (14.27-33); and the view being promulgated in the church
that there was no resurrection (15.12), which led Paul to wonder whether
their faith had been in vain (15.2).

Paul could not have faced problems such as these without his spirit
being stirred and tears welling up in his eyes. As H.A.W. Meyer says, the
calm tone of 1 Corinthians was not due to dissimulation, but 'it was just
his specially tender care for the Corinthians which on the one hand in-
creased his pain that he needed to write such rebukes, and on the other
hand did not allow his vehement emotion to emerge in that Epistle'.[6]

Attitudes to weeping are culturally conditioned. Many of those who find
it difficult to believe that Paul could have written 1 Corinthians with tears
live in Northern regions nearer to the Arctic Circle than to the Equator. It
is characteristic of people who live in Northern regions to keep a 'stiff
upper lip', believing with Sherlock Holmes that 'the emotional qualities
are antagonistic to clear reasoning'.[7] Those who belong to warmer regions
are not on the whole so inhibited.

In Acts 20.31 Paul's ministry at Ephesus is portrayed in the following
terms: 'remember that for three years night and day I did not cease to

brief' und 1 Korintherbrief', *SNTU* 9 (1984), pp. 175-202 (177-78). There is no need
for Borse's theory of a distortion of perspective (*perspektivische Verzerrung*). He
argues that, when Paul wrote 2 Corinthians, his recent traumatic experience in Ephesus
had distorted his vision of the past. But the situation at Corinth was bad enough to
cause any pastor nightmares. Not many modern pastors could feel at ease in such a
situation, and Paul certainly could not.

6. Meyer, *Corinthians*, II, p. 168.
7. A. Conan Doyle, 'The Sign of Four', in *The Complete Sherlock Holmes Long
Stories* (London: Book Club Associates, 1973), pp. 124-239 (136).

exhort every one of you with tears'. Whether we regard this verse as based
on eyewitness evidence or as a free composition by Luke, the picture it
paints rings true: both Luke and Paul were Mediterranean men, to whom a
continuously tearful ministry was something natural. Goudge wisely
remarks that 'tears probably came to the eyes of the Apostle more easily
than to those of his modern commentators; he was not trained, like the
modern Englishman, to an unnatural repression of emotion'.[8]

According to 2 Cor. 7.8 the letter was not only tearful but also hurtful.
Barrett, commenting on this statement, asks whether 1 Corinthians would
have hurt the Corinthians. His reply is: 'Possibly, but one would not have
thought it would do so to such an extent as to make this hurtfulness its
main feature'.[9] This judgment does not take account of the way in which,
in 1 Corinthians, Paul personalizes the whole dispute. You are my spiritual
children, he writes, but you are rebelling against me, your spiritual father
(4.15-16); the 'wisdom' and rhetorical style of your new teachers were
things I deliberately avoided in my own preaching (2.1-5); the triumphalist
theology and lifestyle adopted by your teachers, and embraced by you in
my absence, are diametrically opposed to the lifestyle of myself and my
colleagues (4.6-13); and the ethical teaching of your pedagogues that you
are now following is incompatible with the 'ways in Christ' that I taught
you (4.14-17). Similarly, in chs. 8–10 Paul contrasts the individualism and
appeal to individual rights currently in vogue at Corinth with his own
policy of being the servant of all (9.19-23; 10.33) and ends up: 'be imitators of me, as I am of Christ' (11.1).

In all these passages Paul treats theological and ethical issues in terms
of the loyalty owed by children to their spiritual father. His reason for
adopting this procedure was not merely the desire to apply emotional
pressure. He wanted them to realize that the teaching of his rivals was not
(as they seem to have thought) something new and exciting to be added to
the gospel they had received from him, but was diametrically opposed to
that gospel. Its adoption meant the rejection of Paul's teaching and of his
example, and therefore of Paul himself.

Such an approach would inevitably hurt the Corinthians. Many of them
were Paul's converts, bound to him by close ties of affection. The accusation of disloyalty would cause them surprise, sorrow and repentance.

The language used in 2 Corinthians reflects this situation. The majority
of the church had not only obeyed him in the specific matter of the

8.   Goudge, *Second Epistle*, p. xxxvi.
9.   Barrett, *Second Epistle*, p. 209.

punishment of the offender (2.6), but had completely changed their attitude (7.11). Paul confesses in 7.12 that this change of attitude was what he had hoped to achieve when he wrote the tearful letter. His main concern had not been to punish the specific offence but to reveal to the Corinthians that, when it came to a showdown, their loyalty lay with him and with his gospel, not with his opponents.

2. *The Offender*

In both 1 Corinthians (5.1-13) and 2 Corinthians (2.5-11; 7.12) Paul refers to a man who had committed an offence and become liable to church discipline. It is not surprising that these passages have traditionally been linked together, and the offender of 2 Cor. 2 and 7 has been identified as the incestuous man of 1 Cor. 5.[10] However, this view is currently out of favour.[11] A number of objections are commonly raised against this identification.

a. *The Nature of the Offence*
The offender described in 2 Corinthians had offended Paul personally. In 2.10 Paul talks about his own forgiveness of the offender; and in 2.5 he says the man had caused pain 'not to me but to all of you'. This means 'not so much to me as to all of you', and implies that the man had caused pain to Paul.[12] In 1 Cor. 5, on the other hand, there is no suggestion that

10. In support of this identification, appeal has often been made to the similarities in vocabulary between the passages. However, R. Bieringer correctly points out that the words concerned are too general to justify such an appeal (R. Bieringer, 'Zwischen Kontinuität und Diskontinuität: Die beiden Korintherbriefe in ihrer Beziehung zueinander', in R. Bieringer [ed.], *The Corinthian Correspondence* [Leuven: Leuven University Press, 1996], pp. 3-38 [32]). So also Furnish, *II Corinthians*, pp. 164-65.

11. According to Plummer (*Second Epistle*, p. xv) it 'ought to be regarded as certain' that the tearful letter cannot be 1 Corinthians and the offender of 2 Corinthians cannot be the incestuous man. On the concept of 'certainty' in New Testament scholarship see chapter 2, 'The Argument from Probable Certainty', in Hall, *Seven Pillories*, pp. 21-36.

12. Thrall, *Second Epistle*, p. 171 n. 291. Plummer's comment on the similar οὐκ... ἀλλά construction in 2 Cor. 7.12 is apposite: 'St. Paul is always exhibiting Hebrew modes of thought and language. In Jewish literature we often have two alternatives, one of which is negatived, without meaning that it is negatived absolutely, but only in comparison with the other alternative, which is much more important. 'I will have mercy, and not sacrifice' (Hos. 6.6) does not prohibit sacrifice; it affirms that mercy is much the better of the two' (Plummer, *Second Epistle*, p. 224).

the incestuous man had offended Paul in person. Therefore, it is alleged, the offence referred to in 2 Corinthians must have been, not the case of incest, but a separate incident in which Paul had been personally insulted.[13]

This argument rests on a misunderstanding of the situation. Paul's main concern in 1 Cor. 5 was the attitude of the church. The Corinthians were 'puffed up' (v. 2) and were 'boasting' (v. 6). I have argued in Chapter 2 that the use of the word φυσιοῦσθαι in this passage links the case of incest to the general situation at Corinth described in chs. 1–4.[14] The Corinthians were puffed up with pride because of their new wisdom, which was of an antinomian and individualistic nature. They felt themselves to be free from the shackles of Paul's traditional morality—free to follow the slogan of 6.12: 'I have the right to do whatever I wish'. The man's action, and the Corinthian approval of his action, constituted an open defiance of Paul's moral teaching.

The offence of 1 Cor. 5 was not an isolated act, but was part of an ongoing conflict. This is clearly implied by the structure of the chapter. Between the initial discussion of the man's action in vv. 1-5 and the final exhortation to excommunicate him in v. 13, Paul comments on a previous letter, which had dealt with Christians leading immoral lives (vv. 9-12a).[15] He treats his demand for the disciplining of the offender as an implementation of the principle laid down in the earlier letter.[16] Thus his question in

---

13. Barrett, *Second Epistle*, p. 89; Furnish, *II Corinthians*, pp. 160-68; Thrall, *Second Epistle*, pp. 64-65.

14. See Chapter 2, Section 2.

15. The phrase νῦν δὲ ἔγραψα in 1 Cor. 5.11 must mean 'but in fact I wrote'. It is a clarification of a misunderstanding of his previous letter, in which he had called for the ostracism of deliberate offenders. The phrase has sometimes been translated 'but now I write', treating ἔγραψα as an epistolary aorist. In that case the verse can be read as a correction rather than as a clarification. But the epistolary aorist regards the letter from the point of view of the receiver, whereas νῦν in the sense of 'now' regards the letter from the point of view of the sender. In the sense of 'now' νῦν should be followed by a present tense νῦν δὲ γράφω.

16. The continuity between the 'previous letter' and Paul's argument in 1 Cor. 5 is emphasized by G.W.H. Lampe, 'Church Discipline and the Interpretation of the Epistles to the Corinthians', in W.R. Farmer, C.F.D. Moule and R.R. Niebuhr (eds.), *Christian History and Interpretation: Studies Presented to John Knox* (Cambridge: Cambridge University Press, 1967), pp. 337-61 (344). He thinks it probable that the Corinthian misunderstanding was deliberate, and that this explains the vehemence of Paul's language. 'Not only was the offence peculiarly shocking, even when judged by

5.1: 'Is sexual immorality heard of in Corinth?' does not mean that he was hearing of such immorality for the first time. The question is rhetorical—how can you, as Christians, be guilty of such behaviour?

In all his churches Paul handed on a tradition (παράδοσις) which he himself had been taught. This tradition included not only teaching about the Lord's Supper (1 Cor. 11.23) and the resurrection of Christ (1 Cor. 15.3) but also principles of moral behaviour. He writes to the Thessalonians: 'you received (παρελάβετε) from us how you ought to behave' (1 Thess. 4.1). The verb παραλαμβάνω (which is also used, along with παραδίδωμι, in 1 Cor. 11.23 and 15.2) indicates the handing down of tradition. One prominent item in this moral tradition was abstaining from sexual immorality (1 Thess. 4.1-8). If the prohibition of sexual immorality was a prominent element in Paul's tradition, the enthusiastic endorsement of sexual immorality at Corinth inevitably involved defiance of Paul's tradition. And the case of incest is treated by Paul in 5.1 as an extreme example of such immorality—taking the theory that 'all things are allowable' to its logical extreme.

We must not forget that to reject Paul's teaching meant to reject him as a person.[17] Like the rabbis, Paul taught by example as well as by precept.[18] 'Be imitators of me', he writes, 'as I am of Christ' (1 Cor. 11.1). 'Though you may have countless pedagogues in Christ, you do not have many fathers...I urge you, therefore, be imitators of me' (1 Cor. 4.15-16). Like a natural father he taught not so much a system of doctrine for his children to learn as a way of life for his children to follow, which he demonstrated in his own life as a living visual aid. Timothy was to remind them of his ways (ὁδοί), as he taught them in every church—the lifestyle and the precept being the same (1 Cor. 4.17).

We should therefore regard the case of incest not as an isolated act by one individual but as a test case in the defiance of Paul by members of the church. And this is precisely the situation implied in 2 Corinthians.

---

the standards of pagan morality (verse 1), but it had afforded a focal point for the disobedience of the Corinthian church towards its apostle'.

17. Cf. Thrall, *Second Epistle*, p. 493: 'To repudiate the apostle was to repudiate also the apostolic gospel, represented by his person'.

18. The teaching method of the Jewish rabbis is described as follows by B. Gerhardsson, *Memory and Manuscript: Oral Tradition and Written Transmission in Rabbinic Judaism and Early Christianity* (Lund: Gleerup, 1961), p. 183: 'The pupil is a witness to his teacher's words; he is a witness to his actions as well. He does not only say, "I heard from my teacher" but "I saw my teacher do this or that" '.

According to 2 Cor. 2.9 the 'tearful letter' was written to test whether the Corinthians were 'obedient in all things' (εἰ εἰς πάντα ὑπήκοοί ἐστε). Paul's concern was general, not specific. He wanted them to be obedient not only in their punishment of this one individual, but also in their overall loyalty to his teaching and tradition. In 2 Cor. 7.12 Paul says that the 'tearful letter' was written 'in order that your zeal for me might be revealed to you'. The enthusiastic approval by the church of this man's incestuous behaviour had undermined the relationship of father and children that had previously existed between Paul and the Corinthians, and the most important effect of their repentance was to restore that relationship.

In Furnish's opinion, 'Paul's comment in 2 Cor. 2.9 that he had written to test the obedience of the congregation is not an apt description of what he had been doing in 1 Cor. 5.1-5'.[19] The exact opposite is the case. What was at stake was whether the Corinthians would remain loyal to Paul and to the tradition he had taught them. Their willingness to perform this act of discipline was a symptom and a declaration of that loyalty.

b. *The Nature of the Punishment*

It is sometimes alleged that the punishment prescribed in 1 Cor. 5 was so serious that Paul could not have asked for an immediate pardon for the same offender in 2 Cor. 2. In Furnish's opinion, 'the punishment decreed in 1 Cor. 5 is severe and permanent: that sexual offender is to be totally cut off from the community and left to the ultimately destructive powers of Satan—that is, physical death... Paul's counsel in 2 Cor. 2.6-8 to forgive and restore the offender is simply inexplicable if the same case is in view'. Furnish then cites the stern ascetic Tertullian in support of his judgment.[20]

There are two problems with this argument. The first is that the phrase 'destruction of the flesh' (ὄλεθρος τῆς σαρκός) in 1 Cor. 5.5 does not necessarily imply physical death. Strong arguments against this interpretation have been advanced by Thiselton, Fee and others.[21] The main action

19. Furnish, *II Corinthians*, p. 165, following Allo, *Seconde épître*, p. 58.
20. Furnish, *II Corinthians*, pp. 165-66.
21. Thiselton, 'Σάρξ', pp. 204-28; Fee, *First Epistle*, pp. 210-12; Borse, 'Tränenbrief', pp. 187-88. Cf. the cautious judgment of Lampe, 'Church Discipline', p. 354: 'On balance, then, the probability is quite strong that in 2 Cor. 2.5-11 we have evidence that the severe sentence passed in 1 Cor. 5.5 was not only intended to be, but actually was, remedial: an extreme and painful form of pastoral discipline rather than capital punishment'.

Paul requires the church to take is excommunication. The climax of his argument comes in v. 13: 'remove the evil man from your midst'. Expelling this man from the church into the world meant handing him over to 'the god of this age' (2 Cor. 4.4)—namely, to Satan.[22] What kind of action Satan would take is not specified—in Thiselton's words, 'the whole phrase τῷ Σατανᾷ εἰς ὄλεθρον τῆς σαρκός remains open-ended and in some directions unspecific'.[23] Satan's action could involve physical or spiritual affliction.[24] Had Paul wished to refer to physical death, the use of the phrase ὄλεθρος τῆς σαρκός would have been a most unPauline way of doing so. It is more probable that the distinction between σάρξ and πνεῦμα is similar to that found in other Pauline letters—notably in Gal. 5.16-26, where σάρξ represents sinful human nature.

Moreover, the purpose of the punishment is remedial—so that his spirit may be saved on the day of the Lord (v. 5). It is hard to see how the bare fact of physical death could be the cause of spiritual salvation. As H.A.W. Meyer says, the reference to spiritual salvation suggests that 'the penal procedure of the church...was of a paedagogic nature'.[25] Paul's description of his thorn in the flesh as an 'angel of Satan' in 2 Cor. 12.7 reflects his belief that Satan's activity, however unpleasant at the time, could become a source of spiritual good in the long term.

The second problem with Furnish's argument is that it underestimates the redemptive power of God. The Corinthian Christians were used to lives transformed by the grace of God, and to the amazing scope of God's forgiveness. In 1 Cor. 6.10 Paul reminds them that some of them had been thieves, extortioners, drunkards and foul-mouthed, but they had been washed clean, sanctified and put right with God.[26] Such cleansing was not

---

22. Thrall (*Second Epistle*, pp. 306-308) argues convincingly that the god of this age in 2 Cor. 4.4 is Satan.

23. Thiselton, 'Σάρξ', p. 226.

24. Thiselton ('Σάρξ', p. 223) points out that in inter-testamental Jewish writings Satan pursues his destructive role in a great variety of ways, both physical and spiritual. He quotes the statement of W. Foerster, s.v. 'διάβολος', in *TDNT*, II, pp. 75-81 (80) that 'the destruction which he brings embraces harmful processes of every kind'.

25. Meyer, *Corinthians*, II, p. 169.

26. According to Barrett (*Second Epistle*, p. 213), 'it is hard to think that, after writing 1 Cor. 5.2-5, Paul would be content to have the incident simply washed out'. But it is the washing metaphor that Paul uses in 1 Cor. 6.10 to describe the transforming power of God. Kruse (*Second Epistle*, p. 41) points out that Paul had experienced this power in his own life, having been transformed from a persecutor of the church into an apostle (1 Cor. 15.9).

limited to sins committed before baptism. In Gal. 6.1-2 Paul writes:
'Brothers, if someone is caught in a sin, you who are spiritual should restore him gently. But watch yourselves or you also may be tempted. Carry
each other's burdens, and in this way you will fulfil the law of Christ'.
Paul recognized that there was a constant temptation for Christians from a
pagan background to revert to their former way of life; but, just as fishermen repair their nets, Christians can repair their fellow-Christians, through
carrying each other's burdens.[27] It is this repair work that he advocates in
2 Cor. 2.7-8.[28]

The man concerned may or may not have been a ringleader in the
antinomian movement. He could have been an ordinary member of the
church, caught up in the new teaching and easily persuaded by his teachers
to demonstrate his new-found liberty by doing something outrageous. In
the collective repentance that the church as a whole experienced (2 Cor.
7.9-11) this man also, one assumes, repented. There is no reason why, in
such circumstances, Paul should not put into practice what he preached in
Galatians and revoke the sentence of excommunication on a penitent
fellow-Christian.

c. *The Man who was Wronged*
In 2 Cor. 7.12 Paul refers to the man who did the wrong and the man who
was wronged. Those who regard the offence as a personal insult believe
the man who was wronged to be Paul himself. But if the offence involved
a man and his stepmother, the man who was wronged was presumably the
man's father. This means the father must have been alive at the time of the
offence.[29] The objection has been raised that, if the man's father had been

27. Fee (*First Epistle*, p. 54) makes the point that the word καταρτίζω (which
occurs in Gal. 6.1 and also in 1 Cor. 1.10) is used in Mk 1.19 of fishermen mending
their nets.
28. Furnish (*II Corinthians*, p. 168) tries to deny the relevance of Gal. 6.1 on the
grounds that the principle of that verse would not necessarily apply in all instances and
that Paul was not always consistent. However, his belief that the sentence passed on
the incestuous man was irrevocable implies, not that the principle of Gal. 6.1 was
applied inconsistently, but that in the case of serious sins it did not apply at all. Paul's
understanding of the grace of God was broader than this. He believed in the Old
Testament principle that no judgment (not even the sentence of death) was irrevocable
and that God was capable of changing his mind (Exod. 32.14; 1 Chron. 21.15, 27; Ps.
106.45; Jer. 18.1-8; Amos 7.1-6; Jon. 3.10).
29. Clarke (*Leadership*, p. 84) suggests that, had the father been alive, he would have
been under pressure to bring legal proceedings, or risk being implicated in the crime

alive, the church would not have tolerated his action.[30]

This is a matter of opinion. Walther Schmithals sees the situation very differently. He refers to Paul's 'non-legalistic thinking', and argues that, if the father had been dead, Paul's language and the punishment demanded would have been too harsh, even though such a union was forbidden by Jewish and Roman law.[31] It must be remembered that the current slogan in the Corinthian church was πάντα [μοι] ἔξεστιν: 'I have the right to do whatever I want to do' (6.12; 10.23), and that this right was being claimed as a matter of theological principle. The history of the church warns us not to be dogmatic in laying down what actions are possible or impossible for enthusiastic Christians.

It is true that in 1 Corinthians Paul never mentions the wrong done to the father.[32] The reason for this is that the father's feelings were not his major concern. The most important thing, in Paul's eyes, was not the personal feelings and rights of the participants, but the attitude of the church. He believed that, unless this was changed, the whole church would be polluted, just as the whole of the dough was affected by leaven. His assertion in 2 Cor. 7.12 that he did not write his tearful letter primarily for the sake of either the wrongdoer or the man who was wronged expresses this priority.[33]

d. *Paul's Exercise of Authority*
In Furnish's opinion the disciplinary action in view is of a different kind in the two letters: the handling of the case in 2 Cor. 2 is 'entirely democratic', whereas Paul takes up a more authoritarian position in 1 Cor. 5.[34]

himself. But it is doubtful how far the pressures of upper-class Graeco-Roman society would have applied to the bulk of the church members, whose status was much lower.

30. E.g. Plummer, *Second Epistle*, p. 225: 'Disorderly as the Corinthian Church was, it is difficult to believe that one of its members would be guilty of taking his father's wife while the father was living, and that the rest of the Church, so far from being scandalised, were as much puffed up with complacency as usual'.

31. W. Schmithals, *Gnosticism in Corinth: An Investigation of the Letters to the Corinthians* (Nashville: Abingdon, 1971), p. 237.

32. This point is made by Borse ('Tränenbrief', p. 190, following Windisch, *Der zweite Korintherbrief*, pp. 237-39). However, as Thrall says (*Second Epistle*, p. 65), if the father was not a church member the failure to mention him may not require explanation.

33. I have added the word 'primarily' to represent the force of the idiom οὐ... ἀλλά. See n. 12 to this chapter.

34. Furnish, *II Corinthians*, p. 165.

This is a half-truth. In both letters Paul makes it clear what he wants the Corinthians to do. The difference is that in 2 Corinthians he uses the polite word παρακαλῶ (I urge you to do this), whereas in 1 Corinthians he states that he has already passed judgment himself and expects the Corinthians to ratify that judgment.[35]

The closest parallel to Paul's use of παρακαλῶ in 2 Cor. 2.8 is Phlm. 8-10. Paul wants Philemon to forgive his runaway slave Onesimus and to send him back to Paul. He has the authority to command Philemon to do this (v. 8). But because of his love for him (v. 9) and because he is confident of his obedience (v. 21) he prefers to urge (παρακαλῶ, v. 10) rather than to command. Throughout his ministry Paul tried to avoid using his apostolic authority dictatorially if at all possible, and preferred exhortation to authoritarianism (cf. 2 Cor. 1.24; 13.9-10).[36]

The reason why Paul used the word παρακαλῶ in 2 Cor. 2.8 but did not use it in 1 Cor. 5 was that the situation had changed. When he wrote 1 Corinthians, he was dealing with a man who had defied his moral teaching with the enthusiastic approval of the church. He was not 'confident of their obedience' as he was when writing to Philemon. But when Titus brought him the good news of the Corinthian change of heart, his confidence was restored. He felt able to make a request of the Corinthians, rather than presenting them with a *fait accompli* as he did in 1 Cor. 5.

e. The Importance of the Issue
It is sometimes alleged that in 2 Corinthians the discipline of the offender is treated as though it were the main issue of the tearful letter, whereas in 1 Corinthians the discipline of the incestuous man is only one issue among many.[37] But 2 Corinthians neither states nor implies that the case of discipline was the only matter dealt with in the tearful letter. This theory relies totally on the argument from silence. Paul, it is argued, does not

---

35. Paul's use of παρακαλῶ has been much discussed, especially with regard to 1 Cor. 1.10. For a survey of modern attempts to interpret that verse in the light of Paul's rhetorical structure see Thiselton, *First Epistle*, pp. 111-14. Thiselton rightly inclines to the view of C.J. Bjerkelund (*Parakalo. Form, Funktion und Sinn der parakalo Sätze in den paulinischen Briefen* [Oslo: Universitetsforlaget, 1967]) that παρακαλῶ introduces a personal request, not the *propositio* of a rhetorical argument.

36. This point is elaborated in Chapter 2, Section 3b.

37. Thrall (*Second Epistle*, pp. 58-60) attributes this objection to Bleek, Krenkel and Allo. After discussing Baur's attempt to reply to it, she continues: 'In any case, the contrast remains between a letter concerned (as far as we know) with only one incident and our canonical 1 Corinthians with its extremely wide-ranging subject matter'.

specifically mention any other matter raised in the tearful letter; therefore no other matter can have been raised.

Whenever the argument from silence is used in scholarly debate (as it frequently is), the first question to be asked is: was there a specific reason for Paul to concentrate on one issue to the exclusion of other issues? If there was such a reason, Paul's 'silence' about other issues needs no explanation, and does not imply that such issues cannot have existed. In the case of 2 Corinthians there was a specific reason why Paul had to give further advice about the case of discipline. The punishment he had demanded in the tearful letter had been carried out, and the man had repented (2 Cor. 2.7). This meant that the situation had changed and new advice was needed to deal with the new situation.

If the tearful letter was 1 Corinthians, the case of incest was almost the only matter in that letter that required this kind of follow-up. Most of the problems discussed in 1 Corinthians were of a general nature, and Paul's advice did not need to be modified or repeated in a later letter. When Paul does refer back in 2 Corinthians to some of these problems (at 11.4 and 12.19-21), he does so in summary form, presupposing the detailed discussion in the earlier letter.[38]

There were three matters raised in 1 Corinthians that required follow-up in 2 Corinthians: the case of incest (1 Cor. 5.1-13; 2 Cor. 2.5-11); the collection (1 Cor. 16.1-4; 2 Cor. 8 and 9); and Paul's travel plans (1 Cor. 16.5-9; 2 Cor. 1.15–2.4). In each case it was the Corinthian reaction to what he had written in 1 Corinthians that required Paul to make a response.[39] His decision to engage in further discussion of these three matters was dictated by circumstances, and carries no implication as to their relative importance.

Conclusion

The references in 2 Corinthians to a tearful letter are all appropriate to 1 Corinthians, and the references in 2 Corinthians to an offender and an offence all fit in well with the situation lying behind 1 Cor. 5. This does not logically prove that 1 Corinthians was the tearful letter, but it makes it extremely probable.

---

38. See the detailed discussion of 2 Cor. 11.4 in ch. 7, and of 2 Cor. 12.19-21 in ch. 11.

39. On Paul's travel plans see Chapter 11. On the collection arrangements see Excursus H: 'The Journeys of Titus'.

Chapter 11

PAUL'S TRAVELS AND TRAVEL PLANS

1. *Paul's Travel Plans*

The first thing Paul did in 2 Corinthians, after the initial greeting and thanks-giving, was to defend himself against criticism of his travel plans. He had been accused of fickleness—of saying one thing and doing another. This was clearly a red-hot issue, and Titus had told him how strongly some of the Corinthians felt about it. If the 'tearful letter' was 1 Corinthians, it must have been his announcement of his travel plans in that letter that led to this criticism.

In 1 Cor. 16.5-9 Paul announced that he was planning to visit Mace-donia, and would proceed from there to Corinth, possibly to stay through the winter. He also gave a reason for this plan: 'I do not want to see you now in passing (ἐν παρόδῳ), since I hope to stay with you for some con-siderable time, if the Lord permits'. In other words, he was not intending to cross the Aegean Sea to Corinth and then travel North to Macedonia, thus visiting Corinth ἐν παρόδῳ (on his way to Macedonia). Instead, he intended to travel North through Asia Minor to Troas, cross the sea to Macedonia, and then travel South to Corinth. Thus his next visit to Corinth would not be a fleeting visit on his way to somewhere else, but a longer visit, possibly of several months.

Why did Paul feel the need to explain and justify his plan in this way? The most probable reason is that the Corinthians were expecting Paul to visit them on his way to Macedonia, and he had to give a reason for failing to do so.[1] But if that was the case, the reason he gave for choosing this route—that he did not want to see them 'in passing'—must have seemed to them very unsatisfactory. Why should he not visit them both in passing

---

1. Thrall (*Second Epistle*, p. 71) suggests that Paul could have anticipated a possible misunderstanding of 1 Cor. 4.19, and that the purpose of 16.7 could have been to make it clear that 'soon' in 4.19 did not mean 'on my way to Macedonia'.

and also for a longer time later on? 1 Cor. 16.5-9 is precisely the kind of announcement that 2 Cor. 1.15–2.4 seems to presuppose—an announcement of a journey that bypassed Corinth without a satisfactory explanation for the route chosen.

Those who deny that 1 Corinthians is the 'tearful letter' have to reconstruct a different sequence of events, and this is done in various ways.[2] According to one reconstruction, after writing 1 Corinthians Paul changed his mind from the plan outlined in 1 Cor. 16 to the plan outlined in 2 Cor. 1.15-16—that is to say, he decided to visit Corinth on his way to Macedonia as well as on the return journey. On this theory, his second visit to Corinth was the first stage in this revised itinerary; but this visit proved to be so painful that he cancelled his plan to see them on the return journey, and either went straight back to Ephesus or continued on to Macedonia and returned to Ephesus via Troas.[3] What the Corinthians were objecting to, if this theory is sound, was the cancellation of the *second* half of Paul's itinerary—his promise of a visit on the way back from Macedonia.

The problem with this theory is the emphatic position of πρότερον in 2 Cor. 1.15. What I wanted, Paul writes, was to come to you first, before visiting Macedonia.[4] It is clear from this that it was Paul's cancellation of the first part of his journey—his failure to visit Corinth on the way to Macedonia—that had angered the Corinthians.

An alternative reconstruction is offered by Furnish. Paul's original plan, in his opinion, was the plan given in 1 Cor. 16. But news brought by Timothy of an alarming situation at Corinth persuaded him to make a quick emergency visit. This visit was painful and humiliating, and Paul quickly returned to Ephesus. Before returning to Ephesus he decided that he would have to pay another visit to Corinth on his way to Macedonia to straighten things out. This was the itinerary referred to in 2 Cor. 1.15-16, which involved a double visit. However, by the time he wrote the

2.   For a detailed discussion of various reconstructions of Paul's travel plans see Thrall, *Second Epistle*, pp. 69-74.

3.   Barrett, *Second Epistle*, pp. 7, 86; Martin, *2 Corinthians*, p. 24; Fee, 'ΧΑΡΙΣ', pp. 533-38.

4.   The reasons for taking πρότερον with ἐλθεῖν rather than with ἐβουλόμην are given in Furnish, *II Corinthians*, p. 133 (contra Thrall, *Second Epistle*, pp. 136-37). The point is not that Paul once wanted to come to them and no longer wants to come to them. The point is that he wanted to come to them first (before visiting Macedonia). However, even if πρότερον is taken with ἐβουλόμην, the emphasis is still on the journey *to* Macedonia, not on the return journey.

tearful letter he had changed his mind yet again, reverting to the plan of 1
Cor. 16, and decided to visit Corinth only on the return journey from
Macedonia.[5]

This reconstruction, which assumes that Paul changed his mind on two
separate occasions, would certainly explain why the charge of fickleness
was levelled against him. But there is nothing in 2 Corinthians to suggest
more than one change of mind. Moreover, the purpose Paul had in mind
when planning the double visit was to bring the Corinthians a double
portion of grace (or joy) (2 Cor. 1.15),[6] not to straighten out a difficult
situation.

It is impossible to prove or disprove reconstructions of this kind. We
know so little of the historical background to Paul's letters that almost any
reconstruction is possible. The fact remains that 1 Cor. 16.5-9 is one of
many passages in 1 Corinthians that links up perfectly with the treatment
of the same subject in 2 Corinthians.

2. The Interpretation of 2 Corinthians 12.19–13.4

In 2 Cor. 13.1-2 Paul states that he is about to pay his third visit to
Corinth, and that he intends to carry out on this third visit the threats he
uttered on his second visit.[7] Verse 2 falls naturally into the pattern 'ab-ab-
ab-c', as becomes obvious if the verse is set down in tabular form.[8]

5.   Furnish, *II Corinthians*, pp. 143-44.
6.   There are two readings in the MSS—χάριν and χαράν and commentators are
divided as to which reading to prefer. Whichever reading is chosen, the implication of
Paul's statement is that the plan to pay a double visit was made at a time when
relationships were good, and the visits could be expected to have a happy outcome.
This is equally true if one accepts Fee's view ('ΧΑΡΙΣ', p. 535) that χάρις denotes
benefits conferred by the Corinthians (for a critique of this view see Chapter 8 n. 4, and
Furnish, *II Corinthians*, p. 142).
7.   According to Niels Hyldahl, the words τρίτον τοῦτο ἔρχομαι πρὸς ὑμᾶς in
13.1 do not mean 'this is the third time I am coming to you', but 'on this third occasion
I am indeed coming to you' (N. Hyldahl, *Die Paulinische Chronologie* [Leiden: E.J.
Brill, 1986], p. 103). In his opinion Paul had not visited the Corinthians since his initial
founding visit, but had on two previous occasions intended to come and been prevented. This is a most unnatural way of understanding Paul's words. Equally unconvincing is his translation of 13.2 (see the following note).
8.   2 Cor. 13.2 is set out in tabular form by Hughes (*Second Epistle*, p. 476) and
Martin (*2 Corinthians*, p. 454).
Hyldahl translates ὡς παρὼν τὸ δεύτερον καὶ ἀπὼν νῦν as: 'gleichsam schon
zum zweitenmal anwesend und doch jetzt abwesend'. He thinks that Paul regarded 2

I have stated my intention	and I state my intention
As on my second visit	so now in my absence
To the previous sinners	and to all the rest

That on my next visit I will not spare [the guilty].

Reading the columns vertically, on his second visit Paul warned those who had sinned previously that he would not spare the guilty, and now that he is absent from Corinth he issues the same warning, not only to 'the previous sinners' but also to 'all the rest'. The phrase τοῖς προημαρ-τηκόσιν (to those who have sinned previously), and the fact that only this group was threatened with punishment on the second visit, suggests that the distinction between 'the previous sinners' and 'the rest' is chronological. The actions of the 'previous sinners' took place before or during the second visit, and they were therefore warned on that visit; the actions of 'the rest' took place after the second visit and the warning is now extended to cover them also.[9]

The nature of the behaviour that Paul threatens to punish is explained in the immediately preceding verses—12.20-21. In these verses Paul describes two distinct behaviour patterns—one in v. 20, one in v. 21. They are distinguished from each other in four ways. First, v. 20 is concerned with discord and quarrelling, whereas v. 21 is concerned with sexual

Corinthians, written when he was absent from Corinth, as equivalent to a second visit (*Chronologie*, p. 104). This translation ignores the ab-ab-ab-c structure of the verse, which requires us to take ὡς παρὼν τὸ δεύτερον with προείρηκα and καὶ ἀπὼν νῦν with προλέγω. Hyldahl's grammatical objection that ὡς and καί are not parallel words is unsound—the parallels to this construction cited by Windisch are (pace Hyldahl) convincing (Windisch, *Der zweite Korintherbrief*, p. 414, quoted in Hyldahl, *Chronologie*, p. 104 n. 62).

9.   According to Dieter Georgi and Rudolf Bultmann the word προημαρτηκότες (those who have sinned previously) refers to people who had sinned prior to their conversion and never become Christian in their attitudes (Georgi, *Opponents*, p. 233; Bultmann, *Der zweite Brief*, p. 242). But, as Martin says, 'it is hardly conceivable that Paul would refer to sin committed before conversion as needing to be confessed' (Martin, *2 Corinthians*, p. 467; cf. Barrett, *Second Epistle*, p. 332). The formal structure of 13.2 involves in each of its clauses a distinction of time: 'I have stated my intention' and 'I state my intention'; 'on my second visit' and 'now in my absence'; 'to the previous sinners' and 'to all the rest'. The natural understanding of this parallelism is that the previousness of the previous sinners relates to an earlier stage in Paul's dealings with them, not to the time before their conversion.

immorality. Second, v. 20 contains the hypothetical word πως (perhaps) (I am afraid I may perhaps come across such behaviour); whereas v. 21 is introduced with the word πάλιν (again) (I am afraid God may once again humiliate me when I come).[10] Third, when talking about discord and quarrelling, Paul addresses his remarks in the second person to the church as a whole; whereas his remarks about sexual immorality refer in the third person to 'many people'. Fourth, he refers to those accused of sexual immorality as 'previous sinners', using the same verb προαμαρτάνω as in 13.2. The force of this verb in both verses is to make a chronological distinction between an earlier and a later problem.[11]

If the information gleaned from 13.2 is combined with the information gleaned from 12.20-21, there emerges a clear demarcation of two stages in the conflict. The first stage involved the sexual immorality of the 'previous sinners' which Paul rebuked on his second visit. The second stage involved the discord and quarrelling among other members of the church ('the rest'), which Paul had not experienced at first hand and therefore mentioned only as a possibility (πως). These two problems could, of course, be related. But Paul treats them separately, and by using the verb προαμαρτάνω implies that the immoral behaviour of certain individuals preceded the discord within the church as a whole.

It is a striking fact that in 1 Corinthians there is a chronological sequence very similar to the sequence implied in 2 Corinthians. In 1 Cor. 5.9 Paul refers to a previous letter in which he had urged the Corinthians not to associate with sexually immoral people. In clarifying what he meant by this, he makes it clear that the people concerned were members of the

---

10. The word πάλιν (again) applies to the whole of v. 21 (again, when I come, God will humiliate me), not just to the words ἐλθόντος μου (when I come again, God will humiliate me). Paul has already referred to his forthcoming visit in v. 20 with the word ἐλθών (when I come). It is difficult to imagine a reason why the 'when I come' of v. 20 should be followed by 'when I come again' in v. 21 with reference to the same visit. If, however, v. 21 refers to a repeated humiliation rather than to a repeated visit, the use of πάλιν is natural and appropriate (Plummer, *Second Epistle*, p. 369; Hughes, *Second Epistle*, p. 472 n. 166; Furnish, *II Corinthians*, p. 562).

11. Martin argues that within the group of 'previous sinners' Paul includes not only those guilty of sexual immorality but also those guilty of discord and quarrelling (*2 Corinthians*, pp. 454-55). This interpretation fails to explain why Paul should distinguish the behaviour of v. 20 from that of v. 21 in four different ways, and why in 13.2 he should distinguish 'the previous sinners' he warned on his second visit from 'the rest'.

church.[12] The fact that Paul felt the need to write such a letter indicates the presence within the church, prior to the time of writing of 1 Corinthians, of 'brothers' (church members) whose sexual behaviour Paul considered to be immoral.

1 Corinthians represents the second stage in the conflict. The letter is dominated by the theme of discord. After his initial greeting and thanksgiving Paul plunges straight into this theme—'Chloe's people have told me that there are divisions in the church' (1.11). The problem of discord is explicitly addressed in chs. 1–4 and, as Margaret Mitchell has shown, the whole epistle could be characterized as an appeal for unity (ὁμόνοια) in the face of individualistic and divisive tendencies.[13]

There is thus a close correspondence in this matter between 1 and 2 Corinthians. The sexual behaviour criticized in the 'previous letter' of 1 Cor. 5.9 corresponds to the behaviour of the 'previous sinners' of 2 Cor. 12.21; and the divisions criticized in 1 Cor. 1.10-17 correspond to the divisive behaviour described in 2 Cor. 12.20. This correspondence makes it extremely probable that, when Paul talks about the two problems of discord and immorality in 2 Cor. 12, it is the situation described in 1 Corinthians that he has in mind.

It is commonly believed today that, between 1 and 2 Corinthians, the state of affairs at Corinth radically changed. If this theory is to be upheld, some explanation must be found for the close connection with the 1 Corinthians situation that appears in 2 Cor. 12.19-21. Several explanations have been proposed.

According to Plummer, Paul's fear in these verses is that, by indulging in strife and licentiousness the Corinthians may have returned to their old heathen life. 'With a dread if this kind in his mind, the malice of the Judaising opponents, and the outrageous conduct of ὁ ἀδικήσας (vii.12), appear to be quite forgotten'.[14] This is an astonishing statement. In Plummer's opinion, 2 Cor. 10–13 reflects a new situation created by opponents who have come to Corinth after 1 Corinthians was written. Yet here, according to his theory, Paul voices a fear unrelated to this new situation, a fear so terrible that the main subject of the section fades completely from his mind. This is hard to believe.

Barrett notes that the faults criticized in 2 Cor. 12.20 were also criticized in 1 Cor. 1.11, but he attributes the recurrence of this theme in 2

12. On the translation of νῦν δὲ ἔγραψα in 1 Cor. 5.9 see Chapter 10, n. 15.
13. Mitchell, *Reconciliation*, passim.
14. Plummer, *Second Epistle*, p. 368.

Corinthians to the influence of the rival apostles.[15] He seems to regard these faults as likely to recur at Corinth whenever the right conditions were present, as blossoms appear on trees every year at the appropriate season. Furnish adopts a similar position. He suggests that the boasts and innuendos of the rival apostles (whose activity he believes to be subsequent to 1 Corinthians) could well have revived the discord and jealousy criticized in the earlier letter.[16]

The view of Barrett and Furnish that the Corinthians reacted in an almost identical way to two separate and distinct influences is unnecessarily complicated. It is more probable that Paul refers in both letters to the same divisions caused by the influence of the same teachers.

As for v. 21, Barrett regards the sexual immorality criticized in that verse as an offshoot of the 'gnostic' ideas referred to in 1 Corinthians and comments:

> The theme of gnosis, and that of sexual immorality, have dropped out of 2 Corinthians; new troubles, doctrinal and moral, have taken their place. Yet not entirely; Paul fears that when he revisits Corinth he may find both new sinners, who in accepting the intruding false apostles have fallen into strife, envy, and so forth, and old sinners (προημαρτηκότες) of the gnostic, libertine kind, who have not repented of their fornication.[17]

Barrett here regards the problem of sexual immorality as an old problem, unrelated to the new problem created by the 'false apostles'. But this does not fit the context of 2 Cor. 12. Paul's fear of what he might find at Corinth, expressed in vv. 19-21, was not a subsidiary extra tacked on to his main argument—it was the motivating force behind the main argument. Verse 19 begins with the word πάλαι (all this time)—a reference back to what Paul has been saying either throughout 2 Corinthians or throughout chs. 10–12. All I have been saying, he declares, has been intended not primarily as self-defence but as a means of building you up in your faith (v. 19). My reason for wanting to build you up in your faith is my fear that when I visit you I may find discord and division (v. 20) and the continuance of the sexual immorality I had to mourn on an earlier

---

15. Barrett, *Second Epistle*, pp. 329-30.

16. Furnish, *II Corinthians*, p. 568.

17. Barrett, *Second Epistle*, p. 332. Furnish (*II Corinthians*, p. 568) is undecided between Barrett's view and the view that Paul was afraid of a revival of sexual immorality at Corinth under the influence of his new rivals. The latter view is improbable. Paul's reference to the lack of repentance on the part of the 'previous sinners' indicates continuity rather than revival.

occasion (v. 21). Verses 19-21 constitute a logical whole. The γάρ (for) of v. 20 indicates that Paul's fear of 1 Corinthians-type behaviour is the motivating force behind his attack on the rival apostles in the preceding chapters. This makes the modern theory, that in the two canonical letters Paul faces different opponents and different situations, difficult to maintain.

A further indication that the behaviour criticized in 12.19-21 lay at the heart of the problems Paul faced in 2 Corinthians is the exhortation at the close of the letter. Furnish points out that the phrases 'be of one mind' and 'be at peace' in 13.11 reflect Paul's concern about disunity expressed in 12.20.[18] They also echo Paul's concern about disunity expressed in 1 Corinthians. The words τὸ αὐτὸ φρονεῖτε (2 Cor. 13.11) are a virtual repetition of the exhortation in 1 Cor. 1.10: ἵνα τὸ αὐτὸ λέγητε πάντες. 2 Cor. 13.11 would have been an equally appropriate ending to 1 Corinthians, and can be regarded as a summary of what Paul hoped to achieve in the two letters taken together.

3. *The Second Visit*

If the foregoing interpretation of 2 Cor. 12 and 13 is sound, Paul's second visit to Corinth must have occurred prior to 1 Corinthians. This possibility is today almost universally rejected. Most interpreters favour the alternative hypothesis that the second visit was an intermediate visit between the two canonical letters.[19] Two main arguments are employed in support of this hypothesis.

First, it is widely believed that the letter written 'in anguish of heart and with many tears' (2 Cor. 2.4) was not 1 Corinthians, and that the case of incest in 1 Cor. 5 was not the offence Paul refers to in 2 Cor. 2.5-11. It is therefore assumed that he must have visited Corinth some time after writing 1 Corinthians, been personally insulted, and written a letter (now wholly or partly lost) demanding the punishment of the insulter. If, however, as I have argued in Chapter 10, Paul's references to a tearful letter and to an offence are references to 1 Corinthians, the necessity for positing an intermediate visit between 1 and 2 Corinthians disappears.[20]

---

18. Furnish, *II Corinthians*, p. 585.

19. For a detailed discussion of various theories about the second visit see Thrall, *Second Epistle*, pp. 49-57.

20. Cf. Borse, 'Tränenbrief', pp. 180-81: 'Zum Datum des Zwischenbesuches sagt Paulus nichts. Gewönlich wird angenommen dass er in der Zeit zwischen dem 1 Kor und dem 2 Kor erfolgt sei. Anschliessend hätte der Apostel, wieder nach Ephesus

The second argument is an argument from silence. There is no mention of a second visit in 1 Corinthians. Surely, it is argued, if Paul had paid a visit to Corinth not long before 1 Corinthians was written, and there had been a major confrontation on that visit between Paul and certain members of the church, he would have been bound to refer to these events in the course of the letter.[21]

Behind this argument lies the assumption, characteristic of the use of the argument from silence in New Testament criticism, that someone reading a letter nineteen centuries after its composition is competent to decide what 'ought' to have been in it.[22] This assumption is questionable. The content of a letter is determined by the free choice of the writer, and the choice of what to include and what to omit is not always straightforward.

A case in point is Paul's reference to his 'previous letter' in 1 Cor. 5.9. His only reason for referring to this letter was that it had been mis-interpreted and he needed to correct the misinterpretation. Had this misinterpretation not occurred, he would probably have kept silent about his previous letter. But if he had kept silent, and vv. 9-13a had not been included in 1 Cor. 5, modern readers would probably have assumed that the problem of sexual immorality was a new problem at Corinth, which Paul had heard about for the first time from Chloe's people or from Stephanas. This would have been a reasonable deduction from the wording of 5.1. It is only the 'chance' mention of his previous letter in 5.9 that has saved us from such an assumption.[23]

Whenever an item is not mentioned in an ancient letter that a modern reader thinks ought to have been mentioned, the first question to be asked is: did the author have a reason for failing to mention it? In 1 Corinthians Paul failed to refer to his previous visit because he had two good reasons for not referring to it.

---

zurückgekehrt, den "Tränenbrief" verfasst. Anders stellt sich die Lage dar, wenn auf die Hypothese eines eigenständigen "Tränenbriefes" verzichtet wird, d.h. wenn dieser im 1 Kor vermutet wird. Dadurch wird der Ansatz des Zwischenbesuches in der genannten Periode zwar nicht grundsätzlich ausgeschlossen, es besteht jedoch keine Notwendigkeit mehr, ihn nur dort unterzubringen'.

21. Thrall, *Second Epistle*, pp. 52-53.

22. For examples of this assumption see Hall, *Seven Pillories*, pp. 55-60.

23. A similar case is Paul's brief summary of the historical evidence for the resur-rection in 1 Cor. 15.1-11. He mentioned this only because some people at Corinth were denying the resurrection and their views needed to be refuted. Had these views not been expressed at Corinth, Paul would probably not have mentioned this evidence, and his silence would have been taken to mean that he was ignorant of the historical facts.

The first reason for his 'silence' was that, at the time of writing of 1 Corinthians, some time had elapsed since that visit. The letter that followed the visit could have been the 'previous letter', or could have been an even earlier (now lost) letter.[24] Any comments Paul wished to make about his visit would have been made in that letter.[25] The second reason for his 'silence' was that 1 Corinthians was a conciliatory letter, appealing to the Corinthians as intelligent people with logical arguments (10.15).[26] In a letter of this type, mention of the person or persons who had humiliated him on his second visit would be best left unmentioned.

In 2 Corinthians Paul did refer to his second visit—once directly, once indirectly. But in both cases he did so for a specific reason. In the direct reference (13.2) he promised to carry out on his forthcoming third visit the threats he had uttered during his second visit. Such a reminder and reinforcement of his previous threats was appropriate to the confrontational mood of 2 Cor. 10–13, but would not have been appropriate to the conciliatory mood of 1 Corinthians.

In the indirect reference (2.1) Paul told the Corinthians of his decision not to pay them another painful visit (τὸ μὴ πάλιν ἐν λύπῃ πρὸς ὑμᾶς ἐλθεῖν). The word πάλιν (again) in this verse goes with the whole phrase ἐν λύπῃ πρὸς ὑμᾶς ἐλθεῖν.[27] Paul did not wish his next visit to be as painful as the second visit had proved to be. This allusion to the painful nature of his earlier visit was forced on Paul by Corinthian criticism of his travel plans. He had altered his original plan to visit Corinth on the way to Macedonia, and had been accused of fickleness.[28] In answering this accusation he was forced to reveal that it was the memory of his earlier painful visit that had led to his change of plan. His aim, he declared, was to spare the church—to avoid if possible the pain of further confrontation which a visit at this time would have caused. He had therefore sent a letter

24. It is important to bear in mind that, of all the letters that passed between Ephesus and Corinth during Paul's Ephesian ministry, we probably know of only a small proportion.

25. Plummer, *Second Epistle*, p. xviii n. *; Borse, 'Tränenbrief', pp. 181-82.

26. As I have argued in Chapter 10, Section 1, the deliberative style of 1 Corinthians does not mean that Paul was emotionally detached from the problems that had arisen, and on occasions his emotions break through (4.14; 8.11; 9.15; 16.22).

27. Furnish, *II Corinthians*, p. 140; Thrall, *Second Epistle*, p. 55.

28. The original plan must have been known to the Corinthians, otherwise they would have had no reason to accuse Paul of fickleness in changing it. The view that this plan was not communicated to the Corinthians is, in Thrall's words, 'extremely improbable' (Thrall, *Second Epistle*, pp. 71-72).

instead of coming in person.[29] His hope was that, when he did eventually come to Corinth, the situation would have improved, and his time there would involve, not the kind of confrontation that characterized his second visit, but the sharing of joy (1.23–2.3).

4. *The Sequence of Events*

The sequence of events up to the time of writing of 2 Corinthians may be reconstructed as follows:

i.   Paul paid a visit to Corinth from Ephesus (the 'second visit'). The reason for this visit is not known. During the visit he criticized the sexual behaviour of some members of the church. He warned them that, unless they repented, he would take disciplinary action against them, but took no action at the time (2 Cor. 13.2).

ii.   Sometime after his return to Ephesus he wrote a letter demanding

---

29. The meaning of the words τοῦτο αὐτό in 2 Cor. 2.3 is disputed. Grammatically the words could have two meanings: (i) they could be the direct object of the verb ἔγραψα ('this is precisely what I wrote') with a reference backwards to what he has just said in the previous verses about the motive behind his change of plan; (ii) they could be an adverbial phrase ('for this very reason') looking forward to, and giving emphasis to, the clause governed by ἵνα. The adverbial sense is adopted by BDF (290.4) and by BAGD (sv. αὐτός) 1g, and is more suitable to the context. If Paul had already told them the reasons for his change of mind, there would have been no need for him to explain those reasons again in such detail. The most natural charge for his enemies to lay against him would in that case not have been the charge of fickleness but the charge of cowardice.

Thrall (*Second Epistle*, p. 168 n. 270) objects that the adverbial meaning is contrary to Paul's usage elsewhere, and that 'where the phrase αὐτὸ τοῦτο occurs without a preceding preposition, it acts as the subject or object of the verb'. But in none of the three verses she quotes are the words αὐτὸ τοῦτο the subject or object. In 2 Cor. 7.11 they are in apposition to the subject (τὸ κατὰ θεὸν λυπηθῆναι); in Gal. 2.10 they are in apposition to the object (ὅ); in Phil. 1.6 πεποιθώς is an intransitive verb that does not govern an object in the accusative, and the words αὐτὸ τοῦτο are an adverbial phrase in apposition to the following clause introduced by ὅτι (I am confident in this very respect, that…). Phil. 1.6 is an especially close parallel to the adverbial sense of τοῦτο αὐτό in 2 Cor. 2.3.

It has been argued that the phrase αὐτὸ τοῦτο can only possess adverbial force when the verb is intransitive (Furnish, *II Corinthians*, p. 154 [following Windisch, *Der zweite Korintherbrief*, p. 80] and [more tentatively] Thrall, *Second Epistle*, p. 168 n. 270). But throughout ch. 2 the word ἔγραψα is used intransitively (vv. 3, 4, 9). In this passage Paul is explaining why and how he wrote, not what he wrote.

the ostracism of those leading sexually immoral lives (1 Cor. 5.9).

iii. At around the same time he sent Timothy to Macedonia with a view to his proceeding from Macedonia to Corinth (1 Cor. 16.10; Acts 19.22).[30] Timothy's remit was to remind the Corinthians of the ethical teaching Paul had given them, which he had also exemplified in his own life (1 Cor. 4.17).

iv. Paul met Chloe's people (1 Cor. 1.11),[31] and was also visited by Stephanas, Fortunatus and Achaicus (1 Cor. 16.17), who brought with them a letter from the church at Corinth (1 Cor. 7.1). From these various sources he discovered (among other things) that the church was divided into competitive groups, each supporting a wisdom teacher who operated like a sophist (1 Cor. 1.10-31; 4.6); and that a flagrant case of incest had arisen, which was a source of pride and boasting to a large number of church members (1 Cor. 5.1-13).

v. Paul wrote 1 Corinthians. This letter included condemnation of the competitive allegiance of the Corinthians to their various teachers; condemnation of the wisdom taught by those teachers; a demand for the excommunication of the incestuous man; discussion of a variety of issues of faith and behaviour (many of them raised by the Corinthians in the letter they had sent); arrangements for the collection in aid of the poor Christians in Judaea; and the announcement of Paul's travel plans.

vi. Because Timothy had already left for Macedonia, Titus was sent as the bearer of 1 Corinthians.[32] His remit was to commend to the Corinthians both the general teaching of the letter and its specific demands (*viz.* the excommunication of the offender and the arrangements for the collection).[33] Having done this, Titus was asked to proceed via Macedonia to

---

30. On the meaning of ἐάν in 1 Cor. 16.10 see Chapter 2, Section 3a.

31. See Fee, *First Epistle*, p. 54, for a discussion of the question of whether Chloe's people were Corinthians or Asians.

32. Though Timothy was with Paul at the time of writing of 2 Corinthians (2 Cor. 1.1), it was Titus who was authorized in that letter to continue the organization of the collection (8.16-24). It seems as though Titus took over from Timothy the role of Paul's intermediary at Corinth. Since Titus had gained the confidence of the Corinthians (7.13) and was eager to return (8.17), he was the obvious person to continue the work. Timothy, on the other hand (if we read between the lines of 1 Cor. 16.10-11), seems to have been nervous about going to Corinth. It is probable that Timothy was still in Macedonia when Paul arrived, and never reached Corinth. However, there is not sufficient evidence to justify a detailed reconstruction of Timothy's movements.

33. C.K. Barrett, *Essays on Paul* (London: SCM Press, 1982), p. 123, maintains that the procedure outlined in 1 Cor. 16—private savings, to be collected on Paul's

Troas, to meet up with Paul and inform him of the Corinthian response to his letter.

vii. Paul travelled from Ephesus to Troas, and not finding Titus there moved on to Macedonia. Titus joined him in Macedonia and reported that the Corinthians had been hurt by 1 Corinthians and by its suggestion that they were disloyal to Paul and to his teaching (2 Cor. 2.4; 7.8). On the positive side, they had repented of their arrogance, affirmed their continuing loyalty to Paul, and obeyed his demand for the excommunication of the offender (2 Cor. 2.6; 7.9-12). On the negative side, the wisdom teachers were still at work in the church (2 Cor. 11.18-23), and had made a number of personal criticisms of Paul (2 Cor. 7.2; 10.7-11; 12.16); there was limited enthusiasm for the collection; and some members of the church had taken exception to Paul's announcement in 1 Cor. 16 that he was going to Macedonia via Troas instead of via Corinth.

viii. Paul wrote 2 Corinthians. I hope to show in the next chapter how in 2 Corinthians Paul's confrontation with his opponents at Corinth reached its climax.

EXCURSUS H: THE JOURNEYS OF TITUS

1. *The Relationship between 2 Corinthians 8 and 12*

In 2 Cor. 8 Paul says three things about Titus: that he has urged Titus to complete the work of raising money for the collection (v. 6); that Titus has welcomed his urging and departed for Corinth (v. 17); and that he [Paul] has sent two brothers to accompany Titus (vv. 18-22). The verbs used in vv. 17 and 18 to describe the departure of Titus and the brothers (ἐξῆλθεν and συνεπέμψαμεν) are in the aorist tense. They could be constative aorists, reporting events that had occurred prior to the writing of the letter;[34] or they could be epistolary aorists, whereby the actions are seen

---

arrival at Corinth—did not leave room for the collaboration of Titus or any other agent. But, as any fundraiser knows, the raising of money for charity relies not only on letters written from a distance, but also on the enthusiasm of local advocates. The problem at Corinth was lack of enthusiasm, and that was the problem Titus had to overcome. What 1 Cor. 16.1-4 excluded was Titus *handling* the money, not his advocacy.

For discussion of the references to Titus in 2 Corinthians see Excursus H.

34. The constative aorist is described in Moulton, *Prolegomena*, p. 109; Moule, *Idiom Book*, pp. 10-11; Turner, *Syntax*, p. 72.

from the point of view of the recipients of the letter.[35] In the latter case, 'Titus has departed' means 'Titus is now departing with this letter' and 'we have sent two brothers' means 'we are now sending two brothers'.

There is a further reference to Titus's efforts in fundraising in ch. 12. Paul is defending himself in that chapter against the charge that he is using the collection for his own personal gain. He writes in v. 18: 'I have urged Titus and sent with him the brother. Surely Titus has not defrauded you!' In this verse also the verbs παρεκάλεσα and συναπέστειλα are in the aorist tense, and could be understood either as constative or as epistolary.

There are three main theories about the relationship between these two passages.

1. 8.17-18 and 12.18 refer to two different missions. One argument in favour of this interpretation is the fact that Titus is accompanied by two brothers in ch. 8 but by one brother in ch. 12.[36]

2. 8.17-18 and 12.18 refer to the same mission, but belong to two different letters. In ch. 8 the aorists are epistolary, indicating that Titus and the brothers are bearers of the letter of which ch. 8 forms a part. Ch. 12 belongs to a letter written later than ch. 8; the aorists there are constative, and refer to the mission of ch. 8 as an event in the past.[37]

3. 8.17-18 and 12.18 refer to the same mission within the same letter. In both chapters the aorists are epistolary.[38]

These three interpretations are all grammatically possible. But a strong argument in favour of the third interpretation is Paul's use of παρεκάλεσα in 12.18. He seems to be using this verb in 12.18 in the same sense as in ch. 8, to mean: 'I have urged Titus to complete the work of raising the collection'. But whereas in ch. 8 this meaning is explicit, in ch. 12 it is not.

In ch. 8 Paul states that, inspired by the example of the Macedonian churches, he has urged Titus to complete his fundraising work at Corinth (εἰς τὸ παρακαλέσαι ἡμᾶς Τίτον ἵνα...ἐπιτελέσῃ...τὴν χάριν ταύτην; v. 6). When Paul states later in the chapter (v. 17) that Titus welcomed his urging (τὴν μὲν παράκλησιν ἐδέξατο), the definite article means 'the urging to which I have just referred'. Similarly in 12.18, if

35. Moule, *Idiom Book*, p. 12.

36. Plummer, *Second Epistle*, p. 364; Thrall, *Second Epistle*, p. 15.

37. C.K. Barrett, 'Titus', in *Essays on Paul* (London: SCM Press, 1982), pp. 118-31 (127); Barrett, *Second Epistle*, p. 325; Furnish, *II Corinthians*, p. 559.

38. Menzies, *Second Epistle*, p. 99; R.V.G. Tasker, *The Second Epistle of Paul to the Corinthians* (London: Tyndale Press, 1958); A.M.G. Stephenson, 'Partition Theories on II Corinthians', in F.L. Cross (ed.), *Studia Evangelica*, II (TU, 87; Berlin: Akademie-Verlag, 1964), pp. 639-46 (642-44).

2 Corinthians is a unity, the Corinthians would have understood the words παρεκάλεσα Τίτον in the light of Paul's use of the same word earlier in the letter. But if chs. 10–13 were part of an independent letter, separated from chs. 1–9 not only by time but also by a significant change in the Corinthian situation, such a reference would no longer be understandable. 'I have urged Titus' is a meaningless phrase unless the content of that urging is clearly stated in the context.[39]

The mention of two brothers in ch. 8 and of only one brother in ch. 12 is not a major problem. The reason for the distinction is not that one of the brothers was appointed by the Macedonian churches and one was Paul's nominee.[40] Thrall points out that both of the brothers in ch. 8 are called 'delegates' (ἀπόστολοι) of the churches, and both are sent by Paul.[41] The distinction lies rather in the status of the two brothers. The brother of 8.18-19 had been officially appointed (χειροτονηθείς) by the Macedonian churches to assist in the arrangements for the collection. He was a person of some standing, praised throughout all the churches because of [his preaching of] the gospel. If 'all the churches' includes Corinth, as it should, this man would be known and respected there (at least by reputation). Therefore, in the context of 12.16-18—the rebuttal of the charge of financial dishonesty—the presence of this man would serve as a guarantee of Paul's good faith. The other brother seems to have been of a lesser status. He was probably a younger man, and the other brother's assistant.[42] His role may have been similar to that of John Mark on Paul and Barnabas's missionary journey (Acts 13.5).[43] Paul's only comment in 8.22 is on his enthusiasm.

39. Stephenson, 'Partition Theories', pp. 642-43. By his use of the verb παρα-καλέω, Paul makes a distinction between Titus, an independent colleague (8.23) whom he can only advise, and the two brothers whom he 'sends'.

40. This distinction is made in Barrett, 'Titus', p. 127; Barrett, *Second Epistle*, p. 325; Furnish, *II Corinthians*, p. 566.

41. Thrall, *Second Epistle*, p. 15 n. 90.

42. Cf. Schnelle, *History*, p. 86: 'In 2 Cor. 12.18 Paul names only the brother commissioned by the churches in Macedonia, but not his coworker mentioned in 2 Cor. 8.22. This is appropriate in the context of the accusations made against him in Corinth that he was using the collection to enrich himself personally (cf. 2 Cor. 8.20; 12.14, 16, 17), for only Titus and the brother commissioned from Macedonia were officially responsible for the administration of the collection'.

43. It is interesting that, in Acts 13, vv. 4-5 refer to three people sailing to Cyprus (Barnabas, Saul and John Mark), but v. 7 mentions only two (Barnabas and Saul). This discrepancy does not justify the attribution of vv. 4-5 and v. 7 to two different sources, nor does the similar discrepancy between 2 Cor. 8.22 and 2 Cor. 12.18.

Another noteworthy fact is that, after mentioning both Titus and the brother in 12.18, it is only Titus whose financial integrity Paul affirms. If the aorists are epistolary, this is understandable. Of the men who are now travelling to Corinth bearing the letter, only Titus had previously been involved in the collection arrangements. The rhetorical question μήτι ἐπλεονέκτησεν ὑμᾶς Τίτος; (surely Titus did not defraud you) is a reminder to the Corinthians of what they had personally experienced. The 'brother', on the other hand, despite his reputation as a preacher of the gospel, had not previously been involved with raising money at Corinth, and Paul could not appeal to their personal experience in his case. However, if the aorists of 12.18a were constative, and referred to a fundraising mission in the past, the wording of this verse would be strange. Its natural implication would seem to be: 'Some time ago I urged Titus to visit you and sent the brother with him. Surely Titus did not defraud you (but maybe the brother did!)'

The two aorists παρεκάλεσα and συναπέστειλα in 12.18a should therefore be regarded as epistolary. It is true that they are surrounded in v. 17 and v. 18b by other aorists that are not epistolary. But even if the aorists of v. 18a were constative, their construction would still be different from that of the aorists in v. 17 and v. 18b. Verse 17 reads: μή τινα ὧν ἀπέσταλκα πρὸς ὑμᾶς, δι᾽ αὐτοῦ ἐπλεονέκτησα ὑμᾶς; Here the aorist ἐπλεονέκτησα is used (like the perfect ἀπέσταλκα) to refer to all the various people Paul has sent to Corinth during his time in Ephesus— Timothy, Titus etc. Have I defrauded you, Paul asks, through any of the people I have sent to you? The aorists of v. 18b are similar: surely Titus has not defrauded you! Have we not behaved under the influence of the same Spirit? The word περιεπατήσαμεν (we have behaved) cannot be limited to any particular occasion. It means: have we not been guided by the Spirit in all our behaviour up to the present time? This is what Nigel Turner calls a 'linear' aorist.[44]

In 2 Cor. 12.18a, by contrast, the aorists refer to one particular visit. The contrast with the scope of the aorists preceding and following is equally

44. Turner, *Syntax*, p. 71. Turner quotes the example of Acts 1.21, where Peter states that a twelfth apostle must be chosen from the ranks of those who accompanied the twelve during the earthly ministry of Jesus: τῶν συνελθόντων ἡμῖν ἀνδρῶν ἐν παντὶ χρόνῳ ᾧ εἰσῆλθεν καὶ ἐξῆλθεν ἐφ᾽ ἡμᾶς ὁ κύριος Ἰησοῦς. The aorist tense is used in this verse because the period covered by this intermittent coming and going has been completed at the time of speaking, and the aorists summarize the entire period. The same is true of the aorists of 2 Cor. 12.17 and 2 Cor. 12.18b.

pronounced whether this visit is one that is in the past (constative aorist) or one that is currently taking place (epistolary aorist).

For all these reasons 12.18a is best understood as a reference back to 8.17-18 within the same letter, with the aorists in both cases being epistolary.

2. *How Often did Titus Visit Corinth?*

In 8.1-6 Paul describes how he urged Titus to complete the work of grace at Corinth, in the same way as he had begun it. The words καθὼς προενήρξατο can be interpreted in two ways. Some commentators understand it in the light of Paul's boast in 9.2 that the Achaian churches had been prepared [to give to the collection] since the previous year (ὅτι Ἀχαΐα παρεσκεύασται ἀπὸ πέρυσι). On this view προενήρξατο refers to the preparation of the previous year, and indicates that Titus had already visited Corinth prior to his visit bearing the 'tearful letter'.[45] An alternative view is that προενήρξατο refers to the practical implementation of the arrangements for the collection, which began on the recently completed visit.[46] It is clear from 9.4 that, although Paul had been boasting to the Macedonians about the preparedness of the Achaian churches, he was afraid they might not be prepared. What Titus did, on this view, was to turn the declaration of intent of the previous year into practical arrangements.

In 7.14 Paul reports the joy Titus felt because of the welcome he received at Corinth, and comments: 'I was not made to look foolish over my boasting to him about you. On the contrary, just as we have always spoken the truth to you, so also our boasting in the presence of Titus has proved to be true'. This verse is sometimes taken to imply that Titus had never visited Corinth prior to the visit just completed.[47] But it need not necessarily mean this.[48] If the response of the Corinthians had been disappointing on an earlier visit, Paul may have needed to reassure Titus that they were better than they seemed—a boast which, on this view, was proved to be justified when Titus paid his second visit bearing the painful letter.

45. Plummer, *Second Epistle*, p. 237; Hughes, *Second Epistle*, p. 293; Martin, *2 Corinthians*, p. 447; Horrell, *Social Ethos*, pp. 304-306.

46. Barrett, 'Titus', pp. 125-26; Barrett, *Second Epistle*, p. 221; Furnish, *II Corinthians*, p. 414; Kruse, *Second Epistle*, p. 152.

47. Barrett, *Second Epistle*, p. 215; Furnish, *II Corinthians*, p. 414; Kruse, *Second Epistle*, p. 152.

48. Horrell, *Social Ethos*, pp. 304-305; Thrall, *Second Epistle*, pp. 498-99.

The arguments are well balanced, and it is impossible to be sure which view is correct. Fortunately, this matter is of minor importance, and does not greatly affect our understanding of the two visits Titus definitely paid to Corinth.

Chapter 12

PAUL'S PASTORAL STRATEGY

The preceding chapters have revealed some of the inter-connections between 1 and 2 Corinthians—the opponents Paul faced, the topics he discussed and the historical circumstances he presupposed. However, the unity of the two letters does not consist only in their sharing of a common background and their concern with common issues. It consists also in Paul's implementation, in both letters, of a pastoral strategy. The reason for the contrasts between various sections of the Corinthian correspondence is Paul's pastoral approach to church discipline.[1]

The clearest statement of this approach can be found in 2 Cor. 10.6: 'we are prepared to punish every case of disobedience, when your obedience is complete' (ὅταν πληρωθῇ ὑμῶν ἡ ὑπακοή). In this verse Paul is threatening to exercise discipline against those who are disobedient, but states that he is only prepared to do so when the church is fully obedient. In other words, he wants his disciplinary action to be taken not against the church, but against his opponents with the support of the church. His aim throughout the Corinthian correspondence is to win over the church to his way of thinking, so that discipline will need to be exercised only against a rebellious minority.

The key word here is obedience. In Paul's letters 'obedience' (ὑπακοή, ὑπακούειν) denotes not only obedience to God or to Jesus Christ but also obedience to 'the pattern of teaching' (Rom. 6.17) and 'the teaching you learnt' (Rom. 16.17-19). The reason why Paul lays such stress on this obedience can be seen in the latter passage, which warns against those who 'create divisions and stumbling-blocks contrary to the teaching you learnt' (Rom. 16.17). He tells the Roman Christians that at their baptism they 'obeyed the pattern of teaching and became slaves of righteousness' (Rom. 6.17-18), and appeals to them to continue to express this commit-

1. Much of this chapter is based on, and in some cases quotes directly from, my earlier article: 'Pauline Church Discipline', *TynBul* 20 (1969), pp. 3-26.

ment to righteousness in the way they use their bodies (Rom. 6.19). Similarly he appeals to the Philippians: 'as you have always obeyed... much more now in my absence' (Phil. 2.12), and goes on to talk about avoiding grumbling and arguments and behaving blamelessly (Phil. 2.14-15). Obedience in Paul's letters means a continuing loyalty to Christ and to the tradition of belief and moral behaviour, handed down by the disciples of Christ, of which Paul was the guardian.

In 2 Cor. 10.6, when Paul looked forward to the church's obedience being complete, he was not only thinking of their loyalty to himself as their father in God, but also of their loyalty to the teaching he had given them. That it why he said in 2 Cor. 2.9 that he had written his tearful letter 'to put you to the test, to see whether you are totally obedient' (εἰ εἰς πάντα ὑπήκοοί ἐστε). The case of incest was a test case in a theological and ethical conflict. Their willingness or unwillingness to punish the man concerned would demonstrate whether their loyalty lay with Paul and his teaching or with his opponents and their teaching.[2]

The Corinthian correspondence reveals three stages in the attitude of the Corinthian church.

a. *Disobedience*

This was the situation described in 1 Corinthians: 'independently of us you have become kings' (4.8); 'your boasting is not good' (5.6). They were proudly defying Paul's teaching and example under the influence of their new teachers. In response to this defiance Paul employed reasoned argument throughout 1 Corinthians. He used the 'yes, but' approach, sympathizing as much as possible with the new teaching, but at the same time pointing out its limitations. His reason for adopting this approach was that he was in a very dangerous position. Both his apostolic status and his teaching were under attack, and a large proportion of the church had been won over by the new teaching. Paul had to deal firmly with the test case of incest; but in dealing with other issues he tried to be as conciliatory as possible. It was only when Titus had brought the good news of the church's reaction to 1 Corinthians that he dared to launch the frontal attack on his opponents that we find at the end of 2 Corinthians.

The fact that Paul's personal confrontation of his opponents comes only

---

2. There is one passage in Paul's letters (Phlm. 21) in which he talks of obedience to a personal request. But that request was bound up with the gospel. It was not usual in Graeco-Roman society for slave-owners to treat a runaway slave as 'a beloved brother' (Phlm. 16).

in 2 Corinthians does not prove, as is often claimed, that when the first letter was written these opponents had not yet arrived. It proves rather Paul's conviction that any teaching that undermined his gospel must be opposed first of all with rational argument. He felt free to make a personal attack on his opponents only when the church had been won over by the sympathetic teaching that preceded it.

b. *Partial Obedience*
This was the situation reported by Titus. The Corinthians had obeyed Paul's words about the offender and shown themselves guiltless in that matter (τῷ πράγματι; 2 Cor. 7.11). But the party leaders were still present at Corinth and their influence was only partially broken. Through-out 2 Corinthians Paul is on the defensive as well as on the attack. This is most obvious in chs. 10–13, where he defends himself against various charges his enemies have brought against him. But in chs. 1–7 also, as he describes the ministry of himself and his colleagues, the contrast with other preachers with a different conception of ministry is always latent and sometimes explicit (2.17; 3.1; 5.12). At the same time he is confident (7.16) because the Corinthians have passed the test (2.7). They have demonstrated their loyalty to him and to his teaching over a key issue. He therefore feels free to put off the 'disguise' used in 1 Corinthians and to challenge the rival apostles directly.

However, the direct confrontation of chs. 10–13 is preceded by a detailed exposition of the nature of apostolic ministry in chs. 1–7. The reason for this was Paul's concern that the Corinthians should not only show personal loyalty to him, but should also be convinced in their own minds that the teaching and lifestyle of his opponents was incompatible with the teaching and lifestyle of his colleagues and himself.

c. *Complete Obedience*
This is the stage Paul hopes the church as a whole will have reached at the time of his next visit. Only then, when their obedience is complete, will he punish the disobedient (10.6). This discipline will not mean Paul exercising his apostolic authority against a rebellious congregation. It will be an action supported by the majority of the congregation, in willing obedience to Paul and his teaching, against those who remain loyal to the rival apostles and have refused to repent (12.21). Had Paul used the abusive language of 2 Cor. 10–13 at the time of 1 Corinthians, he would have split the church. By his patient and sympathetic approach at the beginning, he

sought to build up and unify the church. That is how he exercised the authority the Lord had given him 'for building up and not for tearing down' (2 Cor. 13.10).[3]

3.   The evidence suggests that Paul's strategy was successful. When he wrote to the Romans he felt he had fulfilled his ministry of bringing the Gentiles to obedience (Rom. 15.18); his work in the Eastern Mediterranean was completed (Rom. 15.23); and Achaia was joining with Macedonia in contributing to the collection (Rom. 15.26).

BIBLIOGRAPHY

Allo, E.-B., *Saint Paul: seconde épître aux Corinthiens* (EBib; Paris: Gabalda, 1958).

Bailey, K.E., 'The Structure of 1 Corinthians and Paul's Theological Method with Special Reference to 4.17', *NovT* 25 (1983), pp. 152-81.

Balch, D.L., '1 Cor. 7.32-35 and Stoic Debates about Marriage, Anxiety and Distraction', *JBL* 102/3 (1983), pp. 429-39.

Barclay, J.M.G., 'Mirror-Reading a Polemical Letter: Galatians as a Test Case', *JSNT* 31 (1987), pp. 73-93.

—'Thessalonica and Corinth: Social Contrasts in Pauline Christianity', *JSNT* 47 (1992), pp. 49-74.

Barr, J., *The Semantics of Biblical Language* (Oxford: Oxford University Press, 1961).

Barrett, C.K., 'Christianity at Corinth', *BJRL* 46 (1964), pp. 269-97, reprinted in C.K. Barrett, *Essays on Paul* (London: SCM Press, 1982), pp. 1-27.

—*A Commentary on the First Epistle to the Corinthians* (London: A. & C. Black, 2nd edn, 1971).

—'Paul's Opponents in 2 Corinthians', *NTS* 17 (1971), pp. 233-54, reprinted in C.K. Barrett, *Essays on Paul* (London: SCM Press, 1982), pp. 60-86.

—*A Commentary on the Second Epistle to the Corinthians* (London: A. & C. Black, 2nd edn, 1990).

—'Titus', in E.E. Ellis and M. Wilcox (eds.), *Neotestamentica et Semitica: Studies in Honour of Matthew Black* (Edinburgh: T. & T. Clark, 1969), pp. 1-14, reprinted in C.K. Barrett, *Essays on Paul* (London: SCM Press, 1982), pp. 118-31.

Barton, S., 'Paul's Sense of Place: An Anthropological Approach to Community Formation in Corinth', *NTS* 32 (1986), pp. 225-46.

Baur, F.C., *Paul the Apostle of Jesus Christ, His Life and Work, His Epistles and His Doctrine* (2 vols.; London: Williams and Norgate, 1876).

Bengel, J.A., *Gnomon Novi Testamenti* (Berlin: Schlawitz, 1860).

Betz, H.D., *2 Corinthians 8 and 9* (Hermeneia; Philadelphia: Fortress Press, 1985).

Bieringer, R., 'Zwischen Kontinuität und Diskontinuität: Die beiden Korintherbriefe in ihrer Beziehung zueinander', in R. Bieringer (ed.), *The Corinthian Correspondence* (Leuven: Leuven University Press, 1996), pp. 3-38.

Bjerkelund, C.J., *Parakalo. Form, Funktion und Sinn der parakalo Sätze in den paulinischen Briefen* (Oslo: Universitetsforlaget, 1967).

Blue, B.B., 'Acts and the House Church', in D.W.J. Gill and C. Gempf (eds.), *The Book of Acts in its Graeco-Roman Setting* (Carlisle: Paternoster, 1994), pp. 119-222.

Bornkamm, G., 'The History of the Origin of the So-called Second Letter to the Corinthians', *NTS* 8 (1962), pp. 258-64.

—*Paul* (London: Hodder & Stoughton, 1971).

Borse, U., ' "Tränenbrief" und 1 Korintherbrief', *SNTU* 9 (1984), pp. 175-202.

Brown, C.P., *A Telugu-English Dictionary* (Madras: SPCK, 2nd edn, 1903).

Bruce, F.F., *Commentary on the Book of Acts* (London: Marshall, Morgan and Scott, 1965).

—'Commentary on the Epistle to the Colossians', in E.K. Simpson and F.F. Bruce, *The Epistles of Paul to the Ephesians and to the Colossians* (London: Marshall, Morgan and Scott, 1957), pp. 159-313.

Bultmann, R., *Der zweite Brief an die Korinther* (MeyerK, 6; Göttingen: Vandenhoeck & Ruprecht, 10th edn, 1976).

—*Exegetische Probleme des zweiten Korintherbriefes* (Symbolae Biblicae Uppsalienses, 9; Uppsala, 1947).

—'καυχάομαι', in *TDNT*, III, pp. 645-54.

Caird, G.B., *The Language and Imagery of the Bible* (London: Duckworth, 1980).

Callan, T., 'Prophecy and Ecstasy in Greco-Roman Religion and in 1 Corinthians', *NovT* 27.2 (1985), pp. 125-40.

Campbell, R.A., 'Does Paul Acquiesce in Divisions at the Lord's Supper?', *NovT* 33 (1991), pp. 61-70.

Caragounis, C.C., 'ΟΨΩΝΙΟΝ: A Reconsideration of its Meaning', *NovT* 16 (1974), pp. 35-57.

Carson, D.A., D.J. Moo and L. Morris, *An Introduction to the New Testament* (Grand Rapids: Zondervan, 1992).

Chadwick, H., ' "All Things to All Men" (1 Cor. ix.22)', *NTS* 1 (1954–55), pp. 261-75.

Chow, J.K., *Patronage and Power: A Study of Social Networks in Corinth* (JSNTSup, 75; Sheffield: Sheffield Academic Press, 1992).

Clarke, A.D., *Secular and Christian Leadership in Corinth: A Sociological and Exegetical Study of 1 Corinthians 1–6* (AGJU, 18; Leiden: E.J. Brill, 1993).

Collange, J.-F., *Enigmes de la deuxième, épître de Paul aux Corinthiens: étude exégétique de 2 Cor. 2.14-7.4* (SNTSMS, 18; Cambridge: Cambridge University Press, 1972).

Collins, R.F., 'Reflections on 1 Corinthians as a Hellenistic Letter', in R. Bieringer (ed.), *The Corinthian Correspondence* (Leuven: Leuven University Press, 1996), pp. 39-61.

Conzelmann, H., *A Commentary on the First Epistle to the Corinthians* (Hermeneia; Philadelphia: Fortress Press, 1975).

Cranfield, C.E.B., *The Epistle to the Romans* (2 vols.; ICC; Edinburgh: T. & T. Clark, 1975, 1979).

—'Μέτρον πίστεως in Romans 12.3', *NTS* 8 (1961–62), pp. 345-51, reprinted in *idem*, *The Bible and Christian Life* (Edinburgh: T. & T. Clark, 1985), pp. 203-14.

Dahl, N.A., 'Paul and the Church at Corinth according to 1 Cor. 1.10–4.21', in W.R. Farmer, C.F.D. Moule and R.R. Niebuhr (eds.), *Christian History and Interpretation: Studies Presented to John Knox* (Cambridge: Cambridge University Press, 1967), pp. 313-35.

Danker, F.W., 'Paul's Debt to the *De Corona* of Demosthenes: A Study of Rhetorical Techniques in Second Corinthians', in D.F. Watson (ed.), *Persuasive Artistry* (Sheffield: JSOT Press, 1991), pp. 262-80.

Davis, J.A., *Wisdom and Spirit: An Investigation of 1 Corinthians 1.18–3.20 against the Background of Jewish Sapiential Traditions in the Greco-Roman Period* (Lanham, NY: University Press of America, 1984).

de Boer, M.C., 'The Composition of 1 Corinthians', *NTS* 40 (1994), pp. 229-45.

Delobel, J., '1 Cor. 11.2-16: Towards a Coherent Interpretation', in A. Vanhoye (ed.), *L'Apôtre Paul* (Leuven: Leuven University Press, 1986), pp. 369-89.

Deming, W., *Paul on Marriage and Celibacy* (Cambridge: Cambridge University Press, 1995).

Doyle, A.C., 'The Sign of Four', in *The Complete Sherlock Holmes Long Stories* (London: Book Club Associates, 1973), pp. 124-239.

Dunn, J.D.G., *Jesus and the Spirit* (London: SCM Press, 1975).

—*1 Corinthians* (New Testament Guides; Sheffield: Sheffield Academic Press, 1995).

Ellingworth, P., 'Translating 1 Corinthians', *BT* 31 (1980), pp. 234-38.

Ellingworth P., and H.A. Hatton, *Paul's First Letter to the Corinthians* (UBS Handbook; New York: United Bible Societies, 1994).

Fee, G.D., *The First Epistle to the Corinthians* (NICNT; Grand Rapids: Eerdmans, 1987).

—'ΧΑΡΙΣ in 2 Cor. 1.15: Apostolic Parousia and Paul-Corinth Chronology', *NTS* 24 (1978), pp. 533-38.

Field, F., *Notes on the Translation of the New Testament* (Cambridge: Cambridge University Press, 1899).

Findlay, G.G., 'St. Paul's First Epistle to the Corinthians', in W.R. Nicoll (ed.), *The Expositor's Greek Testament* (London: Hodder & Stoughton, 1900), II, pp. 727-953 (repr. Grand Rapids: Eerdmans, 1961).

Fiorenza, E.S., *In Memory of Her: A Feminist Theological Reconstruction of Christian Origins* (London: SCM Press, 1983).

Fisk, B.N., 'Eating Meat Offered to Idols: Corinthian Behaviour and Pauline Response in 1 Corinthians 8–10 (A Response to Gordon Fee)', *TJ* 10 (1989), pp. 49-70.

Fitzgerald, J.T., *Cracks in an Earthen Vessel: An Examination of the Catalogues of Hardships in the Corinthian Correspondence* (SBLDS 99; Atlanta, GA: Scholars Press, 1988).

Foerster, W., 'διάβολος', in *TDNT*, II, pp. 75-81.

Forbes, C., 'Comparison, Self-Praise and Irony: Paul's Boasting and the Conventions of Hellenistic Rhetoric', *NTS* 32 (1986), pp. 1-30.

Furnish, V.P., *II Corinthians: A New Translation with Introduction and Commentary* (AB, 32A; Garden City, NY: Doubleday, 1984).

Gardner, P.D., *The Gifts of God and the Authentication of a Christian: An Exegetical Study of 1 Corinthians 8–11.1* (Lanham, NY: University Press of America, 1994).

Georgi, D., *The Opponents of Paul in Second Corinthians* (Edinburgh: T. & T. Clark, 1987).

Gerhardsson, B., *Memory and Manuscript: Oral Tradition and Written Transmission in Rabbinic Judaism and Early Christianity* (Lund: Gleerup, 1961).

Gill, D.W.J., 'In Search of the Social Elite in the Corinthian Church', *TynBul* 44.2 (1993), pp. 323-37.

Goodspeed, E.J., 'Gaius Titius Justus', *JBL* 69 (1950), pp. 382-83.

Goudge, H.L., *The First Epistle to the Corinthians* (WC; London: Methuen, 1903).

—*The Second Epistle to the Corinthians* (WC; London: Methuen, 1927).

Goulder, M.D., 'Σοφία in 1 Corinthians', *NTS* 37 (1991), pp. 516-34.

Guthrie, W.K.C., *The Sophists* (Cambridge: Cambridge University Press, 1971).

Hafemann, S.J., 'Paul's Argument from the Old Testament and Christology in 2 Cor. 1–9', in R. Bieringer (ed.), *The Corinthian Correspondence* (Leuven: Leuven University Press, 1996), pp. 277-303.

—' "Self-Commendation" and Apostolic Legitimacy in 2 Corinthians: A Pauline Dialectic', *NTS* 36 (1990), pp. 66-88.

Hall, D.R., 'A Disguise for the Wise: μετασχηματισμός in 1 Corinthians 4.6', *NTS* 40 (1994), pp. 143-49.

—*The Gospel Framework: Fiction or Fact? A Critical Evaluation of 'Der Rahmen der Geschichte Jesu' by Karl Ludwig Schmidt* (Carlisle: Paternoster, 1998).

—'Pauline Church Discipline', *TynBul* 20 (1969), pp. 3-26.

—'A Problem of Authority', *ExpTim* 102 (1990), pp. 39-42.

—*The Seven Pillories of Wisdom* (Macon, GA: Mercer University Press, 1990).

Harris, G., 'The Beginnings of Church Discipline: 1 Cor. 5', *NTS* 37 (1991), pp. 1-21.

Harvey, A.E., 'The Opposition to St. Paul', in F.L. Cross (ed.), *Studia Evangelica*, IV (TU, 102; Berlin: Akademie Verlag, 1968), pp. 319-32.

—*Renewal through Suffering* (Edinburgh: T. & T. Clark, 1996).

Hauck, F., 'ἑκών (ἄκων), ἑκούσιος', in *TDNT*, II, pp. 469-70.

Hays, R.B., *First Corinthians* (Interpretation; Louisville, KY: Westminster/John Knox Press, 1997).

Heil, C., 'Die Sprache der Absonderung in 2 Kor 6,17 und bei Paulus', in R. Beiringer (ed.), *The Corinthian Correspondence* (Leuven: Leuven University Press, 1996), pp. 717-29.

Hemer, C.J., *The Book of Acts in the Setting of Hellenistic History* (Winona Lake: Eisenbrauns, 1990).

Hengel, M., *The Charismatic Leader and his Followers* (Edinburgh: T. & T. Clark, 1981).

Héring, J., *The Second Epistle of Saint Paul to the Corinthians* (London: Epworth, 1967).

Hickling, C.J.A., 'Is the Second Epistle to the Corinthians a Source for Early Church History?', *ZNW* 66 (1975), pp. 284-87.

—'The Sequence of Thought in II Corinthians, Chapter Three', *NTS* 21 (1975), pp. 380-95.

Hock, R.F., *The Social Context of Paul's Ministry: Tentmaking and Apostleship* (Philadelphia: Fortress Press, 1980).

Holladay, C.R., *Theios Aner in Hellenistic Judaism: A Critique of the Use of this Category in New Testament Christology* (SBLDS, 40; Missoula, MT: Scholars Press, 1977).

Hooker, M.D., 'Beyond the Things that are Written? St. Paul's Use of Scripture', *NTS* 27 (1980–81), pp. 295-309.

—*Pauline Pieces* (London: Epworth, 1979).

Horrell, D.G., *The Social Ethos of the Corinthian Correspondence: Interests and Ideology from 1 Corinthians to 1 Clement* (Edinburgh: T. & T. Clark, 1996).

Horsley, R.A., 'Consciousness and Freedom among the Corinthians: 1 Corinthians 8–10', *CBQ* 40 (1978), pp. 574-89.

—' "How can some of you say that there is no resurrection of the dead?" Spiritual Elitism in Corinth', *NovT* 20 (1978), pp. 203-231.

—'Wisdom of Word and Words of Wisdom in Corinth', *CBQ* 39 (1977), pp. 224-39.

Hughes, F.W., 'The Rhetoric of Reconciliation: 2 Corinthians 1.1–2.13 and 7.5–8.24', in D.F. Watson (ed.), *Persuasive Artistry* (Sheffield: JSOT Press, 1991), pp. 246-61.

Hughes, P.E., *Paul's Second Epistle to the Corinthians* (London: Marshall, Morgan and Scott, 1962).

Hunt, A.R., *The Inspired Body: Paul, the Corinthians and Divine Inspiration* (Macon, GA: Mercer University Press, 1996).

Hurd, J.C., *The Origin of 1 Corinthians* (Macon, GA: Mercer University Press, 2nd edn, 1983).

Hyldahl, N., 'Die Frage nach der literarischen Einheit des zweiten Korintherbriefes', *ZNW* 64 (1973), pp. 289-306.

—*Die Paulinische Chronologie* (Leiden: E.J. Brill, 1986).

Jenkins, C., 'Origen on 1 Corinthians', *JTS* 9 (1908), pp. 231-47, 353-72, 500-14; *JTS* 10 (1909), pp. 29-51.

Jensen, J., 'Does πορνεία Mean Fornication? A Critique of Bruce Malina', *NovT* 20 (1978), pp. 161-84.

Johnson, L.T., *The Writings of the New Testament: An Interpretation* (Philadelphia: Fortress Press; London: SCM Press, 1986).

Judge, E.A., 'Cultural Conformity and Innovation in Paul: Some Clues from Contemporary Documents', *TynBul* 35 (1984), pp. 3-24.

—'The Early Christians as a Scholastic Community', *JRH* 1 (1960), pp. 4-15 and 125-37.

—'Paul's Boasting in Relation to Contemporary Professional Practice', *AusBR* 16 (1968), pp. 37-50.

—'A Regional κανών for Requisitioned Transport', in G.H.R. Horsley (ed.), *New Documents Illustrating Early Christianity* (5 vols.; North Ryde: Macquarrie University, 1981–89), I, pp. 36-45.

Kamlah, E., 'Buchstabe und Geist', *EvT* 14 (1954), pp. 276-82.

Käsemann, E., 'Die Legitimität des Apostels. Eine Untersuchung zu II Korinther 10–13', *ZNW* 41 (1942), pp. 33-71.

—*New Testament Questions of Today* (London: SCM Press, 1969).

—'The Spirit and the Letter', in *idem* (ed.), *Perspectives on Paul* (Philadelphia: Fortress Press, 1971), pp. 138-66.

Kruse, C.G., *The Second Epistle of Paul to the Corinthians* (Leicester: Inter-Varsity Press, 1987).

Kuck, D.W., *Judgment and Community Conflict: Paul's Use of Apocalyptic Judgment Language in 1 Cor. 3.5–4.5* (Leiden: E.J. Brill, 1992).

Kümmel, W.G., *Introduction to the New Testament* (London: SCM Press, rev. edn, 1975).

Lambrecht, J., *Second Corinthians* (Sacra Pagina, 8; Collegeville, MN: The Liturgical Press, 1999).

Lampe, G.W.H., 'Church Discipline and the Interpretation of the Epistles to the Corinthians', in W.R. Farmer, C.F.D. Moule and R.R. Niebuhr (eds.), *Christian History and Interpretation: Studies Presented to John Knox* (Cambridge: Cambridge University Press, 1967), pp. 337-61.

Lampe, P., 'The Eucharist: Identifying with Christ on the Cross', *Int* 48 (1994), pp. 36-49.

Lim, T.H., ' "Not in Persuasive Words of Wisdom, but in the Demonstration of the Spirit and Power" ', *NovT* 29.2 (1987), pp. 137-49.

Lindemann, A., 'Die paulinische Ekklesiologie angesichts der Lebens-wirklichkeit der christlichen Gemeinde in Korinth', in R. Bieringer (ed.), *The Corinthian Correspondence* (Leuven: Leuven University Press, 1996), pp. 63-86.

Litfin, D., *St. Paul's Theology of Proclamation: 1 Corinthians 1–4 and Greco-Roman Rhetoric* (SNTSMS, 79; Cambridge: Cambridge University Press, 1994).

Lofthouse, W.F., ' "I" and "We" in the Pauline letters', *BT* 6 (1955), pp. 72-80.

Lull, D.J., ' "The Law was our Pedagogue": A Study in Galatians 3.19-25', *JBL* 105/3 (1986), pp. 481-98.

Malherbe, A.J., 'Antisthenes and Odysseus, and Paul at War', *HTR* 76 (1983), pp. 143-73.

Malina, B., 'Does πορνεία Mean Fornication?', *NovT* 14 (1972), pp. 10-17.

Marshall, P., *Enmity in Corinth: Social Conventions in Paul's Relations with the Corinthians* (WUNT [2nd Series] 23; Tübingen: J.C.B. Mohr, 1987).

—'A Metaphor of Social Shame: ΘΡΙΑΜΒΕΥΕΙΝ in 2 Cor. 2.14', *NovT* 25 (1983), pp. 302-317.

Martin, D.B., *The Corinthian Body* (New Haven: Yale University Press, 1995).

—*Slavery as Salvation: The Metaphor of Slavery in Pauline Christianity* (New Haven: Yale University Press, 1990).

Martin, R.P., *2 Corinthians* (WBC, 40; Waco, TX: Word Books, 1986).

Meeks, W.A., *The First Urban Christians: The Social World of the Apostle Paul* (New Haven: Yale University Press, 1983).

Meggitt, J.J., *Paul, Poverty and Survival* (Edinburgh: T. & T. Clark, 1998).

Menzies, A., *The Second Epistle of the Apostle Paul to the Corinthians* (London: Macmillan, 1912).

Merklein, H., 'Die Einheitlichkeit des ersten Korintherbriefes', *ZNW* 75 (1984), pp. 153-83.

Meyer, H.A.W., *Critical and Exegetical Handbook to the Epistles to the Corinthians* (2 vols.; Edinburgh: T. & T. Clark, 1877, 1879).

Mitchell, M.M., 'Concerning περὶ δέ in 1 Corinthians', *NovT* 31 (1989), pp. 229-56.

—*Paul and the Rhetoric of Reconciliation: An Exegetical Investigation of the Language and Composition of 1 Corinthians* (HUT, 28; Tübingen: J.C.B. Mohr, 1991).

Moule, C.F.D., *An Idiom Book of New Testament Greek* (Cambridge: Cambridge University Press, 2nd edn, 1959).

Moulton, J.H., *A Grammar of New Testament Greek*. I. *Prolegomena* (Edinburgh: T. & T. Clark, 1906).

Munck, J., *Paul and the Salvation of Mankind* (London: SCM Press, 1959).

Murphy-O'Connor, J., 'Another Jesus (2 Cor. 11.4)', *RB* 97 (1990), pp. 238-51.

—'Corinthian Slogans in 1 Cor. 6.12-20', *CBQ* 40 (1978), pp. 391-96.

—'Interpolations in 1 Corinthians', *CBQ* 48 (1986), pp. 81-94.

—'Sex and Logic in 1 Corinthians 11.2-16', *CBQ* 42 (1980), pp. 482-500.

—*St. Paul's Corinth: Texts and Archaeology* (Good News Studies, 6; Wilmington, DE: Michael Glazier, 1983).

—*The Theology of the Second Letter to the Corinthians* (Cambridge: Cambridge University Press, 1991).

Newton, D., *The Dilemma of Sacrificial Food at Corinth* (JSNTSup, 169; Sheffield: Sheffield Academic Press, 1998).

Olson, S.J., 'Pauline Expressions of Confidence in his Addressees', *CBQ* 47 (1985), pp. 282-95.

Oster, R.E., 'Use, Misuse and Neglect of Archaeological Evidence in Some Modern Works on 1 Corinthians (1 Cor. 7.1-5; 8.10; 11.2-16; 12.14-26)', *ZNW* 83 (1992), pp. 52-73.

Pearson, B.A., *The Pneumatikos-Psychikos Terminology in 1 Corinthians: A Study in the Theology of the Corinthian Opponents of Paul and its Relation to Gnosticism* (SBLDS, 12; Missoula, MT: Scholars Press, 1973).

Perriman, A., *Speaking of Women: Interpreting Paul* (Leicester: Apollos, 1998).

Phipps, W.E., 'Is Paul's Attitude toward Sexual Relations Contained in 1 Cor. 7.1?', *NTS* 28 (1982), pp. 125-31.

Plummer, A., *A Critical and Exegetical Commentary on the Second Epistle of St. Paul to the Corinthians* (ICC; Edinburgh: T. & T. Clark, 1915).

Plumptre, E.H., 'The Second Epistle to the Corinthians', in C.J. Ellicott (ed.), *A Bible Commentary for Bible Students* (London and Edinburgh: Marshall Brothers, n.d.), VII, pp. 359-417.

Pogoloff, S.M., *Logos and Sophia: The Rhetorical Situation of 1 Corinthians* (SBLDS, 134; Atlanta, GA: Scholars Press, 1992).

Provence, T.E., '"Who is sufficient for these things?" An Exegesis of 2 Corinthians ii.15–iii.18', *NovT* 24 (1982), pp. 54-81.

Robertson, A.T., *A Grammar of New Testament Greek in the Light of Historical Research* (London: Hodder & Stoughton, 1914).

264   *The Unity of the Corinthian Correspondence*

Robertson, A., and A. Plummer, *A Critical and Exegetical Commentary on the First Epistle of St. Paul to the Corinthians* (ICC; Edinburgh: T. & T. Clark, 2nd edn, 1914).
Robinson, J.A.T., *The Body: A Study in Pauline Theology* (London: SCM Press, 1952).
Schenk, W., 'Der 1 Korintherbrief Briefsammlung', *ZNW* 60 (1969), pp. 219-43.
Schmidt, T.E., 'Mark 15.16-32: The Crucifixion Narrative and the Roman Triumphal Procession', *NTS* 41 (1995), pp. 1-18.
Schmithals, W., *Gnosticism in Corinth: An Investigation of the Letters to the Corinthians* (Nashville: Abingdon, 1971).
Schnelle, U., *The History and Theology of the New Testament Writings* (London: SCM Press, 1998).
Schniewind, J., 'Die Leugnung der Auferstehung in Korinth', in E. Kähler (ed.), *Nachgelassene Reden und Aufsätze* (Berlin: Töpelmann, 1952), pp. 110-39.
Schöllgen, G., 'Was wissen wir über die Sozialstruktur der Paulinischen Gemeinden?', *NTS* 34 (1988), pp. 71-82.
Schrage, W., *Der erste Brief an die Korinther* (3 vols.; EKKNT, 7/1-3; Neukirchen-Vluyn: Neukirchener Verlag; Zürich and Düsseldorf: Benziger Verlag, 1991, 1995, 1999).
Schweizer, E., 'The Service of Worship: An Exposition of 1 Corinthians 14', *Int* 13 (1959), pp. 400-408.
Scott, J.M., 'The Triumph of God in 2 Cor. 4.14: Additional Evidence of Merkabah Mysticism in Paul', *NTS* 42 (1996), pp. 260-81.
Scroggs, R., 'The Sociological Interpretation of the New Testament: The Present State of Research', *NTS* 26 (1980), pp. 164-79.
Shanor, J., 'Paul as Master Builder: Construction Terms in First Corinthians', *NTS* 34 (1988), pp. 461-71.
Stephenson, A.M.G., 'Partition Theories on II Corinthians', in F.L. Cross (ed.), *Studia Evangelica*, II (TU, 87; Berlin: Akademie-Verlag, 1964), pp. 639-46.
Stevenson, J., *A New Eusebius* (London: SPCK, 1957).
Stowers, S.K., 'Review of H.D. Betz, *2 Corinthians 8 and 9*', *JBL* 106 (1987), pp. 727-30.
Strange, J.F., '2 Corinthians 10.13-16 Illuminated by a Recently Published Inscription', *BA* 46 (1983), pp. 167-68.
Strecker, G., 'Die Legitimität des Paulinischen Apostolates nach 2 Korinther 10–13', *NTS* 38 (1992), pp. 566-86.
Strugnell, J., 'A Plea for Conjectural Emendation in the NT, with a Coda on 1 Cor. 4.6', *CBQ* 36 (1974), pp. 543-58.
Sumney, J.L., *Identifying Paul's Opponents: The Question of Method in 2 Corinthians* (JSNTSup, 40; Sheffield: Sheffield Academic Press, 1990).
Tasker, R.V.G., *The Second Epistle of Paul to the Corinthians* (London: Tyndale Press, 1958).
Theissen, G., *The Social Setting of Pauline Christianity* (Edinburgh: T. & T. Clark, 1982).
Thiselton, A.C., *The First Epistle to the Corinthians: A Commentary on the Greek Text* (NIGTC; Grand Rapids: Eerdmans; Carlisle: Paternoster, 2000).
—'The Meaning of Σάρξ in 1 Cor. 5.5: A Fresh Approach in the Light of Logical and Semantic Factors', *SJT* 26 (1973), pp. 204-28.
—'Semantics and New Testament Interpretation', in I.H. Marshall (ed.), *New Testament Interpretation* (Exeter: Paternoster, 1977), pp. 75-104.
Thrall, M.E., *A Critical and Exegetical Commentary on the Second Epistle to the Corinthians* (ICC; Edinburgh: T. & T. Clark, 1994).
—*Greek Particles in the New Testament: Linguistic and Exegetical Studies* (NTTS, 3; Leiden: E.J. Brill, 1962).

—'A Second Thanksgiving Period in II Corinthians', *JSNT* 16 (1982), pp. 101-124.

Turner, N., *Syntax* (vol. III of J.H. Moulton, *A Grammar of New Testament Greek*; Edinburgh: T. & T. Clark, 1990).

Verhoef, E., 'The Senders of the Letters to the Corinthians and the Use of "I" and "We" ', in R. Bieringer (ed.), *The Corinthian Correspondence* (Leuven: Leuven University Press, 1996), pp. 417-25.

Vos, J.S., 'Der μετασχηματισμός in 1 Kor. 4.6', *ZNW* 86 (1995), pp. 154-72.

Wagner, J.R., 'Not Beyond the Things that are Written: A Call to Boast Only in the Lord', *NTS* 44 (1998), pp. 279-87.

Wedderburn, A.J.M., 'The Problem of the Denial of the Resurrection in 1 Corinthians XV', *NovT* 23.3 (1981), pp. 229-41.

—*Baptism and Resurrection: Studies in Pauline Theology against its Graeco-Roman Background* (WUNT, 44; Tübingen: J.C.B. Mohr, 1987).

Weiss, J., *Der erste Korintherbrief* (Göttingen: Vandenhoeck & Ruprecht, 2nd rev. edn, 1910).

Welborn, L.L., 'Like Broken Pieces of a Ring: 2 Cor. 1.1–2.13; 7.5-16 and Ancient Theories of Literary Unity', *NTS* 42 (1996), pp. 559-83.

—'On the Discord in Corinth: 1 Corinthians 1–4 and Ancient Politics', *JBL* 106 (1987), pp. 85-111.

Westerholm, S., 'Letter and Spirit: The Foundation of Pauline Ethics', *NTS* 30 (1984), pp. 229-48.

Willis, W.L., 'An Apostolic Apologia? The Form and Function of 1 Corinthians 9', *JSNT* 24 (1985), pp. 33-48.

Winandy, J., 'Un Curieux "Casus Pendens": 1 Corinthiens 11.10 et son interprétation', *NTS* 38 (1992), pp. 621-29.

Windisch, H., *Der zweite Korintherbrief* (MeyerK, 6; Göttingen: Vandenhoeck & Ruprecht, 9th edn, 1924).

—'καπηλεύω', in *TDNT*, III (1965), pp. 603-605.

Winter, B.W., *Philo and Paul among the Sophists* (SNTSMS, 96; Cambridge: Cambridge University Press, 1997).

Witherington, B., *Conflict and Community in Corinth: A Socio-Rhetorical Commentary on 1 and 2 Corinthians* (Grand Rapids: Eerdmans; Carlisle: Paternoster, 1995).

Wordsworth, C., *The New Testament of our Lord and Saviour Jesus Christ, in the Original Greek: With Introduction and Notes* (2 vols.; London: Rivington, 1872).

Young, F., and D.F. Ford, *Meaning and Truth in 2 Corinthians* (London: SPCK, 1987).

Zmijewski, J., *Der Stil der paulinischen Narrenrede* (Bonn: Hanstein, 1978).

INDEXES

INDEX OF REFERENCES

BIBLE

Old Testament

Genesis
15.12 (LXX)	164

Exodus
32.14	232
34	137, 142, 143
34.34-35	142

1 Chronicles
21.15	232
21.27	232

Psalms
10.1 (LXX)	21, 22
11.1 (Heb.)	21
106.45	232

Jeremiah
1.5	194
18.1-8	232
20.7-18	194
31.33	140

Ezekiel
11.19	140
36.26	140

Hosea
6.6	227

Amos
7.1-6	232

Jonah
3.10	232

Apocrypha

1 Esdras
4.47	176

Ecclesiasticus (Sirach)
1.18-20	39
21.11-15	39
24.33	133
39.1	132
39.6	132, 133
39.8	132
39.10	132

1 Maccabees
12.4	176

2 Maccabees
1.10	133

New Testament

Matthew
5.34	36
6.22	27, 28
6.24	7
8.2	26
12.28	218
15.14	26
20.2	118
22.19	118

Mark
1.19	232
3.21	210
6.4	10
14.31	26
15.44	81

Luke
6.33	26
11.20	218
11.34	28
13.3	26
19.31	26
24.29	81

John
5.3	68
5.18	27
5.19-47	27
5.19	27
5.30	27
5.31	27
7.15	123
7.40-43	64
8.12	27
8.14	27
9.16	64
9.31	26
10.19-21	64
11.9	26
11.10	26
13.14	171
13.35	26
15.14	26

19.7	171	2.17-29	64	11.17-24	109
21.4	81	2.25	26, 116	11.18	196
		3.5	108	11.21	195
Acts		3.26	108	11.24	195
1.21	251	4.2	195	11.36	122
5.11	53	4.14	195	12	220
5.38	27	4.19	82	12.1–15.13	108
13.1-3	78	5.10	195	12.3	219, 220
13.4-5	250	5.15	195	13.11	82
13.5	250	5.17	195	14–15	48
13.7	250	6.5	195, 196	14	62
13.36	116	6.8	195	14.2-3	219
15.3	176	6.17	254	14.3	48
15.22	53	6.19	255	14.8	26
15.39	109	7	110, 138,	14.15	195
17.16	68		139	15.1	171
18.1-3	54, 175	7.1-7	25	15.14	108
18.3	54	7.1-6	35	15.18	257
18.5-6	175	7.10	139	15.20-23	193
18.5	105	7.12	139	15.20	193
18.7	55, 175	7.13-25	109	15.23	118, 193,
18.8	53	7.13	139		257
18.17	54	7.14-25	139	15.24	176
18.24-28	12, 17	7.14	139	15.26	118, 257
18.24	18	7.16	195, 196	15.27	171, 195,
18.26	54	7.20	195		196
19.10	87, 118	7.22	139	16	53, 55, 57,
19.21	118	7.25	109		119
19.22	104, 247	8	110	16.1-2	55
20.31	225	8.1-3	139	16.2	55, 182
20.38	176	8.1	109	16.3-5	54
21.5	176	8.3	109, 139	16.6	55
23.6	116	8.4-11	109	16.12	55
25.26	12	8.6-9	139	16.13	55
26.22-23	147	8.10	195	16.16	53
		8.13	195	16.17-20	91
Romans		8.17	195	16.17-19	254
1–8	108	8.25	195	16.17-18	254
1.10	82	9–11	108	16.17	254
1.11-15	126	9.1-13	108	16.23	53, 54, 73,
1.11	176	9.3	109		175
1.12	176	9.5	109, 122	16.24	122
1.15	126	9.19	108		
1.16-17	108	9.29	195	*1 Corinthians*	
1.16	126, 203	9.31	218	1–11	19
1.17	126	11.1	109	1–4	12, 13,
1.18	106, 126	11.12	195		17-21, 24,
1.25	122	11.16	195		30-32, 34,

1 Corinthinans (cont.)

Reference	Pages
	41-44, 65, 228, 241
1–3	15, 39, 40
1–2	43, 150, 152
1	13, 57, 65, 66, 152
1.1–4.21	42, 70, 74
1.1	54
1.2	57, 78, 86
1.4-9	57, 78
1.4-7	74, 78
1.7	78
1.8	95
1.10-31	247
1.10-17	148, 241
1.10-16	14
1.10-12	66, 224
1.10	41, 57, 65, 232, 234, 243
1.11-12	4
1.11	6, 57, 224, 241, 247
1.12	5-7, 9, 11, 21, 57, 69
1.13	41, 43
1.16	118
1.17–2.16	14
1.17-18	154
1.17	16, 150, 155, 160
1.19	146
1.20	145, 146
1.21-25	18
1.22-25	18
1.22	144, 146
1.26-29	59, 77, 79
1.26	51-54, 57, 77, 144, 160, 185
1.27-28	52
1.27	61
1.30	59, 78
1.31	79
2	13, 40, 43, 152, 153
2.1-5	17, 150, 155, 160, 210, 226
2.1-2	18, 154
2.1	16
2.3	155
2.4	16, 201
2.6–3.3	200
2.6-16	37, 201
2.8	39, 195
2.11	39
2.13	16
2.14	153
2.16	39
3–16	152
3	13, 14, 43, 152, 157, 214
3.1-9	7
3.1-4	14, 66
3.1-3	201, 225
3.3-4	4
3.4-9	5
3.4-6	11
3.4	201
3.5–4.5	23
3.5-9	4, 5, 134
3.8	56
3.10-17	4, 5, 8, 12, 14, 24
3.10-15	24, 214
3.10	8, 13, 150
3.12-15	144
3.16-17	8
3.16	11
3.17	10, 11
3.18-20	14
3.18	201
3.20-21	14
3.22	11
4–16	15
4	13, 32, 33, 43, 84, 85, 152, 157, 158
4.1-5	12, 84, 204
4.1-2	13
4.2	13, 196
4.3-5	221
4.3	13
4.6-13	19, 226
4.6-7	82
4.6	3-7, 11, 17, 19-21, 23, 24, 32, 66, 82, 83, 145-47, 247
4.7-21	211
4.7-13	210
4.7	59, 79, 82-85, 153
4.8-13	58, 79, 158
4.8-11	58
4.8-10	59
4.8	59, 77, 79, 80, 82-85, 144, 156, 158, 225, 255
4.9-13	84, 155, 158, 159
4.9	159
4.10	58, 158, 159
4.12	56, 59
4.14-21	29, 42, 44
4.14-17	128, 226
4.14	245
4.15-16	226, 229
4.15	10, 12, 25, 27-29, 34, 158
4.17-21	33
4.17	19, 33, 34, 229, 247
4.18–5.2	32
4.18-21	24, 33, 225
4.18-19	34
4.18	32-34, 144
4.19-21	33

4.19	33, 34, 236	6.9-11	186	8.1–11.1	46, 50, 70, 74	
		6.9-10	36			
4.21	33, 34, 42, 46	6.10	231	8.1–10.22	50, 63	
		6.12-20	36, 37, 40, 61, 225	8.1-13	40, 41, 46, 48, 50	
5–16	19, 30-32, 41-44, 152	6.12	38, 40, 60, 202, 206, 228	8.1-11	225	
				8.1	38, 39, 47, 57, 58, 60, 70, 202	
5–7	30, 44					
5–6	40, 168	6.13	37			
5	33, 36, 39, 124, 227, 228, 230, 233-35, 243, 244	6.18-20	37	8.2	201	
		6.18	37	8.3-4	202	
		7	60, 61, 167, 168	8.4-6	39, 61	
				8.4	14, 47	
		7.1–11.1	168	8.5	28, 70	
5.1-13	36, 49, 227, 235, 247	7.1-2	168	8.7	39, 47, 58, 62, 202	
		7.1	42, 60, 168, 202, 247	8.9-13	47, 192	
5.1-11	33			8.9-12	13, 63	
5.1-5	228, 230	7.7	168	8.9	179	
5.1-2	34	7.8-9	168	8.10-13	48	
5.1	36, 42, 43, 100, 229, 244	7.9	157	8.10	32, 46, 61, 76	
		7.10	167			
		7.11	153	8.11-12	46	
5.2-6	35, 43	7.12	167	8.11	245	
5.2-5	231	7.22	78	8.12	61	
5.2	33-36, 40, 225, 228	7.25	60, 167	8.13	179, 195, 207, 208	
		7.26	167			
5.3-5	225	7.28	60, 168	9	12, 49, 50, 66, 124, 160, 171, 174, 175, 179-81, 183, 189, 192, 193, 204, 207, 208, 214, 222	
5.3	34, 81	7.35	145			
5.5	230, 231	7.36	60, 168, 169			
5.6-8	225					
5.6	35, 225, 228, 255	7.37	168, 169, 172			
5.7-8	49	7.38	168			
5.9-13	244	7.39-40	167			
5.9-12	228	7.40	32, 78, 163, 167, 169			
5.9	87, 240, 241, 244, 247			9.1-27	50	
		8–10	30, 40, 44, 49, 59, 61-64, 124, 179, 226	9.1-14	12, 189, 205	
5.11	36, 228			9.1-2	181, 189	
5.13	49, 228, 231			9.1	13, 180, 205, 207, 208	
6	36, 39, 60, 124	8	30, 39, 40, 46, 49, 50, 63, 64, 179, 207, 208	9.2	28, 179, 180, 189, 196, 208	
6.1-11	36, 76, 124, 225					
6.4	26					
6.7	76, 81			9.3	12, 28,	

1 Corinthinans (cont.)		10.23	40, 48, 60,	11.20-22	66, 225
	179-81,		179, 202	11.20	68, 70, 72
	188, 195,	10.24	206	11.21	67-69
	200, 204,	10.25-27	47, 48	11.22	58, 64, 66,
	207, 208	10.27-29	63		68, 69, 71,
9.4-14	181	10.29-30	47, 48		77, 79
9.4	171, 179,	10.29	47, 206	11.23-26	69, 73,
	181	10.30	48		154
9.5	11, 189	10.33	226	11.23	83, 172,
9.6	186	11–14	30		229
9.10	171	11	65, 70, 73,	11.27-30	225
9.12-15	55, 189		213	11.29	172
9.12	75, 171,	11.1	226, 229	11.31	195
	179, 181,	11.2–14.40	70, 73, 74	11.33	68, 72
	192	11.2-16	71, 72	11.34	67
9.14-27	211	11.2	35, 70, 71,	12–15	19
9.14-15	59		73, 83,	12–14	40, 41, 71,
9.15-27	181, 210		147, 172,		78, 124,
9.15-18	189		173		163, 165
9.15	12, 174,	11.3-16	73	12	40, 41, 43,
	194, 245	11.3-5	71		61, 152,
9.16-18	197	11.3-4	158		166
9.16	26, 194,	11.4-9	173	12.1–14.40	70, 72
	197	11.4	71	12.1-3	165, 166
9.17-18	193	11.6	71	12.1	19, 60, 72
9.17	190, 191,	11.7-9	71	12.2	58, 165
	193-97	11.10	71, 170-	12.4-11	61
9.18	193		73	12.7	78
9.19-23	160, 191,	11.11-15	173	12.8-10	8
	226	11.11-12	71	12.8	39
9.19-22	181	11.13	71	12.10	166
9.22	61, 95	11.14-15	71	12.22-24	61
9.23	181	11.14	26	12.24-25	41
9.24-27	193	11.16	31, 53, 71,	12.24	40
9.27	213, 214,		83, 144,	12.25	40, 41
	222		172, 173	12.27-31	61
10	46, 50,	11.17-34	64, 67, 70,	13	40, 119,
	214		72, 73		124
10.1-22	41, 46, 47,	11.17-22	71	13.2	26
	50	11.17-20	72	13.3	26
10.14-22	48	11.17-18	73	13.4	40
10.14	48	11.17	71, 83,	13.5	109
10.15	48, 211,		172	14	41, 72,
	224, 245	11.18-19	65, 66		163, 164,
10.18	48	11.18	41, 64-66,		166, 173
10.21	46, 48		68, 70, 72	14.1-40	73
10.23–11.1	50, 63	11.19	65, 66, 68,	14.1-25	166
10.23-24	40		213	14.2-5	166

14.12	166	15.29	36, 195	117, 247
14.14	26	15.31	197	1.3-11	120, 127,
14.18	166	15.33-34	31, 113		155, 159,
14.19-23	40	15.34	144		160
14.19	72, 163	15.58	56	1.3-7	160
14.23	53, 72, 73	16	30, 119,	1.5	155
14.24	26		237, 238,	1.8-10	160
14.26-30	166		247, 248	1.11	120, 124,
14.26	41, 69, 72,	16.1-4	76, 235,		127, 160
	73, 163		248	1.12–2.4	100, 120,
14.27-33	225	16.1	60		153
14.27-28	41, 73	16.3	187	1.12-15	127
14.29-33	164	16.4	26	1.12	95, 96,
14.29-31	41	16.5-9	46, 235-		120, 124,
14.29-30	73		38		125, 127,
14.29	166	16.6	175, 177		153, 197
14.30	163	16.7	236, 247	1.13	127
14.31-33	166, 171	16.10-11	177, 247	1.15–2.4	128, 235,
14.31-32	165	16.10	247		237
14.31	164	16.11	68, 177	1.15-24	106
14.32	71, 164	16.12	5, 8, 11,	1.15-19	127
14.33	53		12, 60	1.15-16	237
14.34-35	73	16.15	55, 65,	1.15	176, 237,
14.36	83		118		238
14.37-38	144	16.16-18	118	1.16	176, 177
14.37	32, 71, 78,	16.17-18	175	1.17	95, 120,
	166, 167,	16.17	175, 224		204
	201	16.18	56	1.19	103
14.40	71, 164	16.19	54	1.23–2.3	246
15	30, 44,	16.21	106	1.23-24	127
	153, 154,	16.22	91, 245	1.24	49, 92,
	199				234
15.1-11	244	*2 Corinthians*		2	104, 182,
15.1-3	83	1–9	87-89, 92,		204, 223,
15.2	83, 225,		94, 102,		227, 230,
	229		111-13,		232
15.3	154, 229		250	2.1-7	202, 203
15.5	11	1–7	91, 92, 95,	2.1-3	182
15.9	231		102, 103,	2.1	245
15.10	56		105, 106,	2.3	99, 246
15.12	31, 80,		113, 120,	2.4	99, 223,
	153, 199,		256		243, 246,
	201, 225	1–4	182		248
15.13	195	1–2	120	2.5-11	4, 227,
15.14	195	1	160, 182,		230, 235,
15.16	195		204		243
15.17	195	1.1–2.13	113, 120	2.5	227
15.19	195	1.1	104, 110,	2.6-8	230

2 Corinthians (cont.)		3.7-18	136	6.3-13	120	
2.6	96, 227, 248	3.7	142, 143, 195	6.5	56	
2.7-8	232	3.8	140	6.8-10	99	
2.7	235, 256	3.9	195	6.11-13	121	
2.8	234	3.10	138	6.11	204	
2.9	230, 246, 255	3.11	195	6.12-13	96	
2.10	227	3.12-18	137, 140	6.12	92, 203, 233	
2.11	101	3.12-17	135	6.14–7.1	87, 113	
2.12-17	122, 161	3.12	140, 141	7	92, 94, 96, 104, 105, 120, 203, 223, 227	
2.12-13	99, 104, 162	3.13	143			
2.13	121	3.15	137, 141, 142	7.1	89	
2.14–7.4	104, 113, 114, 120, 121, 123	3.18	137, 142	7.2-4	96, 120	
		4	134	7.2	100, 101, 121, 203, 248	
2.14–7.1	111	4.1-6	134, 135			
2.14–6.10	204	4.1-2	10, 120, 153	7.4-16	96	
2.14–4.6	134, 136			7.4	121, 122, 197	
2.14–3.11	135	4.2	96, 135, 136, 141			
2.14-17	105, 162	4.3-4	142	7.5-16	113, 121	
2.14-16	134	4.3	142, 196	7.5-7	121	
2.14	105	4.4	141, 231	7.5-6	104	
2.16-18	135	4.6	142	7.5	104, 105, 121	
2.16-17	134	4.7–5.10	211			
2.17–3.18	136	4.7-18	155	7.6	105, 121	
2.17	75, 96, 120, 135, 136, 141, 153, 208, 256	4.7-15	28	7.8-12	105	
		4.10	155	7.8-11	202	
		4.11	159	7.8	196, 226, 248	
		4.15	96			
		4.16	28, 196	7.9-12	248	
3–5	162	5	210	7.9-11	232	
3	134-36, 138, 140, 143, 204	5.1-11	154	7.11	96, 227, 246, 256	
		5.1-10	153			
		5.1	153	7.12	4, 100, 128, 196, 227, 230, 232, 233	
3.1-5	135	5.3	153, 154			
3.1-3	105, 137	5.5	153			
3.1	9, 129, 135, 186, 212, 221, 256	5.9-10	214			
		5.11-13	211	7.13-16	94, 105	
		5.12	211, 221, 256	7.13	94, 105, 247	
3.3-11	139	5.13	210, 211			
3.3	140	5.14	154, 211	7.14	105, 197, 252	
3.4-18	204	5.16	28, 196			
3.4-6	200	5.18-21	154	7.15	94	
3.6-11	135	5.19	154	7.16	93, 94, 98, 256	
3.6	138, 140	5.20	212			
		6	96	8–9	119	

8	56, 76, 94, 100, 101, 113-19, 205, 235, 248-50	9.11	95	10.13	217, 219-21		
		9.12	56, 182				
		9.15-19	182	10.14	215-17		
		9.15	87, 116	10.15-16	215		
		10–13	1, 3, 24, 33, 66, 87-89, 91, 92, 94, 95, 98, 102, 103, 105, 111, 112, 134, 143, 145, 149, 151, 155, 158, 159, 199, 200, 205, 223, 241, 245, 250, 256	10.15	56, 219-21		
8.1-15	119						
8.1-6	252			10.16	215, 216		
8.1-5	118			11–12	197, 209		
8.1-2	185			11	7, 98, 157, 158, 184, 209		
8.2	76						
8.4	55						
8.6	115, 116, 248, 249						
				11.1-6	105		
8.14	56, 76			11.1-4	91, 98		
8.16-24	101, 117, 118, 247			11.1-3	89		
				11.1	103, 130, 209, 210, 215		
8.16-19	119						
8.17-18	248, 252						
8.17	101, 247-49			11.2	130		
		10–12	13, 242	11.3	88, 93, 130, 131, 158		
8.18-22	248	10	87, 93, 102, 217, 218				
8.18-19	250			11.4-5	130		
8.18	53, 248			11.4	130, 131, 143, 149-51, 154, 158, 170, 196, 199, 235		
8.19	101	10.1-2	89				
8.20-21	96, 119, 205	10.1	87, 89, 90, 103, 106, 110-12, 205				
8.20	101, 250						
8.22	119, 250						
8.23	101, 119, 250	10.2-4	96, 153	11.5-15	174, 183		
		10.2	95, 103, 110	11.5-7	183		
				11.5-6	130, 212		
8.24	116, 119		205	11.5	130, 131		
9	56, 76, 87, 93, 94, 100-102, 113-18, 182, 205, 235	10.3-6	254-56	11.6	28, 103, 105, 153, 183, 196		
		10.6	248				
		10.7-11	156				
		10.9-11	205				
		10.9	215	11.7-12	103, 208		
		10.10-11	33, 103, 155, 205, 212, 221	11.7-11	55		
9.1-5	93, 101, 117	10.10		11.7	156, 180, 183, 188		
9.1-2	93			11.8-9	178		
9.1	116, 117	10.11	88	11.8	178, 186		
9.2	117, 118, 252	10.12-18	131, 214, 217, 222	11.9-10	118, 178, 189		
9.3-5	116	10.12-13	221	11.9	174, 178, 182, 187		
9.3	117	10.12	136, 199, 215, 221				
9.4	101, 118, 252			11.10	118		
		10.13-16	221	11.11	89, 185, 188, 189		
9.7	169	10.13-14	215				

2 Corinthians (cont.)

11.12-15	189
11.12	75, 188
11.13-15	5, 130, 201
11.14	5, 162
11.18-23	248
11.18	156, 205
11.20	199
11.21-23	140
11.21-22	149
11.21	103, 156
11.22-23	156
11.22	9, 129, 131, 143, 145
11.23	56, 201, 233
11.27	56
11.28-30	162
11.28-29	194, 224
11.28	162
11.29-30	157
11.30	157, 195, 210
12	7, 98, 209, 241-43, 248-50
12.1-5	103
12.1-4	210
12.7	231
12.9	210
12.10	193
12.11-18	174, 183, 184
12.11-14	189
12.11-13	107, 205
12.11	103, 130
12.12	103, 184, 205, 212
12.13-14	187
12.13	75, 103, 186, 189
12.14-15	89
12.14	177, 250
12.16-18	100, 101, 103, 189, 250
12.16-17	96
12.16	153, 187, 188, 205, 248, 250
12.17-18	101, 187, 250
12.17	251
12.18	249-52
12.19–13.4	238
12.19-21	235, 241-43
12.19	89, 242
12.20-21	93, 98, 152, 239, 240
12.20	89, 98, 239-43
12.21	98, 239-43, 256
13	66, 243
13.1-10	33, 212-14
13.1-4	212
13.1-2	238
13.1	238
13.2	33, 238-40, 245, 246
13.3-7	212
13.3	92, 103, 199, 212
13.5-10	66
13.5	92, 93, 213
13.7	213
13.8	96
13.9-10	213, 234
13.10	33, 212, 257
13.11-13	89
13.11	243

Galatians

1–2	217
1.1	107
1.6-9	126
1.10	126, 195
1.11	126
1.12	126
2	131, 217
2.1-10	131, 217
2.7-9	217
2.7	218
2.9	217, 218
2.10	246
2.11-14	24
2.18	195
2.21	195
3.4	153
3.18	195
3.21	195
3.28	71, 73, 173
3.29	195
4.7	195
4.15	195
5.1	35, 47
5.2	107, 110
5.16-26	231
5.18	195
6.1-2	232
6.1	232
6.11-16	91

Ephesians

3.1	107, 108

Philippians

1.6	246
1.12	124, 125
2.5-11	119
2.12	255
2.14-15	255
2.17	196
2.30	56, 175
3	109
3.7	159
3.12-14	110
3.12	81, 153
3.15	110
3.16	218
3.18	224
3.21	5
4.7	178
4.10	82, 153, 179

4.17	179	*2 Thessalonians*		*Hebrews*	
		2.1	124, 125	7.20	116
Colossians		3.17	107	10.31	68
1.13-22	107			11.10	68
1.23	107	*1 Timothy*		12.10	116
1.24	56	1.8	26	13.9-16	91
2.3	39	2.6	56		
2.5	196			*James*	
2.18	32	*2 Timothy*		2.14-16	26
4.18	107	2.5	26	5.7	68
		2.18	80		
1 Thessalonians				*1 Peter*	
1	126	*Titus*		4.17	91
1.1	107	3.13	176	5.1-4	91
1.3	56				
1.7	118	*Philemon*		*2 Peter*	
1.8	118	8-10	234	3.3-7	91
1.9	126	8-9	49		
2.1	126	8	234	*1 John*	
2.9	56	9	234	1.5	26
2.16	218	10-11	49	1.7	26
2.18	107	10	234		
2.19-20	197, 214	13	49	*3 John*	
3.5	56	14	49, 169	6-8	176
3.6	60	15	49		
3.10	56	16	49, 255	*Jude*	
4.1-8	229	18-19	49	17-23	91
4.1	229	19	49, 106, 107		
4.9	60			*Revelation*	
4.14	195	20	49	3.15	209
4.15	217	21	49, 234, 255	22.11	91
5.1	60			22.15	91
5.11	7	22	179	22.18-19	91
5.19-20	35, 71, 173				

CLASSICAL LITERATURE

Appian		*Rhetorica*		Cicero	
Bella Civilia		1419b	98	*De Oratore*	
4.30	11			1.13	15
		Athanasius		1.17	17
Punic Wars		*Deipnosophistae*			
66	161	7.314C	188	Cyril of Alexandria	
				Expositio in Psalmos	
Aristotle		*Vita Antonii*		789A-D	21
Politica		900A-904A	22		
5.1.1301b5	78				

Demosthenes
De Corona
278   91

Dio Chysostom
Orationes
8.9   16, 32
12.5   16
14.16   37, 40,
                    206
15.29   52
19.3-5   16

Diogenes Laertius
Vitae Philosophorum
7.121   40
14.16   206

Epictetus
Dissertations
1.25.26   204
2.1.21-24   206
2.1.23   40
3.5.8-9   191
3.22.46-48   207
3.22.59   161
3.22.113-14   161
4.1.147   169

Enchiridion
1-3   191
1.1-5   206

Fragments
9   191

Eusebius
Historia Ecclesiae
2.4.2   131

Praeparatio Evangelica
8.8.34   131
8.9   133
8.9.38–8.10.18   133
13.11   133

Hermas
Mandatum
11.8   164

Martyrium Polycarpi
7   164

Horace
Odes
4.2.50   161

Isocrates
Antidosis
201-204   184

Nicocles
6-9   17

Juvenal
6.542-47   132

Lucian
The Dream
13   156

Origen
De Principiis
4.2.4   20

Philocalia
1.11   20

Philo
De agricultura
143   15
159–64   32
159   133
160   133

De cherubim
27   133

De decalogo
1   133

*Quod Deus sit
immutabilis*
52   165

Hypothetica
7.13   132

Legum allegoriae
3.159   133

De migratione Abrahami
34–35   133
116   11

*Quod omnis
probus liber sit*
58–61   206
59–61   192
59   37, 40
60–61   192

*Quis rerum
divinarum heres sit*
246–48   32
249–66   164
264–66   165
295   11

De somniis
2.252   133

De specialibus legibus
2.62-63   132
3.1-6   133
3.6   133

De virtutibus
187   52

De vita Mosis
2.188   165
2.212   15

Plato
Lysis
208C   12

Phraedrus
244-53   165

Plutarch
Moralia
131A   32
439E   11
439F   11
452D   11

De Phythiae Oraculis
397C   165

Quintilian
Institutiones Oratoriae
2.15.34   18
12.2.6   18

Seneca
De Beneficiis
2.11.1   161

Strabo
Geography
8.6.20   75
8.6.23   75

Tertullian
On Monogamy
3   168

INDEX OF AUTHORS

Allo, E.-B. 97, 102, 230, 234

Babbitt, F.C. 165
Bailey, K.E. 33, 34
Balch, D.L. 145
Barclay, J.M.G. 31, 58, 59, 62, 84, 145,
    186, 202, 204
Barr, J. 19, 20
Barrett, C.K. 3, 4, 12, 61, 63, 70, 83, 88,
    92, 94, 97, 102, 103, 111, 130, 131,
    135, 147, 149, 152, 153, 159, 186,
    190, 199, 200, 207, 208, 214-17,
    221, 226, 228, 231, 237, 239, 241,
    242, 247, 249, 250, 252
Barton, S. 69
Baur, F.C. 131
Bengel, J.A. 56
Betz, H.D. 99, 100, 114-19
Bieringer, R. 227
Bjerkelund, C.J. 234
Blue, B. 53, 55
Boer, M.C. de 42-45
Bornkamm, G. 86, 91, 218
Borse, U. 224, 225, 230, 233, 243, 245
Brown, C.P. 176
Bruce, F.F. 55, 56
Bultmann, R. 83, 130, 151, 209, 216,
    217, 221, 239

Caird, G.B. 14
Callan, T. 165
Campbell, R.A. 65, 66
Caragounis, C.C. 186
Carson, D.A. 3
Chadwick, H. 169
Chow, J.K. 35
Clarke, A.D. 35, 38, 103, 232
Collange, J.-F. 87, 130, 138

Collins, R.F. 101
Conan Doyle, A. 225
Conzelmann, H. 168, 191, 206
Cranfield, C.E.B. 53, 110, 138, 139, 219,
    220

Dahl, N.A. 35
Danker, F.W. 89-91, 94
Davis, J.A. 39, 52, 132, 133, 144
Delobel, J. 171
Deming, W. 167
Dunn, J.D.G. 14, 36, 39, 166

Ellingworth, P. 73
Ewald, G.H.A. 1

Fee, G.D. 8, 9, 11, 13, 25, 36, 37, 39, 46,
    48, 58, 61, 63, 65, 68, 72, 73, 144-
    46, 157, 159, 164, 169, 171, 176,
    177, 181, 186, 190, 193, 194, 207,
    230, 232, 237, 238, 247
Findlay, G.G. 80, 82
Fiorenza, E.S. 173
Fisk, B.N. 63
Fitzgerald, J.T. 8, 157, 159, 161
Foerster, W. 231
Forbes, C. 157
Ford, D.F. 90, 91, 100, 162
Furnish, V.P. 6, 7, 86, 87, 92, 94, 96, 97,
    102, 124, 125, 130, 134, 136-39,
    142, 143, 150, 151, 156, 161, 178,
    186, 216-18, 221, 227, 228, 230-33,
    238, 240, 242, 243, 245, 246, 249,
    250, 252

Gardner, P.D. 178, 179, 192, 194
Georgi, D. 130, 132-34, 136, 137, 200,
    239

Gerhardsson, B. 229
Gill, D.W.J. 55
Goodspeed, E.J. 55
Goudge, H.L. 48, 95, 96, 100, 226
Goulder, M.D. 7, 14, 40, 148
Guthrie, W.K.C. 15

Hafemann, S.J. 142, 215, 219, 220
Hall, D.R. 4, 23, 42, 114, 121, 152, 153,
    167, 170, 227, 244, 254
Harris, G. 36
Harvey, A.E. 19, 159
Hatton, H.A. 73
Hauck, F. 191
Hays, R.B. 65, 84, 167, 172, 179
Heil, C. 113
Hemer, C.J. 55
Hengel, M. 206
Héring, J. 217
Hickling, C.J.A. 129, 136, 141, 143, 200,
    204
Hock, R.F. 54, 156, 160, 186, 207
Holladay, C.R. 137
Hooker, M.D. 137, 138, 148
Horrell, D.G. 51, 57, 58, 61, 63, 76-78,
    174, 175, 177, 179-82, 252
Horsley, R.A. 80, 84, 144, 200, 202, 203
Hughes, F.W. 90, 91, 102
Hughes, P.E. 89, 224, 238, 240, 242
Hunt, A.R. 165
Hurd, J.C. 70, 202
Hyldahl, N. 223, 238, 239

Jenkins, C. 20
Jensen, J. 36
Johnson, L.T. 168
Judge, E.A. 14, 15, 18, 55, 59, 184, 219

Kamlah, E. 139
Käsemann, E. 129, 130, 138, 149, 151,
    190-93, 200, 205, 217, 220
Kruse, C.G. 4, 223, 231, 252
Kuck, D.W. 80
Kümmel, W.G. 88

Lambrecht, J. 161, 215
Lampe, P. 67, 68, 228, 230
Lietzmann, H. 70, 102

Lim, T.H. 16, 17, 184, 201
Lindemann, A. 69, 77
Litfin, D. 7, 9, 10, 14, 15, 17-19, 90, 156
Lofthouse, W.F. 104, 105
Lull, D.J. 11

Malherbe, A.J. 95, 96
Malina, B. 36
Marshall, P. 6, 80, 147, 155, 161, 178,
    185, 186, 192, 221
Martin, D.B. 60, 61, 155, 182, 184, 192
Martin, R.P. 101, 114, 115, 121, 137,
    138, 149, 156, 161, 215, 217, 237-
    40, 252
Meeks, W.A. 75-77
Meggitt, J.J. 52-55, 62, 63, 66, 67, 74-76
Menzies, A. 97, 223, 224, 249
Merklein, H. 41, 43-47, 57, 70, 71
Meyer, H.A.W. 1, 5, 6, 72, 73, 159, 220,
    225, 231
Milligan, G. 81
Mitchell, M.M. 9, 60, 172, 180, 211, 241
Moo, D.J. 2
Morris, L. 2
Moule, C.F.D. 103, 106, 248, 249
Moulton, J.H. 26, 29, 81, 209, 248
Munck, J. 18, 19
Murphy-O'Connor, J. 37, 38, 53, 54, 88,
    100, 146, 150, 201

Newton, D. 62

Olson, S.J. 93, 94
Oster, R.E. 63

Pearson, B.A. 52, 165
Perriman, A.C. 171
Phipps, W.E. 168
Plummer, A. 25, 35, 87-89, 94, 99, 102,
    104, 134, 150, 155, 159, 194, 209,
    224, 227, 233, 240, 241, 245, 249,
    252
Plumptre, E.H. 210
Pogoloff, S.M. 17-19, 41, 184
Provence, T.E. 134, 135, 139

Ramsay, W. 55
Robertson, A.T. 25-27, 35, 159, 194

Robinson, J.A.T. 56

Saussure, F. de 20
Schenk, W. 43
Schmidt, T.E. 161
Schmithals, W. 233
Schnelle, U. 41, 42, 44, 88, 89, 91, 114,
    129-31, 250
Schniewind, J. 80
Schöllgen, G. 76, 77
Schrage, W. 14, 30, 34, 57, 66, 147, 168,
    171, 191
Schweizer, E. 164
Scott, J.M. 161
Scroggs, R. 77
Shanor, J. 10
Simpson, E.K. 56
Stephenson, A.M.G. 249, 250
Stevenson, J. 20
Stowers, S.K. 115, 116
Strange, J.F. 219
Strecker, G. 90, 217
Strugnell, J. 146, 147
Sumney, J.L. 131, 136, 140, 157, 205

Tasker, R.V.G. 249
Theissen, G. 8, 9, 51-70, 75, 207
Thiselton, A.C. 6, 12, 20, 32, 34-37, 39,
    40, 46, 48, 49, 61, 68, 70, 71, 73-75,
    110, 141, 145, 146, 157, 159, 163,

165, 168-73, 184, 191, 194, 197, 230,
    231, 234
Thrall, M.E. 86, 91, 92, 96, 99, 102, 113,
    114, 121, 127, 134, 136-38, 142,
    153, 154, 161, 162, 177, 210, 227-
    29, 231, 233, 234, 236, 237, 243-46,
    249, 250
Turner, N. 26, 45, 104, 149, 248, 251

Verhoef, E. 105
Vos, J.S. 4, 5, 10, 19-24

Wagner, J.R. 147
Wedderburn, A.J.M. 31, 80, 84
Weiss, J. 46, 120, 121, 123, 193, 195,
    197
Welborn, L.L. 7, 9, 12, 78, 114, 120-24,
    147
Westerholm, S. 139
Willis, W. 13, 179, 180
Winandy, J. 171
Windisch, H. 135, 143, 233, 239, 246
Winter, B. 15-17, 52, 78, 182
Witherington, B. 9, 98, 119
Wordsworth, C. 187

Young, F. 90, 91, 100, 162

Zaas, P.S. 36
Zmijewski, J. 98, 99

This JSOTS book forms part of the *Journal for the Study of the Old Testament* series

We also publish

Journal for the Study of the Old Testament
Edited by
John Jarick, *University of Oxford, UK*
Keith Whitelam, *University of Sheffield, UK*

You can read about the most up-to-date scholarship and research on the Old Testament by subscribing to the *Journal for the Study of the Old Testament*, which is published five times a year. The fifth issue comprises of the *Society for Old Testament Study Book List*, a book containing reviews of the most important works being published on the Old Testament from authors and publishers world-wide.

The *Journal for the Study of the Old Testament* is published by Sheffield Academic Press, a Continuum imprint and you can find out more including current subscription prices by visiting:

www.continuumjournals.com/jsot

FREE Sample Copy
Please request a no obligation sample copy by contacting:

Orca Journals
FREEPOST (SWB 20951)
3 Fleets Lane, Stanley House
Poole, Dorset BH15 3ZZ
United Kingdom

Tel: +44 (0)1202 785712
Fax: +44 (0)1202 666219
Email: journals@orcabookservices.co.uk

OR

Visit **www.continuumjournals.com/jsot** and request a FREE sample copy from our website

SHEFFIELD ACADEMIC PRESS
A Continuum imprint
www.continuumjournals.com